THE NEW BOOK OF KNOWLEDGE ANNUAL

THE
NEW BOOK
OF
KNOWLEDGE
ANNUAL

The Young People's Book of the Year

Grolier Incorporated, Danbury, Connecticut

1987

Highlighting Events of 1986

ISBN 0-7172-0618-1
ISSN 0196-0148
The Library of Congress Catalog Card Number: 79-26807

COPYRIGHT © 1987 BY GROLIER INCORPORATED

Copyright © in Canada 1987 BY GROLIER LIMITED

STAFF

CONTENTS

CONTRIBUTORS

FREEDMAN, Russell
Author, *Animal Instincts; Tooth and Claw; How Animals Learn; Growing Up Wild; Getting Born; How Animals Defend Their Young; Animal Architects; The Brains of Animals and Man; How Birds Fly; Animal Superstars; Children of the Wild West; Immigrant Kids; Cowboys of the Wild West*

WHY ANIMALS DO WHAT THEY DO

GOLDBERG, Hy
Sports journalist; former co-ordinator of sports information, NBC sports

SPORTS, 1986

GORDON, Cyrus H.
New York University, Gottesmann Professor of Hebraic Studies; author, *Ugaritic Literature; Ugaritic Manual; The World of the Old Testament; Before the Bible; The Common Background of Greek and Hebrew Civilizations*

BABYLONIA

HACKER, Jeffrey H.
Author, *Carl Sandburg; Franklin D. Roosevelt; Government Subsidy to Industry; Spectator's Guide to the 1984 Olympics;* editor, *The Olympic Story*

NOVEL VIEWS OF THE SOUTH
INCIDENT AT THE HAYMARKET

HAHN, Charless
Stamp editor, *Chicago Sun-Times;* co-author, *British Pictorial Envelopes of the 19th Century*

STAMP COLLECTING

HRNCIR, Elizabeth J.
University of Virginia, Assistant Professor, Early Childhood Development and Education, Curry School of Education

DAY CARE

KELLY, Richard
University of Tennessee at Knoxville, Professor; author, *Lewis Carroll; George du Maurier; Grahame Greene*

KENNETH GRAHAME

LEMKE, Robert F.
Assistant to the publisher, Krause Publications *(Numismatic News);* author, *Standard Catalog of United States Paper Money, 1981; Coin Finder—Consumer Guide, 1980, 1981; How to Get Started in Coin Collecting*

COIN COLLECTING

LUND, Sharon Disney
Burbank, California

WALT DISNEY

MATH, Irwin
President, Math Associates, Inc.; author, *Wires and Watts: Understanding and Using Electricity; Morse, Marconi, and You; Bits & Pieces*

BATTERIES

PASCOE, Elaine
Author, *South Africa: Troubled Land; Racial Prejudice; The Horse Owner's Preventive Maintenance Handbook*
SOUTH AFRICA: A NATION UNDER PROTEST

REUNING, Winifred
Science writer/editor, Division of Polar Programs, National Science Foundation
ARCTIC

SCHAFFNER, Cynthia V.A.
KLEIN, Susan
Authors, *Folk Hearts*
HEART TO HEART

SHAW, Arnold
University of Nevada—Las Vegas, Director, Popular Music Research Center; author, *A Dictionary of American Pop/Rock; Black Popular Music in America; Honkers and Shouters; 52nd St.: The Street of Jazz; The Rockin' 50's; The World of Soul*
THE MUSIC SCENE

SILVERSTEIN, Alvin
SILVERSTEIN, Virginia
Authors, *Guinea Pigs; Hamsters; Gerbils; So You're Getting Braces*
DIGESTIVE SYSTEM

SKODNICK, Ruth
Statistician
INDEPENDENT NATIONS OF THE WORLD

TESAR, Jenny
Designer, computer programs; series consultant, *Wonders of Wildlife;* author, *Introduction to Animals* (Wonders of Wildlife series)
THE RETURN OF HALLEY'S COMET
COMPUTER BULLETIN BOARDS

TOSH, Nancy
Editor, *Crafts 'n Things* magazine
POPULAR CRAFTS

WALLACE, G. David
Corporate Strategies Editor, *Business Week* magazine; author, *Money Basics*
DOLLAR

WEISMAN, Robert A.
State University of New York at Albany, Meteorologist, Department of Atmospheric Science
DROUGHT

WHITING, Robert M.
University of Chicago, Research Associate, the Oriental Institute
ALPHABET

ZIMMERMAN, Everett
University of California—Santa Barbara, Professor, Department of English; author, *Defoe and the Novel; Swift's Narrative Satires*
DANIEL DEFOE

IN THE PAGES OF THIS BOOK...

How closely did you follow the events of 1986? Do you remember the people who made news during the year? What about the trends—what was in and what was out? Who won in sports? What were the top songs, films, and television shows? What important anniversaries were celebrated? All these things helped make up your world in 1986—a year that was like no other.

Here's a quiz that will tell you how much you know about your world—about what took place during the past year and about other things as well. If you're stumped by a question, don't worry: You'll find all the answers in the pages of this book. (The page numbers after the questions will tell you where to look.)

In April, 1986, explosions at the _____ nuclear power plant in the Soviet Union resulted in the worst accident in the history of nuclear power. (*23;44*)

What 18-year-old was crowned a world champion and became the first black woman to win a major figure-skating title? (*173*)

The U.S. national debt, which is the accumulation of all the yearly budget deficits, has reached a staggering ($2 million/$2 billion/$2 trillion). (*56*)

In January, Voyager 2 became the first space probe to visit _____, the third largest planet in the solar system. (*122*)

What flower officially became the "national floral emblem" of the United States? (*32*)

In June, the best-selling novel of all time celebrated the 50th anniversary of its publication. Name the book. (*192*)

These sleepy, oh-so-slow-moving animals do little more than hang around their tropical habitats—which are disappearing at an alarming rate. Name these animals and their homes. (*84;106*)

Despite increasing internal violence and massive worldwide criticism, South Africa clings to its racial policy of apartheid. South African activist and Nobel peace prize winner _____ has said that government concessions have created only "the appearance of change." (*49*)

In July, Greg LeMond became the first non-European cyclist to win the Tour de France, the world's premier bike race. What country was LeMond from? (*158;180*)

The Short Snout Society is (a fan club for pigs/probably "hogwash"/a group of gourmets who love pork). (*82*)

"Aroma therapy" is currently being studied by scientists. The scent of spiced apples, for example, has been shown to lower _____. (*116*)

What movie won the 1986 Academy Award for best motion picture? (*252*)

The contras are (a rock band/rebels fighting in Nicaragua/a TV serial). (*59*)

"World in Motion, World in Touch" was the slogan of Expo 86, one of the most successful world's fairs in North America. Where was this fair held? (*100*)

Looking like a giant exclamation point in the sky, Halley's comet made its (10th/20th/30th) recorded appearance in 1986. (*99*)

In June, Kurt Waldheim, a former Secretary General of the United Nations, was elected president of Austria. What events in this man's past made the election so controversial? (*26;65*)

In 1986 the Montreal Canadiens won their (15th/11th/23rd) Stanley Cup title, giving them the most championships of any professional sports team in North America. (*170*)

Waterfronts all over the United States and Canada have been restored as marketplaces and are being visited by thousands of people every day. What Boston waterfront complex celebrated its 10th anniversary in 1986? (*206*)

PANDA HERE HAD NAP is an example of a _____. (*137*)

Who became Chief Justice of the U.S. Supreme Court in September? (*26;64*)

The *Challenger* space shuttle disaster in January resulted in the deaths of seven astronauts, including schoolteacher _____, the first "ordinary" person in space. (*17;121*)

What great Hollywood actor, known for his elegance and wit, died in November? (*37*)

Once looked down upon as the ultimate in bad taste, what kind of signs have made a "dazzling" revival and are even being displayed in art galleries? (*244*)

In 1986 the U.S. Treasury issued its first gold _____ coins—coins whose values are determined by the amount of precious metal they contain rather than by their denominations. (*152*)

What country won the 1986 World Cup tournament, the soccer extravaganza that is held every four years? (*174*)

The Statue of Liberty celebrated its 100th birthday in 1986. Frédéric Auguste Bartholdi, the French sculptor, used his _____ as the model for Liberty's face. (*187*)

Immigration was a popular subject of discussion in 1986, the year of the Statue of Liberty's centennial celebrations. Why did many immigrants change their surnames when they came to the United States? (*211*)

Twenty-three-year-old _____ set the music world on its ear when her very first album became the most successful solo debut album of all time. (*254*)

The Soviets launched their new space station Mir in February. Larger and more sophisticated than previous space stations, Mir has (4/6/2) docking ports for visiting spacecraft. (*19;123*)

In 1986, _____ won the Masters golf tournament for a record sixth time. (*169*)

With "people power" behind her, _____ replaced Ferdinand Marcos as president of the Philippines in February. (*18;40*)

A new First Dog was in the White House in 1986 when frisky Lucky was replaced by a Cavalier King Charles spaniel named _____. (*80*)

What made the Pied Piper "pied"? (*280*)

In 1986 a robot helped researchers finally "get to the bottom" of an event that had occurred on April 14, 1912. What happened in 1912 and 74 years later? (*113*)

(Louis L'Amour/Roy Rogers/Don Quixote), a writer known primarily for his Westerns, is currently the third best-selling U.S. novelist of all time. (*266*)

In recent years, inner space has become a huge garbage dump filled with nonfunctioning satellites, burned-out rocket stages, and fragments of satellites. In fact, about (20%/60%/95%) of all objects orbiting Earth are "space junk." (*128*)

The *Protoavis* has knocked the *Archaeopteryx* from its perch as the world's earliest bird. The discovery of the 225,000,000-year-old fossils supported the theory that birds evolved from (pigs/dinosaurs/butterflies). (*30*)

THE WORLD IN 1986

Soviet leader Mikhail Gorbachev and U.S. President Ronald Reagan met in Reykjavik, Iceland, in October, 1986. The two leaders discussed nuclear disarmament and missile reduction. The meeting lasted two days but ended in stalemate, leaving the future of arms control in doubt. Nevertheless, some people viewed the talks as an encouraging step toward world peace.

THE YEAR IN REVIEW

The year 1986 saw troubles deepening in many parts of the world. Fighting in the Middle East and Central America, cool relations between the superpowers, and a wave of terrorism were among the year's darker events. But there were also bright spots and encouraging signs.

Hopes for a new arms-control agreement were raised early in the year by the news that U.S. President Ronald Reagan and Soviet leader Mikhail Gorbachev would seek a summit meeting. But those hopes were dashed in October, when the two leaders met in Iceland but were unable to agree on arms reductions. One major stumbling block was a U.S. plan for a space-based anti-missile defense system, which the Soviets opposed. Relations between the two countries remained strained after the talks.

Throughout much of the year, Western countries tried to untangle a web of international terrorism that seemed increasingly complex. A string of bombings in Europe, the hijacking of a Pan American airliner in Pakistan, and an attack on a synagogue in Turkey were among the terrorist attacks that took the lives of many innocent people in 1986. Middle Eastern groups were linked to these and other incidents. And such groups were holding a number of Westerners, including several Americans, hostage in Lebanon.

There was evidence that several Middle Eastern countries—Libya, Syria, and Iran—were supporting the terrorist groups. In April, the United States staged a bombing raid on what it believed were terrorist centers in Libya, in retaliation for that country's involvement. In the fall, after evidence of Syrian involvement emerged, the United States and many Western European countries limited their trade and diplomatic ties to that country. These steps, however, did not seem to immediately reduce terrorist attacks.

A year-end controversy erupted over secret dealings between the United States and Iran. As the facts became known, it was learned that the Reagan administration had sold weapons to Iran in an effort to obtain the release of U.S. hostages held by Iranian-backed groups in Lebanon. Such sales went against a U.S. policy that had been in effect since 1979, when Iranians had seized the U.S. embassy in Teheran, Iran, and taken more than 50 Americans hostage. They also ran counter to the United States' assertions that it would not negotiate with terrorists. The controversy widened into a scandal that shook the Reagan administration when it was discovered that top administration officials had secretly channeled money from the arms sales to revolutionaries in Nicaragua.

The conflicts and problems that have plagued the Middle East itself also continued: civil war in Lebanon, war between Iraq and Iran, and no progress on the question of a homeland for Palestinian Arabs who were displaced when Israel was created in 1948. In Central America, too, long-running civil wars continued in El

Salvador and Nicaragua. But not all international news was bad. In two island countries—the Philippines, in the Pacific, and Haiti, in the Caribbean—repressive dictatorships that had held power for many years were overthrown by mostly peaceful means. Both countries continued to face serious problems, but their steps toward greater freedom were seen as encouraging.

Blacks in South Africa continued to protest against apartheid, the policy of strict racial segregation enforced by the minority white government. A state of emergency remained in effect through the year, banning demonstrations and gatherings. But international pressure on the South African government increased. The U.S. Congress, overriding a veto by President Reagan, imposed stronger limits on trade with South Africa. And a number of major U.S. corporations sold their South African assets. Elsewhere in Africa, the severe drought and famine that had marked 1985 eased somewhat.

The year saw more than its share of accidents and disasters, among them the worst nuclear accident in history. In April, an explosion at a Soviet nuclear power plant at Chernobyl, near Kiev, spewed radiation over a wide area. More than 30 people died from the immediate effects, and it was feared that thousands might die from the long-term effects of the radiation.

Tragedy also struck in the United States, when the space shuttle *Challenger* exploded just after liftoff on January 28. Seven astronauts were killed, among them Christa McAuliffe, a New Hampshire teacher who was to have been the first ordinary person in space. People everywhere mourned the deaths. And the space shuttle program was put on hold while design flaws thought to have caused the explosion were corrected.

In other U.S. news, Congress wrestled with two major economic problems: tax reform and budget deficits. A sweeping tax-reform law, passed in September, was expected to lower taxes for many individuals while increasing the amounts paid by business and industry. Congress also sought ways to cut the annual deficit in the federal budget, which has mushroomed in recent years. Late in 1985, it passed a law calling for set annual reductions in the amount of the deficit. But the 1986 budget exceeded the target, and despite Congressional efforts there were fears that the 1987 budget would do the same.

A bit of good news for many people in the United States and other Western countries was a drop in oil prices. Increased oil production, lower consumption, and the failure of members of the Organization of Petroleum Exporting Countries (OPEC) to agree to price and production controls produced the drop. While the oil industries in the United States, Canada, and other countries saw their incomes fall off sharply, the individuals and industries that buy petroleum products benefited.

The world also had a notable visitor in 1986: Halley's comet, which circles the sun in an orbit that brings it past Earth every 76 years. Several countries took part in scientific studies of the comet. And there were hopes that by the time of the comet's next visit, in 2061, people would find solutions to at least some of the world's many problems.

JANUARY

7 President Ronald Reagan announced that the United States would sever economic ties with Libya. He also ordered all Americans living in Libya to leave immediately. These actions were in response to Libyan support for international terrorism, which Reagan called "a threat to the national security and foreign policy of the United States."

18 The space shuttle *Columbia* ended a six-day mission. The seven-member crew included Representative Bill Nelson of Florida, the first member of the House of Representatives to go into space, and Franklin Chang-Diáz, the first Hispanic-American astronaut. During the mission a communications satellite was launched, and many scientific experiments were performed.

13-24 A coup against the president of Yemen (Aden), Ali Nasser Mohammed, widened into twelve days of fierce civil war. By January 24 the rebels had gained control of most of the country, and Haider Abu Bakr al-Attas was named president.

20 France and Britain announced that they would build two rail tunnels under the English Channel. The proposed "chunnel," to be completed in 1993, would be 30 miles (48 kilometers) long. It

As thousands of people at the Kennedy Space Center in Florida watched in horror, the space shuttle *Challenger* exploded in a ball of fire, leaving plumes of smoke streaking across the skies.

would run between Dover, England, and Calais, France. One tunnel would be for high-speed trains; the second would be for special trains designed to carry cars and buses. Two previous attempts to construct channel tunnels, in the 1870's and 1970's, were canceled for political and economic reasons.

In Lesotho, Prime Minister Leabua Jonathan was ousted in a military coup. Jonathan, who had been in power since Lesotho gained its independence in 1966, was succeeded by Justin Lekhanya.

26 In Uganda, President Tito Okello was overthrown in a coup. Yoweri Museveni succeeded Okello, who had been in power since July, 1985.

28 A little over a minute after liftoff, the space shuttle *Challenger* exploded, killing all seven astronauts aboard. It was the worst disaster in U.S. space history. The crew consisted of Gregory B. Jarvis, Ronald E. McNair, Ellison S. Onizuka, Judith A. Resnik, Francis R. Scobee, Michael J. Smith, and Christa McAuliffe—a high school teacher from New Hampshire who was to have been the first ordinary citizen in space.

29 President Ronald Reagan nominated Richard E. Lyng as U.S. Secretary of Agriculture, to succeed John R. Block. Block had announced his resignation on January 7. (On March 6, the Senate confirmed the nomination.)

The *Challenger* crew: Front row—Michael Smith, Francis Scobee, and Ronald McNair. Back row—Ellison Onizuka, Christa McAuliffe, Gregory Jarvis, and Judith Resnik.

FEBRUARY

2 In national elections in Costa Rica, Oscar Arias Sánchez, the National Liberation Party candidate, was elected president. He succeeded Luis Alberto Monge, who had been president since 1982.

7 Following presidential elections in the Philippines, both President Ferdinand E. Marcos and his main opponent, Corazon C. Aquino, claimed victory. The elections had been held amid charges of widespread government bribery and fraud. (On February 15 the National Assembly proclaimed Marcos the winner, although an independent tally found that Aquino had received a majority of the votes. In the succeeding days, there was increasing domestic and international pressure on Marcos, urging him to step down. On February 25, Marcos accepted a U.S. offer of asylum and fled to Hawaii, ending twenty years of rule. Aquino assumed the position of president.)

Following three months of increasing unrest, Haiti's President Jean-Claude Duvalier fled to France, ending a 28-year dictatorship by the Duvalier family. A military-civilian council headed by Henri Namphy took over the government. Duvalier (nicknamed ''Baby Doc'') had assumed the presidency in 1971, after the death of his father, François (''Papa Doc''). The elder Duvalier had been elected president in 1957 but had refused to allow any further elections.

16 In a runoff election in Portugal, Mário Soares, the Socialist candidate, was elected president—the nation's first civilian president in 60 years. Soares, a former prime minister, succeeded António Ramalho Eanes, who had been president since 1976.

20 The U.S. Senate approved a United Nations treaty against genocide, nearly 37 years after it was first submitted by President Harry S. Truman. (Genocide is the deliberate extermination of a racial, religious, or ethnic group.) The treaty, formally called the Convention on the Prevention and Punishment of the Crime of Genocide, was adopted by the U.N. General Assembly in 1948 and has since been endorsed by more than 90 nations. The treaty declares that genocide is an international crime, and it obliges nations that adhere to it to punish those who commit the crime. Approval by the Senate had long been blocked by people who, while not necessarily disagreeing with the purpose of the treaty, stated that the United States should not be subject to international criminal laws.

20 The Soviet Union launched the space station Mir ("peace") into orbit around Earth. Mir is designed to be the central module of a permanently manned space research complex. Visiting spacecraft will be able to dock at the station's six ports.

28 Olof Palme, premier of Sweden, was assassinated in Stockholm. Palme, 59, was leader of the Social Democratic Party. He had been premier from 1969 to 1976 and from 1982 until his death. He was an important participant in international politics and was known as a spokesman for peace and nuclear disarmament. Ingvar Carlsson was named to succeed Palme.

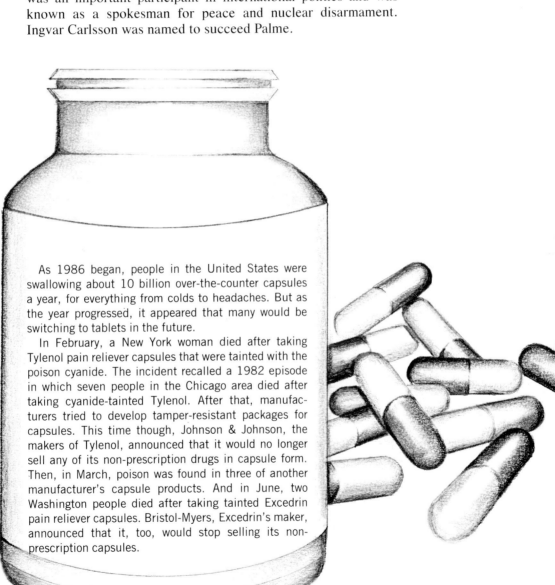

As 1986 began, people in the United States were swallowing about 10 billion over-the-counter capsules a year, for everything from colds to headaches. But as the year progressed, it appeared that many would be switching to tablets in the future.

In February, a New York woman died after taking Tylenol pain reliever capsules that were tainted with the poison cyanide. The incident recalled a 1982 episode in which seven people in the Chicago area died after taking cyanide-tainted Tylenol. After that, manufacturers tried to develop tamper-resistant packages for capsules. This time though, Johnson & Johnson, the makers of Tylenol, announced that it would no longer sell any of its non-prescription drugs in capsule form. Then, in March, poison was found in three of another manufacturer's capsule products. And in June, two Washington people died after taking tainted Excedrin pain reliever capsules. Bristol-Myers, Excedrin's maker, announced that it, too, would stop selling its non-prescription capsules.

MARCH

6 Georgia O'Keeffe, the American artist, died at the age of 98. O'Keeffe, whose career spanned 70 years, was a key figure in 20th-century American art. She was known for her paintings of natural forms and objects, including animal bones, huge flowers, and landscapes of New Mexico, and for her use of brilliant colors.

16 In elections for the French National Assembly, an alliance of conservative parties won a narrow victory against the ruling Socialist Party. As a result, Socialist President François Mitterrand asked conservative Jacques Chirac to become premier. It was the first time since France's Fifth Republic was established in

Georgia O'Keeffe, the American artist, died at the age of 98. She was best known for her dramatic paintings of flowers, landscapes, animal skeletons, and other natural forms.

French elections resulted in a sharing of power between Socialist President François Mitterrand (*right*) and conservative Premier Jacques Chirac (*left*)—the first time since 1958 that the president and the premier were from opposing political camps.

1958 that the president and premier were from opposing political camps. The elections also ended five years of Socialist rule, the longest period France had spent under a left-wing government in almost 200 years. (Chirac assumed the post on March 20, succeeding Laurent Fabius, who had been premier since 1984. Ordinarily the president, supported by a premier from his own party, is the most powerful figure in French politics. But under the new arrangement, called cohabitation, it was expected that Mitterrand would wield less power.)

18 Bernard Malamud, the American author, died at the age of 71. Winner of the Pulitzer Prize, Malamud once said that his novels and short stories were primarily about ''simple people struggling to make their lives better in a world of bad luck.'' His works include *The Natural, The Assistant,* and *The Magic Barrel.*

30 James Cagney, the American actor, died at the age of 86. He appeared in more than 60 movies. With his first film, *The Public Enemy,* Cagney became known as the screen's most popular tough guy. One of his best-known roles was in *Yankee Doodle Dandy,* for which he won an Academy Award in 1942.

APRIL

2 A bomb smuggled aboard a Trans World Airlines jet flying from Rome to Athens exploded and killed four passengers, all of them Americans. Nine others were wounded. An Arab terrorist group claimed responsibility for the explosion.

5 A bomb exploded in a discotheque in West Berlin, killing two people, including an American soldier, and wounding 230 others. The U.S. government later said it had "irrefutable proof" of Libyan involvement in the bombing.

14 U.S. planes bombed "terrorist-related targets" in the Libyan cities of Tripoli and Benghazi. President Ronald Reagan said the attack was in retaliation for the April 5 bombing in West Berlin and, more generally, for the "reign of terror" that Libyan leader Muammar el-Qaddafi had launched against the United States. The U.S. bombing killed at least 15 people and wounded 60 others. One U.S. plane was downed and its two crew members killed.

Simone de Beauvoir, the French author, died at the age of 78. Her best-known book, *The Second Sex,* published in 1949, helped lay the foundation for the feminist movement.

23 The South African government announced that it would abolish the laws that severely restricted the movements of blacks within

Miami, Florida, became the first city with a "people mover" when its Metromover system began operations in April. The system consists of automated cars that move on an elevated track, making a loop through the city's downtown business area. The cars stop at nine stations along the 2-mile route. Similar people movers are being used at some airports.

On April 26, the world's worst nuclear accident occurred at the Soviet Union's Chernobyl nuclear power plant. Radioactive material was spewed into the atmosphere and was carried around the globe by high-level winds. Here, an engineer at Chernobyl is being checked for radiation.

the country. Included were the pass laws, which required blacks to carry identification passes and were among the most hated aspects of apartheid, the white government's official policy of racial segregation. Blacks who wish to move from one black area to another will now be allowed to do so, but residential areas will continue to be segregated on the basis of race.

Otto Preminger, the Austrian-born motion picture producer and director, died at the age of 80. Among his most notable films were *Laura, The Moon Is Blue, Anatomy of a Murder,* and *Exodus.*

25 In Swaziland, 18-year-old Prince Makhosetive was crowned King Mswati III. He succeeded his father, King Sobhuza II, who had died in 1982.

26 Explosions ripped through the Soviet Union's Chernobyl nuclear power plant, igniting fires, crippling a nuclear reactor, and spewing radioactive material into the atmosphere. The accident, which occurred some 70 miles (112 kilometers) north of Kiev, was the worst in the history of nuclear power. Countries around the world strongly criticized the Soviets for having withheld information about the disaster for almost two days, until Sweden detected radioactivity in the atmosphere. About 300 people living near the power plant were injured, and at least 31 people died—most from radiation and burns. It was the first time people were known to have died from radiation emitted by a nuclear power plant. Radioactivity from the accident was carried around the globe by high-level winds. The levels were considered too low to be hazardous in North America.

2 Gro Harlem Brundtland was named premier of Norway. She succeeded Kaare Willoch, who had resigned after losing a vote of confidence in the nation's parliament. Willoch had been premier since 1981.

4 In Afghanistan, Najibullah was named general secretary of the Communist Party, the most important position in the country. He succeeded Babrak Karmal, who had held the position for seven years.

6 Sudan's ruling military leaders handed over power to a civilian coalition government. A five-member council was chosen to act as collective head of state in place of a president. Sadiq al-Mahdi was named prime minister.

The leaders of seven major industrial nations ended a three-day meeting in Tokyo, Japan. The countries represented were Britain, Canada, France, Germany, Italy, Japan, and the United States. The talks focused on world economic issues and on the need for measures against terrorism.

9 Tenzing Norkey, the Nepalese-born mountain guide, died at the age of 72. In 1953, Norkey and Sir Edmund Hillary of New Zealand became the first people to climb Mount Everest, the world's highest mountain.

15 Yugoslavia's parliament chose Branko Mikulic as premier of the country. Mikulic succeeded Milka Planinc, who had been premier since 1982.

16 In national elections in the Dominican Republic, Joaquín Balaguer was elected president. He succeeded Salvador Jorge Blanco, who had been president since 1982. (Balaguer had previously been president from 1966 to 1978.)

25 Some 5,000,000 people joined hands to participate in Hands Across America, a fund-raising event to help the hungry and homeless in the United States. The chain of people, most of whom contributed money to the cause, reached from New York to California, with only a few gaps in the line (in the Arizona desert, for example). Other people, in states not on the route, joined hands to form smaller, local chains.

In national elections in Colombia, Virgilio Barco Vargas of the Liberal Party was elected president. He succeeded Belisario Betancur Cuartas, who had been president since 1982.

25 A river ferry carrying about 1,000 people capsized and sank in the Meghna River in southern Bangladesh. More than 500 passengers lost their lives.

28 In national elections in Barbados, the Democratic Labor Party won a majority of seats in parliament. Errol Barrow, the party's leader, thus became prime minister. He succeeded Bernard St. John, who had been prime minister since March, 1985.

Hands Across America: To raise money for the poor, some 5,000,000 people joined hands and formed a nearly unbroken line that snaked through sixteen states and the District of Columbia.

8   In a runoff presidential election in Austria, Kurt Waldheim of the Conservative People's Party was elected president of the country. He became the first non-socialist to hold the position since the end of World War II. During the campaign Waldheim, a former Secretary General of the United Nations (1972–81), was the focus of great controversy because of his war record. He was accused of having served in a German Army unit involved in Nazi war crimes during World War II. After repeated denials, Waldheim admitted that he had known of the atrocities but insisted that he hadn't personally committed any war crimes.

9   Franz Vranitzky was named chancellor of Austria. He succeeded Fred Sinowatz, who resigned after three years in office.

A special presidential commission, reporting on the January 28 space shuttle *Challenger* disaster, severely criticized the National Aeronautics and Space Administration (NASA). The commission said that the direct cause of the explosion was a faulty seal on a booster rocket, but that both NASA and the rocket manufacturer had failed to fix the seal problem after having become aware of it.

13   Benny Goodman, the American clarinetist and bandleader known as the King of Swing, died at the age of 77. Goodman was credited with starting the age of swing—the type of big-band dance music popular from the mid-1930's to the mid-1940's.

14   Alan Jay Lerner, the American lyricist and playwright, died at the age of 67. Lerner's best-known works are the musicals he created with composer Frederick Loewe, including *Brigadoon, Paint Your Wagon, My Fair Lady, Camelot,* and *Gigi.*

17   It was announced that Warren E. Burger, Chief Justice of the U.S. Supreme Court since 1969, would retire. President Ronald Reagan nominated Associate Justice William H. Rehnquist, a member of the Supreme Court since 1971, to succeed Burger. He also nominated Antonin Scalia, a judge of the Court of Appeals for the District of Columbia, to the Supreme Court. (The Senate confirmed the nominations on September 17.)

Kate Smith, the American singer, died at the age of 79. She was best known for her rendition of ''God Bless America,'' which she introduced in 1938 and which became an unofficial national anthem, especially during World War II.

Benny Goodman, known as the King of Swing, died in June. The clarinetist and band-leader was famous for having brought about the sound of swing, a blend of jazz and popular music. This type of big-band dance music was ''the thing'' about 50 years ago.

JULY

3 Rudy Vallee, the American singing idol for whom the term "crooner" was coined, died at the age of 84. Vallee, whose theme song was "My Time Is Your Time," was one of the country's most popular radio, theater, and nightclub performers in the 1930's and 1940's.

4 Festive events that included a parade of sailing ships in New York Harbor and the biggest fireworks display in U.S. history marked the 100th birthday of the Statue of Liberty—America's monument that symbolizes the concepts of hope and freedom.

14 Truong Chinh was named secretary general of Vietnam's Communist Party, the most important political office in the country. He succeeded Le Duan, who died on July 10. Le Duan had been Communist Party leader since 1969.

26 W. Averell Harriman, the U.S. diplomat, died at the age of 94. Harriman had served as an adviser to four presidents (Franklin Roosevelt, Harry Truman, Lyndon Johnson, and John Ken-

The summer's biggest fling was a space-age flying toy called the Aerobie, shown here with its inventor, Alan Adler. Adler, a California engineer, used computer simulations to design the rubber and plastic rings, which can soar the length of three football fields. That's about twice the distance that the popular flying Frisbees can travel.

About 1,500 farmers in drought-stricken South Carolina got together and spelled out a human "thank you" for the hay donated by Midwestern farmers to feed starving cattle.

nedy). One of his most important posts was ambassador to the Soviet Union during World War II. He also served one term as governor of New York and held high positions in business and finance.

31 By the end of the month, most of the states in the U.S. Southeast were experiencing the effects of the region's worst drought in 100 years. Springs and wells dried up, and reservoirs fell to dangerously low levels. Corn and other crops were ruined. And cattle starved to death because there was no food for them. Agricultural losses totaled an estimated $2 billion. Adding to the crisis was a record heat wave, which resulted in the deaths of more than 60 people. Congress approved a relief package providing grain, feed, cash, and other forms of aid to tens of thousands of farmers in the region. And farmers around the country donated thousands of tons of hay to feed the starving livestock.

AUGUST

6   William J. Schroeder, the longest-surviving recipient of a permanent artificial heart, died at the age of 54. Schroeder had received the heart on November 25, 1984.

13   It was reported that fossil bones found in western Texas may be the remains of the world's earliest birds. The 225,000,000-year-old fossils were from birds that scientists have named *Protoavis* (for "first bird"). *Protoavis* is 75,000,000 years older than *Archaeopteryx,* which was formerly believed to have been the earliest bird. The bones were dug out of ancient mud in 1984, and they belonged to two birds the size of crows. The discovery supported the theory that birds developed from reptiles—because the ancient birds were like dinosaurs in some ways.

21 In northwest Cameroon, a cloud of toxic gases escaped from a lake in a volcanic crater. More than 1,500 people were killed as the poisonous fumes from Lake Nios spread over four mountain villages. Poisonous gases are often present in the vapors released by volcanoes, even without a major volcanic eruption. These gases are usually trapped at the bottom of crater lakes. But some unexplained occurrence in Lake Nios made the gases shoot up to the surface, explode, and fill the air. (Thirty-seven people died in a similar unexplained incident that occurred in 1984, at a lake in the same mountain chain as Lake Nios.)

31 Henry Moore, the British sculptor, died at the age of 88. Moore, one of the greatest artists of the 20th century, created huge abstract sculptures in stone, wood, and metal. His best-known works are his graceful sculptures of human figures.

A Soviet passenger ship, the *Admiral Nakhimov*, sank in the Black Sea after colliding with a Soviet freighter. Of the 1,234 people aboard the ship, 398 lost their lives.

Opposite page: Fossil bones found in Texas may be the remains of the world's earliest birds. The drawing at left shows the bones (black) as part of a reconstruction of what these ancient birds looked like. They had teeth, long bony tails, clawed fingers, and powerful hind legs—characteristics that link them to dinosaurs.

5 cm

4 Harvard University, the oldest university in the United States, began a week-long celebration of the 350th anniversary of its founding. Prince Charles of Britain was the main speaker at opening ceremonies on the school's Cambridge, Massachusetts, campus. Special seminars, fireworks, and parties filled the rest of the week.

5 Four Arab terrorists seized a Pan American jumbo jet in Karachi, Pakistan. The airplane, en route from India to West Germany and the United States, carried 389 passengers and crew members. After holding the plane on the ground for sixteen hours, the gunmen panicked when its generator ran out of fuel and the lights dimmed. They herded the passengers to the middle of the plane, opened fire, and threw hand grenades at them. Some passengers began to escape through emergency doors, and the terrorists were then captured by Pakistani commandos who stormed the plane. Twenty-one people, including two Americans, were killed. About 100 more were injured.

6 In Istanbul, Turkey, two Arab terrorists attacked worshippers at a synagogue during the morning Sabbath service, killing at least 21 people. The terrorists failed to escape and were killed when one of their grenades exploded.

16 The 41st annual session of the United Nations General Assembly opened at U.N. headquarters in New York City. Humayan Choudhury of Bangladesh was elected to serve as assembly president for one year.

17 A bomb exploded in front of a crowded department store in Paris, France, killing at least five people and injuring about 50 others. The attack was the latest in a series of five Paris bombings that had begun September 8. French investigators suspected that the bombs were the work of Lebanese terrorists.

23 The U.S. House of Representatives voted to make the rose America's national flower. (The Senate had passed the resolution in 1985.) The action ended a debate that went back to the late 1800's. Over the years, people had proposed many flowers as the "national floral emblem"—including the dogwood, the marigold, the mountain laurel, and the corn tassel.

THE TAX REFORM ACT OF 1986

The most sweeping revision of U.S. income tax laws since the 1940's was passed by Congress in late September. (The bill was signed into law by President Reagan on October 22.) The new law was expected to eliminate taxes for low-income groups and reduce taxes for many other taxpayers. At the same time, it would raise taxes for businesses and end many "tax shelters" that had allowed wealthy people to pay less. The provisions of the new tax law were to be phased in over a four-year period. Below are some highlights of the law:

	OLD LAW	NEW LAW
INDIVIDUAL TAX RATES	14 brackets, 11 to 50 percent	2 brackets, 15 and 28 percent
PERSONAL EXEMPTIONS	$1,080	Rising in stages to $2,000 in 1989
STANDARD DEDUCTIONS	$2,480 (single returns) $3,670 (joint returns)	$3,000 (single returns) $5,000 (joint returns)
MORTGAGE INTEREST	Fully deductible	Deductible for first and second homes only
OTHER PERSONAL INTEREST (on car loans, credit cards, etc.)	Deductible	Deductions phased out over four years
BUSINESS ENTERTAINMENT	Fully deductible	80 percent deductible

OCTOBER

2 As a protest against South Africa's racial policy of apartheid, the U.S. Congress imposed strong economic sanctions on the country. In doing so, Congress overrode President Ronald Reagan, who had earlier vetoed the bill. The new law banned American loans to and investments in South Africa; halted imports of South African iron, steel, coal, uranium, textiles, and agricultural products; and ended landing rights for South African Airways in the United States.

3 A fire and explosion crippled a Soviet nuclear submarine in the Atlantic Ocean. Three crew members died; the remaining men were evacuated to Soviet ships. Efforts to keep the submarine afloat and tow it home were unsuccessful, and after three days it sank. The Soviet government said that there was no danger of radioactive pollution.

9 The U.S. Senate found Federal District Judge Harry E. Claiborne guilty on three articles of impeachment and removed him from office. Claiborne was serving a prison sentence for filing false income tax returns. He had refused to resign from the judgeship and continued to collect his salary while in prison. The only way to remove him from office was to have the House of Representatives impeach him (bring charges against him) and the Senate convict him. A number of government officials have been impeached, but this was the first conviction in 50 years.

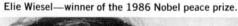

Elie Wiesel—winner of the 1986 Nobel peace prize.

10 A strong earthquake hit San Salvador, the capital of El Salvador. The quake killed an estimated 500 people and left another 20,000 homeless.

12 U.S. President Ronald Reagan and Soviet leader Mikhail Gorbachev completed two days of talks in Reykjavik, Iceland. Their discussions focused on arms-control issues, but no agreements were reached.

19 Mozambique President Samora M. Machel died in a plane crash. Machel, 53, had led the nation since its independence in 1975. (On November 3, Joaquím A. Chissano was named president.)

20 Yitzhak Shamir, leader of the Likud coalition of parties, became prime minister of Israel. He succeeded Shimon Peres, head of the Labor Party. The switch was in accordance with a power-sharing agreement reached in September, 1984, following an election in which neither group won enough seats in parliament to form a government. Under the agreement, Peres served for the first 25 months of the term, and Shamir was to serve the second 25 months.

THE 1986 NOBEL PRIZES

Chemistry: Dudley R. Herschbach of the United States; Yuan T. Lee, a Taiwanese-born American; and John C. Polanyi, a German-born Canadian, for developing techniques that led to the first detailed understanding of chemical reactions.

Economics: James McGill Buchanan of the United States, for his work in showing how economic principles apply to political decision making.

Literature: Wole Soyinka of Nigeria (the first African to win the prize), for his plays and poetry, which portray ''the drama of existence.'' Soyinka is a member of the Yoruba tribe, and his writings often detail its rich culture and mythology.

Peace: Elie Wiesel, a Rumanian-born American, for his commitment to ''peace, atonement, and human dignity.'' Wiesel, who has written and lectured widely about his experiences in Nazi concentration camps, was cited as ''one of the most important spiritual leaders and guides in an age when violence, repression, and racism continue to characterize the world.''

Physics: Ernst Ruska of West Germany, for his invention of the electron microscope; and to Gerd Binnig of West Germany and Heinrich Rohrer of Switzerland, for their invention of the scanning tunneling microscope.

Physiology or Medicine: Rita Levi-Montalcini, a citizen of both the United States and Italy, and Stanley Cohen of the United States, for their discovery of chemicals that stimulate and regulate the growth of cells.

NOVEMBER

1 Tons of poisonous chemicals spilled into the Rhine River when a fire destroyed a chemical storage building near Basel, Switzerland. The chemicals endangered drinking-water supplies and killed hundreds of thousands of fish. The four countries through which the Rhine flows—Switzerland, France, West Germany, and the Netherlands—closed plants that process Rhine water for drinking, banned fishing in the river, and took steps to prevent the polluted water from seeping into streams and underground water reserves.

4 In U.S. elections, Democrats kept their majority in the House of Representatives and regained a majority in the Senate. Republicans gained eight governorships. Among the Democrats running for office were two children of former U.S. Senator and Attorney General Robert F. Kennedy (Joseph P. Kennedy II, who won the House race in Massachusetts, and Kathleen Kennedy Townsend, who was defeated in a House race in Maryland). A former basketball player, Democrat Tom McMillen, won another House race in Maryland. And Republican Fred Grandy, who played Gopher on the TV show ''The Love Boat,'' won a House race in Iowa. A record number of women also ran for office. In some cases, such as Nebraska's governor race (won by Republican Kay Orr) and Maryland's Senate contest (won by Democrat Barbara A. Mikulski), women ran against women.

6 U.S. President Ronald Reagan signed a major immigration reform bill aimed at solving the problem of illegal aliens (people who enter the country without the government's permission). Several million illegal aliens are thought to live in the United States, mostly to obtain better jobs than they could find in their home countries. The new law set stiff penalties for employers who hire illegal aliens. But it also offered legal status to illegal aliens who had entered the country before 1982 and lived there continuously since then.

9 Atef Sedki was appointed premier of Egypt. He succeeded Ali Lotfi, who resigned after fourteen months in office.

28 With the deployment of a B-52 bomber equipped to carry cruise missiles, the United States exceeded the limits of SALT II (the second U.S.–Soviet Strategic Arms Limitation Treaty). Signed in 1979, SALT II set limits on the number of long-range bombers and missiles each country could have. The treaty never formally took effect because it wasn't ratified by the U.S. Senate. But both nations had complied with it.

Cary Grant, the British-born actor who starred in sophisticated Hollywood films, died at the age of 82. Known for his elegance and wit, he made 72 movies over a period of more than 30 years. Among his most famous were *The Philadelphia Story, To Catch a Thief,* and *North by Northwest.* In 1970, Grant was awarded a special Academy Award for "his unique mastery of the art of film acting."

Debonair Hollywood actor Cary Grant, a box-office favorite for more than 30 years, died in November.

1 *La Rue Mosnier aux Paveurs,* a painting by the French artist Édouard Manet (1832–83), was sold for $11,088,000, the highest price ever paid at auction for an Impressionist painting.

2 Desi Arnaz, the Cuban-born actor, bandleader, and producer, died at the age of 69. Arnaz is best remembered for the 1950's situation comedy "I Love Lucy," in which he starred with Lucille Ball, his wife at the time. The series was the most popular TV program in history, and reruns are still shown around the world.

8 Democratic members of the U.S. House of Representatives chose Jim Wright of Texas to be the new Speaker of the House. The position is an important one: The Speaker is the presiding officer of the House and, should anything happen to the president of the United States, is second in line (after the vice-president) for the presidency. Wright succeeded Thomas P. (Tip) O'Neill, Jr., who retired after ten years as Speaker.

9 Scientists announced that maps of the Earth's internal structure showed that Earth's molten metal core isn't a smooth sphere but has mountains and valleys that are far bigger than those on the surface. The peaks and valleys are formed when hot magma rises into the mantle (the layer of Earth that surrounds the core), and sinks again. The scientists said that the peaks and valleys of the core might help explain some scientific puzzles—such as variations in Earth's magnetic field and a slight jerkiness in the planet's rotation.

15 In national elections in Trinidad and Tobago, the National Alliance for Reconstruction won a majority of seats in the House of Representatives. A. N. R. Robinson, the party's leader, thus became prime minister. He succeeded George Chambers, who had been prime minister since 1981. The elections ended thirty years of leadership by the People's National Movement party.

18 In Vietnam, Nguyen Van Linh was named general secretary of the Communist Party, the most important political office in the country. He succeeded Truong Chinh, who resigned after five months in office. Prime Minister Pham Van Dong also resigned. He had been prime minister of North Vietnam since 1955, and he continued to hold the position after North and South Vietnam were reunified in 1976.

THE WHITE HOUSE CRISIS

As 1986 drew to a close, the United States was embroiled in a scandal over secret sales of weapons to Iran and secret aid to rebels in Nicaragua. Top members of the Reagan administration were involved, but just who was responsible was unclear.

The scandal began to develop in early November, when the United States admitted that it had sold weapons to Iran in an effort to obtain the release of Americans held hostage by Iranian-backed terrorists in Lebanon. Iran needed the weapons because it was fighting a war with Iraq, its neighbor. But the United States had previously said that it wouldn't negotiate with the terrorists and that it would be strictly neutral in the Iran-Iraq war. And arms sales to Iran had been banned since 1979, when Iranians had stormed the U.S. embassy in Teheran, their capital, and held more than 50 Americans hostage for over a year.

President Ronald Reagan at first said that the arms secretly sent to Iran had consisted of small amounts of spare parts and defensive weapons. Later, it was revealed that more than 2,000 anti-tank and anti-aircraft missiles had been sent over a period of at least eighteen months. To manage the undercover scheme, the administration had worked with Israelis and with a network of private arms dealers. Secret Swiss bank accounts had been set up to handle the cash.

The Justice Department began an investigation, and in late November it turned up a startling twist to the affair: Profits from the arms sales, estimated at $10,000,000 to $30,000,000, had been diverted to provide military aid to rebels in Nicaragua. In 1985, Congress had barred such aid to the contras, as the rebels were called, although it had lifted the ban in mid-1986.

President Reagan, who had campaigned hard for aid to the contras, said that he hadn't known of the diversion of funds. Two White House officials who were involved in the scheme—Vice Admiral John M. Poindexter, the president's national security adviser, and Lieutenant Colonel Oliver L. North, one of Poindexter's aides—resigned from their posts. A presidential commission and several congressional committees began their own investigations. Since laws might have been broken, the Justice Department recommended that an independent counsel be appointed to investigate the affair and to prosecute, if necessary, those involved.

As the investigations proceeded, many questions remained. It appeared that more people might have known of the scheme than had first been announced. The exact path of the money was also unclear—contra leaders claimed that they had never received it. There were also questions about the effect the scandal would have. Foreign governments were highly critical of the secret dealings and indicated that they had lost faith in U.S. foreign policy. At home, polls showed Reagan's popularity plummeting, and there was concern that the growing controversy would interfere with his effectiveness as president.

Corazon Aquino's supporters: "People power" helped her to become the new president of the Philippines in 1986.

PEOPLE POWER IN THE PHILIPPINES

In a dramatic chain of events that kept the world spellbound for months, a new government came to power in the Philippines in February, 1986. The episode was hailed as a victory of democracy over repression.

The new Filipino leader was Corazon C. Aquino, who replaced Ferdinand E. Marcos as president. To win the post, she and her supporters struggled against voting fraud and harassment from the Marcos government, which had held power for twenty years.

People in the United States watched the struggle with special interest. The United States has strong historical ties to the Philippines. In addition, the Pacific island country is of great strategic importance, and the United States maintains naval and air bases there. Many Filipinos have moved to the United States, further strengthening the ties between the countries.

THE BACKGROUND

From the late 1500's until 1898, the Spanish ruled the Philippines. By the late 1800's, the Filipinos were in revolt against them. Then the United States won control of the islands in the Spanish-American War. The Philippines thus became the first—and only —U.S. colony.

The United States immediately began to plan for Philippine independence. It helped build roads, schools, and other public services. And it introduced the concept of democratic government, a concept that took hold strongly among the Filipinos. Japan seized the islands during World War II. But independence was finally granted in 1946, after the United States defeated Japan and regained control.

The new country faced many problems, including poverty and a Communist-led rebellion. The United States continued to help with economic aid. But some central problems remained. For example, wealthy landowners held most of the farmland, while most of the workers were poor. And the government was plagued by corruption.

Ferdinand Marcos was elected president in 1965. At first, his government was popular. He stepped up the building of roads, bridges, schools, and airports, and he began a land-reform program that would break up some of the holdings of wealthy landowners. Agricultural production increased. But the Marcos government was troubled by many of the same problems that previous governments had faced, including charges of corruption. The landowners resisted the land-reform efforts. Communist guerrillas increased their activities in the north, and a Muslim separatist group began fighting in the south.

Faced with rising opposition, Marcos declared martial law in 1972. The legislature (National Assembly) was suspended, and opposition leaders were arrested. The following year, Marcos announced a new constitution. It granted him sweeping powers and an unlimited term of office as president. Martial law remained in effect.

Secure in his power, Marcos placed many of his close associates and members of his family (including his wife, Imelda) in top positions in government and business. And arrests of opposition leaders continued. One of those arrested was Benigno Aquino, Jr., the husband of Corazon Aquino. He was sentenced to death. But the sentence was stayed, and in 1980 Marcos allowed him to leave the country for medical treatment in the United States.

Marcos lifted martial law in 1981 and, in an election that same year, won a new term of office. But observers charged that the vote had been rigged. Opposition to Marcos grew. In August, 1983, Benigno Aquino decided to return to the Philippines to lead the opposition in a campaign for legislative elections, which were scheduled for early 1984. As he stepped off his plane in Manila, he was shot dead.

The government said that Communists were behind the shooting. Many people didn't believe this. Some said that soldiers who had been assigned to guard Aquino had shot him, under orders from government officials. A million Filipinos turned out for Aquino's funeral and heard speeches calling for an end to "tyranny and oppression."

A commission of inquiry charged 25 military officers with conspiracy in Aquino's death. But a special court appointed by Marcos acquitted them in December, 1985. The verdict was widely criticized by Filipinos and by foreign countries, including the United States.

This, then, was the atmosphere that surrounded the 1986 presidential election.

THE ELECTION

Corazon Aquino declared her candidacy in December, 1985. Her running-mate was Salvador Laurel, a politician who had broken with Marcos in 1980. Laurel had previously announced his own candidacy for president, but he joined forces with Aquino at the last minute.

Aquino made Marcos the focus of her campaign. She charged that economic problems, corruption, and police and military brutality had run rampant during his years in power. She promised reforms in business, government, and the military, and she said she would seek a cease-fire with the Communist rebels. She also raised the issue of Marcos' health, which was said to be failing. Many people suspected that, should he become too ill to serve as president, Imelda Marcos would run the government either openly or from behind the scenes.

Marcos' running-mate was Arturo Tolentino, one of his long-time associates. Their slogan was "Marcos for national recovery."

Former president Ferdinand E. Marcos and his wife, Imelda. Marcos had held power for twenty years.

41

THE WOMAN IN YELLOW

Corazon Aquino worked sixteen-hour days in her 1986 election campaign against Philippine President Ferdinand Marcos. Dressed in yellow, her husband's favorite color, she greeted huge crowds who shouted "Cory! Cory!" to show their support. She fielded tough questions from reporters. And when the campaign succeeded, she took the reins of government with confidence.

Aquino's show of strength surprised many people —she had been known as a shy, private person. The daughter of a wealthy Filipino family, she had studied in the United States and toyed with the idea of becoming a lawyer. But when she met her future husband, Benigno Aquino, she gave up the idea of a career.

Throughout their marriage, she stayed in the shadows, devoted to family life. Benigno Aquino, known as Ninoy, became a senator and one of Marcos' leading opponents. He was imprisoned for seven years. After his release in 1980, she went with him to a self-imposed exile in the United States.

Three years later, he returned alone to the Philippines and was murdered as he stepped off his plane. Corazon Aquino followed immediately—first to arrange his funeral, then to work with other opposition leaders. Filipinos rallied around her. In 1985 she was presented with a petition signed by a million people, asking her to run for president.

In the campaign and the confrontation with Marcos that followed, the 53-year-old widow blossomed into a tough, courageous leader. As president, she was firm but low-key—she made it clear that she was in charge, but she refused to live in the lavish presidential palace. She was also aware of her strength. Her victory, she said, had come "because I was the widow of Ninoy—and also because I am Cory Aquino."

Marcos, too, promised economic and military reforms. He also said that Aquino was supported by the Communists, a charge she denied.

Aquino drew large crowds at her rallies. She won the backing of the Roman Catholic Church—an important force in the Philippines, where 84 percent of the people are Catholic. Marcos also drew large crowds. But his critics charged that he used bribery and intimidation to get the support. In outlying regions, some opposition politicians were apparently assassinated by Marcos supporters.

The United States was officially neutral in the contest. But it called repeatedly for an honest election, without the fraud that had colored earlier votes in the Philippines. In addition, the United States supported an independent poll-watching group called Namfrel, which planned to monitor the voting and the ballot counting. American and international delegations also arrived to watch the vote. But the Marcos government limited their access to the polls.

On election day, February 7, 1986, observers said that fraud and intimidation were evident. Marcos was said to have substituted pre-stuffed ballot boxes and false tally sheets for the true ones, bribed voters, and used "flying voters" who registered and voted in several polling places.

The official government count showed Marcos winning, and the legislature confirmed that result. But Namfrel's unofficial count showed Aquino leading, and Aquino also claimed victory. She vowed to lead her supporters in peaceful protests and demonstrations until Marcos bowed to their pressure and resigned. "People power," she said, would win the day.

A NEW GOVERNMENT

Aquino was backed in her demands not only by many Filipinos but by leaders in many foreign countries. The United States condemned the voting fraud. Then, just days before Marcos was to be inaugurated, two important military leaders, Juan Ponce Enrile and Fidel Ramos, quit their posts. They took control of military headquarters in Manila, and declared support for Aquino. Cheering crowds gathered outside the headquarters building. When Marcos sent troops to break up the crowds, the soldiers refused to fire on the demonstrators. And some defected to the rebel camp.

The United States urged Marcos to resign. At first, he refused. On February 25, he went ahead with his inauguration—while, at the same time, Aquino staged a rival inauguration. But that night, Marcos quietly fled the presidential palace with his family and close associates. U.S. helicopters ferried them to the Pacific island of Guam. From there, they flew to Hawaii. The United States promptly recognized Aquino's government, and she announced, "The long agony is over. A new life starts for our country tomorrow."

One of the new government's first acts was to free political prisoners. Aquino also dismissed the Marcos-controlled legislature and many local politicians who had backed Marcos. She appointed a panel to write a new constitution. And she began talks on a possible cease-fire with Communist rebels.

Meanwhile, evidence emerged that Marcos and his supporters had used their power to amass vast personal fortunes. When Aquino's supporters entered the presidential palace, they found incredible luxuries—including closets and storerooms filled with thousands of dresses and shoes for Imelda. The Marcos holdings were said to be worth $5 billion, mostly invested in gold, oil, and land abroad. Most of the money, it was suspected, had been diverted from public funds. With the country facing a severe economic crisis, the new government began legal action to recover some of this money.

Some Marcos loyalists hoped that the ex-president would return to the Philippines. And there were disagreements within the new government. Enrile, who had become defense minister, strongly criticized Aquino's moderate policy toward the Communists. Late in November, after reports that Enrile was planning a coup, Aquino dismissed her entire cabinet and named a new one without him. A few days later, the government signed a 60-day cease-fire with the Communist rebels.

A referendum on the new constitution was set for January, 1987. Aquino still faced many problems, including an economy that had been weakened by years of corruption. But, at least for the time being, she had "people power" behind her.

CHERNOBYL: A NUCLEAR NIGHTMARE

On the morning of April 28, 1986, workers at a nuclear power plant in Sweden saw alarming signals on their computer screens —signals that indicated abnormal levels of radiation in the air. Immediately, they began checking their plant for a possible leak. Nothing was found.

Meanwhile, other nuclear plants in Sweden, Finland, Denmark, and Norway reported similar signals. Officials plotted the wind direction—from the southeast—and checked maps. And they found a possible source for the radiation: the Chernobyl nuclear power station, a group of four reactors near Kiev in the Soviet Union.

Demands for information from the Soviets at first brought silence. That evening, however, in a televised announcement, the Soviets revealed that one of Chernobyl's reactors had been damaged. It was eventually learned that the accident had actually occurred on April 26, at about 1:30 A.M., in reactor 4—and it was no minor mishap.

The Chernobyl event was, in fact, the worst nuclear accident on record. According to official Soviet figures, at least 31 people died (most from radiation exposure); about 300 were hospitalized; and more than 135,000 were evacuated from contaminated areas. It was feared that thousands more might die, as some of the long-term effects of radiation began to be felt.

WHAT HAPPENED?

The Soviets said that the accident was mainly caused by careless workers. But Western scientists said that flaws in the plant's design were also involved. Like other nuclear plants, the Chernobyl nuclear reactor had a core of radioactive fuel rods, each filled with pellets of uranium. Interspersed among the fuel rods were control rods, made of boron, that were raised or lowered to speed up or slow down the reaction in the core. When the control rods were raised, the atoms of uranium in the fuel rods would undergo fission (begin to break down) and produce tremendous heat. This heat was used to boil water. The steam from the boiling water powered a turbine generator, which produced electricity.

The greatest danger at a nuclear plant is that the reaction will grow too hot and get out of control. When this begins to happen, explosions of steam or gas can release radioactivity into the air. The worst kind of trouble is a meltdown. In a meltdown, the radioactive fuel grows so hot that it melts through the floor of the reactor building— usually made of concrete many feet thick— and into the ground. Once there, it can contaminate land and water for miles.

The Chernobyl reactor differed from most Western reactors in one important respect. In most Western reactors, vast amounts of water cool the fuel rods and also act as a "moderator," controlling the reaction. More water can be poured in at the first sign of trouble. At Chernobyl, the fuel rods were cooled by a small amount of water. And they were surrounded by a graphite block. Graphite, like water, acts as a moderator in the chain reaction. But it has a drawback: At extremely high temperatures, it can burn. And because the temperatures of burning graphite are so high, water can't put out the fire—it simply evaporates on contact.

Several months after the Chernobyl accident, the Soviets reported what had gone wrong. They said that workers had closed down some of the reactor's emergency systems while they were conducting tests. Then, when the reaction in the core began to speed up, they tried but failed to shut down the plant. The reactor grew hotter, releasing steam and explosive gases. Explosions rocked through the plant, blowing the roof off the building and setting off raging fires. The graphite began to burn. And vast amounts of radiation were released into the air.

As the graphite continued to burn, workers rushed to smother it. Flying over the plant in helicopters, they dumped thousands of tons of sand, clay, lead, and boron onto the damaged building. And they burrowed beneath the building to construct a barrier of concrete, lead, and boron, to stop the fuel if it began to melt and descend through the floor. It took days to bring the fire under control, and it smoldered for weeks. But it appeared to stop short of a full meltdown.

THE EFFECTS OF THE ACCIDENT

Because technicians at the plant were slow to realize the danger, people living nearby weren't alerted immediately. Thirty-six hours after the fire started, people were evacuated from Pripyat, the town closest to the reactor. More people were evacuated weeks later, when concentrations of radiation were discovered farther away. Because radioactive contamination can linger for years, no one knew when they would be able to return to their homes. The Soviets insisted that people 70 miles (112 kilometers) away in Kiev, the nearest large city, were safe. But many chose to leave.

Those who had received heavy doses of radiation were hospitalized. Radiation can have many immediate effects, including burns and the destruction of bone marrow. Bone marrow produces blood cells, and when it is destroyed, people die. A team of U.S. doctors was flown in to perform bone marrow transplants on the victims, but many died despite their efforts.

How many people would ultimately be affected was unknown. Radiation's long-term effects include cancers and birth defects, but they may not show up for years. In the Soviet countryside and in other European countries, there were fears that the radiation had contaminated crops, milk, and other farm produce. People in some areas were warned not to drink rainwater or to eat certain foods.

Previous nuclear accidents had been nowhere near this damaging. Three people had died in an explosion at an experimental reactor in Idaho in 1961. In the most serious accident at a U.S. power plant—Three Mile Island in Pennsylvania, in 1979—no one had been injured.

Chernobyl made people think again about the risks of nuclear power, which accounts for about 15 percent of the world's electricity. Opponents of nuclear power staged demonstrations in many countries. Plans for new plants in Finland and the Netherlands were delayed. But other people remained convinced that nuclear power held promise for the future—if it could be made safe.

A Soviet worker hoses radioactive dust off buildings near the Chernobyl nuclear plant. The world's worst commercial nuclear disaster took place at the plant in April.

South Africa's racial policy of apartheid has brought the nation to the brink of civil war.

SOUTH AFRICA: A NATION UNDER PROTEST

South Africa found itself on the brink of civil war in 1986. Ruled by whites, who are a small minority but control the government and the economy, the country has long been torn by racial conflict. In recent years, the white government has been under increasing pressure—internationally and from within the country—to allow greater equality. And more and more, black South Africans have turned to violence as a way of gaining rights.

South Africa is among the wealthiest African countries, with great reserves of gold and other natural resources. It occupies a strategic location at the southern tip of the continent—half the world's shipping passes around the Cape of Good Hope. The country also provides a market or a shipping point for many of the goods produced elsewhere in Africa. For these reasons, people everywhere watched the 1986 events closely.

The focus of protest was on the government's policy of apartheid—a legal framework by which racial groups are kept strictly segregated. Apartheid laws divide South Africa's 32,000,000 people into four groups: white, Coloured (people of mixed race), Asian (chiefly Indian descent), and black. Each group must live separately and be educated separately. Each has certain economic and political rights. The approximately 4,500,000 whites enjoy the most privileges. Blacks, who number over 20,000,000, have virtually no political rights, and their opportunities are severely limited.

Many of the laws that established formal apartheid were passed in the 1940's and 1950's. But the concepts behind them are as old as the history of white settlement in South Africa.

SOUTH AFRICA'S EARLY DAYS

The first white settlement was founded at Cape Town in 1652 by the Dutch East India Company. At that time, darker-skinned people had long lived in the region. In the west were two groups of nomadic hunters and herders, the San and the Khoikhoi (called Bushmen and Hottentots by the early whites). In the east were various groups that spoke Bantu languages. Most of the blacks in modern South Africa are descended from these early Bantu-speaking groups.

The early white settlers—mostly Dutch, German, and French—traded for cattle with the Khoikhoi. They also imported slaves from the East Indies and from farther north in Africa. At first, there was some intermarriage between the whites and the other groups, and this gave rise to the group that is today known as Coloured. But racial attitudes hardened as the colony began to grow.

As the colony's borders spread, the San and the Khoikhoi were all but wiped out by wars and disease. About 1800, the British took control of the colony, and English settlers began to arrive. The whites spread eastward, farther into black territory, and their guns allowed them to defeat any opposition they met.

But the descendants of the early Dutch and German settlers (called Afrikaners or *Boers,* from the Dutch word for "farmer") objected to the new British government. Chief among their complaints was the fact that the British were willing to grant blacks and Coloureds more rights. The Afrikaners believed that these groups were meant to serve whites.

In 1834, the British abolished slavery. Angered by this and other issues, many Afrikaners headed northeast. Beyond the borders of the Cape Colony, they established two republics, the Orange Free State and the South African Republic (Transvaal). The British, meanwhile, kept extending their borders to the east.

By the late 1800's, most of modern South Africa was under white control. Blacks were kept as servants or herded onto reserves that were too small or too poor to support them. Then diamonds and gold were discovered. The richest mineral deposits were in the Afrikaner republics, but the British found fabulous diamond fields in their lands.

Whites now needed black labor to bring the minerals to the surface. So they adopted contract labor laws, laws that restricted the movements of blacks, and taxes (to pay the taxes, blacks had to leave their reserves and work for cash). The laws were harshest in the Afrikaner republics, but the British also adopted strict labor laws.

The discovery of diamonds and gold also led to conflict between whites. In the Anglo-Boer war of 1899–1902, the British took control of the Afrikaner republics. But the Afrikaner regions were allowed to keep their restrictions on blacks. Thus, while blacks and Coloureds could hold property and vote in the Cape, only whites had these rights in the Afrikaner regions.

In 1910, the British South African colonies gained independence as the Union of South Africa. Although the Afrikaners had been defeated, they outnumbered the British. And Afrikaners controlled the Union government from the beginning. Their racial views soon influenced the country's laws.

THE RISE OF APARTHEID

Among the first laws passed by the Union were restrictions on black workers, banning strikes and limiting them to low-level jobs in the mines. Other laws kept blacks from buying land. In the 1920's, as industry began to develop in the cities and blacks flooded in to look for jobs, the restrictions were tightened. The government set up separate townships, outside the cities, where black workers were to live. In the 1930's, the government took Cape blacks off the regular voter rolls and gave them token representation in an all-white parliament.

This was only the beginning, however. After World War II, a conservative Afrikaner group, the National Party, came to power. It was this group that brought apartheid to full flower. The word "apartheid" means "separateness," and under the National Party plan each of South Africa's racial groups was to live separately—there would be no racial mixing of any kind.

All South Africans were classified into one or another racial group. Interracial marriage was forbidden. And new laws gave the government the power to declare what racial group might live where. Thousands of Coloured and Indian families, as well as blacks, were turned out of their homes when areas were suddenly declared "for whites only." Beaches, theaters, sports events, and social services were also segregated. In the Cape, Coloured voters were taken off the regular rolls and given token representation.

Next, the government decided that blacks should be ruled by local chiefs in their segregated areas, under white trusteeship. The reserves were declared "homelands" for various tribal groups, and all blacks were assigned to one or another of these areas. They lost even their token representation in parliament. Ultimately, the government said, the black homelands would become independent (although South Africa would retain control of many of their affairs). Then blacks would no longer be citizens of South Africa—and thus have no claim to political rights.

Several of the black homelands have been declared independent, but no country except South Africa recognizes them as such. And while all blacks are assigned to homelands, only about half live in them—they are too small and too poor to support the black population. The rest of the blacks leave to find work, and they live in the townships near white cities or in illegal squatter camps.

When it set up the homelands in the 1950's, the government realized that this would happen. So, to control the flow of blacks to the cities, it required all blacks outside the homelands to carry special passes. Failure to produce a pass on demand was a criminal offense, and over the years this law became one of the heaviest burdens for blacks. Blacks were also barred from a growing number of jobs, to keep them from competing with white workers. And a separate educational system was set up for blacks —concentrating on tribal traditions and practical skills.

The effect of apartheid was to condemn blacks to a life of poverty and oppression. Coloureds and Asians, too, found their opportunities cut off. Not surprisingly, resistance to apartheid grew. Groups such as the African National Congress (ANC), which had formed to promote black interests in the early years of the Union, organized nonviolent demonstrations in the 1950's and 1960's. The government responded by banning the groups and arresting their leaders. Frustrated and driven underground, the demonstrators turned increasingly to violence. And the government turned increasingly to force in its effort to silence the protest.

Two incidents stand out in this downward spiral to violence. On March 21, 1960, the police fired on a group of demonstrators in Sharpeville, near Johannesburg, killing 69. On June 16, 1976, they fired on a student demonstration in the huge black township of

Nelson Mandela, the leader of the banned ANC, has been in jail since 1963. He has become a symbol of the determination of South Africa's blacks to be free. His wife, Winnie, is also a strong crusader for black rights.

Demonstrators in Washington, D.C., protest against apartheid. Many countries have imposed trade sanctions as a way of pressuring South Africa to give more equality to its black majority.

Soweto, killing about 1,000. Both incidents were followed by riots, a government crackdown, and waves of arrests.

These incidents were also followed by international protests against the South African government. After Sharpeville, the government responded by withdrawing from the Commonwealth of Nations and becoming a republic. But in the late 1970's, after Soweto, more whites began to question apartheid. And there were signs of change in South Africa.

Black trade unions were allowed to form in 1978. In 1984, a new constitution gave limited political rights to Coloureds and Asians —although blacks were still ignored. In 1985, bans on interracial marriage were lifted, as were many of the minor, social segregation laws. The government declared that apartheid was dead. But these changes stopped short of giving anything like true equality to blacks. They produced only what Desmond Tutu—a South African church leader, black activist, and 1984 Nobel peace prize winner—called "the appearance of change."

Thus blacks continued their protests. And violence increased. Much of the fighting was among blacks themselves—between radicals who sought a quick end to white rule and people who thought that support of the government was in their best interests. In 1985, the government declared a state of emergency in some black areas, sharply limiting civil rights and making wide arrests in an effort to end the unrest.

EVENTS OF 1986

The state of emergency was lifted in March, 1986, and the government released the last of the 8,000 people it had detained. It also abolished the hated pass laws, replacing the passes with identity documents that were to be carried by *all* South Africans. But these moves didn't end segregation or give blacks equality. Unrest didn't end, either. And violence began for the first time to spread into white areas—in several incidents, bombs were planted in white shopping and business sections. There were also nonviolent protests, such as strikes and consumer boycotts of white-owned stores.

In May, the government cracked down again. South African troops staged raids on three neighboring countries—Botswana, Zambia, and Zimbabwe—where ANC guerrillas were said to be training. A month later, just before the tenth anniversary of the Soweto uprising, the government declared a new, sweeping state of emergency. It also passed laws that would allow many restrictions—such as detaining people for up to six months without trial—to remain in place after the emergency ended. An estimated 10,000 people, including labor leaders and entire church congregations, were detained in the following weeks. The press was forbidden to report news of violent protest, except that released by the government.

In contrast, the government offered blacks the prospect of elections—a vote for an advisory black council—although it would retain the right to approve the candidates. Thus the government seemed to waver between reform and harsh repression. And, as before, the restrictions and arrests led to more demonstrations, strikes, school boycotts, and violence.

The situation in South Africa touched off new protests abroad. In the United States, churches and student organizations led demonstrations against apartheid, and government officials and celebrities joined in. Two main kinds of economic pressures were proposed: sanctions, or limiting trade with South Africa; and divestment, or selling stock in companies that did business in South Africa. Divestment was seen as a way of forcing foreign companies to sell their South African assets, such as factories.

Those who favored economic pressures argued that sanctions and divestment would make a firm moral statement—one that the South African government couldn't ignore. Furthermore, they said, whites in South Africa controlled industry and enjoyed the greatest benefit from it. If countries stopped trading with and investing in South Africa, they argued, white incomes would be hurt. Then whites would quickly pressure their government for change.

Opponents of economic pressures said that blacks would be hurt most—they would be the first to lose their jobs. Even those who kept their jobs might be worse off if foreign employers left, the opponents said. The reason was that most foreign companies followed principles of equality in employment, while white South Africans (who would buy the factories sold by the foreign companies) did not. There was also some question about how effective such pressures would be. South Africa is self-sufficient in most areas and doesn't rely greatly on imports.

Nonetheless, the movement for economic pressures gained steam through 1985 and 1986. By mid-1986, nineteen U.S. states and dozens of cities had voted to divest, and many universities and private groups had done the same. Many U.S. corporations, including General Motors, IBM, and Warner Communications, had sold their South African assets. And many countries had imposed trade sanctions. In September the European Economic Community barred all new investment in South Africa, along with imports of South African iron, steel, and gold coins. Britain, South Africa's major trading partner, had been reluctant to go along with these steps but agreed when other Common Market members supported them.

The United States government at first took only limited steps, such as a ban on South African gold coins and on sales of computer equipment to agencies that enforced apartheid. One of the reasons that the administration didn't take stronger measures was that the South African government, for all its flaws, opposed Communism, while the ANC was suspected of having links with Communist groups. In the fall of 1986, however, Congress voted overwhelmingly for much stiffer sanctions, including bans on coal, uranium, and textiles, as well as iron and steel. New investment was also barred. President Reagan vetoed the sanctions bill, but Congress overrode his veto. The sanctions were imposed in October. The United States also named Edward J. Perkins, a black diplomat, as its new ambassador to South Africa.

But South Africa showed no sign of easing its stand. In December, the government tightened the emergency decree, banning peaceful protests such as boycotts and imposing near-total press censorship. Meanwhile, the number of people who had died in violence since late 1984 rose to about 2,300. And unrest seemed likely to continue.

ELAINE PASCOE
Author, *South Africa: Troubled Land*

50

THE MIDDLE EAST

Violence and terrorism colored events in the Middle East in 1986 as a number of long-running conflicts continued through the year. In Lebanon, torn by civil war since the 1970's, disputes raged between various religious and political groups. War between Iran and Iraq entered its seventh year with no sign of a settlement.

One of the region's biggest problems remained unsolved: the question of whether a separate homeland should be created for Palestinian Arabs, many of whom were displaced when Israel was created as a Jewish homeland in 1948. This question remained at the heart of the animosity between Arabs and Israelis.

The problems drew worldwide attention because of the importance of the Middle East. The region lies at the crossroads of three continents and produces much of the world's oil. Moreover, in recent years terrorism sponsored by several Middle Eastern groups has reached out to touch people in Western countries, especially in countries that—like the United States—have supported Israel.

LEBANON

The year opened on a promising note in Lebanon. This country, once among the most prosperous in the region, has been devastated by a civil war that has left tens of thousands of people dead. But in the closing days of 1985, the country's rival factions—which include various Christian and Muslim groups—signed a peace pact. It had been sponsored by Syria, which has had troops in Lebanon since 1976 in an effort to control the fighting.

The pact, however, didn't last even a month. Supporters of Lebanese president Amin Gemayel said that it reduced the president's authority and gave too much power to Muslims. Fighting broke out again. In addition to pitched battles between the militias of the various groups, there were car bombings and other terrorist attacks in Beirut, the capital, and other areas of the country.

In July, Syria moved troops into West Beirut, the Muslim sector of the city, and restored a temporary measure of calm. But fighting between rival Christian groups continued in East Beirut. And although Muslims

In 1986 violence continued in Lebanon, which has been torn by civil war for many years. Beirut, the capital, was especially hard hit with car bombings and other terrorist attacks.

and Christians attempted to reach a new pact in September, violence continued to flare up between them.

A group that reappeared in Lebanon during 1986 was the Palestine Liberation Organization (PLO). The Arab fighters of this group oppose Israel. During the 1970's they established bases in Lebanon, from which they launched attacks against Israel. Israel invaded Lebanon in 1982 and drove most of the PLO fighters out of the country. But by 1986 many were back.

One result was an increase in fighting in southern Lebanon, where Israel had kept some troops in a "security zone" along the Lebanese-Israeli border. PLO and other Arab groups attacked Israeli troops, and Israel responded with raids and air strikes on their bases.

The fighting in Lebanon also took its toll on a United Nations peacekeeping force, which throughout the year attempted to maintain a buffer zone just north of the Israeli zone. Four French soldiers were killed in September in attacks against a French battalion that was part of the U.N. force. The attackers were Iranian-backed Muslims who opposed what they called France's support of Iraq in the Iran-Iraq war.

THE HOSTAGES

Throughout the year citizens of several countries—including Britain, France, Italy, and the United States—were held hostage in Lebanon by various terrorist groups. A French embassy official was assassinated in September, and Iranian-backed Muslim groups took responsibility for kidnapping several Frenchmen. At the beginning of the year, one of these groups, Islamic Holy War, said it was holding four French captives. One of these was shot. In March, four members of a French television crew were kidnapped. Two were released in June, and two other Frenchmen were released in November. Other French citizens were also seized during the year.

Islamic Holy War said it was also holding three American hostages: Terry A. Anderson, David P. Jacobsen, and Thomas M. Sutherland. A fourth, Lawrence Martin Jenco, was freed in July. The group demanded the release of seventeen terrorists being held in Kuwait in exchange for the oth-

ers, a demand that was turned down. The United States said firmly that it wouldn't negotiate with terrorists.

But in November, Jacobsen was freed, and there were reports that the United States had negotiated with Iran for his release. The United States had ended diplomatic relations with Iran in 1979, when Iranians seized the U.S. embassy in Teheran, Iran's capital, and took more than 50 Americans hostage. Those hostages were held for over a year, and the United States since then had said it wouldn't sell the Iranians arms or spare parts for the U.S. weapons they already owned. After Jacobsen's release, however, President Reagan admitted to secret contacts with and arms sales to Iran, and it appeared that a deal had been made. The secret actions were widely criticized. And a furor erupted in the United States when it was learned that millions of dollars from the arms sales had been secretly diverted to aid revolutionaries fighting in Nicaragua.

Meanwhile, two British hostages and an American, Peter Kilburn, were killed by a Libyan-backed group in April. And three other Americans, Joseph James Cicippio, Frank Herbert Reed, and Edward Austin Tracy, were reported kidnapped by other terrorist groups in the fall.

SYRIA

Besides the fighting in Lebanon, Syria was involved in other Mideast disputes during the year. This country, which has ties to the Soviet Union, was accused of sponsoring terrorist acts abroad.

Syria's link to terrorism had long been debated. But in 1986, the British found what they said was conclusive evidence of Syrian involvement in an incident that took place in April. In this incident, a Jordanian, Nezar Hindawi, attempted to plant a bomb aboard an Israeli airliner at Heathrow Airport, near London. Evidence released later showed that Hindawi had been provided with a false Syrian passport and had fled to Syria's London embassy after the attempt failed.

In October, Britain broke off diplomatic relations with Syria, and the United States and Canada recalled their ambassadors from Syria in a show of support. The United States also imposed restrictions on trade with Syria. Most of the members of the European Community supported Britain by banning new arms sales to Syria and taking other measures. Concerned that French hostages in Lebanon might be harmed, French officials also met with Syrian officials, seeking their cooperation in reducing terrorism.

Syria also faced increased tension with Israel. One focus of dispute was the Golan Heights, a strip of land along the Israeli-Syrian border that Israel had seized in a 1967 war with several Arab states. Syrian President Hafez al-Assad, a firm opponent of Israel, has continued to demand the return of the land. In recent years Syria has built up its armed forces. And in 1986 it began to dig trenches in southern Lebanon, possibly in preparation for a war with Israel.

THE PALESTINIAN QUESTION

Several attempts to settle the Palestinian question failed in 1986. Mostly, these attempts focused on whether the West Bank, an area Israel had captured from Jordan in 1967, might be set up as a Palestinian homeland. Israel and Egypt agreed in principle on this question in the Camp David accords of

1978. Since then, the United States has pressed for negotiations, but no progress had been made. One reason is that the parties most directly involved—Israel, Jordan, and the PLO—have refused to talk to each other.

Early in 1986, the United States agreed that the PLO should represent Palestinian Arabs in future discussions. But preliminary talks between Jordan and the PLO broke down after the PLO again refused to recognize Israel's right to exist. Jordan's King Hussein announced in February that he was giving up his efforts to negotiate a settlement. Meanwhile, the PLO itself was torn by divisions between moderates who wanted to negotiate and more radical members who favored violence and terrorism.

Later in the year, King Hassan II of Morocco attempted to get negotiations moving again. Hassan, who had great prestige in the Arab world, met with Israeli Prime Minister Shimon Peres in July in Morocco. But the talks, which were described as "exploratory," produced no agreement. Other Arab leaders denounced the meeting, and Syria broke ties with Morocco.

Moroccan King Hassan (*below*), greatly respected in the Arab world, met with Israeli Prime Minister Shimon Peres in July. He tried to negotiate a solution to the Palestinian problem, but no agreement was reached.

ISRAEL

Israel was involved in other important negotiations during the year. In August, Israeli and Soviet representatives met for the first time since the 1967 war, when the Soviets had broken off relations with Israel. Although the meeting lasted only 90 minutes, it was seen as an encouraging sign for the future. And in September, Peres met with Egyptian President Hosni Mubarak in Egypt. Relations between the two countries had cooled since the signing of the Camp David accords and a peace treaty in 1979, and this was the first summit they had held in five years.

One topic of the talks was a border dispute over a small area of beachfront in the Sinai Peninsula. Israel had seized the Sinai from Egypt in 1967 but returned most of it under the terms of the 1979 treaty. The two leaders agreed to submit the dispute to a team of international arbitrators.

Yitzhak Shamir succeeded Shimon Peres as prime minister of Israel in October, under an agreement that had been worked out in 1984. In elections that year, neither Shamir's Likud coalition nor Peres' Labor Party had been able to win a majority of seats in the Knesset, Israel's parliament. They had agreed to share power, with Peres turning over the prime minister's post to Shamir after 25 months.

THE PERSIAN GULF

The long-running war between Iran and Iraq, which began as a border dispute in 1980, continued to take a tremendous toll on both countries. Iraq's armed forces were better equipped. But they were unable to make headway against Iran, which threw larger numbers of soldiers into the fight. During 1986, the fighting included attacks on oil installations and on shipping in the Persian Gulf, an important route for oil tankers.

Most other Persian Gulf states backed Iraq in the war and opposed the Iranian government, led by Ayatollah Ruhollah Khomeini. Khomeini, who came to power in a revolution in 1979, was a fundamentalist Muslim cleric. He advocated similar revolutions in other Arab countries. And Iran, like Syria, was believed to have sponsored terrorist attacks abroad.

But in 1986, the Iranian government faced problems at home. By some estimates, more than 665,000 Iranian soldiers had been killed or wounded in the fighting. Iran's income from oil, its chief export, had fallen drastically because of the disruption caused by the fighting and because of a drop in world oil prices. There were rumors that Khomeini, who was 86, was ill. And there were signs of dissent, including several car bombings in Teheran, the capital. All the same, the government appeared to be firmly in control.

Despite great economic problems and a long-running war with Iraq, Iran's religious leader Ayatollah Ruhollah Khomeini seemed firmly in control of the country in 1986.

LIBYA AND TERRORISM

On April 14, 1986, U.S. jets bombed targets in Libya. It was the most dramatic of several steps the United States took during the year in an attempt to stop Libyan support of terrorism.

Links between international terrorists and their backers are shadowy and difficult to trace. Libya wasn't the only state accused of supporting terrorism. But the United States said it had clear evidence of Libyan involvement in some of the worst incidents.

At the center of the issue was Libya's flamboyant leader, Muammar el-Qaddafi, who came to power in a coup in 1969. Qaddafi has used Libya's oil wealth to modernize the country. But he also dominates most aspects of Libyan life. The press is censored, and there are no political parties. Children undergo mandatory military training. Posters and pictures of Qaddafi hang everywhere. "Revolutionary committees" monitor all aspects of life and promote the ideas laid out in the "Green Book," Qaddafi's outline of social theories.

Qaddafi has also made statements supporting Arab terrorists who strike against the West. And he is thought to have helped plan and finance some of their acts. For example, the United States has said that he supports the group led by Abu Nidal, a Palestinian terrorist. After terrorists thought to belong to this group killed nineteen people in the Rome and Vienna airports in late December, 1985, the United States broke economic ties with Libya and ordered Americans there to leave.

But this was only the beginning of the 1986 events. In March, Libya fired on U.S. naval forces that were on maneuvers off the Libyan coast. The U.S. forces fired back, sinking two Libyan ships. Then, on April 2, a terrorist bomb ripped a hole in a U.S. airliner bound from Rome to Athens, killing four Americans. An unknown Arab terrorist group claimed responsibility. Days later, another bomb exploded at a West Berlin nightclub frequented by U.S. soldiers. Two people were killed, and some 230 were wounded.

The United States said it had evidence that the West Berlin bombing was carried out on Libyan orders. Its response was the April 14 bombing of "terrorist-related targets" in two Libyan cities, Tripoli and Benghazi. One U.S. jet was lost in the attack. The full extent of damage and casualties in Libya wasn't known.

The strike was popular in the United States and

was supported by the British government, but most Western European countries expressed dismay. The Soviet Union and Arab countries condemned the United States. And a U.S. envoy in Sudan and three Britons and an American being held hostage in Lebanon were killed in retaliation.

Qaddafi disappeared from public view for a few months and was said to have been shaken by the bombing. It was said that opposition to his rule was increasing in Libya. But terrorist acts continued. They included a wave of bombings in Paris and other European cities; the hijacking of a U.S. airliner in Pakistan, in which 21 people died; and an attack on a synagogue in Istanbul, Turkey, in which 21 members of the congregation were slain.

Various Arab and Muslim groups were behind these and other attacks, and Syria and Iran, as well as Libya, were said to be their backers. There was also new evidence of Syrian links to some earlier incidents, such as the Rome airport attack. The web of international terrorism, it seemed, was a tangled one indeed.

THE UNBALANCED BUDGET

In 1986, the U.S. national debt reached a staggering sum—more than $2 trillion, a figure difficult for most people to comprehend. How did the country get so deeply in debt?

The government got into debt exactly the same way that individuals do—by spending more money than it took in. Each year the government takes in money from taxes and other revenues and spends it on programs that range from defense to school lunch subsidies.

The federal budget outlines how money is obtained and spent in each fiscal year. (A fiscal year runs from October 1 to September 30.) It starts with a proposal from the president to Congress. Congress makes changes and passes a resolution showing budget goals. Then it passes individual bills to authorize taxes, spending on various programs, and borrowing. Like other bills, these must be signed into law by the president.

The reason the government borrows money is because spending has exceeded income. When that happens, the budget is said to show a deficit. (For instance, let's say you are planning next year's budget. You will take in $80 from taxes and spend $100 on various projects. Your deficit will be $20— one fifth of your total budget.) Each year there is a separate budget, and thus each year there is a separate deficit. The accumulation of all the yearly deficits equals the national debt.

Budget deficits aren't new. In fact, only once did the federal government earn more than it spent—about 150 years ago. In most years since then, the deficits have been small enough to be manageable. But by 1986, they were growing at an alarming rate, and it was feared that they might do serious harm to the country's economy.

DEFICIT DANGERS

Deficits tend to grow in two situations, war and economic recession. During a war, the government spends more on defense. During a recession, it spends more on social programs and efforts to stimulate the economy, to help bring the country out of the recession. At the same time, because the economy has slowed down and many people are out of work, the government takes in less money in taxes. As a rule, the annual budget deficit shrinks when the economy recovers from a recession and starts to grow again, because the government's income rises.

In 1981–82, the United States suffered a severe recession. Budget deficits grew. But when the economy began to recover in 1983, the deficits did *not* shrink. At first, the government was unwilling to raise taxes or cut spending sharply because it feared that these moves would halt the recovery. By 1985, the year's deficit had topped $212 billion—about one fifth of the total budget figure. Many people agreed that something had to be done.

President Ronald Reagan opposed tax increases. He said that spending on domestic programs should be cut, but that spending on defense should be increased. His administration was confident that the economy would continue to grow and that, as a result, the deficits would disappear automatically.

Many members of Congress felt otherwise. They said that economic growth was sluggish and that cuts should be made in both domestic and military programs. And many said that taxes would have to increase. Although such steps would be unpopular, they said, they were necessary because the budget deficits had reached dangerous levels.

The deficits were dangerous because the government borrows from the same pool of money as other borrowers in the United States. This pool is made up of the savings that individuals put aside in bonds and bank accounts. People borrow from the pool for mortgages and other loans. Businesses borrow to expand and build new factories. And the government borrows to make up its deficit. In 1981, the amount required by the government was a third of national savings. By 1985, it had grown to two thirds.

The government's growing requirements meant that there was greater competition among all borrowers. Interest rates remained low in 1986, but it was expected that the greater competition would soon cause them to rise. High interest rates, in turn, might touch off another recession—businesses wouldn't be able to expand if they couldn't afford the high rates of loans.

But even those who believed that cuts and tax increases were necessary couldn't agree on how they should be made. Dozens of special interest groups pressed Congress for favorable treatment when budget time came around. Many politicians, worried about re-election, didn't want to lose votes by cutting popular programs or raising taxes. And some budget areas couldn't be cut—for example, the government had to spend a lot of money just to pay the interest on its loans.

BALANCING THE BUDGET

Late in 1985, Congress passed a law calling for a gradual reduction in the yearly budget deficits. Nicknamed the Gramm-Rudman-Hollings Act (for three senators who sponsored it), the law required the government to meet certain budget goals or face automatic cuts in spending. The cuts would be divided equally between military and domestic programs. In 1986, the yearly deficit was to drop to $172 billion, and cuts would be voluntary. In 1987, it was to drop to $144 billion, and cuts would be mandatory. The deficits would continue to drop until 1991, when the budget would be balanced and spending would equal revenues. (Even at that point, however, the national debt of more than $2 trillion would still exist.)

The Supreme Court ruled part of the law unconstitutional in July, 1986. This was the part that stated how the automatic cuts would be put into effect. Congress said that it would vote cuts through anyway, and that it would find another way to make them automatic. But even with cuts, the 1986 goals weren't met—the deficit was over $220 billion. One reason was that the economy was sluggish, so that revenues weren't as high as had been expected.

President Reagan sent his budget proposal for fiscal year 1987 to Congress in February, 1986. It increased military spending, but it met the 1987 goal by making deep cuts in domestic programs. Many members of Congress said that these cuts were too severe. The legislators debated several plans and, in June, finally settled on one that offered less for defense but spared a number of domestic programs and met the deficit goal.

But the economy remained sluggish throughout the year, and the government had to revise its budget forecast. It seemed that revenues would be lower than expected in 1987—and thus the deficit would be higher.

Congress continued to work on the budget problem. But it seemed unlikely that the deficits could be permanently brought under control.

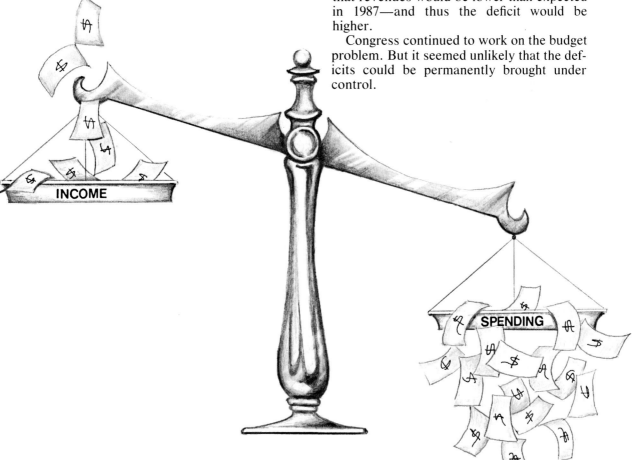

U.S. President Ronald Reagan and Soviet leader Mikhail Gorbachev meet for two days of talks in Reykjavik, Iceland.

AROUND THE WORLD

The United States and the Soviet Union dominated newspaper headlines in 1986, with relations between the two superpowers remaining strained despite several meetings and agreements. Continuing conflict in Central America, and the U.S. role in that conflict, was also in the news. A roundup of these and other events follows.

U.S.–SOVIET RELATIONS

Arms-control and human rights issues were on the agenda when U.S. President Ronald Reagan and Soviet leader Mikhail Gorbachev met in Reykjavik, Iceland, on October 11 and 12. The meeting, called a "pre-summit" conference, was supposed to bring the two leaders closer to agreement on these issues, in preparation for a full summit meeting later in the year. But the Iceland meeting ended with no agreement, and plans for the second meeting were dropped.

Earlier in the year, both sides had made new proposals on arms control. In January, the Soviets proposed eliminating all nuclear arms by the year 2000. The proposal wasn't considered practical by the West, and the United States responded with a plan to gradually eliminate medium-range missiles in Europe and Asia.

By summer, in arms-control talks in Geneva and in other high-level talks, the two sides appeared to be moving closer to agreement. But a major stumbling block remained: The Soviets insisted that no new pacts on nuclear arms could be made unless the United States agreed to abandon research and testing for the Strategic Defense Initiative. This plan, popularly known as Star Wars, called for a space-based antimissile defense system. It had been proposed by President Reagan in 1983. The Soviets contended that it violated a 1972 treaty banning the testing and deployment of antimissile weapons.

The Soviets also extended a halt in nuclear weapons testing that they had begun in 1985, and they invited a team of Western scientists to monitor their main test center for the first time ever. The United States declined to join the testing halt, however, saying that such tests were necessary for national security. And it said that verification—proving that tests hadn't taken place—still remained a problem.

There was disagreement, too, about the future of the second U.S.–Soviet Strategic Arms Limitation Treaty (SALT II), which was signed in 1979. The U.S. Senate had never ratified the treaty, but both countries had said they would abide by it. Each had also accused the other of breaking it. In 1986, Reagan announced that the United States would no longer be bound by the agreement.

These were some of the issues that the October summit was expected to help clear up. The meeting itself was nearly scuttled by several incidents. Earlier in the year, the United States had ordered the Soviets to cut the size of their U.N. mission in New York City, and a Soviet U.N. employee was arrested in August as a spy. The Soviets promptly arrested Nicholas Daniloff, a U.S. reporter, in return. But both men were released a month later (although more diplomats were expelled by both countries later in the year). And the Iceland meeting took place as planned.

The two leaders at first made great progress on several of the arms-control issues. But in the end, the talks foundered once again on the Star Wars plan. Each side blamed the other for the impasse. And there were conflicting reports about how far each had gone in making concessions to the other. Arms talks continued in Geneva, but their future course was unclear.

One important East-West agreement was reached in 1986. In September, the North Atlantic Treaty Organization (made up of the United States and its Western European allies) and the Warsaw Pact (the Soviet Union and its Eastern European allies) concluded a pact designed to reduce the risk of accidental war. It stated that each side would inform the other of troop maneuvers and exercises, and that both would allow inspection of their forces to show that no surprise attack was being planned.

CENTRAL AMERICA

Civil war continued to trouble Central America in 1986. In El Salvador, fighting between leftist rebels and the government entered its seventh year. Government troops made gains against the rebels early in the year but were unable to defeat them. In June, Salvadoran President José Napoleón Duarte issued a call for peace talks, and a date in September was set. But when the day arrived, the rebels refused to go to the talks, saying that government troops in the area posed a danger to them. Thus fighting continued, and the death toll rose to 60,000.

Duarte, a moderate, had been elected in 1984. He had helped control right-wing extremists, in and out of the army, who through murder and kidnapping had fueled the conflict. But the army was still accused of human rights abuses. And El Salvador faced other troubles in 1986, too. The war had drained its economy, and Duarte increased taxes and took other steps designed to help the economy recover. Most of these measures were unpopular with the people.

In the United States, much attention was also focused on Nicaragua, whose leftist government has supported the Salvadoran rebels with arms and supplies. In response,

the United States has supported rebels (called the contras) in Nicaragua since 1981. And each year, Congress has argued intensely over the merits of this aid. In addition to fears that granting aid would eventually lead to U.S. military involvement in Nicaragua, there were charges that some of the contra leaders were misusing the funds.

In 1985, Congress had approved economic aid but had barred military aid for the contras. In mid-1986, after several heated debates, military aid was restored and a total of $100,000,000 was approved. The International Court of Justice (World Court) ruled in June that the aid was a violation of international law and ordered it stopped. But the World Court's decisions aren't binding or enforceable, and the Reagan administration said the court had no power to rule on the question.

Then, late in the year, a scandal broke out. It appeared that during the time when Con-

Nicaraguan government troops in Honduras look for contra rebels. The United States has supported the contras.

Haiti's despotic president was overthrown in 1986, but the country remained among the poorest of nations.

gress had barred military aid to the contras, the Reagan administration had secretly sold weapons to Iran. It had then diverted millions of dollars from those sales to the contras to buy arms. During that time it had claimed that only private groups were providing military aid. Reagan denied any personal knowledge of the undercover scheme. But polls showed that public confidence in him had dropped, and an investigation was launched to determine who was responsible and whether any laws had been broken.

Whatever aid the contras may have received, they made little headway in their fight in 1986. Concern that the conflict might widen emerged in March and again in December, when Nicaraguan government troops crossed into Honduras to attack contra camps there. The United States rushed helicopters and crews to the area.

Meanwhile, in October, a U.S. citizen, Eugene Hasenfus, was shot down while flying a cargo plane loaded with contra supplies over southern Nicaragua. He was taken prisoner and later sentenced to 30 years in prison on charges of terrorism and other crimes. The United States denied that it had directed the supply operation, as Nicaragua claimed. Then in December, in a surprise move, Hasenfus was released. But in that same month, another American, Sam Nesley Hall, was arrested in Nicaragua and charged with spying.

HAITI

Haiti's President Jean-Claude Duvalier was deposed in a coup in February, 1986, ending nearly 30 years of despotic rule. Duvalier had assumed the presidency in 1971 after the death of his father, François (Papa Doc) Duvalier, who had become president in 1957. The Duvaliers ruled with an iron hand. Their secret police, the Tontons Macoute, spread terror through murder, kidnapping, and torture. A former French colony that was once a favorite Caribbean tourist spot, Haiti suffered, and its economy was all but ruined by government corruption.

On February 7, 1986, after a series of riots and demonstrations against his rule, Duvalier fled the country. A military council led by Lieutenant General Henri Namphy took control. Duvalier and his family and closest aides were flown to France aboard a U.S. military jet, and wild celebrations broke out in Port-au-Prince, Haiti's capital.

But the celebrations were short-lived. In some areas, they turned ugly as people vented their anger against Duvalier's supporters with violence and looting. And when calm returned, Haiti still faced many problems. It remained the poorest nation in the Western Hemisphere. The United States released $26,000,000 in economic aid that had been promised to Haiti but suspended because of the human rights abuses of the Duvalier regime, and it offered more aid to the new government.

Many Haitians were impatient with the new government's reforms, however—they wanted the problems solved quickly. Fresh antigovernment protests broke out. And while Haitians enjoyed civil liberties for the first time in many years, they also faced a wave of robberies and other crimes that the Tontons Macoute had kept in check.

The military junta promised a quick return to democratic rule, and it said presidential elections would be held before the end of

A group of Tamil refugees, originally from Sri Lanka, fled West Germany and made a dangerous voyage across the Atlantic Ocean to reach Canada.

1987. In October, elections were held for a council that would write a new constitution for the country. But the turnout was extremely light. Many people said they didn't understand what the vote was about or hadn't been told about it.

SRI LANKA

Sri Lanka (formerly Ceylon), an island country in the Indian Ocean known for its tea and spices, was torn by strife between two groups in 1986. The two groups were the Sinhalese, who form the majority in the country and control the government, and the Tamils, the largest minority group. Both groups are descended from people who migrated to the island from India centuries ago. They speak different languages and follow different religions—the Sinhalese are Buddhists, and the Tamils are Hindus.

From the 1100's to the 1500's, the Tamils ruled a kingdom in the north of the island, and the Sinhalese ruled a kingdom in the south. Then Europeans took control of the island—first the Portuguese, then the Dutch, and finally the British. In 1948, the island became independent once again. Disputes broke out between the Tamils and Sinhalese on various issues, but for the most part they were settled peacefully.

But many Tamils wanted a greater share of power, especially in the northern provinces where most of them lived. A few wanted an independent state. By the early 1980's, some of these had formed guerrilla groups and begun to attack government troops. The troops retaliated with sweeping arrests, and there were charges of brutality and torture. As the conflict increased, Tamils and even some Sinhalese fled the country.

In 1986, an estimated 300,000 Tamils were refugees. Most of them were in camps in India, but some had fled to the West, mostly to Europe. The Western European countries weren't prepared for an influx of refugees, however, and the Tamils often found a cold reception. One group of 155 Tamils, unable to obtain permission to live in West Germany, reportedly paid $2,500 each to make a cramped, dangerous journey across the Atlantic Ocean on a freighter. They arrived in Canada in August, having been put off their ship in lifeboats a few miles offshore.

Meanwhile, in Sri Lanka, the government held talks with Tamil groups and worked out ways to share more power with them, chiefly by giving more independence to the provinces. But several issues remained unsolved, and the guerrilla groups rejected the reforms. Because most of the guerrillas were based in India, it was thought that India's help would be needed to solve the deadlock.

Not everyone was happy with cheap oil. Sinking prices led to the closing of thousands of oil rigs and discouraged exploration for new fields.

CHEAP OIL

In 1986, car travel was up in the United States and most other industrial countries. In fact, many families did more driving than they had in years. The reason was a sharp drop in the price of oil.

This was a switch from previous years. In the 1970's and early 1980's, rising petroleum prices were a fact of life. Crude oil that sold for less than $3 a barrel in 1972 was selling for $34 a barrel in 1981. Gasoline prices just kept going up, and so did the prices of oil used for heating and in industry. Because oil is used to make many products—from gasoline to plastics to fertilizers—the increases affected nearly every aspect of life.

In 1982, prices started to level off and drift downward. Then, in 1986, they took a nosedive, dropping to below $10 a barrel. Most people were delighted—cheaper oil meant lower prices for gas at the pump and for all the other products that involve petroleum. But the falling prices weren't a blessing for everyone. And some people warned that cheap oil now might only spell trouble for the future.

WHAT MADE PRICES RISE AND FALL

Both politics and economics were behind the ups and downs in the oil market. The world's oil supply isn't evenly distributed—countries that have a lot of oil sell to those that need more. Many of the oil-rich countries, particularly those in the Middle East, belong to a group called the Organization of Petroleum Exporting Countries (OPEC). In the 1970's, OPEC succeeded in driving prices up.

The first step came in 1973, when Israel became involved in a war with some of its Arab neighbors. In protest against the support given to Israel by the United States and some European countries, Arab oil producers cut their exports and stopped shipping oil to the United States altogether. Because demand for oil was great, oil prices in the United States soared. Oil shipments resumed early in 1974, but the OPEC countries had doubled their prices.

The next step came in 1978. A revolution in Iran interrupted oil production in that country, which produced about 10 percent of the world's oil. The new Iranian government that came to power the next year resumed production, but at lower levels. Again, demand for oil allowed OPEC to raise its prices. By 1981, oil reached a peak of $34 a barrel, with some premium grades higher. In the United States, the price of gasoline had risen from an average of 38 cents a gallon in 1973 to $1.35 a gallon in 1981.

By then, however, other factors were beginning to work to bring prices down. Countries that imported oil were trying to use less. People turned down thermostats, drove their cars less, and drove at slower speeds to use less gas. They added insulation to their homes and sometimes turned to alternate sources of energy, such as solar power and wood-burning stoves. Industries, too, tried to save oil. Worldwide, oil consumption dropped from about 65,000,000 barrels a day in 1979 to about 59,000,000 in 1985.

At about that same time, oil-producing countries that weren't members of OPEC began to increase their production. They included Mexico, Norway, and Britain. OPEC's share of the world market dropped from 60 percent in the late 1970's to 38 percent in 1983. The prices set by OPEC were still important, but they could no longer control the market.

With less demand and more oil available, prices began to fall. Saudi Arabia and some other countries cut their oil production in an effort to reduce the supply and keep prices up. But other oil-producing countries—even some other OPEC members—wouldn't follow suit.

Late in 1985, Saudi Arabia switched tactics. In an effort to flood the market with oil, it increased production. The Saudis knew that this would make prices plunge, and they hoped that other oil-producing countries

would be hurt. If it cost these countries more money to produce oil than they could earn by selling it, the Saudis reasoned, they would agree to limit the amount they produced. In that way, the OPEC countries could regain their share of the market and control prices again.

The first part of the plan worked—prices dropped to their lowest levels in a decade. But the second part was harder. At first, the OPEC countries and other oil-producing nations couldn't agree on limits of production. OPEC finally reached an agreement in August, 1986, but the non-OPEC nations weren't bound by that agreement.

WINNERS AND LOSERS

For most people in oil-importing countries, the drop in prices was like a gift. People and businesses alike had more money to spend on items other than fuel, and that was expected to help economic growth.

For people in oil-exporting countries, cheaper oil was bad news. Hardest hit were developing countries such as Mexico and Nigeria. They depend on their oil income to buy essential goods from other countries and also to make payments on their huge debts.

For countries like the United States, the drop in oil prices was a mixed blessing. That was because the United States is both an oil producer and an oil importer—it produces enough oil to meet about two thirds of its needs and imports the rest. Most of the country benefited from cheaper oil. But in the oil-producing Southwest—especially Oklahoma, Louisiana, and Texas—there were problems. Since oil companies couldn't make a profit with prices so low, they cut back production and laid off workers. Unemployment rose. Banks that had lent money to oil companies were also in trouble —some companies couldn't meet their payments. In addition, there was concern that the cutback in oil production would lead to greater U.S. dependence on foreign oil.

No one knew just how long prices would stay low. But everyone agreed that, eventually, they would have to rise again. The reason was simple: The world has only so much oil. And as supplies begin to run low, demand for this shrinking oil supply will drive prices up again.

NEWSMAKERS

William H. Rehnquist, 61, became Chief Justice of the U.S. Supreme Court on September 26, 1986. He succeeded Warren E. Burger, who retired after serving as chief justice for 17 years. Rehnquist had served on the court as an associate justice since 1971. Widely regarded as a brilliant legal scholar, he had a reputation as a conservative. The Senate vote confirming him as chief justice was 65 to 33— the largest number of opposing votes in the Court's history.

In a ceremony filled with pomp and splendor, 26-year-old **Prince Andrew** of Britain married **Sarah Ferguson**, also 26, on July 23. Spectators lined up ten deep to catch a glimpse of the royal wedding procession on its way to London's historic Westminster Abbey. Just hours before the wedding, Andrew, who is fourth in line to the British throne, received a new title: Duke of York. That made Fergie (as the bride is known to her friends) a duchess.

In a historic gesture, **Pope John Paul II** visited Rome's central synagogue on April 13. It was the first time in the history of the Roman Catholic Church that a pope had been known to visit a synagogue. Speaking to the congregation, the pope condemned anti-Semitism "at any time and by anyone." **Chief Rabbi Elio Toaff** (right) called the visit a "true turning point in the policy of the church."

Kurt Waldheim, 67, was elected to a six-year term as president of Austria in June. Waldheim's campaign for the largely ceremonial post was colored by charges that he had been involved in war crimes during World War II. During the war, he had served as an officer in a German army group that carried out brutal reprisals against Yugoslav partisans and sent thousands of Greek Jews to Nazi death camps. Waldheim, a former Secretary General of the United Nations, had tried to keep this part of his war record secret. When it became known, he said that he had had no authority over the events and hadn't known of many of them.

Anatoly B. Shcharansky was one of several dissidents who were allowed to leave the Soviet Union in 1986. Shcharansky, 38, had campaigned for human rights. In 1974, he was barred from emigrating to Israel with his wife, Avital. Later, he spent nine years in prison. He was released in Berlin in a U.S.–Soviet prisoner exchange in February and, with his wife, flew to Israel.

Prince Makhosetive of Swaziland was installed as King Mswati III in April. The 18-year-old ruler was still a student at Sherborne, a British boarding school, where his friends called him "Mac." He was one of about 90 children of the former Swazi king, Sobhuza II, who had had 50 wives and who died in 1982.

Six **Canadian and U.S. explorers**, assisted only by 20 sled dogs, reached the North Pole on May 1. They had braved bitter cold for 55 days and crossed 900 miles (1,450 kilometers) of ice, refusing fresh supplies. They were the first to make such a trek since Robert E. Peary and Matthew Henson in 1909.

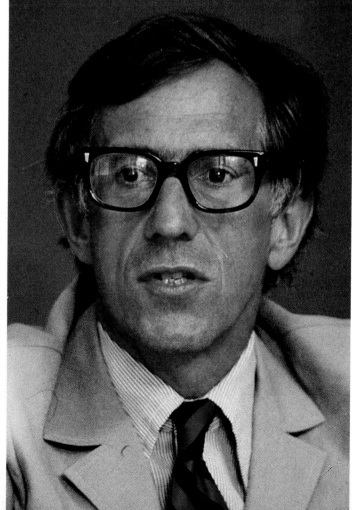

An international furor developed when the Soviet Union arrested **Nicholas Daniloff**, a U.S. reporter, in Moscow on August 30. The Soviets said Daniloff was a spy, a charge the United States denied. The arrest came a week after the United States had seized a Soviet U.N. employee on espionage charges. It was feared that the incident would disrupt plans for a summit meeting between the two nations in October. But a month after the arrest, both men were freed.

ANIMALS

Do fish kiss? No, scientists say. The French grunts shown here may be having an argument over territory— although just what the mouth-to-mouth position means isn't clear. These glittering, yellow-striped swimmers, with their fascinating behavior, are residents of the colorful underwater world of the coral reef.

Sea anemone

Angelfish

Psychedelic dragonet

UNDER-WATER-COLORS

Far more vivid than any watercolors in an artist's paintbox are the hues found beneath the tropical seas. Intense reds, brilliant blues, and bright greens and yellows create an underwater world that vibrates with color. Much of this fantastic variety of shades is produced by the animals that live in the tropical waters. But these animals haven't taken on their colors just for decoration.

There are several reasons for the dazzling colors and patterns. One is camouflage—color helps protect a fish or another sea animal from its enemies. On land, camouflage usually means drab colors such as brown or gray, which blend with earth, trees, and

Pipefish

Soft coral

rocks. But in the tropics, from the Caribbean Sea to the Indian Ocean, the coral reefs and marine plants are usually brilliantly colored. Thus bright colors and stripes and spots help sea animals stay hidden.

The animal that sports vivid coloring may also be warning predators that it is poisonous. An octopus that attacks a brilliant red fish and gets stung with poison will remember that fish's pattern and color—and avoid it. Color also helps sea creatures identify others of their species at mating time. The tropical reef is crowded with hundreds of different species of fish, crabs, and other sea animals. Still, males and females of each species manage to find each other to mate— thanks to the distinctive colors that mark each one.

But whatever the reasons for these fabulous under-water-colors, the result can be summed up in one word: beautiful.

Spotted grouper

WHY ANIMALS DO WHAT THEY DO

Before the first astronaut rocketed into space, a chimpanzee named Ham led the way. Early in the U.S. space program, Ham was strapped in a capsule and sent into orbit. When he returned to Earth, he was grinning. The ground crew thought that Ham was pleased with his space ride, but the chimp knew better. That smile on his face wasn't really a smile at all.

An animal's behavior doesn't always mean what it appears to mean. Actions that seem similar to human actions may in fact be very different. When a chimp smiles, is it happy? When a snake flicks out its tongue, is it going to sting an enemy? When a raccoon washes food, is it practicing habits of good sanitation? Scientists who study animal behavior have come up with some surprising answers to these questions.

A full, open grin is usually shown by a chimp who is frightened. It is often accompanied by loud screaming.

WHY CHIMPANZEES SMILE. When a person smiles or frowns, you usually know what it means. The human face expresses a wide range of moods and emotions. The face of a monkey or ape expresses many emotions, too—but it's easy for a human observer to be fooled.

A British scientist named Jane Goodall studied the facial expressions of wild chimpanzees in Africa. As she watched the animals, she learned to recognize feelings like fear, anger, joy, and frustration in a chimp's mobile face. For instance, if a chimp is angry or intends to attack, it presses its lips together tightly. If it's in a friendly mood and wants to be groomed by a companion, it purses its lips and pushes them forward in a pout. In the chimpanzee's world, a pout is both a greeting and an invitation.

When a chimp opens its mouth, pulls back its lips, and shows its teeth, it appears to be smiling or grinning. But its grin isn't a sign of pleasure. Instead, a grinning chimp reveals fear. A chimp grins during and after an attack, or when it's threatened by a stronger chimp. Grinning is almost always accompanied by loud screaming. History doesn't record whether Ham the astrochimp was screaming when he landed on earth, but his wide grin showed clearly that he was scared out of his wits.

If a chimp keeps its teeth closed when it grins, it is more nervous than frightened. This kind of grin is accompanied by squeaking sounds and whimpers. A low-ranking chimp approaches a higher-ranking one by displaying a closed grin, which is very much like a nervous smile in a human.

A chimp does have a genuine smile, what Jane Goodall called a "play-face." When a chimp is happy or having fun, it opens its mouth, juts out its chin, and shows its lower teeth. This play-face is accompanied by grunting sounds, or chimpanzee laughter.

WHY WOLVES HOWL. Once heard, the haunting sound of wolves howling on a moonlit night can never be forgotten. There have always been legends and superstitions about those wild, spine-tingling howls that seem so eerie and sinister. Are the wolves baying at the moon? Are they closing in on a deer or warning human listeners that it's time to climb a tree? What do the howls really mean?

Wolves actually have a number of calls. And they don't just howl when the moon is out, or even at night. As a rule, a pack of wolves will howl together every evening, moon or not, and again in the early morning. Pack howling is always started by one wolf. The animal shapes its mouth carefully, closes its eyes, and utters a long, low, moaning sound, which rises higher and higher. Then the other wolves join in, each with its own distinct voice, producing the wild harmony that seems to fill the wilderness. Usually the performance lasts about 30 seconds, but it may continue for a minute or more. As each wolf stops howling, it may bark sharply.

A group howl seems to be connected with the pack's hunting territory. Many animals utter calls and cries on their home territory, warning rivals to keep their distance. A wolf pack will defend its territory against other packs, and howling is a way of proclaiming property rights. If wolves of a neighboring pack are within hearing, they will answer the howl—but they will also keep away.

When a single wolf howls alone, it seems to be calling to the rest of the pack. Usually, its fellow wolves will answer. By howling, individual pack members can keep in touch with each other and signal their positions when separated.

Howling may have other meanings, too. It's quite possible that wolves enjoy howling together simply because they're glad to be together.

WHY RATTLESNAKES RATTLE. Is anything more frightening than the sound of a rattlesnake rattling in the wilderness? First you hear a sound that resembles the rapid clicking together of dried bones. As the rattler shakes its tail faster, it sounds more like the angry buzz of an insect or the hiss of escaping steam.

That sound doesn't mean that the rattler is about to attack. A rattlesnake shakes its tail to warn away enemies and give itself time to escape. Its rattle can save the snake from being stepped on by a horse, or attacked by a dog. A rattler would rather rattle than fight.

A pack of wolves will howl together to proclaim their hunting territory. When a single wolf howls, it is usually trying to make contact with the rest of the pack.

If possible, a rattlesnake will always move away from danger by slithering into a hole or behind a rock. But if it's cornered or taken by surprise, then it may strike and bite without rattling. People are bitten because they step on rattlesnakes, get too close, or try to pick one up.

A baby rattlesnake has no rattle. All it has is a small hard "button" at the tip of its tail. The first time it sheds its skin, it loses its baby button and gains its first real rattle. From then on, it gets a new rattle every time it sheds its skin. Each rattle is a dry, hollow scale connected loosely to the scales on either side.

To warn away enemies, a rattlesnake makes a fearsome noise by shaking its tail. To smell, a snake flicks its tongue in and out to pick up odors from the air and ground.

Since a rattler may shed its skin several times a year, you can't tell its age by counting its rattles. Also, it may lose some of its rattles as it squeezes between rocks or hooks its tail on twigs. And it may shake its tail so hard, it actually shakes off a rattle or two.

Strangely enough, a rattlesnake can't hear its own rattle. Snakes have no ears, and they can't hear sounds as we do.

WHY SNAKES FLICK OUT THEIR TONGUES. A snake's tongue is often called a "stinger," but it doesn't sting. The tongue is harmless to other creatures but very important to the snake.

All snakes have a keen sense of smell. They smell in two ways—with their nostrils and with their tongues. When a snake slithers along flicking out its dark forked tongue, it's testing the air and ground for odors, much as a dog sniffs along a country path.

A snake's flicking tongue picks up odors from the air and the ground. Then the tongue carries the odors inside the snake's mouth. On the roof of its mouth are two pits, called Jacobson's organs. When the snake presses its tongue against these pits, it can both smell and taste every odor its tongue has picked up. Its tongue helps it to hunt, find other rattlers, and stay away from trouble.

WHY ELEPHANTS TAKE MUD BATHS. An African elephant may be ten feet high and weigh six tons, but when it wallows in the mud it seems as playful as a puppy. A whole group of elephants will join together in a riotous mud bath. They'll sit in the mud, lie down at full length, roll on their backs, and wallow about noisily. That's why a muddy area visited by elephants is called a wallow.

Mud can be comforting on a hot afternoon. It feels cool and soothing, and it relieves itching. And when the bath is over, the coating of mud protects the elephant's hide from the hot sun and from annoying insects and parasites. Elephant hide is an inch thick in places, but it's very sensitive, especially to fly and mosquito bites.

WHY RACCOONS WASH THEIR FOOD. The raccoon is called "the washer" because it seems to wash its food in water before eating. Away from streams and lakes, it eats all sorts of fruit, grains, and small creatures without bothering to wash them. But when a raccoon is near water, every morsel is washed and scrubbed until there would seem to be no flavor left.

A raccoon's favorite hunting grounds are shallow pools along the banks of streams. It digs under rocks, gravel, and sand, and whatever it fishes up is sloshed, dunked, and scrubbed repeatedly before being eaten.

Is the raccoon being sanitary? Not really. In fact, it isn't washing its food at all. It's actually hunting for small water creatures. As it probes and shifts the sand and gravel, it rolls every handful between its nimble black fingers until it finds what it wants—a tasty crayfish, mussel, or snail. Then it pops the creature into its mouth and starts "washing" again.

WHY OPOSSUMS "PLAY POSSUM." An opossum is small, shy, and seemingly defenseless. It has no special armor to protect itself or weapons to fight with. But it does have a special trait that helps it survive and flourish.

When an opossum is cornered, it falls on its side and lies absolutely still with its eyes closed and its tongue hanging out of its mouth, just as though it were dead. Its heartbeat slows down. It may actually be in a state of shock caused by fright. If picked up, the opossum is as limp as a rag. It can be

An elephant wallows in the mud to protect its sensitive hide from the sun and annoying insects.

When a raccoon appears to be washing its food, it is actually hunting for small water creatures.

carried about by its tail for some time without moving before it suddenly comes "alive" again. That's how the expression "playing possum" originated.

A baby opossum will "play dead" the first time it faces danger, even if it has never seen another opossum behave that way. The act is an instinct, and it's very effective. An attacking animal, after a few sniffs at the "corpse," will usually move away. A few minutes later the opossum will come to life, shift position, look cautiously around, scramble to its feet, and scamper away.

Playing dead is a common defensive technique among many insects, reptiles, and birds, and among a few other mammals. The jackal, the honey badger, and the striped hyena all "play possum."

WHY DUCKLINGS FOLLOW THEIR MOTHER. When you walk through the park on a spring day, you sometimes see a platoon of ducklings waddling single-file behind their mother. They'll follow her wherever she goes. They've been doing that since the day they hatched.

The urge to follow is a powerful instinct among newly hatched ground birds like ducks, swans, chickens, geese, and turkeys. These birds are able to stand up and run around soon after they hatch. Usually they start to follow their mother. But if for some reason their mother isn't around, they'll look for something else to follow.

Farmers noticed this behavior a long time ago. If a farmer takes a newly hatched ground bird from its mother and keeps it with him long enough, the baby bird will try to follow him. If it is returned to its mother, it doesn't seem to recognize her. It will still run after the farmer.

An Austrian scientist named Konrad Lorenz was the first to investigate this following instinct. He hatched some goose eggs in an incubator, and after they hatched he conducted some experiments. He found that newly hatched goslings will run after the first moving object they see. It may be their mother, or it may be a person, a dog, a rolling ball, a toy car, or almost anything else the goslings see moving away from them. And after following something for just a brief time, they'll refuse to follow anything else.

This following instinct is strongest during the first few hours of a gosling's life. If a newly hatched bird is kept in a room by itself and isn't given a chance to follow, it gradually loses the urge to follow. At the end of only one day, it hesitates and seems fearful of anything that moves. At the end of two days, it won't follow at all.

Dr. Lorenz called this behavior *imprinting,* because a baby bird's first impressions seem to become so deeply imprinted in its mind. By following its mother, a newly hatched gosling learns to recognize her and associate with others of its kind. But if it follows a farmer and accepts him as its mother, then it may want to associate with humans for the rest of its life. Such a bird has become imprinted to humans.

Imprinting is important in the lives of other creatures as well. Hoofed animals like cows, sheep, and deer also struggle to their feet and start to walk a few minutes after they are born. Ordinarily, they follow their mother. In this way they learn to recognize her and stay with the rest of the herd. But if a hoofed animal is taken from its mother and raised on a bottle by humans, it will learn to follow humans. A bottle-reared lamb becomes so strongly attached to humans, it will ''baa'' plaintively when left alone with other sheep. If it is forced to return to its flock, it will go off by itself to graze and may stay apart from the flock for the rest of its life. That's why Mary's little lamb followed her everywhere she went.

RUSSELL FREEDMAN
Author, *Animal Instincts*

Above: The small, shy opossum has a special trait that helps it survive—it "plays dead." Below: Newly hatched ground birds such as swans follow the first object they see—usually their mother. This is how they learn to associate with others of their kind.

ANIMALS IN THE NEWS

A diver feeds a dolphin at the Living Seas, the newest attraction at Walt Disney World's Epcot Center in Florida. The exhibit, which opened in 1986, presents a dazzling array of 6,000 sea creatures in an ocean tank so large that you move through it down window-lined tunnels.

The ivory-billed woodpecker is among the rarest birds in North America—so rare that many people thought it was extinct. But in April, 1986, Cuban and U.S. scientists sighted at least two of the birds in Cuba. The species hasn't been seen in the United States since 1941; logging destroyed most of its natural habitat. This 1938 picture shows a young ivory-bill.

Macombo and Mosuba are rare in the world of gorillas, but they have a lot in common with each other—they are identical twins! When this picture was snapped in early 1986, the youngsters were 2½ years old. Inseparable, they spend part of the year at the Columbus, Ohio, zoo, with their father, and part at a zoo in Omaha, Nebraska, with their mother. A private plane takes them back and forth.

Quetzalcoatlus northropi, with a wingspan of 36 feet (11 meters), soared over North America some 65,000,000 years ago. The creature, a pterodactyl, has long been extinct. But in 1986, researchers built a half-size mechanical replica of the reptile. It flew over the California desert for a film, *On the Wing,* made for the National Air and Space Museum. But in its public debut, near Washington, D.C., in May, the creature crashed.

The title of First Dog changed paws in 1986 when Rex (below) replaced Lucky (left) as the White House pet of U.S. President Ronald Reagan and his wife, Nancy. Lucky, a sheepdog, was given to the Reagans in late 1984, but he proved too bouncy (and hard to White-House-break) for life in Washington. Less than a year later, Lucky retired to the Reagans' California ranch, where he can roam happily without a leash. And the President gave his wife Rex, a Cavalier King Charles spaniel who proved to be more suited to White House life.

Bird or beast? The platypus swims like a duck, has webbed feet and a duck's bill, and lays eggs. But it also has fur and produces milk to feed its young. Scientists have classified the platypus as a mammal, but it's still a puzzling creature. In 1986, research showed that the animal has another odd trait: It can sense electrical currents with its bill. The ability may help the platypus find food under water, because muscle movement (of a shrimp, for example) can produce small electrical currents.

Black-and-white pandas are rare enough, but Dan Dan is the only known brown-and-white panda in the world. This 1985 picture, one of the first of the female panda, shows her at her home in the Xian Zoo in China.

HAVE YOU HUGGED A PIG TODAY?

Pigs are no longer confined to the barnyard. Instead, they are turning up on T-shirts and greeting cards, in movies and cartoons, as car ornaments and belt buckles. People wear plastic pig snouts and hats with pig ears to parties, plant flowers in pig-shaped pots, decorate the walls of their homes with paintings and posters of pigs. In short, pigs are IN.

There's even a fan club for pigs—the Short Snout Society, whose primary objective is to improve the public image of pigs. To join, you have to take a Pig Aptitude Test. Once you're a member you can attend the Swine Ball and take part in other social events—including the pig-kissing contest at the Short Snout Gala.

Probably the biggest fans of these often maligned animals are those people who have pet pigs. Not just people who live on farms, but even people who live in cities and suburbs. They'll tell you that pigs aren't dirty, lazy, fat critters good only for eating, but are cute, cuddly, clean animals that can bring much pleasure into your life.

A LOT OF HOGWASH

Pet pigs may lead pampered lives, but many people still hold false beliefs about the animals. Some of this "hogwash" is even part of everyday language. You may, for instance, have called someone a "sweat hog" or said he "sweats like a pig." This is unfair. Pigs barely sweat—they can't, because they have few sweat glands. To cool off in hot weather, they have to lie in something wet. They would much rather wallow in nice clean water than in the gooey muck of a pigsty, but usually only the latter is available to them.

On the other hand, calling a stubborn person "pigheaded" *isn't* unfair. Pigs are quite willful and hard to deter when they want something. Like a chocolate chip cookie, perhaps. Pigs love sweets—in fact, they like all sorts of foods. One pet pig named Norma Jean eats whatever her owners eat, including clams, lobsters, and fancy hors d'oeuvres.

Unlike people, however, pigs don't overeat. Nor are they particularly messy eaters. "To eat like a pig" should be used as a compliment, not a criticism.

Pigs are among the most intelligent of all domestic animals, and they can be trained to do all sorts of things—pull wagons, chew bubble gum, carry banners that read "BOYCOTT BACON." In the 19th century one circus featured pigs that played "Yankee Doodle" and other songs on a xylophone. More recently, a woman in Houston, Texas, taught her pet pigs to swim. One of the pigs, a 3-month-old named Priscilla, became a heroine when she saved a boy from drowning in a lake.

Pet owners who have raised both dogs and pigs say that it's easier to housebreak a pig than a dog. They've even taught pigs tricks that are usually associated with dogs—such as how to sit, lie down, and roll over.

Pigs are curious animals and love to explore. Their favorite pastime is nosing, or rooting, about in the soil. They push the flat, leathery end of their snout along the ground like a miniature plow, unearthing anything in their path. They have a great sense of smell, too. The French have long taken advantage of these attributes to train pigs to sniff and root out truffles, rare fungi that grow underground and are considered food delicacies.

HOGGING OUR HEARTS

Throughout history there have always been at least some people who have been great admirers of pigs. Artists have captured the appeal of well-rounded pigs; poets have extolled their virtues; children have memo-rized nursery rhymes about them . . . and saved pennies in all kinds of piggy banks.

Perhaps the most famous literary pig is Wilbur, the friend of Charlotte the spider in E. B. White's story *Charlotte's Web*. On television there's the elegant Miss Piggy of "The Muppet Show," and Arnold of the former "Green Acres" series (who likes to sip soda through a straw). Another popular actor is Porky Pig, star of numerous movie cartoons. And in newspapers you can follow the adventures of Salomey, Li'l Abner's beloved pet.

But these storyland pigs can't be snuggled up to while watching TV. You can't take them for a walk or for a drive in your new car. You can't hold conversations with them. And, as one pigmaniac says, "You just haven't lived until you've kissed a pig!"

Pigs are in! And people who have them for pets say that they're cute, cuddly, and clean.

SLOTHS: JUST HANGIN' AROUND

Even its name is an insult—sloth, a synonym for laziness. The sleepy, slow-moving sloth has been called moronic, wretched, an "imperfect sketch" drawn by nature, even a "defective monster."

In fact, the sloth has been much misunderstood. Scientists are learning that these mammals are actually perfectly tailored to their environment. Sloths live in the treetop canopies of the tropical rain forests in South and Central America. They survive on a low-energy diet made up mostly of leaves. Since the sloth takes in so little energy in its food, it also expends very little energy—and its body and habits are perfectly designed to save effort.

One of nature's slowest creatures, the sloth spends its life just hanging around. Specifically, it hangs upside down on the branches of trees in the rain forests. With their long, hooklike claws, sloths can cling so tightly to the branches that sometimes the only way to capture one is to cut off the branch it's gripping.

TWO TOES OR THREE

There are two types of sloths: the two-toed sloth (with two claws on its front paws) and the three-toed sloth (with three claws in front). They are the last survivors of an animal family that once included giant ground sloths, some of which were as big as elephants. Ground sloths died out about 10,000 years ago. The two modern sloth types differ from each other in many ways, and there are several species of each type. But all have become specially adapted to life in the green and leafy world of the treetops.

All sloths have thick, shaggy fur; long limbs (longer in front than behind); short, stubby tails; and flat faces with short snouts and tiny ears. The shape of a three-toed sloth's muzzle gives the impression that the animal is always smiling, even when it's asleep. These sloths also have dark markings around their eyes, to fool predators into thinking they're awake when they're not.

The sloth's body structure helps it save energy. Its weight is low—about 20 pounds

(9 kilograms) for a two-toed sloth, half that for a three-toed sloth. And sloths have very little muscle, only half the amount that most similar-sized mammals have. Maintaining muscle tissue requires a lot of energy—and, after all, you only need muscles if you're going to move around.

Two-toed sloths are slightly more active than three-toed sloths. They have sharp canine teeth and will bite or lash out with their claws if they are disturbed. A three-toed sloth will just cling tighter to its branch; it can't bite because it has no front teeth. Some don't move even when a gun is fired at close range. In any case, sloths are nearsighted and don't see very far. They're also somewhat hard of hearing, but their sense of taste is good.

Sloths are the most numerous mammals in the rain forest; there are many more sloths than monkeys. But visitors to the forest rarely notice the sloths because they move so little and are usually silent. Three-toed sloths have a distinctive cry of distress—"ay-ee"—which has led Brazilians to name them ais. But the cry of distress isn't often heard.

Sloths are so lethargic and unaware of their surroundings that you'd expect them to be easy marks for predators. But in fact, many sloths survive to enjoy a peaceful old age. Not only are they hard for predators to spot, they're also well protected with shaggy fur, thick skin, and extra ribs. They may live as long as 30 or 40 years—and all that time, they do as little as possible.

A SLOTHFUL LIFE

Most of the time—up to twenty hours a day—the sloth is asleep, curled up in the crotch of a tree or hanging from a branch. When it tucks in its head and its short, rounded tail to doze off, a sloth looks like what one scientist called a "hanging animal basket." It also looks something like a wasps' nest, so predators tend to pass by. Predators also ignore the sloth because it blends in with the background of branches and leaves. The sloth's fur is naturally brownish gray. But each hair is scored with tiny grooves, where algae grow. Thus the sloth's coat has a greenish tinge.

The coat is unusual in another way: It's parted along the animal's stomach, instead of along its back (as is the case with most other mammals). This means that the coat sheds rainwater well when the sloth is hanging upside down, so there's no need to run for cover in the rain forest's frequent showers. The thick fur also acts as an excellent insulator—so the sloth doesn't have to waste energy keeping its body temperature up.

Even with their fur coats, sloths don't maintain a constant body temperature the way most mammals do. To save energy, their body temperature drops when they're asleep. Three-toed sloths climb (slowly) to the tops of their trees to warm themselves in the sunlight when they awake. Two-toed sloths are nocturnal (active at night). Being a bit more lively by nature, they can warm themselves by moving around.

When the sloth isn't sleeping, it's doing next to nothing—munching a few leaves, perhaps, or moving (ever so slowly) from branch to branch. The animal's curved claws, long arms, and flexible joints ensure

The sloth spends most of its life hanging upside down from tree branches. When it tucks in its head and tail to doze off, it looks just like a "hanging animal basket."

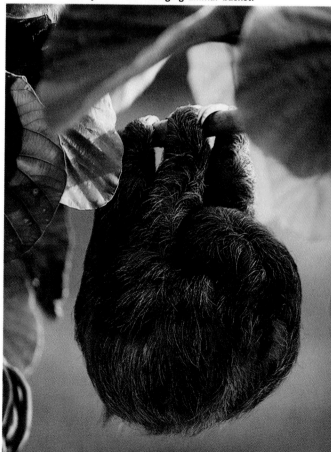

that it doesn't have to move too much to get a meal. It just reaches out in a leisurely fashion to grab a leaf. Its head can rotate as much as 270 degrees on its neck, so it doesn't have to move its body to look around. Three-toed sloths have extra vertebrae in their necks, making it even easier to reach nearby leaves. The sloth tears off a bit of leaf with its leathery lips and (slowly) chews it with its peglike back teeth.

Two-toed sloths can get along on just about any leafy diet, and they eat fruit and flowers as well. They may also raid birds' nests for eggs. But three-toed sloths have more finicky eating habits. Scientists think that each three-toed sloth learns from its mother to eat the leaves of only certain types of trees. Since different sloths learn different feeding patterns, many can live in the forest together without competing against each other for food. But three-toed sloths are almost impossible to keep in captivity because each requires an individual diet. The sloths you see in zoos are two-toed sloths.

Just as the sloth eats slowly, it digests slowly. A sloth's stomach is usually full because the supply of leaves in the rain forest is ample. The stomach is so large that, together with its contents, it may make up more than a fourth of the animal's weight. Bacteria in the stomach help digest the leaves, but the process is measured in days. Three-toed sloths eliminate about once every eight days; two-toed sloths, only slightly more often. Both types laboriously climb down to the bases of their trees to deposit their dung and then slowly climb up again.

As you might expect, sloths don't put a great deal of effort into grooming themselves. A sloth's coat is, often, a mess. It's also home to many other creatures—hundreds of beetles, ticks, and mites, as well as moths that lay their eggs in the fur. When the moth larvae hatch, they feed on the algae growing there.

Sloths are rarely seen on the ground—and with good reason. Some two-toed sloths can

The slow-moving sloth survives on a low-energy diet made up mostly of leaves.

A newborn sloth clings to its mother's fur until it's six to nine months old.

walk awkwardly on the ground, but three-toed sloths have so little muscle that they can't even stand on all fours. They must crawl, reaching out with their front claws to grasp something and then dragging their bodies up to it. For this reason, most sloths use the branches to move from tree to tree: The sloth crawls out to the tip of a branch and waits for a gust of wind to blow a branch from a neighboring tree within its reach. Then it grasps the new branch and lets itself be pulled into the new tree.

Sloths are excellent swimmers, however. Their fur traps air, and this, combined with their light weight and large stomachs, helps them bob along like floats when they must cross forest streams.

A SLOTH FAMILY

In the wild, sloths live alone. Baby sloths are born singly, usually once a year. Often the birth takes place as the mother is dangling from a tree branch. The newborn sloth clings to the fur of its mother's chest and stays hidden, nursing, for the first few weeks of life. Then it begins to reach out and grab leaves to sniff them, and also to nibble some

of the mother's food. The female raises her baby on her own; the male takes no part in the family.

A baby sloth is a little acrobat, with many times more energy than its parents. It has to be, because its mother takes no notice of it as she climbs about the trees. If the young sloth doesn't pay attention, it may be squeezed or scraped off by a passing branch. So it nimbly hops off, scampers around the obstacle, and jumps back on its mother on the other side. At the rate adult sloths move, there's plenty of time.

The young sloth continues to cling to its mother's fur until it's six to nine months old. During this time it learns which leaves are edible and which trees should be avoided. Then the mother leaves, and the young sloth is on its own in its familiar territory. Six months later, the mother returns, often with a new baby. Then the young sloth must move off to find a territory of its own.

Sloths are full-grown when they're about 6 years old. By that time, they've acquired all the laziness of their parents. They're ready for a long and drowsy life of doing nothing—slowly.

Honeybee

BEE MY LOVE

Few things are as lovely as flowers, with their bright colors, delicate forms, and soft scents. But if it weren't for animals, most flowers wouldn't exist. The reason is that animals help flowering plants reproduce.

Flowering plants form seeds by combining male and female cells, through a process called pollination. The reproductive parts are in the flowers. At the center of the flower is a vase-shaped post called the pistil. This is the female part, and it's where the ovules, or eggs, are produced.

Around the pistil is a ring of slender stalks called stamens. These are the male parts, and it's where the pollen develops. When the pollen grains are ripe, they must be transferred from stamen to pistil. When this occurs, the pollen grains fertilize the ovules, which then develop into the seeds that will form new plants.

If pollen is transferred from the stamen to the pistil of the same flower, the process is called self-pollination. But not every plant can fertilize itself. In many plant species, some flowers contain only pistils and others have only stamens. Even when flowers contain both stamens and pistils, they often can't self-pollinate—because this usually

Hummingbird

Moth

isn't the best method of reproduction. Cross-pollination, which combines the pollen of one plant with the ovules of another plant of the same kind, mixes the genetic material of the two plants. The result is usually stronger plants and better fruit.

And this is where animals help—they carry the pollen from one plant to another. They don't know they're helping. Usually they go to the flowers to drink the sweet nectar inside or to eat the pollen itself. But in the process, their bodies pick up a few grains of pollen, which are then carried to the next flower they visit.

Bees are the most famous pollinators—and the busiest, visiting flower after flower after flower. You'll often see hives of honeybees set beneath the trees in orchards, placed there specifically so that the bees will pollinate the fruit trees. Beetles, moths, and butterflies are other pollinating insects.

Some birds help, too—tiny hummingbirds hover in the air as they drink the nectar from a flower, and then dart off to the next. There are even small mammals that help pollinate flowers. They include bats and the tiny Australian honey possum.

These animals and others like them are so important to plants that they are actually the reason that flowers even exist. The bright petals, wonderful scents, and sweet-tasting nectar of flowers are there for one purpose: to attract animals that will help the plant reproduce.

Honey possum

Beetle

DOING WHAT COMES NATURALLY

When you come home from school, your dog runs to greet you, jumping up and licking your face. When you go out, it howls for hours—and all your neighbors complain.

Your cat doesn't seem to care very much whether you're home or not. Sometimes it's affectionate, curling up next to you and purring warmly. At other times, it's not so sweet —like the time it ripped the living room drapes to shreds with its claws.

What makes cats and dogs act the way they do? The answer lies in their natures. Their behavior—which may seem strange or funny to you—is natural and right to them. After all, our pet cats and dogs are descended from wild animals. While life with people has changed them in many ways, their instincts aren't all that different from those of their wild relatives.

ALL IN THE FAMILY

No matter how much you train your pets, a cat will never act like a dog, and a dog will never act like a cat. Most dogs want company, and they thrive on affection. They worship their owners, and they're always looking for a kind word and a pat. Cats, on the other hand, seem to regard their owners as equals. They like to play and be stroked, but they're also content to spend long periods of time alone.

The lives of wild dogs and cats provide a clue to these differences in nature. In the wild, wolves and dogs hunt in packs. They are runners who exhaust their prey in a long chase and then bring it down in a final group effort. Each wolf pack has a strict social order, or hierarchy. The pack leader is usually the biggest, strongest, smartest male; all the other wolves hold positions below him.

You can see how this way of life affects the way a dog behaves when it lives with a human family. The family takes the place of the pack, and the dog feels insecure when it's left alone. The dog also works out its spot in the social hierarchy of the "pack"—

usually at or near the bottom. In most cases, the dog decides that one of the adults in the family is the pack leader. That's why dogs are always looking up to people and hoping for approval—they need to belong.

In contrast, cats in the wild hunt alone. (Lions, who hunt in small groups called prides, are an exception.) Rather than chasing its prey, a cat stalks it quietly, unseen, and then springs at the last minute. This kind of hunting is best done alone—lots of cats stalking the same prey would make too much noise. And the cat's powerful forelegs and sharp claws permit it to bring down prey without help.

Thus a domestic cat doesn't feel as dependent on people as a dog does. People may be its friends, but the cat won't feel insecure when it's left alone. And it has no need to win approval from its human family.

Many other things that cats and dogs do can also be traced back to their ancestors' lives in the wild. A lone wolf will howl to find his pack—if the others hear the howling, they'll howl back. In the same way, your dog may howl when it's left alone. Many dogs also love to dig, in the flower garden or wherever they find loose dirt. Digging is an important skill for wild dogs and wolves. They may dig to find small burrowing animals, and they dig underground dens in which to raise their young.

Barking at (and even biting) strangers is another natural behavior for dogs. Wolf packs establish territories and keep out all strange wolves. Your dog establishes a territory, too. It may include your yard or the whole block, but the dog will bark at any stranger who enters it. Dogs and wolves mark the boundaries of their territories with scent marks, made by urinating on bushes, trees, and posts. When you take your dog for a walk and it sniffs each bush you pass, it's reading the ''calling cards'' left by other dogs.

Cats also establish territories and mark their boundaries with scent. A domestic cat may ''own'' an area from one third of a mile to three miles across. Whether or not the cat fights to defend its territory depends on how aggressive it is. But cats usually save their hissing and fighting for other cats—they rarely consider people to be intruders.

In the wild, cats are efficient hunters. But when a domestic cat catches a mouse or another small creature, it will often play with it —flipping it about with its paws for quite a while before making the kill. Scientists who study animals say this is because the cat is just working off its pent-up hunting energy.

Cats scratch to keep their claws sharp. Sharp claws are essential for hunting and also for climbing—something else a cat does with ease. In the wild, cats will use a tree

It's instinctive for cats to hiss and dogs to bark. Usually, they're just defending their territories.

Cats scratch and dogs dig. In the wild, cats need sharp claws for hunting and climbing, and dogs dig to find burrowing animals or to make underground dens.

trunk for claw-sharpening. But unless your house cat has a scratching post, it may use your furniture.

Cats are also known for two other traits: cleanliness and curiosity. They groom themselves for hours with their forepaws and tongues, and they bury their wastes neatly in a litterbox. In the wild, both these habits help prevent parasites and disease. Curiosity

is also an advantage for cats in the wild—being sharp observers and investigators helps cats avoid danger and find prey.

Both cats and dogs love to play, and that's another trait that serves their relatives well in the wild. Through play, young wolves and wild cats learn to hunt. And domestic cats and dogs work out their hunting instincts through play. Dogs love to chase balls (and sometimes cars), and cats love to stalk and pounce on their toys.

With so many instincts governing their behavior, how is it that cats and dogs have learned to live with people? One reason is another trait dogs and cats share: a long socialization period. The socialization period is the time when young animals learn who they are and how to behave, by copying the older animals around them. In many species, the young are socialized within hours or days of birth. But for cats and dogs, the socialization period doesn't even begin until a few weeks after they're born. And it continues until they're ten or twelve weeks old. So pups and kittens who grow up with people learn how to behave in a human household.

BODY TALK

Cats and dogs have dozens of ways to tell us how they feel and what they think. But their ways of communicating are sometimes quite different.

Both animals communicate dominance and submission through eye contact. If you meet your pet's gaze, who looks away first? Whoever stares longest is top dog (or cat). Don't try this with a strange dog, though. Dogs sometimes interpret a long stare as a threat and may attack as a result. If you meet a strange dog that may be aggressive, avoid eye contact altogether. But don't run away —that would tell the dog that you're afraid.

Body position also helps tell you whether an animal is feeling submissive or aggressive. A dog may roll over on its back to show submission; that's its way of saying "you're the boss." If the dog thinks *it's* the boss, it may jump up and put its paws on your shoulders. If a dog is aggressive, it will often stand with ears and tail perked up and its hackles —the hairs on its back—raised. The raised hackles make the dog seem larger to its opponent. When the dog is ready to fight, it may lower its head to protect its throat.

Cats also fluff up their fur—all over their bodies and even on their tails—to look larger to an opponent. When they're afraid or worried, they sit with their tails curled around their bodies. When they're *very* frightened, they arch their backs and hold their tails straight up in a "Halloween cat" pose. But a cat that brushes against your leg and arches its back usually just wants to be petted.

If the cat rubs your leg with its head and tail, it's marking you with scent that says you're a friend. A cat may also pat your face with its paw to show friendship—with its claws carefully retracted, of course. A dog that wants to show friendship will lick you, especially on the face.

Tails are great indicators of mood. When a dog is frightened or ashamed, it tucks its tail between its legs. A level, wagging tail is a sign of happy friendship. But be careful if the tail is carried high, even if it's still wagging—the dog may be showing aggression. Cats twitch their tails when they're annoyed and when they're stalking prey—even if the prey is just a scrap of paper or a rubber mouse.

When your cat wants to play, it may lie on its side and bat the air with its paws. Your dog may nudge you with its nose, raise a paw, or crouch down in front with its hindquarters raised. Dogs also have a "play face"—a silly sort of grin—that they put on when they want to romp.

Cats and dogs can also produce a whole range of vocal expressions to tell you how they feel. Dogs whine and whimper to show submission or to get attention, bark when they're happy or excited, yelp when they're hurt, and snarl and growl when they want to make a threat. Cats meow when they want attention—or food—but they rarely meow to each other. They may chatter when they spot a bird and yowl when they gather outside at night. And they hiss and spit to show anger. People don't know exactly why cats purr, but it's usually connected with the pleasure of being petted or groomed.

Once you understand why your pet does the things it does and what it's trying to tell you through its body language and the sounds it makes, you'll enjoy your pet more. And you may be better able to keep it from doing the wrong (but natural) things—like howling all day or shredding the drapes.

To show trust, friendliness, and affection, a dog will lick your face, and a cat will brush its body up against you.

SCIENCE

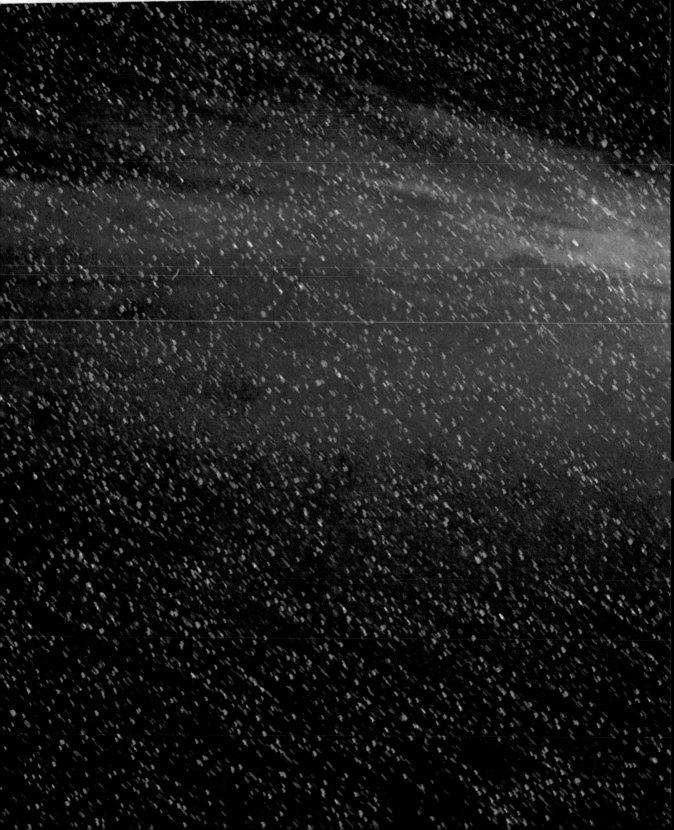

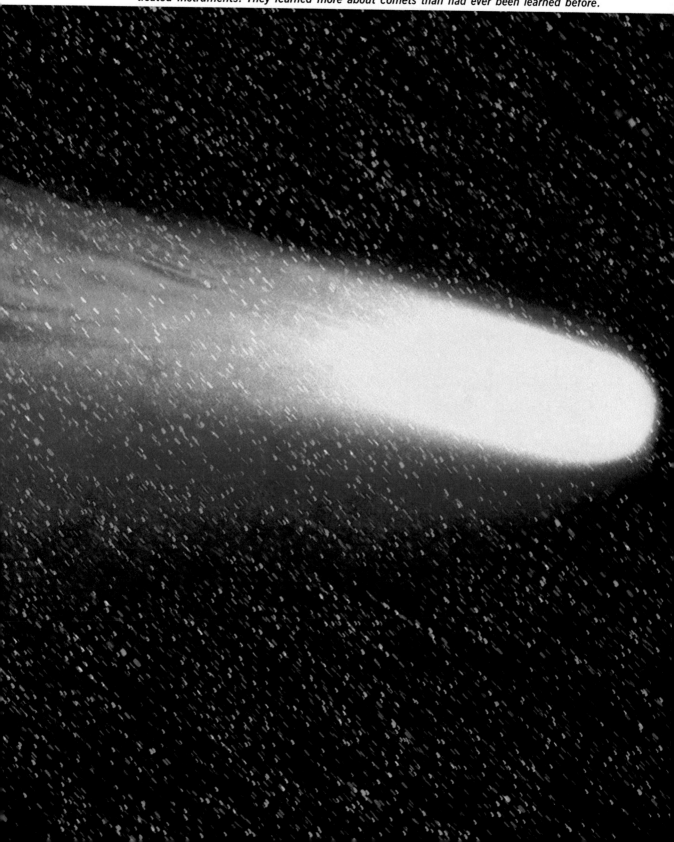

Halley's comet streaks across the night sky in March, 1986. The comet, with its glowing tail of gas and dust, visits Earth once every 76 years. During the 1986 visit, more than 1,000 astronomers took part in an international study of the comet, using spacecraft and sophisticated instruments. They learned more about comets than had ever been learned before.

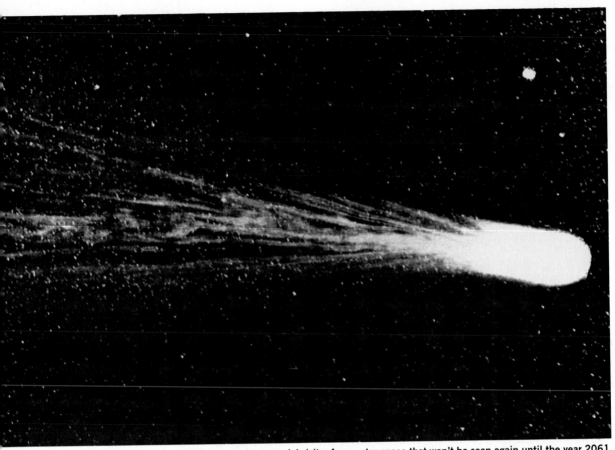

Halley's comet—a special visitor from outer space that won't be seen again until the year 2061.

THE RETURN OF HALLEY'S COMET

In 1986, a very special visitor from outer space returned—Halley's comet. People had waited 76 years for the event. The comet's last visit had occurred in 1910. "It was scary then . . . like a blowtorch in the sky," said an elderly man who remembered that visit.

"This is a poor excuse for what it was in 1910," the man said when he saw the comet in 1986. Indeed, the view of the comet from Earth was nowhere near as brilliant as in the previous encounter. This was largely due to the fact that Earth was a month further back on its orbit than it had been in 1910. So instead of coming within 14,000,000 miles (23,000,000 kilometers) of Halley's comet, as we had in 1910, our closest encounter was 39,000,000 miles (63,000,000 kilometers).

Despite the disappointment felt by some people, the 1986 visit was a huge success as far as scientists were concerned. More than 1,000 astronomers participated in International Halley Watch, using the world's most powerful telescopes to track the comet. They also had an array of sophisticated instruments aboard five unmanned spacecraft that had been launched especially to obtain data on the comet.

Two of the spacecraft, Suisei and Saki-gake, were launched by Japan. Their primary objective was to study the interaction of the comet with the solar wind. (The solar wind is a stream of charged particles—mostly protons and electrons—that flow away from the sun.)

Two more craft, Vega 1 and Vega 2, were launched by the Soviet Union. They carried cameras and various instruments, including dust collectors provided by American scientists. In early March, these craft flew within 5,300 miles (8,500 kilometers) of the comet and returned many excellent photographs and other data.

The closest approach to Halley's comet was made by the European Space Agency's craft Giotto. (This vehicle was named after the 14th-century Florentine painter Giotto di Bondone. It is believed that he used a 1301 sighting of Halley's comet as the model for the Star of Bethlehem in his famous nativity scene, *Adoration of the Magi*.) On March 14, Giotto flew within 335 miles (540 kilometers) of the comet's nucleus. Its television cameras and instruments provided extremely detailed information about the nucleus.

As a result of all these investigations, more was learned about comets in 1986 than had been learned in all the centuries before.

A GIANT EXCLAMATION POINT!

Halley's comet travels in an elliptical orbit that is more than 7 billion miles (11 billion kilometers) long. During most of its travels it consists only of a small, solid, icy nucleus. But as the comet approaches the sun, solar radiation causes the nucleus' ice particles to vaporize and form gases. These gases, together with some dust that escapes from the nucleus, form a fuzzy cloud, called the coma, around the nucleus. This glowing coma makes it impossible to see the actual nucleus from Earth.

The long tail is formed by the solar wind, which pushes some of the coma material away from the sun. A comet's tail is always

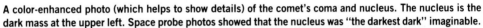

A color-enhanced photo (which helps to show details) of the comet's coma and nucleus. The nucleus is the dark mass at the upper left. Space probe photos showed that the nucleus was "the darkest dark" imaginable.

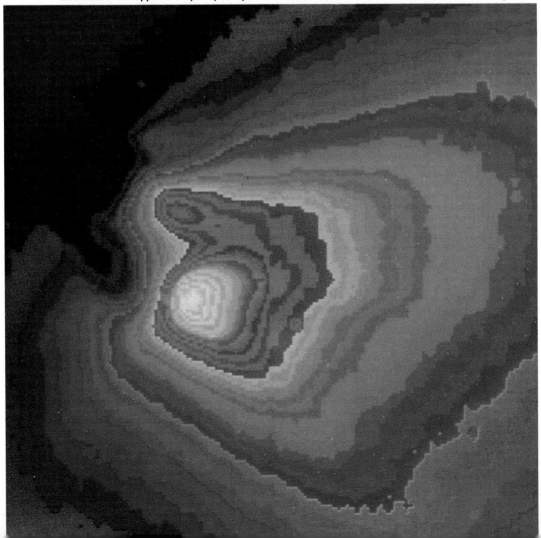

HOW THE COMET GOT ITS NAME

Most comets are named after their discoverers. But Halley's comet had been seen by people long before it was named after Edmund Halley (his name rhymes with "alley").

Edmund Halley was an English astronomer who lived from 1656 to 1742. At that time, the people believed that each comet was on a one-way trip—that it streaked through the solar system only once, never to be seen again. But Halley believed that comets traveled in orbits that would periodically bring them back to Earth's vicinity. And he believed that the comet he had seen in 1682 was the same one that people had seen in 1531 and 1607. In his book *Synopsis astronomiae cometicae,* Halley predicted that this comet would return again in or about the year 1758.

On Christmas night, 1758, sixteen years after Halley's death, a German farmer and amateur astronomer studied the sky through his telescope and became the first person to witness the return of the comet that year. Halley's prediction that comets travel in orbits around the sun was confirmed. And the comet has carried his name ever since.

on the side *away* from the sun. It's behind the nucleus as the comet races toward the sun—and ahead of the nucleus as the comet streaks past the sun.

The nearer a comet gets to the sun, the brighter and longer its tail becomes. Soon the comet looks like a giant exclamation point in the sky. (Comets, like planets, don't emit light. Rather, they are visible primarily because they reflect sunlight.)

The tail may be tens of millions of miles long and easily visible through telescopes. But it contains very little material. It is a better vacuum than any vacuum scientists can create on Earth. In fact, if all the matter in a comet's tail could be gathered together, it would easily fit into your home.

A BLACK SNOWBALL

Before 1986, the composition of comets was unknown. The most widely accepted theory, proposed in 1950 by astronomer Fred L. Whipple, suggested that a comet's nucleus resembled a dirty snowball. This "snowball" was thought to be a mass of frozen matter, consisting of ice, carbon dioxide and other frozen gases, and small particles of dust and minerals. Data collected by Giotto and the Vegas confirmed Whipple's theory, but with some unexpected twists.

First, Halley's nucleus was bigger than expected. It measured 10 miles (16 kilometers) long and 5 miles (7.5 kilometers) wide. And it wasn't a round ball. Instead, it was shaped like a peanut or a lumpy potato.

The surface of the nucleus was uneven, with ridges and valleys. And it was black—"very dark, the darkest dark you can imagine," said a European Space Agency scientist. This black coating acts as an insulator. It keeps the surface of the nucleus warm despite the underlying ice. An infrared scanner on Vega 1 found that surface temperatures in one region of the nucleus were about 85°F (28°C).

More than 80 percent of the gas blowing out from the nucleus, as it neared the sun, was water vapor. And there was a lot of it: The sun's heat caused the nucleus to lose at least 40 tons a second! Furthermore, it appeared that this evaporation was occurring only from certain parts of the nucleus: Photographs taken by Giotto showed narrow jets of gas and dust coming from six or seven vents, and all the vents were on the side of the nucleus facing the sun.

Every time Halley's comet nears the sun, part of its nucleus evaporates. Eventually, the comet will disintegrate completely. This has happened to many other comets. But it won't happen to Halley's comet for a long time. Scientists expect this comet to continue on its orbit for hundreds of thousands, perhaps millions, of years.

A HISTORY OF FEAR AND SUPERSTITION

Halley's comet has been known to people for thousands of years. Chinese astronomers were believed to have sighted it in 240 B.C. The Babylonians recorded its appearances in 164 B.C. and in 87 B.C.

In those long ago times, people had little knowledge of astronomy. Many myths arose to explain these objects that blazed across the night skies. The Chinese thought comets were "broom stars," used by the gods to sweep evil out of the heavens. The evil then fell to Earth, bringing disasters.

People elsewhere also believed that comets foretold terrible events. In A.D. 66, Halley's comet was said to hang like "the blade of a sword" over Jerusalem. Historians viewed this as a warning that told of the city's fall to the Romans four years later. The 1066 appearance of the comet was blamed for the Norman conquest of England. And its 1456 appearance was associated with the fall of Constantinople to the Turks and future Turkish victories. The victors in these battles, however, may have viewed the comet's appearance in a more positive light!

Edmund Halley's discovery that comets travel in orbits and don't just "appear" helped dispel many of the superstitions about comets. But some people continued to fear them. In 1910, after astronomers announced that Earth would pass through the tail of Halley's comet, thousands of people panicked. Fearing they would die from poisonous gases in the tail, they bought "comet pills" and gas masks. In many places, people refused to work, children asked teachers for permission to stay home from school, and priests and ministers were besieged by calls asking for reassurance.

People were once afraid of Halley's comet. In 1986 there was no fear, just a lot of fuss as people tried to glimpse it.

The year 1986 marked the 30th recorded passage of Halley's comet. There was no fear, but lots of fuss. People took out their telescopes and binoculars to try to get a glimpse of the comet. They signed up for trips to the Australian outback and other exotic viewing places. They bought commemorative stamps, T-shirts, gym bags, posters, pins, and other trinkets.

For many people, the views were disappointing. But perhaps more spectacular views will occur in 2061, when Halley is scheduled to make its next visit. So mark your calendar!

JENNY TESAR
Designer, Computer Programs

99

VANCOUVER'S WORLD'S FAIR

A rolling ribbon of concrete, jammed with vehicles that ranged from Cadillacs and helicopters to skateboards . . . a Roman chariot from ancient times . . . antique locomotives . . . visions of travel in space. These are snapshots from Expo 86, the world's fair held in Vancouver, Canada, from May 2 through October 13, 1986. During that time, about 22,000,000 people visited the exposition, making it one of the most popular fairs in recent years.

The fair took transportation as its theme, with the slogan "World in Motion, World in Touch." Nearly 100 exhibitors were on hand. They included over 50 countries and more than 30 corporations, along with Canadian provinces, U.S. states, and international organizations. The Vancouver fair was the first major world's fair at which three rival nations—the United States, the Soviet Union, and China—all exhibited.

Perhaps the greatest attraction of the fair was its spectacular setting. Downtown Vancouver is located on a fist-shaped peninsula, with Burrard Inlet to the north and False Creek to the south. Most of the fair exhibits were placed along False Creek. The major exception was Canada's pavilion, which was on the shore of Burrard Inlet and was connected to the rest of the fair by a special train (part of a brand-new transit system the city installed for the fair). From any point, however, fairgoers could glimpse beautiful views of the water and the snow-capped mountains to the north.

HIGHLIGHTS OF THE FAIR

The exhibits at the fair covered the history of transportation from ancient times to the distant future. The future was the theme at Expo Centre, a 17-story geodesic dome that was designated the symbol of the fair. Inside it were displays showing how people will travel from place to place in years to come, as well as a giant-screen film called *A Freedom to Move*. Watching the film, visitors could see what it would be like to travel in a high-speed train or on an ultra-light plane.

Near this glimpse of the future was a view of the past: the Roundhouse, a renovated train shed. It housed an antique steam locomotive with polished brass fittings, a car

from the 1890's, and other transportation devices from the 19th century—some real and some from the pages of Jules Verne and other fiction writers. An even deeper glimpse into the past could be had in the Great Hall of Ramses II, part of an exhibit that showed the beginnings of transportation. There, nearly 100 artifacts and objects from ancient Egypt were displayed.

Three large outdoor areas were set aside as Theme Plazas—one each for land, air, and sea travel. In the Land Plaza, huge outdoor sculptures picked up the transportation theme. *Highway 86* was the title of the concrete road clogged with every sort of vehicle imaginable. Another traffic sculpture showed vehicles from all over the world spiraling up a tower. In the Air Plaza, a steel cage enclosed all kinds of different flying machines. And in the Marine Plaza were 150 boats from around the world, ranging from sleek racing yachts to a reed boat used by fishermen in Peru.

The fair's most popular exhibits, however, were inside the pavilions set up by the various countries and corporations. The Canada pavilion, Canada Place, was one of the largest ever built for a world's fair. It contained nine theaters, an outdoor stage, restaurants, and a television studio. There was also a vast exhibit hall—so large that a small saucer-shaped aircraft made flights down its length every half hour. The exhibits in this hall presented the theme of transportation as interpreted by Canadian artists and inventors. From the outside, the pavilion looked like a ship, with a fiberglass roof shaped like five great sails.

At the main fair site on False Creek, Canada was represented by seven provinces and both of its territories. Several of these pavilions showcased the characteristics of the provinces and territories. Saskatchewan's, for example, was a huge, mirrored-glass grain elevator. The entrance to the Alberta pavilion was guarded by two model dinosaurs, reminders of the ancient time when the province's vast oil reserves were formed. Ontario used special effects—light, smoke, film, sound, and a shaking floor—to give visitors the feeling of standing beneath Niagara Falls. British Columbia, as the host province, put up a large two-building pavilion dedicated to the themes of discovery and challenge. Inside, performers put on nine separate shows highlighting the province's nine tourist regions.

The United States exhibit featured space

travel. It opened with a special gallery paying tribute to the ten U.S. astronauts who had died in the space program, including the seven *Challenger* astronauts who were killed in 1986. From there, visitors walked down a corridor past displays showing U.S. firsts in space, saw a film that gave the sensation of blast-off, and entered a special room that conveyed the sense of the vast emptiness of space. (The United States was also represented by pavilions from three states, California, Oregon and Washington.)

Space travel was also the theme for the Soviet Union's pavilion. Outside the exhibit was a statue of Yuri Gagarin, the first cosmonaut. Inside were full-size models of the Soviet space station and other spacecraft.

Japan's pavilion was a favorite with children. Outside, it was covered with reproductions of old wood-block road maps. Inside was the world's largest exhibit of transportation models—an entire model city, filled with moving cars, trains, and overhead gondolas. It showed the problems of transportation in a crowded island nation.

Italy displayed an ancient Roman chariot and something for the future, too: a racing bicycle made of the lightweight, space-age materials titanium and carbon. West Germany, Japan, Britain, and France featured models of the high-speed trains that operate in their countries. West Germany also showed a special car, designed for the disabled, which could be controlled by using voice commands. Czechoslovakia featured a computer-controlled simulation of a flight from Vancouver to Prague.

General Motors had one of the most popular corporate pavilions. Its highlight was a multimedia show called "The Spirit Lodge," in which a live performer portrayed an Indian storyteller—who illustrated the stories with ghostlike, three-dimensional holographic images. Several other corporations

Canada's shiplike pavilion dramatically carried through Expo 86's theme of transportation. The pavilion was also one of the largest ever built for a world's fair.

showed eye-catching films. At the Teleglobe Canada Theatre, for example, visitors saw *The Taming of the Demons,* a film that used nine screens and an eight-track sound system, and *Portraits of Canada,* a Walt Disney film shown on a screen that surrounded the viewers in a full circle.

JUST FOR FUN

While many of the exhibits at the fair were designed to provide information about various methods of transportation, there were plenty of attractions that were just plain fun. Canada made the most of some of the features it's known for: A huge hockey stick and puck towered over the fairgrounds. Visitors to Canada Place were greeted by Callithumpians, mummers who taught moose calling. And inside, actors dressed as a beaver and a Canada goose put on a show.

Five different amusement park rides offered thrills and chills. One, the Looping Star Ship, flipped riders into 360-degree loops and simulated the weightlessness of outer space. Getting around the fair site was also fun. An overhead monorail train and gondolas carried visitors from one attraction to another. Those who wanted to stay on the ground could try some other unusual transportation methods: horse-drawn buggies and pedicabs.

Dozens of restaurants offered good things to eat. There were tried-and-true favorites like hamburgers, and novelties like Sputnik sausages and Siberian orange drink (at the Soviet pavilion) and buffalo steaks (at Canada's First Nation restaurant). The Northwest Territories pavilion offered reindeer and whale meat.

There were also special events throughout the fair season. Britain's Prince Charles and Princess Diana were on hand to open the fair in May. Singers, comedians, orchestras, and ballet and theater companies from around the world made appearances in Vancouver while the fair was running. The Kirov Ballet, the famous Soviet troupe, made its first North American appearance in more than 22 years. The Peking People's Art Theater made its first North American appearance ever. And countless smaller productions were presented at the seventeen theaters on the fair site itself.

So that the theme of the fair wouldn't be

A popular outdoor exhibit was a colorful traffic sculpture that showed numerous vehicles spiraling up a tower.

forgotten, fair organizers scheduled special events that were tied to transportation. These events were organized around specific aspects of the theme, such as polar transportation, automobiles, human-powered transportation, and modern rail travel. They included a hot-air balloon festival, car rallies, races between colorful dragon boats specially shipped from Hong Kong, parades of work boats and rescue boats, and contests in parachuting and skateboarding.

If visitors tired of the fair, they could always turn to the attractions of the city of Vancouver and the beautiful country surrounding it. The people of Vancouver hoped that, long after the fair was closed, the millions of visitors who had attended it would remember their city and, perhaps, return.

COMPUTER BULLETIN BOARDS

"For Sale: 10-speed bike; new tires. Best offer."

"Is anyone out there taking computer classes at the community college? I'd like to talk to you."

"Missing! 8-year-old collie named Shaggy. Reward."

"50's dance at Rogers H.S. Friday night, beginning at 8. Bring your parents' old dance records."

These messages and ads are just like the ones on the bulletin boards in your school and in the local supermarket—except in one very important way. Instead of being written on paper and posted on corkboard, they appear in glowing letters on a computer screen. They're on a computer bulletin board, one of the newest ways to communicate with other people.

A computer bulletin board is an electronic "warehouse" for messages—messages are actually stored in a computer's memory. If you have the right equipment, you can contact the computer to read the messages. You can also contact the computer to have your own message "posted" on the bulletin board, for other users to read.

KINDS OF BULLETIN BOARDS

Some bulletin boards are set up by individuals, churches, clubs, schools, small organizations, and other such groups. These bulletin boards are generally local and free. That is, they are open to anyone who calls in.

Other bulletin boards, such as those within corporations and government agencies, are private. Codes or passwords prevent outsiders from gaining access to private boards.

Still other bulletin boards are part of commercial information networks such as The Source and CompuServe. To use these boards, a person must subscribe to the network and pay a fee.

Some computer bulletin boards are small, devoted to specific subjects, such as computer games, genealogy, airplanes, jokes, food, astronomy, and dating, to name just a very few. Other boards are so large that they are divided into subject categories. Callers who connect with such boards are offered a choice of message lists—each one covering a different subject.

New bulletin boards are constantly springing up, so it's difficult to know exactly how many are in existence. But there are at least 2,500 public bulletin boards across the United States. The New York City area alone has more than 100 boards, with names both straightforward and strange-sounding— Board of Ed, NY Computer Society, Time Tunnel, Coco Creations, The Worm Hole.

To learn about bulletin boards in your area, check computer publications or ask local computer retailers. Many bulletin boards provide telephone numbers of other boards. Once you've contacted one board, you may become part of a whole new world.

USING BULLETIN BOARDS

Do you want to read the messages on a computer bulletin board? Or leave messages of your own? To do so,

you need a computer, a modem (a device that connects the computer to a telephone), and communications software (a program that will allow your computer to "talk" over the telephone lines). You also need the telephone number of the bulletin board you would like to reach.

Turn on your computer, load the communications program, and dial or key into the computer the phone number of the bulletin board. When the bulletin board's main computer answers the phone, you'll hear a tone that tells you that your computer is connected to it. The bulletin board computer may send a welcoming message, which will appear on your screen. Next, it may ask whether you want to read messages on the board or add a message of your own.

If you want to add a message, you simply type it on your computer and then tell your computer to "send" it through the modem and telephone line to the bulletin board. You'll be asked if your message is for retrieval by anyone or only by a specific person. If it's for a specific person, you need to know the name that person uses. Some people use their real names when communicating through a bulletin board. Others use nicknames or codes, such as "Fat Cat" or "VX-27."

Let's say a computer game has you flummoxed. You just can't figure out how to escape from "jail." You call up a bulletin board and leave a message for anyone to read: "How do I get into the guard's house

or past the oooga-oooga lady?"Leave your name, too—or a code name, such as "Red Rody." Later, check to see if there are any messages for you. If another player knows the game and reads your message, he or she may send you a private message: "Red Rody, look for a pilot's license in the mailbox near the guardhouse."

BECOME A "SYSOP"

The person who runs a computer bulletin board is called a system operator, or "sysop." Many sysops are teenagers.

Sysops usually leave their computers turned on 24 hours a day. People can contact the computers and leave messages even if the sysops are elsewhere.

To set up a bulletin board and become a sysop, you need a computer, a modem, and a bulletin board software package. This type of software can be purchased from a computer store. Some bulletin board software is in the public domain, which means it's available free (usually through computer clubs and similar groups). And if you know computer programming, you can write your own software. Which is the best choice for you? Why not ask for help on someone else's bulletin board?

JENNY TESAR
Designer, Computer Programs

NATURE'S VANISHING RAIN FORESTS

Enter the dim, green world of the tropical rain forest. As you walk down the forest trail, huge trees surround you. Tropical vines hang from their limbs, and far above you their leafy branches form a rooflike canopy that blocks out the sun. The air is warm, damp, and heavy.

High above, you hear the calls of howler monkeys and parrots and other exotic birds. But on the forest floor, you see few signs of life. Every so often you hear a soft rustle as a toad or some other small creature hops away, startled by your footsteps. And now and then you spot a brilliant blue butterfly, fluttering through the dim light. Be careful to stay on the trail—the tree trunks look so much alike that it's easy to get lost. And keep your eyes open for snakes.

Tropical rain forests like the one you have entered cover a narrow band of the Earth near the equator. They are found in Africa, South and Central America, Asia, and Oceania. (The world's largest rain forest is around the Amazon River, in Brazil.) They get their name from the fact that it rains there almost every day—which also accounts for the heavy, damp air. And, although you may see few animals as you walk along the forest floor, rain forests actually teem with life. More than a third of the world's animal and plant species live there, and scientists believe that the tropical habitat is home to many others that haven't even been discovered yet.

But the rain forests are disappearing at an alarming rate: More than 50 acres (20 hectares) of forest are cut every minute, as people take the trees for lumber and the land for farms, roads, and other types of development. Thus scientists are rushing to study these exotic living laboratories before they vanish. And conservationists are working on plans to save as much of the rain forests as they can.

THE RAIN FOREST FLOOR

Tropical rain forests are one of the world's last great wilderness areas. Few people live in them, and many regions of the forests have never been explored. The forests took centuries to develop—some of the tropical trees that now tower hundreds of feet above the ground were saplings when Columbus sailed to the New World. Unlike northern forests, where you will see many trees of the same species grouped together in clumps and stands, the tropical rain forest contains a seemingly endless variety of different types of trees.

The dense shade cast by the canopy of the treetops means that there is no tangle of underbrush on the forest floor—without sunlight, plants can't grow. Instead, just a few species of ferns and similar plants survive in the open spaces between the tree trunks. Some trees have huge "buttress" roots that flare out from the trunks 20 feet (6 meters) above the ground. The roots extend down into the soil, and scientists think they help anchor the trees in the thin leaf mold that carpets the forest floor.

The soil of the floor isn't rich, and some trees and plants have developed other ways of getting the nutrients they need. For example, special types of fungi grow around the tree roots and help the trees break down the few nutrients that the soil does contain. And some trees have developed above-ground roots that trap water and minerals in the air. The soil is so poor, in fact, that when land has been cleared for farming, people often find that it will support crops for only a year or two.

Sometimes there's a break in the canopy —because a tree has fallen, or because a stream has cut its way through the forest. Then sunlight can enter, and the forest produces a riot of vines, shrubs, and flowering plants. Animals congregate in these spots, too—monkeys, iridescent butterflies, and brightly colored birds such as parrots, toucans, and orioles. In the South American forests, there are brilliant red and blue arrow poison frogs, whose bright colors warn predators of the deadly poison they secrete on their skins. And always, there are snakes that hang like vines from tree limbs.

Forest streams also teem with life. In many places, there are strange species of fish. In the forests around the Amazon, for

Most of the life of the tropical rain forest is found far above the ground, in the treetop canopy. There, huge leafy branches spread horizontally, forming a dense "forest above the forest." And that layer supports an almost endless variety of plants and animals.

Marmoset

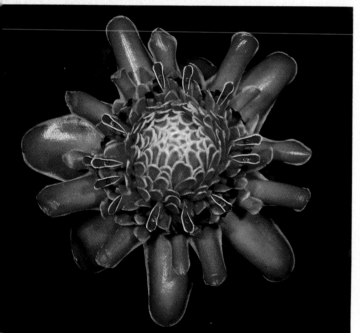

Torch ginger flower

Quetzal

108

Heliconia

Variegated squirrel

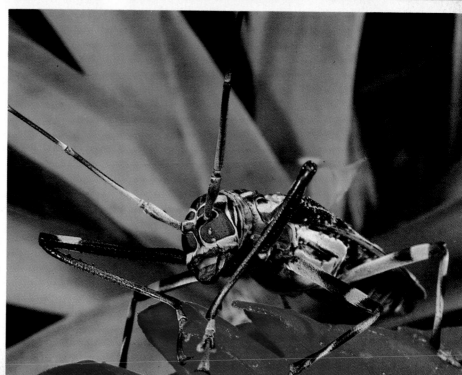

Harlequin beetle

example, one type of fish has flat-topped teeth like those found in cows and other grazing animals. The teeth have a purpose—for two to four months a year, when the Amazon's waters are high, the river spills over its banks and floods the forest floor. Then the fish can swim out through the forest and eat the seeds, fruit, and nuts that they find there. Other fish have the remarkable ability to breathe air during the brief dry seasons when forest ponds shrink. They do this through a special collection of blood vessels in their foreheads. These vessels work much like human lungs, pumping oxygen directly into the bloodstream.

One reason you see so few signs of life as you walk through the forest is that many of the animals are nocturnal—they sleep during the day and come out to hunt for food at night. But the biggest reason is that most of the life of the forest is found far above the ground, in the treetop canopy.

STUDYING THE CANOPY

Scientists are racing against time to study the rain-forest canopies before they are destroyed. But they face special risks and problems in their work. The first problem is getting up to the treetops.

Climbing the trees isn't a good solution—snakes and scorpions lie in wait along the branches. Some researchers build towers up to treetop level. Others use "cherrypickers"—the mechanical lifts often used in tree work and fruit harvesting. One scientist studying the rain forest in Costa Rica climbs into the trees on ropes and constructs a platform in the branches. Then he assembles a network of ropes, like a spider web, that allows him to move from tree to tree.

The dangers don't end when the researchers are in the trees. Violent storms can uproot the trees, and there's always the risk of a fall. Still, dedicated researchers continue to climb into the canopy, to see first-hand one of the least-studied habitats on Earth.

Scientist Donald Perry studies Costa Rica's rain-forest canopy by constructing a weblike network of ropes.

THE TREETOP CANOPY

The rain-forest canopy is a completely different world. Here, in the sunlight 50 to 200 feet (15 to 60 meters) above the ground, the huge trees send out massive horizontal branches. And they support an almost endless variety of life forms—from birds, bats, and butterflies to mice, monkeys, and countless other, more exotic animals. Many of the creatures that live here spend their entire lives in the treetops, rarely or never setting foot on the ground.

The key to life high above the ground is interdependence: The plants and animals of the canopy depend on each other to stay alive. For example, a strange plant called the trashbasket plant anchors itself to tree limbs. It traps debris that falls from higher in the canopy and turns this material into nutrient-rich humus. The humus supports not only the plant but also insects like earthworms and centipedes.

Many other plants grow in the treetops, too. Most of these are epiphytes—plants that grow on tree limbs and take the moisture and nutrients they need from the air rather than from the soil. There are countless epiphytic varieties of orchids, mosses, lichens, and ferns. One epiphyte, a spiky-topped plant called the bromeliad, helps nurture baby frogs. The leaves of this plant trap water, and tree frogs place their eggs there. When the eggs hatch, the tadpoles can swim about in the water caught by the plant.

A few of the mightiest trees depend on single species of insects to reproduce. The flower of the Brazil nut, for example, is so tightly closed that only one bee, the carpenter bee, is able to open it. Without this bee, the flowers couldn't be pollinated, and no seeds would be produced. The many species of tropical fig trees in the rain forest depend on tiny fig wasps for pollination. The wasps in turn lay their eggs in the tree's fruit.

Some species of insects also depend on each other. In South America, for example, wasps bore holes in the long hanging nests of Azteca ants. The Azteca ants then protect the wasps from their main predators, the army ants. And the stinging wasps in turn protect the Azteca ants from anteaters that climb into the trees in search of food.

Sometimes the chain of interdependence extends back down to the forest floor. Several species of birds, for example, follow army ants as they march across the floor looking for food. The birds eat insects that the army ants flush out, and they in turn are followed by butterflies that feed on their droppings.

One of the best-known treetop dwellers is the sloth—a mammal that hangs upside-down from the tree limbs and sleeps most of the time. More than twenty species of insects, including several moths and beetles, live in the sloth's furry coat. A type of algae also grows on the coat, giving the animal a greenish tint that helps it stay camouflaged among the leaves.

Like other tree-living animals, the sloth is specially adapted to its home: It has long limbs and grasping hands that help it reach and hold vines and tree branches, and its eyes are positioned looking forward, for good depth perception. The many species of monkeys that live in the canopy also have these traits. Treetop animals seem to share still another trait—intelligence. Parrots, which are said to be among the smartest of birds, live in the rain-forest canopy. And the coati, a raccoonlike animal that also lives in the treetops, uses basic reasoning to get its food, much as a chimpanzee does.

THE FUTURE OF THE RAIN FORESTS

It seems likely that as more acres of forest are cut, many of the rain forest plants and animals will become extinct. This is because so many of these plants and animals depend closely on each other. Yet the outlook for saving the forests isn't good. Most of the forests are in developing countries that badly need both farmland and the income from lumber that cutting the forests provides.

But there are ways in which the uncut forests can provide income. Brazil nuts already are an important crop in South America. And some countries have started to experiment with other ways of producing crops from the rain forest—oil from oil palms, for example, and certain fast-growing trees that can be raised and harvested for lumber. Other tropical plants provide valuable chemicals that can be used in medicines and insecticides, and they might be grown for those purposes. With careful planning and good conservation, the tropical rain forests may yet be saved.

Voyager—designed for record-breaking flights.

THE FLIGHT
OF THE VOYAGER

In 1927, Charles Lindbergh made the first nonstop solo flight from New York to Paris, a distance of 3,610 miles (5,810 kilometers). His distance record was broken the same year. And as airplanes improved, nonstop distance records were broken repeatedly. In 1962, a U.S. Air Force pilot set a record for nonstop distance flown without refueling by flying from Okinawa to Spain—an astounding 12,532 miles (20,168 kilometers).

In 1986, two private pilots from California broke that record—by just about doubling the distance. The pilots, Richard Rutan and Jeana Yeager, flew nonstop around the world without refueling, covering a distance of 25,012 miles (40,253 kilometers). They were the first to circle the globe on a single load of fuel.

The feat would have been impossible in a conventional airplane. But their plane—named *Voyager*—was far from conventional. Built almost entirely of lightweight plastics and stiffened paper, it weighed less than a compact car. But *Voyager* could carry up to five times its own weight, and it had a wingspan longer than that of many commercial airliners.

Voyager was designed by Burt Rutan, Richard Rutan's brother, especially for record-breaking flights. Basically, it was a flying fuel tank—even its long, hollow wings were filled with fuel. Two propellers, fore and aft, pushed and pulled the plane to a top speed of 100 miles (161 kilometers) an hour. To save weight, the cockpit was as small as possible—not much bigger than a bathtub. While one pilot sat halfway up to fly the plane, the other would lie down. The pilots carried the same packaged food used by astronauts, as well as a supply of oxygen for high altitudes.

In July, the pilots broke their first records with the plane. On a test flight, they flew back and forth over California for 111 hours, covering a total of 11,600 miles (18,670 kilometers). That was the longest closed-circuit flight (a flight that begins and ends at the same place) on record, and also the longest time that any plane had ever stayed aloft.

Voyager set off on its around-the-world flight on December 14. Right away there were troubles. On takeoff, the tips of the plane's fuel-laden wings scraped the runway and were damaged. The pilots decided to continue anyway, heading west across the Pacific Ocean. Over the South Pacific they had to alter their route to avoid a typhoon—and that was only the first of many storms they skirted. Near South America, rough air even tipped the plane over on its side.

Mechanical problems also developed. At one point the plane's oil pressure dropped dangerously low. Hours before landing, one engine stalled for five minutes. And a faulty gauge raised worries that *Voyager* would run out of fuel.

Voyager landed at Edwards Air Force Base in California on December 23 with fourteen gallons of fuel to spare. Tail winds had helped the plane along, cutting the time of the flight to nine days from the original estimate of twelve. Rutan and Yeager were exhausted and bruised from the long ride. But they had won a coveted place in the record books.

THE FATE OF THE TITANIC

She was the largest ship of her day—over 882 feet (269 meters) long. With a double-bottomed hull, she was said to be unsinkable. She embarked on her maiden voyage from England to New York City with about 2,200 people on board. But on that voyage, just before midnight on April 14, 1912, the luxury liner *Titanic* struck an iceberg. She sank within three hours. Because the ship carried too few lifeboats, only about 700 people, mostly women and children, were saved.

The *Titanic* disaster became a legend. And until September, 1985, the ship's exact whereabouts in the deep Atlantic Ocean remained a mystery. Then a team of American and French researchers announced that they had found the wreck, lying beneath 2½ miles (4 kilometers) of water several hundred miles southeast of Newfoundland. And in 1986, U.S. researchers reached the sunken hulk and explored it.

Special equipment was required for the job. At such depths, the water pressure is so great that it can crush the hull of a normal submarine. The researchers took thousands of pictures with a remote-controlled sledlike device, the Angus, which was loaded with cameras, tethered to a surface ship, and dragged back and forth over the wreck.

In addition, three researchers descended to the upper deck of the *Titanic* in a special minisub, *Alvin*, that was designed to withstand the water pressure. From *Alvin*, they released Jason Jr. ("JJ"), a robot that some crew members called a "swimming eyeball." Controlled by a cable attached to the sub, JJ entered the wreck through a skylight, wandered through the interior, and took many pictures.

The researchers learned some surprising things about the disaster. For one, the *Titanic* seemed to have broken in two long before it reached the bottom of the ocean. The rust-covered stern section was some 1,800 feet (550 meters) from the bow, swiveled to face the opposite direction. Otherwise, the ship was upright and remarkably intact. The researchers found no gash in the hull from the iceberg. Instead, they suggested, the impact may have buckled the steel hull's seams, so that water rushed in.

JJ found that the ship's ornate wood paneling had been eaten away by marine worms. But the ship's brass, ceramic, and glass fixtures were intact. Crystal chandeliers still hung in their places. More wreckage lay around the hull—copper kettles from the galley, an old shoe. A teacup rested atop one of the ship's boilers.

The researchers brought up no artifacts. Instead, they left two plaques on the wreck. One honored the *Titanic*'s victims, and the other urged future explorers to leave the ship undisturbed "as a memorial to deep-water exploration."

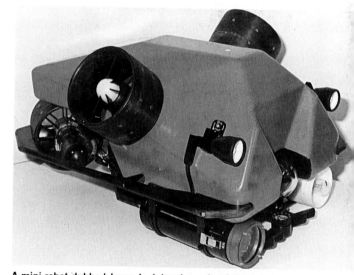

A mini-robot dubbed Jason Jr. (*above*) wandered through the *Titanic*, taking pictures. One photo showed a still-hanging, coral-encrusted crystal chandelier (*below*).

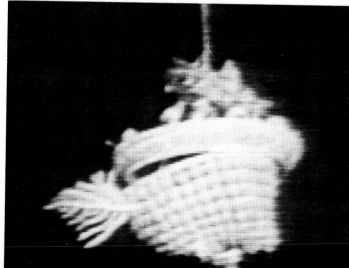

THE SWEET SUCCESS OF SMELL

New mown grass . . . a cake baking in the oven . . . the first daffodils of spring . . . the spicy scent of a Christmas tree. These aromas probably make you feel warm and happy all over. Did you ever wonder why?

People often think about what they see or hear, but rarely about what they smell. And scientists have only recently begun to study the sense of smell, the oldest and deepest of our senses. What they've learned so far, however, is leading them to recognize smell's true importance. Smell, it seems, is closely linked to our emotions—and perhaps to our health. Some doctors are even exploring aroma therapy, using scents to help treat a variety of medical problems.

HOW YOU SENSE A SCENT

When you see something, your eyes register patterns of light. When you hear something, your ears pick up sound waves. And when you smell something, your nose detects chemicals—odor molecules that are given off by the item you're smelling.

When you sniff a flower, for example, odor molecules rise through your nostrils to the back of your nose. There, the molecules are absorbed by the membranes and microscopic hairs that line the nasal passages. One small patch of this nasal lining—called the olfactory epithelium—is packed with nerve cells that are stimulated by odors.

As soon as the odor molecules hit, these cells fire off signals along direct nerve pathways to the brain. The signals are received in the brain's olfactory bulb, a small area just behind the eyes. From there, the signals are carried deeper into the brain and the odor is identified.

The sense of smell is closely linked to the sense of taste. In fact, many of the flavors we "taste" in food are really aromas. Odor molecules enter the nose as we lift food to our mouths, or they enter through the back of the mouth, where the nasal passages connect with the throat. Many distinct flavors, such as coffee and chocolate, can't be detected when the sense of smell is blocked.

Some scientists think that the human sense of smell evolved to its present state long before the rest of the human brain developed. Our sense of smell, they say, basically isn't much different from that of a fish. And some animals have more highly developed smell centers than ours. The part of a dog's brain that is concerned with smell, for example, is much larger than the part of the human brain that does the same thing. And a dog's sense of smell is much sharper than a human's.

Still, the human brain is capable of distinguishing more than 5,000 aromas, although most people can't give a name to even half that many. Newborn infants react to odors, and babies just a few days old can smell the difference between their mothers' milk and that of other mothers. The ability to tell one odor from another is thought to peak in adulthood, between the ages of 20 and 40. After age 70, it declines. But scientists don't know how the brain tells one scent from another. One theory is that the receptor cells in the nasal passages are specialists—certain cells are stimulated only by certain aromas.

MEMORY AND EMOTION

Another aspect of smell that scientists are only just beginning to learn about is its relation to other brain functions, such as memory and emotion. The link between smell and memory is found in many animals. For example, scientists were long puzzled by the way ocean salmon manage to return each year to the streams where they were born, in order to breed. The answer was the sense of smell: Every stream has its own distinct odors, and the fish were able to smell their way back home.

People remember smells longer and better than they remember sights and sounds. If you hear a song on the radio, you may not be able to place it when you hear it again several months later. But if you smell an aroma you've once smelled before, chances are you'll remember what it belongs to and also how that item looked, tasted, or felt.

You'll probably even be reminded of where you were and how you were feeling the first time you smelled that scent. That's one reason why certain odors make you feel good—the scent of daffodils, for example, reminds you of a warm spring day. Your sense of smell can remind you of unpleasant experiences as well as happy ones. In one research study, students smelled a particular odor while they were told they had scored poorly on a test. Later, when they smelled that odor again, more than half of them felt unhappy.

Many manufacturers make use of this aspect of the sense of smell when they market their products. Cleaning products, for example, are often given lemon or pine scents because people seem to associate those scents with cleanliness. And, even when they aren't linked to specific memories, certain smells seem to bring out emotions in people. The scent of almond, for instance, makes people think of happy events. Peach, strawberry, and apple scents seem to help people relax.

The reason for smell's close link to memory and emotion may lie in the make-up of the brain itself. Nerves travel from the olfactory bulb to distant points throughout the brain—including the centers for memory and emotion. Researchers who placed dye in the scent-sensitive nasal passages of animals found that the dye was carried all the way to these areas by the nerve cells. Thus, when you smell a flower, your memory and emotions are stimulated automatically.

AROMA THERAPY

For many years, people have thought that certain scents had medical properties. Mint, for instance, was supposed to be a stimulant. Lavender was said to cure headaches. Eucalyptus was supposed to prevent sleep. Now researchers are finding that some of these beliefs may be more than folklore, and aromas may actually play an important role in medicine.

Some smells, particularly spiced apple, have been shown to lower blood pressure and reduce muscle tension. They may be used to help people deal with stressful situations or to treat high blood pressure. And the scent of peaches seems to ease pain and may also help control panic attacks and epilepsy.

Other scents have been found helpful in controlling appetite, depression, and migraine headaches. Some aromas help people get to sleep, and others seem to wake them up. One researcher has even invented a scent alarm clock that sends a mist of wake-up aroma out into the room.

One day, odors may even be used to deliver drugs to the brain—to treat neurological diseases and serious mental disorders such as schizophrenia. Usually, drugs circulate in the blood and pass through the blood-vessel walls to reach body cells. But in the brain, a membrane called the blood-brain barrier surrounds the blood vessels and prevents the drugs from getting out. That means that the brain cells can't be reached by most drugs. Now researchers are looking for ways to link drug molecules to odor molecules. By hitching a ride with the odor molecules, the drugs may be able to act directly at sites of disease deep within the brain.

Such medicines are for the future. Scientists are still studying the role of smell in health. Meanwhile, you might want to do some research into your own smelling power.

TEST YOUR SMELL POWER

How sharp is your sense of smell? Can you sniff out the difference between chocolate and cherries? Between tunafish and tomatoes?

Your nose may not be as sharp as you think it is. Researchers say that people's sense of sight often prejudices their judgment when it comes to identifying odors. In other words, if you see a rose, you expect it to smell like a rose—and when you sniff it, it does.

It's easy to test your sense of smell. Ask a friend to help you. Put on a blindfold, and then have your friend hold different substances under your nose—ketchup, spices, onions, fruit, cheese, and other foods; toothpaste, soap, and similar household items; flowers and plants from the garden.

Most people can identify about 70 percent of all odors, the researchers say. If you can do better than that, you may have the makings of a great nose!

THE CAPITAL OF SCENT

If you visit Grasse, in southern France, the first things that strike your eye may be the fields of flowers that surround the city. And the first thing that strikes your nose may be the aroma of those flowers—jasmine, roses, narcissus, lavender, and others—carried by the warm Mediterranean breezes.

Grasse is a city that scent made famous. It's the center of the French perfume industry, which is known the world over. The land and the sunny climate of the region make it the perfect growing spot for flowers, and since the 1600's flowers have been grown there specifically for perfume.

The flowers are hand-picked in the early morning, when their scents are freshest and strongest. Then, through a long distilling process, they are reduced to scented oils. It takes 4,000 pounds of rose petals to make a pound of rose oil—and that pound of oil may sell for more than $1,500.

A fine perfume is made by blending different floral oils with aromatic chemicals and alcohol. It takes a keen nose to develop such a blend, and the master perfumers of Grasse are known for their noses. At schools run by the perfume industry, students are taught to distinguish some 1,500 aromas. The top professionals—the master "noses" —can identify as many as 3,000 at first sniff.

Today perfume makers are relying more on computers and laboratory equipment to make their blends. To keep costs down, some are also using artificial scents and less expensive floral oils from North Africa and other regions. But the flowers of Grasse are still prized above all others, and this city remains the scent capital of the world.

SHIFTING SANDS

A dunescape is a landscape in motion, shifting like the patterns in a kaleidoscope. Wind continually shapes and reshapes the sand dunes, like a sculptor who cannot decide on a final design. Pushed by the wind, the dunes creep across the land, swallowing vegetation as they go. Their surfaces, bathed in light, reflect a constantly changing range of colors.

Sand dunes are found around the world, primarily in deserts and along coastlines. Most began to form long ago, as wind piled up particles of sediment. The main difference between coastal and desert dunes is the plant life they carry. Because there is more moisture along the coasts, the dunes there are often covered with scrubby plants and grasses. But plant life is rarer in desert dunes like those shown here.

Wind determines a dune's shape. When the wind shifts and blows from many directions, towering pyramids of sand form, with arms reaching out like the points of a star.

When winds blow alternately from opposite directions, S-shaped dunes that snake across the desert may form.

When the wind blows mainly from one direction, dunes may form in long bars that run in the same direction as the wind. But more often, they form at right angles to the wind. In the desert these transverse dunes, as they are called, slope gradually on the windward side and drop off sharply on the leeward side (away from the wind). But along the coast, where the wind blows off the water, plants anchor the leeward side. The force of the wind hollows out the windward side instead.

Two factors give dunes their color. The first is the type of minerals in the sand. In New Mexico, gypsum makes dunes a gleaming white. In Arizona, yellowish dunes have formed from sandstone. Some Utah dunes are pink. Dunes also reflect the light around them. From the brilliant white or yellow of midday, they deepen to pink and dusky blue at sunset. Moonlight and dawn paint the sand with still other colors. Dunescapes seem to be nature's art studio—a place to experiment with form and color.

Plumes of smoke streak across the sky as the *Challenger* space shuttle explodes shortly after take-off. Seven astronauts lost their lives in the worst accident in the history of the U.S. space program.

SPACE BRIEFS

The 1986 space year was filled with both triumph and tragedy. The triumphs included a dramatic flight past Uranus, the launching of a sophisticated new space station, and visits to Halley's comet by five space probes. But for people everywhere, these events were overshadowed by the worst accident in the history of the U.S. space program—the explosion of the space shuttle *Challenger,* in which seven astronauts lost their lives.

SETBACKS FOR THE SPACE SHUTTLE

The year was to have been a busy one for U.S. space scientists and astronauts. The National Aeronautics and Space Administration (NASA) had scheduled fifteen shuttle flights.

Mission 24. Things got off to a shaky start with the 24th shuttle mission, the first in 1986. *Columbia* was launched on January 12, after a record seven postponements. Once aloft, however, the mission was a success. Led by mission commander Robert L. Gib-

son, the crew included Charles F. Bolden, Jr., Robert J. Cenker, Steven A. Hawley, George D. Nelson, Franklin Chang-Diáz (the first Hispanic-American to fly in space), and Congressman Bill Nelson of Florida (the first member of the House of Representatives in space). They launched a communications satellite, observed Halley's comet, and performed more than a dozen experiments before returning to Earth six days later.

The Challenger Disaster. People had begun to take shuttle flights for granted. But enthusiasm for the January 28 *Challenger* flight was high because, for the first time, the shuttle would carry an ordinary citizen into space: Christa McAuliffe, a teacher from New Hampshire.

Thousands of spectators watched as *Challenger* left the launch pad at the Kennedy Space Center in Florida. Millions more, including many classes of schoolchildren, watched on TV. Their excitement quickly turned to horror when, just a little over a minute after launching, the shuttle's external fuel tank exploded. A huge orange cloud of flame and smoke engulfed the spaceship. The two booster rockets flew off, their paths marked by white trails of smoke across the sky. For an hour, debris from the disintegrated craft continued to fall into the Atlantic Ocean.

The explosion killed all seven crew members: mission commander Francis R. Scobee, Gregory B. Jarvis, Ronald E. McNair, Ellison S. Onizuka, Judith A. Resnik, Michael J. Smith, and Christa McAuliffe.

People everywhere were stunned by the tragedy and mourned the astronauts. More than 10,000 people, including President Ronald Reagan, attended a memorial service held at the Johnson Space Center in Houston, Texas. People across the country contributed money for memorial funds. Messages of condolance were received from many world leaders. Seven asteroids discovered by the Lowell Observatory in Flagstaff, Arizona, were named for the astronauts in their memory. And the Soviets, who had made the first maps of Venus, named two craters on the planet for McAuliffe and Resnik. (Venus is named after the Roman goddess of love and beauty. In keeping with this, Soviet mappers had decided to name Venusian features only for women.)

What Caused the Accident? Immediately after the *Challenger* accident, efforts were begun to determine what had gone wrong. Aircraft and ships searched for remains of the craft, and many parts, including the crew compartment, were recovered. In addition, engineers studied the vast amount of computer data that *Challenger* had sent back to Earth in the brief moments before it exploded. There had been more than 2,000 sensors aboard the craft, monitoring everything from fuel tank pressure and combustion temperatures to the astronauts' heart rates.

President Reagan appointed a special commission to review the evidence and to

AN "ORDINARY" PERSON

Among those who died in the *Challenger* explosion was the woman who was to have been the first "ordinary" person in space: Christa McAuliffe, a 37-year-old social studies teacher from Concord, New Hampshire. She had been chosen in July, 1985, from 11,000 teachers who had applied for the honor.

Until then, McAuliffe had led a quiet life. She was born Sharon Christa Corrigan on September 2, 1948, in Boston, Massachusetts, and decided on her career—teaching—while she was still in high school. Soon after graduating from college, she married Steven McAuliffe, a high school classmate. They later had two children, a boy and a girl.

In her history classes at Concord High School, McAuliffe taught that the contributions of ordinary people were as important as those of generals and statesmen. She often told her students to "reach for the stars" and not set any limits on their goals. She brought these feelings with her to the space program. After her selection, she went through a six-month astronaut training program that included zero-gravity flights in diving planes, riding in centrifuges that simulated the forces of takeoff, and practicing emergency escape tactics.

With her bubbling enthusiasm and cheerful personality, McAuliffe quickly became a celebrity. But she never forgot that she was an ordinary person— signing autographs, she joked, reminded her of signing hall passes in school. That ordinariness helped people identify with her, and made her death on January 28, 1986, all the more tragic.

121

make recommendations for future action. In June, the commission issued its report. It said that the accident had occurred because one of the synthetic rubber rings used to seal the joints of the right booster rocket had failed. Hot gases shot through the joint and ignited the fuel in the external tank, causing the explosion.

The report said that engineers had suspected since 1977 that these rings didn't work properly in cold temperatures. And it was very cold when *Challenger* was launched on January 28—much colder than for any previous launch. But, reported the commission, both NASA and Morton Thiokol Inc., the manufacturer of the booster rockets, "first failed to recognize [the joint seal] as a problem, then failed to fix it and finally treated it as an acceptable flight risk." The commission criticized NASA for poor management and for not paying enough attention to safety, saying: "A well-structured and managed system emphasizing safety would have flagged the rising doubts about the . . . joint seal."

The commission recommended major design and structural changes for the shuttle. As a result, future flights were delayed until 1988, so that changes could be made. There was also to be a major change in how future shuttles would be used: In August, 1986,

President Reagan ordered NASA to stop using shuttles to launch commercial satellites—such as those from private communications and weather-tracking companies. Instead, shuttles would be used to launch only U.S. government military and scientific satellites. Commercial satellites would have to be carried by private space-launching companies. Because there were no such companies in the United States, the order meant that commercial satellites would have to be launched by foreign firms.

THE EUROPEAN LAUNCHING PROGRAM

The United States and the Soviet Union have the world's major—but not the only—space programs. Western Europe, Japan, and China also launch satellites, although none have as yet sent up manned vehicles. Of the three, Western Europe's European Space Agency (ESA) is the most advanced.

Operated by fourteen countries, ESA has a special division called Arianespace that launches commercial satellites for private companies. Like the U.S. space program, Arianespace had both successes and setbacks in 1986. On February 21, it launched SPOT, a powerful remote-sensing satellite. Cameras on this craft could take highly detailed photos of Earth.

But on May 30 an Arianespace rocket was destroyed in midair after its third stage failed to ignite during a launch. It was the fourth failure in eighteen launchings. The Arianespace program was put on hold while the problem was investigated, leaving Western countries temporarily without a way to launch commercial satellites. But Arianespace was confident that it could overcome the difficulties. It had contracts to launch some 40 satellites, including several owned by U.S. firms—enough to keep its rockets booked through 1990.

A VOYAGE TO URANUS

Before 1986, little was known about Uranus, the third largest planet in the solar system. But on January 24, the U.S. unmanned craft Voyager 2 became the first space probe to visit the planet. And in six hours, more information about Uranus was collected than astronomers had gathered during the 205 years since the planet's discovery.

The United States had launched the Voy-

A color-enhanced photo of Uranus, taken by Voyager 2.

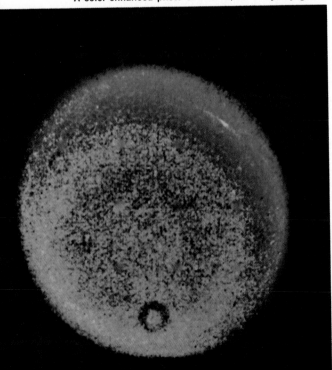

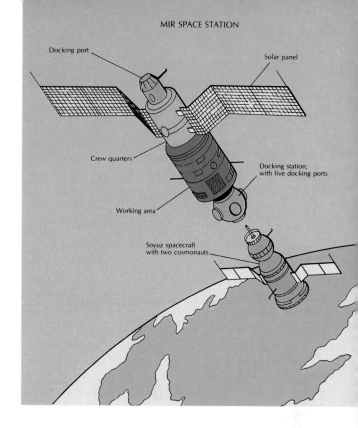

Docking port

Solar panel

Crew quarters

Docking station, with five docking ports

Working area

Soyuz spacecraft with two cosmonauts

ager spacecraft in 1977. The probe had flown by Jupiter in 1979, and Saturn in 1981. When it flew by Uranus in 1986, it was about 1.8 billion miles (3 billion kilometers) from Earth.

Scientists already knew that Uranus was different from other planets in the solar system. All the other planets rotate on nearly vertical axes. They spin like tops moving at full speed. Uranus, however, has a horizontal axis, and the planet sort of rolls on its side like a dying top or a bowling ball. But Voyager transmitted information that revealed the planet to be different in many other surprising ways.

The planet has a small, rocky core about the size of Earth. Voyager's instruments indicated that this surface is completely covered by a deep ocean of extremely hot water. And all this is hidden by a very thick bluish-green gaseous cloud layer.

Using Earth-based telescopes, astronomers had discovered nine rings and five moons circling Uranus. Voyager discovered a tenth ring and ten more moons (for a total of fifteen). The rings are made up of chunks of black material—unlike Saturn's rings, which are made up of bright, fine-grained particles.

The most interesting photographs sent back were of the moon Miranda. Its surface is marked with wide craters, deep valleys, long ridges, terraces, a large V-shaped pattern, and even something that resembles a racetrack. One scientist commented: "If you took all the bizarre features in the solar system and put them on one object, that would be Miranda."

A NEW SOVIET SPACE STATION

In terms of space exploration, 1986 was a banner year for the Soviets. The highlight came in February, when they launched their new space station, Mir (for "peace"), into orbit around Earth. The station was planned as the first step in the creation of a permanently manned research complex in space.

Mir was larger and more sophisticated than the previous Soviet space stations. Shaped like a cylinder, it was powered by two huge solar panels that extended like wings from its midsection. There were six docking ports for other spacecraft—one at each end and four grouped in a docking sec-

tion at the forward end. Both manned and unmanned spacecraft could dock at the front and rear ports; the other four ports were designed primarily for research modules. Inside the station, there were living and working areas for up to six people.

On March 13, cosmonauts Leonid D. Kizim and Vladimir A. Solovyov were launched aboard a Soyuz T-15 spacecraft. Two days later they docked with Mir. "As we came close, it looked like a white-winged seagull, soaring above the world," said Kizim. The cosmonauts conducted a variety of experiments and photographed Earth. On May 5 they detached their craft from the space station and traveled to and docked with another, older space station: Salyut 7. It was the first time that astronauts had moved from one space station to another.

On May 28, Kizim and Solovyov spent almost four hours outside their spacecraft and constructed a tower 50 feet (15 meters) long, which they attached to Salyut. The activity provided valuable experience in building large structures in space.

The cosmonauts flew back to Mir on June 26. Finally, on July 16, after having spent 125 days in space, they boarded Soyuz T-15 one more time, for their return to Earth.

and leaves. The ancestors of modern ferns appeared some 300 million years ago. During the Mesozoic era—the age of the dinosaurs—ferns reached the size of tall trees. Ferns provided some of the vegetable matter that formed Earth's coal deposits millions of years ago.

There are still some treelike ferns, but the ones most of us know today are much smaller—3 feet (1 meter) tall or less. Still, ferns remain remarkable plants. Their method of reproduction—without flowers or seeds—is completely unlike that of most of the other plants we're familiar with. Their soft green beauty makes them a favorite of gardeners and woodland strollers. And, over the years, people have found many uses for these appealing plants.

ENDLESS VARIETY

There are about 10,000 different kinds of ferns. Together, they form an order called the Filicales. Ferns grow all over the world, anywhere that the ground isn't covered by ice year-round. But most ferns prefer warm climates, and most also need a great deal of moisture. For that reason, almost three-fourths of the fern species are found in the tropical and subtropical rain forests near the equator. Even in cooler climates, ferns usually prefer a moist and shady spot—along the banks of a forest stream, for example.

Most ferns plant their roots in soil. But some grow from cracks in rocks and stone walls, some grow in water, and some are air plants, or epiphytes. The epiphytes grow on the branches of trees and get their nourishment from damp air and from decaying matter that accumulates in the tree bark. One epiphyte, the oak or moss fern, grows on oak trees. It was honored by the Druids of ancient Britain, who held their religious ceremonies in oak groves.

In size, ferns range from minute to monstrous. Some ferns that grow in water are no more than a quarter of an inch (0.6 centimeter) tall and could easily be mistaken for bits of moss. At the other extreme are the tree ferns of South America and the Pacific islands. Some of these ferns grow 60 feet (18 meters) tall or higher, supported by strong, woody stems. They look rather like palm trees.

THE PERFECTION OF FERNS

"Nature made ferns for pure leaves, to see what she could do in that line," wrote the 19th-century American author Henry David Thoreau. And indeed, leaves are what ferns are all about—delicate, feathery, intricate leaves, arching up from the ground. Ferns have no flowers to steal the show from their greenery; they don't need flowers to add to their beauty.

Ferns have another distinction: They were among the first plants to have proper roots

Ferns are noted for their delicate, feathery, intricate leaves, arching up from the ground. They come in a great variety of sizes and shapes, and their soft green beauty makes them a favorite of both gardeners and woodland strollers. Clockwise, from right: maidenhair fern; lady fern; shiny fan fern.

On the underside of a fern frond are clusters of spore cases—the secret to the plant's method of reproduction.

About 300 different species of ferns grow in North America. Apart from their size, they vary mostly in their leaves, which are called fronds. The fronds may be slender and tapering or wide and heart-shaped. They may be covered with fine hairs or scales. They are usually divided into many leaflets, and the leaflets themselves vary in shape from one species to the next.

Some plants that are often thought to be ferns are not, however. The "asparagus fern," which is often used in florists' arrangements, is really the flowering shoot of the asparagus plant. Resurrection fern, which curls into a ball when dry and uncurls when wet, is actually a kind of spike moss.

HOW FERNS GROW

In most ferns, the fronds are the only part of the plant you see. The fronds rise on long stalks out of a rhizome, a sort of horizontal stem. Roots grow out of the rhizome to bring nourishment to the plant. Usually the rhizome is below the ground. Some ferns, however, have stems that travel above the ground or on other plants. And on the tree fern, the rhizome actually forms the trunk.

If you look at the underside of a full-grown fern frond, you'll probably see groups of brownish or whitish dots. These are clusters of spore cases, and they're the secret to the fern's method of reproduction. Each spore case is packed with microscopic spores. When the spores are ripe, the cases open and release them like fine dust into the air.

The spores fall to the earth. If they land in a spot with ample moisture and good growing conditions, they begin to develop into tiny plants. These plants look nothing like the ferns that produced them. They consist of single heart-shaped leaves, about a quarter of an inch across. In fact, the little plants aren't new ferns; they're just intermediate steps in the reproduction process.

The tiny plant is called a gametophyte ("reproductive plant") or prothallus ("first growth"). It develops special tissues that produce male and female sex cells (like the pollen and ovules in flowering plants). A female egg cell develops near the notch in the heart shape. Male sperm cells develop at the bottom point of the heart.

For the male cells to fertilize the egg cell, another ingredient is needed—water. When the little plant is covered with a film of moisture, the sperm cells swim across to reach the egg. This is why ferns like a moist habitat: Without moisture, they can't reproduce.

Once the egg has been fertilized, a new fern starts to grow, and the gametophyte withers away. In most ferns, the fronds emerge tightly coiled and uncurl as they grow. Coiled up, they look something like the head of a violin—and for that reason, they're called fiddleheads.

Some ferns have other ways of reproducing. One of the most unusual reproduction methods is that of the walking fern. When one of this fern's fronds touches the ground, it takes root and produces a new plant.

USES FOR FERNS

One of the simplest uses people have found for ferns is to eat them. Both the rhizomes and the new shoots, or fiddleheads, of certain varieties have been prized as delicacies in certain parts of the world, and the leaves of some types have been used to make tea. Today some supermarkets even carry fiddleheads, fresh (in season) or frozen.

In times gone by, people also made medicine from ferns. Several types of maidenhair ferns, native to North America and Europe, were used to make cough syrups and similar medicines. Oak fern was used against arthritis as well as respiratory problems. Wall rue, a common European fern that grows in rock crevices, was thought to cure swollen glands. The American Indians made a tonic from the rhizome of the common lady fern, and they treated snake bites with a poultice made from the roots of the rattlesnake fern. A concoction made from the root of the male fern is still used in many countries to rid people and animals of intestinal parasites.

Ferns were also used to make a primitive sort of shampoo, said to be especially good for preventing baldness. Sweet-scented dried ferns were included in potpourri and sachets. Bracken, a common fern that grows along roadsides and in open areas in Europe and North America, was used as bedding for farm animals and thatched roofing for houses. In medieval times, ash from burned bracken was used as an ingredient in glass and in soap. The reason the ashes were used was that they were high in alkali, which is necessary for both materials.

People also entertained some strange beliefs about certain ferns. Wall rue, for instance, was fed to cows to ward off evil spells that might sour their milk.

GROWING FERNS

Today ferns are valued mostly for their beauty. They are favorites in shady gardens, as houseplants, and in florists' bouquets. The Boston fern, the maidenhair fern, and the holly fern are some of the types often seen in gardens.

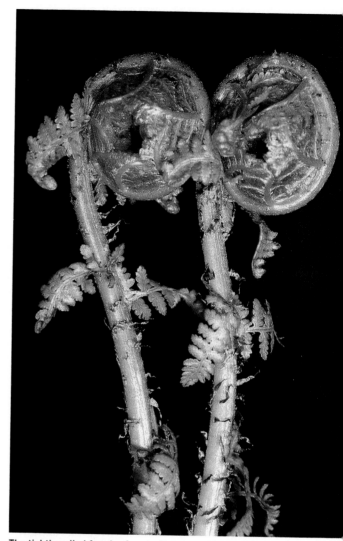

The tightly coiled fronds of a new fern resemble the head of a violin, and that's why they are called fiddleheads.

The trick to growing ferns is to duplicate their natural habitat as closely as you can. Tropical ferns and epiphytes can be difficult; they need special conditions that are best provided in a greenhouse. But ferns that are hardy outdoors where you live will do well if they have a shady, moist spot in your garden. Indoors, they need moderate sunlight and plenty of water. Regular fertilizing will help keep your ferns growing. They'll reward you with masses of delicate green fronds, so that you can have a bit of woodland beauty in your home.

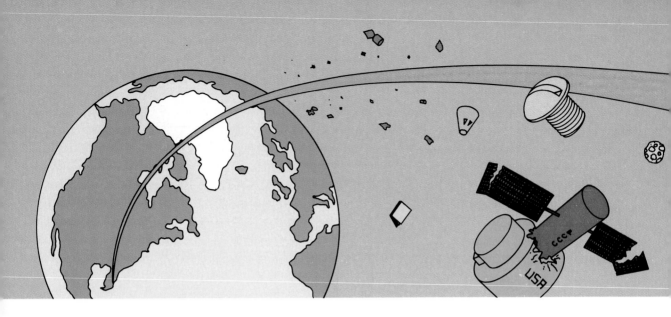

SPACE JUNK

In thirty or forty years, when you finally get to take your long-awaited ride in space, what do you think you'll see? A beautiful view of Earth, no doubt, and a clearer sight of the stars than you ever thought possible. Chances are, however, that you'll also see a lot of space junk.

Ever since people started sending satellites and rockets into space, inner space has been turning into a vast garbage dump. Inner space is the area from 100 to 22,000 miles (160 to 35,400 kilometers) above Earth, and it's where Earth-orbiting satellites and spacecraft (such as the shuttle) are placed. Most space junk is found in lower Earth orbits, at altitudes of about 300 to 900 miles (480 to 1,450 kilometers).

The orbiting trash isn't made up of old tin cans and wrappers from fast-food restaurants, of course. Instead, it consists of nonfunctioning satellites, burned-out rocket stages, and fragments from satellites and rockets that have exploded or disintegrated. U.S. and Soviet tests of antisatellite weapons account for a lot of the litter—such weapons can smash their targets into thousands of pieces.

Estimates of just how much space junk there actually is vary. But scientists say that there are several thousand large chunks of litter orbiting Earth, and perhaps 40,000 smaller pieces. And there are as many as 100 billion tiny objects, such as paint chips. Al-together, about 95 percent of all the objects orbiting Earth are trash.

TRASH TROUBLE

Space junk isn't just messy—it's dangerous. Many people think that objects left in space will fall to Earth, usually burning up from the friction created when they re-enter the Earth's atmosphere. In fact, most objects in high Earth orbit will never return to Earth. Even at an altitude of 700 miles (1,125 kilometers), objects may remain in orbit for hundreds of years. Objects at lower altitudes usually do fall back to Earth, but they don't always burn up in the atmosphere. In 1978, chunks of a Soviet nuclear-powered satellite littered northern Canada (fortunately, there was no radioactive contamination). And in 1979, the enormous U.S. Skylab space station broke up and scattered its pieces over Australia and the Indian Ocean.

The risks from falling space junk are very small, though. Many more meteors enter the atmosphere than do pieces of space junk, and no one has ever been hit by a meteor. The real danger is the junk that *stays* in space, as most of it does.

Items that orbit Earth don't all drift along at the same speed in the same direction. Each satellite and bit of space junk is in its own orbit, changing altitude and turning according to its own plan. When two objects pass each other, they often do so at a speed

ORBITAL GARBAGE SERVICE

of 22,000 miles (35,400 kilometers) per hour. And at a speed like that, a collision can be catastrophic. A particle the size of a grain of sand would have enough force to punch through the shell of a manned craft like the space shuttle, causing the cabin to lose its pressure and oxygen.

Scientists suspect that collisions may have already wiped out a number of satellites that have exploded without explanation. They are fairly certain that collisions between pieces of space junk have taken place. And pits in the windows of the Apollo spacecraft and Skylab seem to be evidence of collisions with tiny bits of junk.

The risk of a collision, however, is still slight. There may be a lot of orbiting junk, but it's spread out over a vast area. For the space shuttle, which orbits about 300 miles (480 kilometers) above Earth, the risk of a collision is about one in a million during the few days of a mission. The risk is greater the longer an object stays in space. A space station, for example, might face a one-in-ten chance of a collision over a ten-year period.

As space becomes more and more littered with junk, however, scientists are concerned that people may be creating an artificial asteroid belt about Earth. Soon, they worry, space travel may become too risky. The question is, what can be done to clean up space?

CLEANING UP

There are several plans, some more practical than others. One idea is to send up a sort of orbiting trash collector that would sweep dead satellites and other debris into a container. When it was full, it could be towed back to Earth. So far, this is just an idea—no space garbage truck has been built. Another plan is to have the space shuttle collect debris. But the shuttle wouldn't have enough fuel to chase more than one satellite per trip, and in any case much of the debris is out of its reach.

Another approach is to improve the protective cladding on spacecraft, so that they would be better able to withstand a collision. However, this would add to their weight—and thus make them harder and more expensive to launch.

Still another idea is to plan for the disposal of satellites and other spacecraft before they're even launched. Small rockets could be mounted on satellites, for example. When the satellite was finished with its work, the rockets would be fired to move it into a low orbit. From there, gravity would pull it into the atmosphere, and it would burn up.

The debris created by antisatellite weapons tests may require a different solution: an international treaty. Countries might agree to ban such tests, or at least to conduct them at low altitudes so that the debris would be pulled back into the atmosphere.

These plans are on the drawingboard. Chances are, however, that the problem of space junk will grow in years to come. So when you take your space flight, don't be surprised if you see a warning posted in your craft: DON'T BE A LITTERBUG.

MAKE & DO

Create your own version of Hands Across America! Take a long strip of colorful wrapping paper and draw lines dividing it into equal widths. Fold the paper in accordion pleats along these lines. Draw the outline of a figure on the top pleat. Then cut around it, keeping the paper folded. Unfold the paper to see your chain.

PRETTY PETALS

A delicate bouquet of violets . . . a romantic arrangement of roses in a vase . . . an exotic lei of gardenias—almost everyone loves flowers. But because fresh flowers soon die, many people enjoy creating items using preserved, fabric, or paper flowers. In this way, they can have pretty petals around them all the time.

PRESSED FLOWERS

Have you ever opened up an old book and come across a flower pressed between the pages? Perhaps someone had saved the flower as a remembrance of a special day or person. Even though the flower was in the book for many years, it kept its shape and beauty. It could still be recognized as a pansy or a daisy or a honeysuckle blossom.

Pressing is one of the most common ways to preserve fresh flowers. The process doesn't require expert skill or elaborate equipment. You simply place the flowers between sheets of absorbent paper, such as paper towels or newspaper, and weigh them down with a book or other heavy object. Because the paper is porous, it draws moisture from the flowers. Depending on how much water is in the flowers, drying time ranges from a few days to a few weeks.

Pressed flowers can be assembled into pictures that can be framed and hung on walls. They can be arranged to create placemats. And they can be used to decorate stationery, gift cards, candles, and bookmarks.

Before you start to make an item, think about the design: Have a clear picture in mind of what you want to do. Consider what background—perhaps paper, perhaps fabric —would look best with the flowers you have pressed. Generally, soft, solid colors are better than bright colors and patterns. Queen Anne's Lace, for instance, would look dramatic on black velvet. Autumn flowers might look nice on olive green. And a horseshoe of four-leaf clovers would be striking on beige.

Pressed flowers are fragile. It's a good idea to use tweezers to pick up and position them. This is easier than using your fingers, and you'll be less likely to damage the flowers.

If you've planned a design using a variety of overlapping flowers, leaves, and grasses, begin by positioning the pieces that will form the outline of the design. Then add the main flowers and, finally, the smaller flowers and leaves. When everything is exactly as you want it, glue each piece to the background. Use as little glue as possible. You don't want any glue to leak out around the edges of stalks or to form lumpy blobs under petals.

Finally, you may wish to protect your flower print under glass or plastic. This is especially important if the item will be handled a lot or if you want it to last a long time.

PAPER FLOWERS

Colorful flowers made from crêpe paper can be used in many ways. They can be strung together in garlands to edge a tablecloth or hang over a window. They can be placed in a vase, just as you would a bouquet of roses. And they can be used to decorate gifts. A single pink poppy, for example, looks elegant on dark wrapping paper.

Crêpe paper flowers can be made to look very much like real flowers. Or you can use your imagination and design flowers that have no equal in nature. Even stylized flowers, however, should have the same parts as real flowers: petals, stamens, stems, and leaves.

Crêpe paper stretches easily and can be molded into many different shapes. By wetting the paper and causing its color to run, you can also obtain various shades of color. This can be done by wetting just one color of crêpe paper, in which case you will get a range of shades of that color. Or it can be done by folding together several different colors and simultaneously wetting them and squeezing them together. For instance, you

might combine orange, yellow, and white crêpe papers to achieve tints ranging from deep orange to pale beige.

Stems are made by wrapping lengths of wire with green crêpe paper. Green paper is also used to shape leaves, which are then sandwiched over a piece of wire to add support and flexibility.

FABRIC FLOWERS

Even more fanciful than paper flowers are flowers made with cotton, silk, velvet, and other fabrics. Fabric flowers can be formed into corsages, used to decorate hats and gift packages, and arranged in vases.

Almost any type of fabric can be used, but stiff fabrics are easier to work with than those that are thin and delicate. Try to match the fabric to the type of flower you want to make and to the function it will serve. An informal bouquet in a kitchen might be made of calico; an arrangement for a formal dining room would be better made out of satin.

In addition to the fabric, you need fine thread-covered wire (which comes in many colors) to form the petals, and heavier wire for the stems. You also need artificial stamens, green florist's tape, and a latex glue. All these materials are available from craft shops.

To form a petal, bend the thread-covered wire into the desired shape. If all the petals of the flower are to be the same shape, form all of them before attaching the fabric.

134

Lay the fabric right side up. Put glue on the entire underside of the wire shape and press it onto the fabric. Be sure that all parts of the wire attach to the fabric. After the glue is dry, cut around the outside of the wire shape. Cut as close to the wire as possible.

To assemble a flower, begin by cutting a piece of the heavy wire for the stem. Tie together a bunch of stamens and attach them to the stem. Position the petals around the stamens and wire them in place. Then wrap florist's tape around the bottom of the flower head and down along the entire length of the stem. Finally, bend and arrange the petals until the flower has the desired shape.

Whether pressed or crêpe paper or fabric, these beautiful blossoms will add an enchanting touch to your surroundings. And they'll continue to look fresh and lovely for months and years to come.

MADAM, I'M ADAM

What do the following words have in common with each other?

MOM, EYE, SEES, LEVEL, REDDER

What do these words have in common with the title of this article?

All are palindromes. A palindrome is a word, phrase, or sentence that reads the same forward and backward. Read the title from left to right. Then, from right to left. It says the same thing both ways: "Madam, I'm Adam." (When reading a palindrome backward, you may have to re-arrange the punctuation.)

Many people greatly enjoy palindromes—both collecting them and inventing them. They even make up crossword puzzles in which the answers to the clues are palindromes. Try to guess the one-word palindromes that these clues define:

1. The middle of the day
2. Male parent
3. Young dog
4. Female sheep

In many two-word palindromes, each of the words forms the other word when the letters are reversed. For example:

POOL LOOP
TOP POT
STRAW WARTS

In other two-word palindromes, you must change the spacing between letters when you read them backward:

Senile Felines

Panda here had nap

TIP IT
STOP SPOTS
SENILE FELINES

Here are some three- and four-word palindromes that use both techniques:

MAY SEES YAM
PAT DID TAP
POOR DOG, GO DROOP
NEVER ODD OR EVEN
TEN AT A NET
PANDA HERE HAD NAP

The longer the palindrome, the more difficult it is to create. The best method is to start with a word that can be written backward. Place it at the beginning and end of the palindrome, leaving lots of space in between:

PAM .... MAP

Now try using various words in the middle until you come up with a phrase or sentence:

PAM SAW RADAR WAS MAP
or
PAM SEES NEIL, AN ALIEN SEES MAP

People's names, particularly those that end with vowels, are often useful in creating palindromes:

NORMA, I AM RON
IMA! NO LEMON, NO MELON AM I!

It's fun making up a story to go along with the palindrome. When would a person insist he was neither a lemon nor a melon?

Make up stories—ludicrous, serious, or mysterious—for these palindromes:

BOB SAW RATS. STAR WAS BOB.
MA'S PALS SLAP SAM.
NO, IT IS OPEN ON ONE POSITION.

Some palindromes are famous. One of the best-known is "ABLE WAS I ERE I SAW ELBA." This refers to the famous French ruler Napoleon I, who was sent to the island of Elba after he was forced to abdicate in 1814. He later escaped from Elba and tried once again to rule Europe, but he was defeated by the British and their allies at the Battle of Waterloo.

Another famous palindrome is "A MAN, A PLAN, A CANAL: PANAMA." It most probably refers to Ferdinand de Lesseps, the 19th-century French engineer who made the first attempt to build a canal across the Isthmus of Panama.

There's even a palindrome that can be made almost infinitely long:

NEVER EVER EVER EVER EVER EVEN

You can keep inserting "ever" forever, and this will continue to be a palindrome. But no matter how long you make it, it must always have a beginning and an end, so that it can be read from either direction.

Pam sees Neil, an alien sees map

137

CUTE CATERPILLARS

Liven up your room with CUTE CATERPILLARS! These crazy, creepy critters can be made from kneesocks or from a combination of anklesocks and leg warmers. Wildly patterned ones work best. First make the caterpillar's head by stuffing the toe of a sock with fiberfill or some other material. Tie off the head with a colorful ponytail elastic or piece of yarn.

Then stuff the next section and tie it off. Keep going until you reach the end of the sock. Now add the details. Try brightly colored pipe-cleaner antennas. Glue on plastic eyes or make eyes and other parts out of felt. How about a glittering rhinestone nose? Give the caterpillar false eyelashes, pipe-cleaner legs, and a giant pompom tail. Be creative.

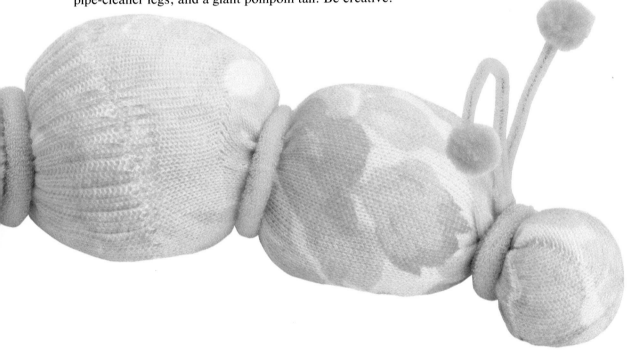

STAMP COLLECTING

The largest-ever North American stamp show was held near Chicago, Illinois, from May 22 to June 2, 1986. Ameripex 86 was the first international show in the United States since 1976, and it drew collectors from far and wide. The show provided stamp collectors with a chance to view magnificent collections from around the world and to get a first peek at some of the many new stamp issues of 1986.

U.S. STAMPS

In connection with the Ameripex show, the United States issued a set of miniature stamps showing the portraits of all deceased U.S. presidents. Thirty-five presidents were shown together with their signatures on the stamps, which were issued in four sheets of nine each. The 36th stamp in the set showed the White House.

As always, famous Americans were featured on several U.S. issues during the year. Two new additions to the Great Americans series honored former Supreme Court justice Hugo L. Black, known for his defense of individual liberties, and Paul Dudley White, who gained fame as a cardiologist (a doctor specializing in heart disease). Other new stamps in this series depicted two famous scholars: John Harvard (for whom Harvard University is named) and Bernard Revel, the first president of Yeshiva University in New York City.

Sojourner Truth, who was born a slave in 1797 but gained her freedom and became a famous human rights activist, was honored by a stamp in the Black Heritage series. The poet T. S. Eliot was pictured on a 22-cent stamp in the Literary Arts series, and a stamp in the Performing Arts series showed Duke Ellington, a master of jazz.

Stamps were also part of the celebration of the 100th birthday of the Statue of Liberty in 1986. To mark the event, the United States produced a joint issue with France, which had given the statue in 1886. Both countries used the same design, a view of the statue's head.

Among other popular U.S. issues were two that focused on folk art. The first of these, a block of four stamps, depicted colorful, hand-woven Navajo blankets. Another block of four, issued as part of the Folk Art series, showed carved wood figurines that were used as ships' figureheads and as advertising for shops from colonial times through the 1800's.

The 1986 Love stamp, issued around Valentine's Day, showed a cartoonlike sketch of a puppy. And a set of five stamps depicted fish common to U.S. waters—the Atlantic cod, the bluefin tuna, the muskellunge, the catfish, and the largemouth bass.

OMNIBUS ISSUES

Collectors could choose from a number of omnibus issues—stamps issued by several countries on a common theme—during 1986. Britain, West Germany, San Marino, and several other countries marked the return of Halley's comet with stamps. (Many other countries had issued Halley's comet stamps in 1985.) Britain and other countries also issued stamps in honor of the marriage of Prince Andrew and Sarah Ferguson.

Since soccer is the world's most popular team sport, dozens of countries issued stamps honoring the 1986 World Cup soccer championship, held in Mexico City. Typical was a design from the African country of Gabon, showing flags of many nations and a soccer ball suspended over a soccer stadium. The Commonwealth Games, held every four years, were also marked with stamps from several countries.

The theme for the annual Europa issue, put out by members of the Congress of European Posts and Telecommunications, was nature and conservation. Britain depicted four of its endangered species: the wild cat, barn owl, pine marten, and natterjack toad. Belgium showed the effect of pollution on fish. Turkey depicted a bird of prey on one stamp and litter cluttering a pastoral scene on another.

An omnibus issue that proved popular with young collectors honored the Brothers Grimm—with fairy tale scenes portrayed by Walt Disney characters such as Mickey Mouse. Fourteen countries took part, and most also included miniature portraits of Jacob and Wilhelm Grimm.

Wood Carving: Nautical Figure

Folk Art USA 22

1986 STAMPS
FROM AROUND
THE WORLD

LOVE

USA **22**

PHILATELY
– THE
INTERNATIONAL
HOBBY

UNITED
NATIONS

44c

中華民國郵票

溥心畬畫
松枝山鳥

REPUBLIC OF CHINA **2**

中華民國郵票

溥心畬畫
空庭松鶴

REPUBLIC OF CHINA **8**

中華民國郵票

溥心畬畫
楊富靜態

REPUBLIC OF CHINA **10**

nations unies

ANNÉE INTERNATIONALE DE LA PAIX

0,**45**

'LORD AMHERST'
Wrecked 1778

E↑R

BERMUDA

$2

Mangrove Flycatcher

Cardinal Honeyeater

Blue-faced Parrotfinch

Dusky White-eye

Bridled White-eye

PALAU 44c — **PALAU 44c**
PALAU 44c — **PALAU 44c**

80

Halleyscher Komet GIOTTO-Mission der esa

DEUTSCHE BUNDESPOST

Love Art Museum
Navajo Art USA 22

Museum of the American Indian
Navajo Art USA 22

Vereinte Nationen
AFRIKA IN NOT **$8**

United Nations
AFRICA IN CRISIS **22c**

EUROPA

13

BELGIË BELGIQUE

RÉPUBLIQUE GABONAISE

350F

COUPE DU MONDE DE FOOTBALL - MEXICO 1986

Canada 34

'86

A TOPICAL
COLLECTION OF
TRANSPORTATION STAMPS

14ᴾ CENTURY OF MOTORING
ISLE OF MAN

SULTANATE OF OMAN
100 BAISA
POLICE DAY 1985

Brasil 84   Brasil 84
610,00   620,00

1883 1983
CENTENARIO DE LOS ASCENSORES DE VALPARAISO
$40 CORREOS CHILE

12ᴾ   12ᴾ   12ᴾ   12ᴾ

LIVERPOOL AND MANCHESTER RAILWAY 1830 LIVERPOOL AND MANCHESTER RAILWAY 1830 LIVERPOOL AND MANCHESTER RAILWAY 1830 LIVERPOOL AND MANCHESTER RAILWAY 1830

British Virgin Islands
35ᶜ USCy
Fishing Boat

LEADERS OF THE WORLD · LEADERS OF THE WORLD
AUTO 100   1903 WINTON BRITAIN
GRENADINES OF ST. VINCENT 5ᶜ

AUTO 100   1903 WINTON BRITAIN
GRENADINES OF ST. VINCENT 5ᶜ
LEADERS OF THE WORLD · LEADERS OF THE WORLD

25

1874-1974

CORREO AEREO
13 PTA
españa   CICLISMO   F.N.M.T. 1983

TÜRK HAVA KURUMU
POSTA
TÜRKIYE CUMHURIYETI   20 LIRA

12

BELGIË - BELGIQUE

Brasil 85
Crs 220

BUSCA E SALVAMENTO MARITIMO

Christmas 1974
Niue 10ᶜ

The United Nations declared 1986 the International Year of Peace, and many countries issued stamps on that theme. Most bore the year's official symbol—a dove within the U.N. wreath—along with other designs. New Zealand, for example, showed a stylized drawing of the tree of life. Kenya's stamp was more ominous: It showed an atomic explosion with the words "Disarmament (Ban the Bomb)." The United Nations itself produced stamps in U.S., Swiss, and Austrian denominations. Even the Vatican, which doesn't usually join in omnibus issues, had stamps for the International Year of Peace.

STAMPS FROM AROUND THE WORLD

Among popular issues from Canada was a block of four stamps honoring explorers of North America. The first stamp showed tents and implements used by the first explorers—the peoples who migrated from Siberia to Alaska some 12,000 years ago. Another stamp showed two Viking ships sailing toward America. The third and fourth stamps showed two British explorers, John Cabot and Henry Hudson, who sailed to America searching for trade routes to Asia.

Four Canadian stamps saluted Expo 86, the world's fair held in Vancouver during the year. They showed the Canadian Pavilion, Expo Centre, and designs illustrating the communications and transportation aspects of the fair. A 1986 addition to Canada's National Parks set depicted a view of La Mauricie National Park in Quebec, which shelters more than 150 species of birds. Other Canadian stamps honored the 1988 Winter Olympics and the "mail from home" military mail program.

Argentina issued a number of stamps that all related to Antarctica, including eight that depicted the continent's wildlife. Belize, in Central America, released eight stamps marking the diverse ethnic heritage of its people, whose ancestors hail from many parts of the world.

Taiwan issued a series of stamps showing the delicate paintings of P'u Hsin-yu, a famous Chinese artist who was a member of the Manchu royal family. Another colorful group of four stamps from Taiwan depicted the art of Chinese flower arranging.

The Pacific island of Palau released two striking issues. One set showed songbirds, and the other was a sheet of stamps that, together, showed a coral reef. Bermuda issued a three-part set showing famous ships that have gone down in the treacherous waters around that Caribbean island.

Popular European issues included a Love stamp from Ireland showing a letterbox in the shape of a heart, as well as several sets from Yugoslavia. One of these showed artworks from nonaligned countries; another, butterflies and moths of Europe; and a third, folk costumes from eight regions.

Drought and famine in Africa were highlighted in stamps issued by the United Nations. Three stamps, designed by Ethiopian artists and bearing the words "Africa in Crisis," were released in U.S., Austrian, and Swiss denominations. Half the income from their sales was to go to aid people in Africa.

The United Nations also honored the hobby of stamp collecting in a set of stamps issued at the Ameripex show. Two stamps, in U.S. and Swiss denominations, showed one of the U.N.'s most valuable earlier issues—the 1954 human rights stamp—under a collector's magnifying glass. Other stamps in the group showed a sheet of various older stamps and a stamp engraver at work.

A TOPICAL COLLECTION

Transportation was an important theme at the 1986 world's fair in Vancouver, Canada. It would also make an excellent theme for a topical collection—a collection built around a single idea. You could begin your collection with some of the stamps issued in 1986. For example, an Alaskan dogsled from the 1920's was featured on a new stamp in the U.S. Transportation series. And a set of stamps from New Zealand showed vintage motorcycles.

Your collection can dip into past years' issues from other countries. And it can span all methods of transportation—from bicycles to balloons, antique cars to aircraft, ships to space shuttles. You'll find plenty to choose from because transportation is one of the most popular themes for stamps.

CHARLESS HAHN
Stamp Editor
Chicago Sun-Times

FANCY FILES

Need a place to store magazines, school reports, or stationery? In very little time you can create fancy file boxes to place on top of your desk. All you need are cereal or soap boxes, colorful wrapping paper, and tape or glue.

There are two styles of files. To make a side-opening file, tape closed the top of the box and then cut out one of the narrow sides. For a top-opening file, cut out the top of the box; then cut downward at an angle on the two wide sides and across the connecting narrow side. To make sure the files don't tip over, place several strips of cardboard in the bottom of each box. Cover the boxes with wrapping paper. Tape or glue the paper in place.

Try making a matching pencil holder from a small tin can.

144

TAKE NOTE

Here's a note-taker just perfect for hanging next to your telephone. The doll holding this notepad is made from a small food strainer. The mesh part of the strainer forms the doll's face; the handle holds the notepad.

Begin by covering the mesh part of the strainer with a piece of skin-toned, stretchy fabric. Pull the fabric over the underside of the strainer until it forms a smooth surface. (Don't cover the hanging hook at the top.) With needle and thread, sew the ends of the fabric together in the back—over the strainer's open side.

Make hair from yarn and glue it around the top and sides of the face. Cut out eyes, a nose, and a mouth from felt and glue them onto the face. Make a felt bow and tie it around the neck. Now, use strong tape to attach the strainer's handle to the back of the pad of paper. And finally, tape two loops of felt onto the back of the notepad (at the bottom), and insert a colorful pencil.

HATS OFF!

People wear all sorts of hats for all sorts of occasions. There are work hats and party hats. There are hats for special events, such as the mortarboards worn by graduating students. There are even hats, such as nightcaps, that you wouldn't want your best friend to see you wearing!

Through the ages, fashions in headwear have changed often. Some styles that were once very popular are no longer seen. For instance, in medieval Europe wealthy women often wore tall, pointed hats called hennins. The hats looked a bit like ice-cream cones, and some reached incredible heights.

The hennin and seventeen other types of hats are illustrated below. Match the illustrations with the names in the list on the right. If some of the hats are unfamiliar to you, look in your dictionary for descriptions of them.

1. boater
2. beret
3. bonnet
4. bowler (or derby)
5. cloche
6. coolie
7. deerstalker
8. fez
9. hennin
10. miter
11. mortarboard
12. nightcap
13. sombrero
14. ten-gallon
15. top hat
16. tricorn
17. turban
18. tyrolean

Next, go on a word hunt. Hidden in this search-a-word puzzle are the names of all eighteen hats. Try to find them. Cover the puzzle with a sheet of tracing paper. Read forward, backward, up, down, and diagonally. Then shade in the letters of each hat as you find it. One hat has been shaded in for you.

D	R	A	O	B	R	A	T	R	O	M	N	C
I	E	H	E	N	N	I	N	O	G	L	O	H
N	I	E	L	I	V	A	M	P	P	O	L	E
T	R	U	R	K	U	P	A	M	L	H	L	Y
E	E	V	A	S	H	C	H	I	Q	N	A	R
N	O	R	M	U	T	Y	E	U	A	U	G	T
P	N	U	S	E	H	B	A	X	E	Q	I	N	R	O
S	O	Z	E	G	B	O	W	L	E	R	K	E	I	S
L	B	J	I	U	B	P	O	O	K	I	S	T	C	H
E	Z	N	F	O	U	R	X	N	R	E	T	S	O	F
M	O	V	A	L	Y	F	I	G	A	I	R	I	R	M
N	I	T	O	T	H	E	W	I	L	B	A	R	N	E
N	E	T	O	A	S	Z	S	O	M	B	R	E	R	O
R	A	Y	E	C	L	O	C	H	E	R	P	U	T	E
M	E	R	R	Y	O	U	T	I	M	E	S	T	S
	E	K	S	E	Q	B	I

POPULAR CRAFTS

When you turn your hand to crafts, there's no end to the things you can do—and the materials you can use. Scraps of fabric can be turned into a decorative hooked rug. Designs from paper napkins find their way onto, of all things, jewelry. A few strips of wood and some paint, and artificial flowers become a beautiful wall decoration.

This Victorian-looking hooked rug was made from strips of fabric, and it would make an unusual wall hanging.

Today people are enjoying both old crafts and new ones. Rug hooking, needlework, and many of the fabric crafts have been around for many, many years. Now these traditional crafts have been joined by some other ones that your grandparents would never have thought of. But whether you work in old crafts or new, you'll find great satisfaction in making useful and decorative objects by hand.

RUG HOOKING

Pretty hooked rugs were a feature of many homes a few generations ago. Today such a rug can highlight a spot in your entryway, in front of your fireplace, or at the foot of your favorite chair. Or it can serve just as well as an attractive and unusual wall hanging. The Victorian-looking rug shown here was made from strips of fabric worked through a burlap backing, using a rug-hooking tool available in craft and needlework shops.

The first step is to prepare the backing, stretching the burlap and tacking it to a wooden frame, so that it stays taut and straight while you work. Then, following a pattern, draw the oval shape of the rug and its design onto the burlap. Use a permanent felt marker (one that won't bleed later, when the rug is washed).

Next, cut the fabric into long, narrow strips, each three eighths of an inch (1 centimeter) wide. The actual hooking process involves drawing the strip through the burlap repeatedly, making a succession of little loops on the top of the burlap. To do this, hold the hook above the burlap, and the fabric strip underneath. Push the hook down through the burlap, catch the fabric strip underneath, and pull a loop of it up through the burlap. Then push the hook down again, close to the first loop, and bring up another loop. Keep the loops even, about a quarter of an inch (0.6 centimeter) high, and spaced close together for a nice, dense coverage.

Begin in the center of the design and work outward toward the edge of the rug. When the rug is finished, remove it from the frame. Trim the edges of the burlap to within 2

The folded star, a classic quilting pattern, works beautifully when used on a small piece such as a pillow.

This Teddy-bear-design set for baby's room includes a crib quilt, a pillow, and a baby book.

inches (5 centimeters) of the hooked area, fold the edge under, and hem.

Who knows—your rug may one day become a family heirloom!

QUILTED STARS

Quilting is another traditional craft. In days gone by, people spent days and weeks making the sections of quilts, stitching them together by hand, and turning them into beautiful finished bed coverings. There were many classic patterns for quilts. And the folded star pattern was one of the most beautiful and popular.

Without spending the time you'd need to make an entire quilt, you can still enjoy the old-fashioned, "country" look of quilting. You can use the folded star pattern on a small piece, such as a pillow or a guest towel. Choose lightweight fabric in coordinating prints and solids for your piece. (If you are a beginning quilter, you may wish to use a simpler pattern, because the folded star is a somewhat complicated one.)

To make the petal star pillow shown here, cut pieces of fabric into circles and then fold them into wedges and triangles. Working from the center out, sew the sections to a stiff fabric backing. Finish off the rim of the circle with a bias-cut fabric edging and a wide piece of lace, and add a ruffle. Then attach the star to a small, round pillow stuffed with polyester fill.

CROSS-STITCH EMBROIDERY

If you're clever with a needle and thread, you can turn out beautiful gifts for special occasions. A gift set for a new baby, for example, could include a crib quilt, a pillow, and a baby book—all featuring the same design. The set pictured here shows a teddy bear with Irish flair, on a set that takes green as its dominant color.

The teddy-bear design is done in cross stitch, a basic embroidery technique, using six-strand embroidery floss. While the design is the same on all three pieces, the size and scale are different for each one. The pillow and crib quilt are made by stitching together the finished embroidery pieces with squares and strips of coordinating fabrics; the quilt is attached to a prequilted backing. The baby album is a special type designed to take an insert.

Using one basic design, you can make a special gift or a coordinated set. You might even want to adapt the design to carry the teddy bear theme throughout the nursery, stenciling or painting on the crib and other baby furniture.

A TRELLIS OF FLOWERS

Springtime in the garden . . . lilacs blooming . . . warm breezes . . . a trellis filled with flowers. Now you can enjoy the feeling of spring all year long with a pretty wall decoration made of wood lattice and silk flowers. It will bring back the feeling of an old-fashioned garden, where roses grew over latticed arches and people passed warm afternoons sitting in the garden gazebo.

The background of the wall decoration is made with strips of wooden lath, which are sold in lumber and hardware stores. The lath strips are cut into the desired lengths and sanded smooth.

The lattice is assembled in two layers. First, place the strips for the bottom layer

A trellis of flowers: This wall decoration made of wood lattice and pretty petals brings spring into your home.

Using a simple craft technique, paper party napkins can be turned into smashing bangle bracelets.

parallel to each other on heavy paper (an opened grocery bag will do). Glue them to the paper to hold them in place. Then lay the top layer of strips at right angles to the first, and glue these strips to the bottom layer.

When the glue is dry, pull off the paper backing and give the lattice several coats of paint, sanding between coats.

Now the flowers can be attached. Position the blooms in a way that is pleasing to you, and then wire them to the lattice. You can buy flowers ready-made, or assemble them yourself from individual petals and leaves sold in craft stores.

Finally, attach a picture hanger to the back of the lattice. Then hang it up and enjoy spring all year!

BEAUTIFUL BRACELETS

Pretty designs are all around you—in magazines and books, even on supermarket shelves. Some of the most clever and colorful designs are on paper goods, especially paper party napkins. New craft techniques will let you turn those designs to new uses.

You can, for example, transfer them onto big wooden bangle bracelets, like the ones shown here.

To begin, buy raw wood bangles and beautifully designed paper napkins. Sand the bangles smooth. Then give them at least two coats of paint inside and out. On the bracelet shown here, white was used on the outside, and a color coordinating with the paper design was used on the inside.

To transfer the design, first separate the top ply, or layer, of the napkin from the rest. (Only the top layer of the napkin carries the design.) Spray this layer with a special waterproofing product—sold in craft stores for this purpose. From this layer, cut out strips of paper carrying the design, and glue them to the bracelet. Finally, apply two coats of spray sealer to protect the finished bracelet.

The result? A beautiful piece of jewelry to give with love or wear with pride—because you made it yourself.

NANCY TOSH
Editor
Crafts 'n Things magazine

COIN COLLECTING

Gold coins from around the world were the new issues that attracted the most attention from collectors in 1986. There were also special commemorative issues marking events of the past, present, and future.

U.S. COINS

In 1986, the U.S. Treasury issued its first gold bullion coins—that is, coins whose value is determined by the amount of precious metal they contain, rather than by their official denominations.

U.S. $50 gold bullion coin (containing 1 ounce of gold)

In recent years, one of the most popular bullion coins has been South Africa's Krugerrand. In September, 1985, however, the U.S. government had banned imports of Krugerrands as a protest against the racial policies of the South African government. The new U.S. gold coins were expected to take the Krugerrand's place with collectors.

The first of the series was a $50 gold piece issued in September, 1986, and containing 1 ounce of gold. It was followed by $5, $10, and $25 coins, containing ¹⁄₁₀ ounce, ¼ ounce, and ½ ounce each. All bore the same design, a combination of classic and new U.S. coin motifs. On the obverse was a figure of Liberty striding out of the rising sun, bearing the torch of freedom and the olive branch of peace. A tiny U.S. Capitol dome appeared in the lower left. This design was used on $20 gold pieces from 1907 to 1933 and has been considered one of the most beautiful of all time. The backs of the gold coins showed a new design: a nest of eagles with a male, a female, and two hatchlings.

Since gold was selling at more than $400 an ounce at the time the first coins were released, they were priced at about eight times their face value. Thus, while the coins could be used at their face values as legal tender, it was highly unlikely that any would turn up in circulation.

A new U.S. silver dollar, containing an ounce of silver, was issued as a companion piece to the gold coins. Its obverse featured a figure of Liberty walking—a design that was used on half dollars from 1916 to 1947. On the reverse was a version of the eagle and shield design that has appeared on many U.S. coins.

That U.S. collectors were eager for new coins was shown by the success of another 1986 issue, the three-coin Statue of Liberty commemorative series. The group consisted of a gold $5 coin, a silver dollar, and a half dollar produced to mark the 100th anniversary of the Statue of Liberty. By September, all the 500,000 gold coins had been sold, along with 5,000,000 silver dollars and 5,500,000 half dollars. The sales raised $64,000,000 for restoration of the statue and of the Ellis Island immigration station in New York City.

COINS AROUND THE WORLD

Joining in commemorating the Statue of Liberty was France, which had given the statue to the United States in 1886. The French government issued 100-franc gold

French 100-franc gold coin commemorating the centennial of the Statue of Liberty

Canada's $20 silver coins honoring the 1988 Winter Olympics, to be held in Calgary, Alberta

Mexico's 50-peso coin commemorating the 1986 World Cup soccer championship

and silver coins that showed a close-up view of the statue's head, with a flock of birds flying behind.

Canada, which will host the 1988 Winter Olympics in Calgary, Alberta, released four coins featuring designs of Winter Games competitions. (The coins formed part of a series of ten $20 silver coins, the first two of which were issued in 1985.) The 1986 coins depicted free-style and cross-country skiing, hockey, and the biathlon.

Besides the Olympic coins, Canada released a silver dollar marking the centennial of the city of Vancouver, site of the 1986 World's Fair. This coin also marked the anniversary of the 1886 arrival in Vancouver of the country's first transcontinental train. The coin showed the old train chugging away from the modern skyline of Vancouver.

Since 1976, Canada has issued a $100 gold coin annually, each marking a special event. Since the United Nations designated 1986 as the International Year of Peace, the 1986 coin took peace as its theme. It showed olive branches—a symbol of peace—intertwined with maple leaves, Canada's symbol.

Mexico hosted the 1986 World Cup soccer championship, and it issued eight new gold and silver coins to mark the event. Their denominations ranged from 25 to 500 pesos (a peso was worth about 15 U.S. cents at the

time of the issue). All the coins featured various soccer designs. They joined eight similar coins that had been released in 1985.

Several members of the Commonwealth of Nations issued coins to honor the July, 1986, wedding of Prince Andrew, son of Queen Elizabeth II of Britain, and Sarah Ferguson. The Isle of Man released two coins with a denomination of one crown (25 pence, or about 37 U.S. cents). One showed portraits of the royal couple, while the other showed their familial coats of arms. The Falkland Is-

The Falkland Islands' 25-pound coin honoring the marriage of Britain's Prince Andrew and Sarah Ferguson

lands issued a silver coin with a denomination of 25 pounds (about $37) that pictured the royal pair facing each other.

Meanwhile, in London, the British Royal Mint staged a special exhibition marking 1,100 years of government minting. The date commemorated was 886, when the British ruler Alfred the Great drove Danish invaders from London. One of his first steps after the victory was to re-establish the mint, which has produced British coins ever since.

ROBERT F. LEMKE
Numismatic News

A HATFUL OF FLOWERS

"Plant" a country garden on a straw hat! The hat can be worn or hung on a wall in your room. It also makes a charming gift.

You need a straw hat, ribbons, and a variety of dried leaves and flowers—you can buy these or dry them yourself. It's easiest to work with a glue gun, which can be purchased at a craft shop.

Begin by making a bow with long streamers. Center the bow on the back of the hat or set it on one side; then glue it in place. Try positioning the leaves and flowers in different ways. When you're completely satisfied with the arrangement, carefully glue the pieces to the hat.

ALL IN THE PHYLUM

Members of the animal phylum Arthropoda are everywhere: on the ground, in the air, in all the waters of the world. There are more than 1,000,000 different kinds of arthropods, and many of them are familiar to you. Spiders, scorpions, and centipedes are arthropods. So are ants, butterflies, and all other insects.

Most of the water arthropods are also familiar to you. In fact, these ocean animals are so common that they have been called "the insects of the sea." To discover the more popular name of this group, you need a pencil and a sheet of lined paper. Number the lines 1 through 14, leaving a line of space between numbers. Carefully follow the directions given below. They will lead you to the name. Hint: It will be easier if you rewrite the complete words at each step.

The solution is on page 381.

1. Print the words INSECTS OF THE SEA.

2. Remove all spaces between the words.

3. Place an R after the fourth letter from the left.

4. Remove all letters that appear in the word OH!

5. Find the second letter from the left. Move it between the seventh and eighth letters from the right.

6. Replace the second vowel from the left with a U.

7. Find the third vowel from the right. Change it to the letter that comes first in the alphabet.

8. Remove the seventh and eighth consonants from the left.

9. Insert a C between the third and fourth consonants from the right.

10. Find the third vowel from the left. Place it between the fourth and fifth consonants from the left.

11. Find the third and thirteenth letters from the right. Remove them.

12. Find the second S from the left. Place it after the second A from the left.

13. Find the letter that comes after M in the alphabet. Move it between the A-S combination.

14. Reverse the order of the first four letters of the word.

When's the last time you saw one of these arthropods? Was it in the ocean . . . or on your dinner plate?

MANY FRIENDS COOKING

SURPRISE RICE PUDDING, from Sweden

Christmas Eve in Sweden. Friends and families have gathered together. Candles flicker. Faces glow. Everyone's ready for a holiday game of chance. This is the way it's played: Creamy rice pudding is spooned into bowls and passed around. Everyone watches. Waits. When each person has been served, the eating begins . . . slowly . . . carefully.

Legend says that the person who finds an almond in his or her pudding will have good luck all year long. You might try serving this rice pudding at a party. Then the finder of the almond could be given a prize.

INGREDIENTS

- 3 tablespoons butter
- 1 cup rice
- ¾ cup water
- 1 quart milk
- 1 teaspoon cinnamon
- 4 tablespoons sugar
- ¼ teaspoon salt
- 1 teaspoon vanilla
- 1 whole almond

EQUIPMENT

measuring spoons
saucepan
measuring cups
mixing spoon

HOW TO MAKE

1. Melt the butter in the saucepan. Add the rice and water. Bring to a boil and cook, stirring with the mixing spoon, for about 5 minutes.

2. Add the milk, cinnamon, sugar, salt, and vanilla.

3. Simmer for about 20 minutes, stirring every few minutes. Be careful not to let the milk boil over.

4. When the milk is nearly evaporated and the rice is soft, turn off the heat and stir in the almond. Pour into a serving bowl and serve warm.

This recipe serves 6 to 8 people.

COCONUT CHICKEN, from Indonesia

Have a *rijsttafel*—that means "rice table"—a unique Indonesian way of eating. Here's how Indonesians do it. First they make a pot of fluffy rice. Then they prepare an assortment of meats, vegetables, and relishes. Indonesian cooks vary the tastes between spicy and bland, hot and cold, crisp and soft, sweet and sour. The one rule in planning a *rijsttafel:* Flavors shouldn't be repeated.

When everything is ready, each diner heaps the rice in the middle of the plate and carefully spoons the other foods in a ring around the rice. You can begin your *rijsttafel* with rice and coconut chicken.

INGREDIENTS

1 3-pound chicken, cut into serving pieces
3 cups coconut milk
    (available at health food stores)
⅛ teaspoon cayenne
¼ teaspoon salt
5 mint leaves
1 medium onion

EQUIPMENT

paper towels
deep frying pan, to hold the chicken
measuring spoons
measuring cups
paring knife
baking or broiling pan
cooking fork or kitchen tongs

HOW TO MAKE

1. Wash the chicken and dry it with paper towels.

2. Place the chicken in the frying pan. Add the coconut milk, cayenne, salt, and mint leaves.

3. Cut up the onion into small pieces and add to the frying pan.

4. Bring the chicken and the other ingredients to a boil. Then turn down the heat and simmer for 20 minutes or until the liquid is nearly gone and only a thick sauce remains.

5. Preheat the broiler.

6. Remove the chicken from the frying pan and put it into the baking or broiling pan. Save the sauce.

7. Broil the chicken for 20 to 30 minutes. Use the cooking fork or tongs to turn the chicken while it cooks so that it doesn't burn.

8. When the chicken is done, transfer it to a platter and pour the sauce over it. Serve.

This recipe serves 6 people.

SPORTS

On each leg of the 2,500-mile Tour de France bicycle race, the overall leader has the honor of wearing the maillot jaune, or yellow jersey. At the end of the race, after pedaling through the streets of Paris, the victor keeps the jersey and is celebrated as perhaps no other figure in European sports. In 1986, the maillot jaune went to a non-European cyclist for the first time ever—America's Greg LeMond.

BASEBALL

The record shows that the New York Mets rolled up an impressive 108 victories in the regular season, enough to win the National League Eastern Division title by 21½ games. It also shows that they defeated the Houston Astros, 4 games to 2, in the National League playoffs. Finally, it shows that they became the 1986 champions of major league baseball by beating the Boston Red Sox, 4 games to 3, in the World Series.

What the bare statistics fail to show is that, once the Mets had completed their romp through the regular season, they reached the brink of elimination several times. Only with a series of miraculous come-from-behind victories did they emerge as champions.

The Astros had clinched the National League Western Division on a no-hitter by Cy Young Award winner Mike Scott. In the league championship series, Scott proceeded to defeat the Mets twice: 1–0 in the first game and 3–1 in the fourth game. The New Yorkers took the second game by a 5–1 score and pulled off their first miracle in the third game. Trailing in the 9th inning, the Mets' Len Dykstra hit a two-run homer to gain a 6–5 victory. In the fifth game the hero was Mets catcher Gary Carter, who gave New York a 2–1 victory with a run-scoring single in the 12th inning. The most gripping contest was the sixth game. Trailing 3–0 into the 9th, the Mets rallied for three runs to send the game into extra innings. Each team scored in the 14th, and New York tallied three times in the top of the 16th. Houston fought back in the bottom of the stanza but fell short. The Mets won, 7–6, to capture the National League pennant.

Similar suspense hung over the American League playoffs. The California Angels, champions of the Western Division, had an 8–1 victory in the first game. Boston tied it up with a 9–2 triumph in the second. Then on their home field, the Angels took an apparently insurmountable lead with a 5–3 win in the third game and a 4–3 victory (11 innings) in the fourth game. In the fifth contest, California carried a 5–2 lead into the top of the 9th inning and moved within one strike

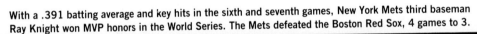

With a .391 batting average and key hits in the sixth and seventh games, New York Mets third baseman Ray Knight won MVP honors in the World Series. The Mets defeated the Boston Red Sox, 4 games to 3.

of eliminating the Red Sox. But Don Baylor and Dave Henderson hit clutch home runs to give Boston the lead. The Angels tied it in the bottom of the 9th, but Henderson's sacrifice fly in the 11th sent home the winning run. The pumped-up Sox won the next two games easily, 10–4, and 8–1, to capture the American League pennant.

Only once before had any team won the World Series after losing the first two games on its home field (the Kansas City Royals in 1985). But that is exactly what the Mets accomplished in 1986. The Red Sox, who hadn't won a World Series since 1918, took the first game in New York's Shea Stadium, 1–0, behind the pitching of Bruce Hurst. Boston had an easier time in the second game, coming out on top 9–3.

In the third contest, played at Boston's Fenway Park, the Mets' Dykstra led off with a home run, and New York proceeded to a 7–1 victory. The following night, two homers by Carter led the Mets to a series-tying 6–2 win. But in the fifth game, Hurst and the Red Sox came back for a 4–2 triumph, and Boston was only one game away from its long-awaited championship.

Back in Shea for the sixth confrontation, the Mets faced Boston ace Roger Clemens—the American League Cy Young Award winner and Most Valuable Player (MVP). The Red Sox jumped to a 2–0 lead, but the Mets climbed back. Back and forth it went. By the bottom of the 10th, the Red Sox were ahead 5–3 and within one strike of winning the series. But the Mets refused to die, coming up with three runs for a dramatic 6–5 victory. No team had ever scored three times in extra innings to win a World Series game.

And the excitement wasn't over. Facing the stingy Hurst in the final contest, the Amazin' Mets came from behind again. Overcoming an early 3–0 deficit, they took a 6–3 lead in the 7th inning and added two more in the 8th. The 8–5 victory gave them the second championship in the team's 25-year history.

Mets third baseman Ray Knight, who had a key single in the sixth game and the winning home run in the seventh, was named MVP of the World Series. Philadelphia Phillies' third baseman Mike Schmidt won his third National League MVP award for the

Boston's Roger Clemens was named the Cy Young Award winner and MVP in the American League.

regular season. Red Sox third baseman Wade Boggs beat out New York's Don Mattingly (.357 to .352) for his fourth American League batting championship. And Montreal's Tim Raines took the National League crown with a .334 average.

1986 WORLD SERIES RESULTS

		R	H	E	Winning/Losing Pitcher
1	Boston	1	5	0	Bruce Hurst
	New York	0	4	1	Ron Darling
2	Boston	9	18	0	Steve Crawford
	New York	3	8	1	Dwight Gooden
3	New York	7	13	0	Bob Ojeda
	Boston	1	5	0	Dennis Boyd
4	New York	6	12	0	Ron Darling
	Boston	2	7	1	Al Nipper
5	New York	2	10	1	Dwight Gooden
	Boston	4	12	0	Bruce Hurst
6	Boston	5	13	3	Calvin Schiraldi
	New York	6	8	2	Rick Aguilera
7	Boston	5	9	0	Calvin Schiraldi
	New York	8	10	0	Roger McDowell

Visiting team listed first, home team second

MAJOR LEAGUE BASEBALL FINAL STANDINGS

AMERICAN LEAGUE

Eastern Division

	W	L	Pct.	GB
*Boston	95	66	.590	—
New York	90	72	.556	5½
Detroit	87	75	.537	8½
Toronto	86	76	.531	9½
Cleveland	84	78	.519	11½
Milwaukee	77	84	.478	18
Baltimore	73	89	.451	22½

Western Division

	W	L	Pct.	GB
California	92	70	.568	—
Texas	87	75	.537	5
Kansas City	76	86	.469	16
Oakland	76	86	.469	16
Chicago	72	90	.444	20
Minnesota	71	91	.438	21
Seattle	67	95	.414	25

NATIONAL LEAGUE

Eastern Division

	W	L	Pct.	GB
*New York	108	54	.667	—
Philadelphia	86	75	.534	21½
St. Louis	79	82	.491	28½
Montreal	78	83	.484	29½
Chicago	70	90	.438	37
Pittsburgh	64	98	.395	44

Western Division

	W	L	Pct.	GB
Houston	96	66	.593	—
Cincinnati	86	76	.531	10
San Francisco	83	79	.512	13
San Diego	74	88	.457	22
Los Angeles	73	89	.451	23
Atlanta	72	89	.447	23½

* pennant winners

MAJOR LEAGUE LEADERS

AMERICAN LEAGUE

Batting
(top 10 qualifiers)

	AB	H	Avg.
Boggs, Boston	580	207	.357
Mattingly, New York	677	238	.352
Puckett, Minnesota	680	223	.328
Tabler, Cleveland	473	154	.326
Rice, Boston	618	200	.324
Yount, Milwaukee	522	163	.312
Fernandez, Toronto	687	213	.310
Bradley, Seattle	526	163	.310
Bell, Toronto	641	198	.309
Franco, Cleveland	599	183	.306

Home Runs

	HR
Barfield, Toronto	40
Kingman, Oakland	35
Gaetti, Minnesota	34
Canseco, Oakland	33
Deer, Milwaukee	33

Pitching
(top qualifiers, based on number of wins)

	W	L	ERA
Clemens, Boston	24	4	2.48
Morris, Detroit	21	8	3.27
Higuera, Milwaukee	20	11	2.79
Rasmussen, New York	18	6	3.88
Witt, California	18	10	2.84

NATIONAL LEAGUE

Batting
(top 10 qualifiers)

	AB	H	Avg.
Raines, Montreal	580	194	.334
Sax, Los Angeles	633	210	.332
Gwynn, San Diego	642	211	.329
Bass, Houston	591	184	.311
Hernandez, New York	551	171	.310
Hayes, Philadelphia	610	186	.305
Ray, Pittsburgh	579	174	.301
Knight, New York	486	145	.298
Webster, Montreal	576	167	.290
Schmidt, Philadelphia	552	160	.290

Home Runs

	HR
Schmidt, Philadelphia	37
Davis, Houston	31
Parker, Cincinnati	31
Murphy, Atlanta	29

Pitching
(top qualifiers, based on number of wins)

	W	L	ERA
Valenzuela, Los Angeles	21	11	3.14
Krukow, San Francisco	20	9	3.05
Ojeda, New York	18	5	2.57
Scott, Houston	18	10	2.22
Gooden, New York	17	6	2.84
Knepper, Houston	17	12	3.14

LITTLE LEAGUE BASEBALL

Spearheaded by pitcher Wu Chun-Liang, the team from Tainan City in Taiwan captured the 40th Little League World Series in Williamsport, Pennsylvania. In the final contest, played before 32,000 spectators and an international television audience, Wu and his teammates shut out the team from Tucson, Arizona, 12–0. It marked the 16th time in 20 years that a team from the Far East had won the championship, and the 11th time that a team from Taiwan had taken the honors. The Taiwanese also continued their streak of never having lost a Little League championship contest.

Wu Chun-Liang, whose fastball was clocked at 71 miles per hour, limited the Arizonans to only two singles in the final game —one in the fourth inning and one in the sixth inning. Wu struck out fourteen batters and walked none. He also performed well at the plate, knocking a home run in the first inning. But the big hitting star was teammate Chen Ching-Chan, who slammed a pair of two-run homers in the contest. The 12-run margin of victory for Tainan City tied the record for the championship game.

The youngsters from Taiwan were impressive in all three of their tournament games at Williamsport. In the opener, Wu hurled a no-hitter against Valleyfield, Quebec. He struck out twelve batters and kept the Canadians from hitting the ball beyond the infield. Tainan's hitters, meanwhile, rolled up an amazing 26 runs.

In their semifinal game against Maracaibo, Venezuela, the Taiwanese showed their championship spirit in a different way. Behind by two runs in the sixth (and final) inning, they tied the score at 4–4 with a dramatic home run by Yen Hsin-Ho, sending the game into extra innings. Then, in the eighth, Tainan City exploded for seven runs, winning the contest 11–4. Yen contributed two more hits in the final outburst.

Tucson, meanwhile, reached the championship game with a 6–0 victory over Norridge, Illinois, and a 4–1 triumph over Sarasota, Florida. Philip Johnston, who pitched the shutout for Tucson against Norridge, was the primary victim of Tainan City's 13-hit barrage in the championship game.

In the finals of the Little League World Series, Wu Chun-Liang of Taiwan pitched a two-hit shutout.

BASKETBALL

In winning their 16th league championship, the Boston Celtics continued two traditions in the National Basketball Association (NBA). The first was their own success in the final playoff series. Only once since

Larry Bird soared again, winning his third straight MVP award and leading the Celtics to their 16th NBA title.

1958 have the Celtics failed to win the title after reaching the final round. That came in 1985, when they were defeated by the Los Angeles Lakers. The other tradition was the crowning of a new NBA champion. Not since 1969 has any team won back-to-back titles.

From the beginning of the 1985–86 season, it was widely assumed that the Celtics and Lakers would meet in the playoff finals for the third year in a row. But in the Western Division championships, the Lakers came up against the ever-improving Houston Rockets and were ousted 4 games to 1. The Celts, meanwhile, reached the league finals after losing only one game in their first three playoff rounds. Against the fired-up Rockets, Boston completed another banner season with a hard-fought six-game triumph.

The 1985–86 Celtics were considered one of the best teams in NBA history. Their total of 67 wins during the regular season was only two shy of the league record. And their 15 wins in the playoffs gave them a record 82 victories for the season. In 51 appearances on their home court (including playoffs), they lost only once.

Boston was led once again by the spectacular Larry Bird. The 6-foot, 9-inch forward was named the league's most valuable player (MVP) for the third year in a row, and he rounded out his season with MVP honors for the playoffs as well. Nevertheless, it was brilliant team play that made the Celts so great. The other starters were center Robert Parish, forward Kevin McHale, and guards Dennis Johnson and Danny Ainge. Center Bill Walton and guard Jerry Sichting were major contributors off the bench.

With all their fire power, the Celtics had no easy time against Houston in the championship round. The Rockets were led by the "Twin Towers"—7-foot Akeem Olajuwon and 7-foot, 4-inch Ralph Sampson. In only his second season, Olajuwon had already proved to be one of the best centers in the league. The giant Sampson had tossed in a miraculous buzzer shot to oust the Lakers in the fifth game of the Houston–Los Angeles series.

NBA FINAL STANDINGS

EASTERN CONFERENCE
Atlantic Division

	W	L	Pct.
Boston	67	15	.817
Philadelphia	54	28	.659
New Jersey	39	43	.476
Washington	39	43	.476
New York	23	59	.280

Central Division

	W	L	Pct.
Milwaukee	57	25	.695
Atlanta	50	32	.610
Detroit	46	36	.561
Chicago	30	52	.366
Cleveland	29	53	.354
Indiana	26	56	.317

WESTERN CONFERENCE
Midwest Division

	W	L	Pct.
Houston	51	31	.622
Denver	47	35	.573
Dallas	44	38	.537
Utah	42	40	.512
Sacramento	37	45	.451
San Antonio	35	47	.427

Pacific Division

	W	L	Pct.
L.A. Lakers	62	20	.756
Portland	40	42	.488
L.A. Clippers	32	50	.390
Phoenix	32	50	.390
Seattle	31	51	.378
Golden State	30	52	.366

NBA Championship: Boston Celtics

COLLEGE BASKETBALL

Conference	Winner
Atlantic Coast	Duke
Big East	St. John's, Syracuse (tied, regular season) St. John's (tournament)
Big Eight	Kansas
Big Ten	Michigan
Ivy League	Brown
Metro	Louisville
Missouri Valley	Bradley (regular season) Tulsa (tournament)
Pacific Ten	Arizona
Southeastern	Kentucky
Southwest	Texas, Texas A&M, Texas Christian (tied, regular season) Texas Tech (tournament)
Western Athletic	Texas–El Paso, Utah, Wyoming (tied, regular season) Texas–El Paso (tournament)

NCAA: Louisville

NIT: Ohio State

The Celtics got off to a quick start in the finals, winning the first and second games in Boston by scores of 112–100 and 117–95. In the third game, played in Houston, the Celts had an eight-point lead with only three minutes left and seemed in command. But the Rockets, led by Olajuwon and Sampson, came back for a 106–104 victory. The fourth game, also played in Houston, was perhaps the best of the series. In an exciting back-and-forth contest, Walton put in a key rebound shot with 1 minute, 39 seconds of play remaining, and Boston went on to win 106–103.

Though they trailed 3 games to 1, the Rockets refused to give in. Paced by Olajuwon's 32 points, they scored an easy 111–96 victory in the fifth game. The contest was marred by a fight involving Sampson, who was ejected from the game. The incident, however, did seem to ignite the Rockets.

Back in Boston Garden for the sixth game, the Celtics were ready to wrap things up. And wrap things up they did. With Bird at his best—29 points, 11 rebounds, 12 assists—the Celts rolled to a 114–97 victory that clinched the title.

College Play. In the National Collegiate Athletic Association (NCAA), no single team was dominant, at least among the men. In the title contest, the Louisville Cardinals emerged as champions with a 72–69 victory over Duke. Duke had entered the tournament as the top-ranked team in the country. It breezed through the early rounds and then defeated No. 2-ranked Kansas, 71–67, in the semifinals. Louisville, ranked No. 7, reached the finals with an 88–77 victory over upstart LSU. In the championship contest, Louisville's freshman center Pervis Ellison scored 25 points and was named the game's MVP. Junior center Walter Berry of St. John's won most of the college player-of-the-year awards.

In women's competition, the University of Texas was by far the best of the field. The Lady Longhorns compiled a 34–0 record and defeated the University of Southern California (USC), 97–81, in the NCAA tournament finals. Texas' Clarissa Davis won game MVP honors. USC's Cheryl Miller was voted the women's player of the year for the second straight time.

FOOTBALL

In 1986, the world of football saw the Bears roll and a league fold; Walter Payton continued his run through the record book; a team with a mediocre record grabbed the Grey Cup; and a college player with a great arm snared the Heisman Trophy.

THE NFL PLAYOFFS AND SUPER BOWL XX

Championship football games are usually filled with suspense. Who will win is often in doubt until late in the last quarter. For the Chicago Bears, however, the 1985–86 National Football League playoffs and Super Bowl XX had plenty of excitement but not much suspense. Chicago's "Monsters of the Midway" were by far the best team in the NFL and steamrolled to the title.

The Bears entered the playoffs with a spectacular 15–1 regular season record, which put them high atop the National Conference's Central Division. The other playoff teams in the National Conference were the Eastern Division champion Dallas Cowboys,

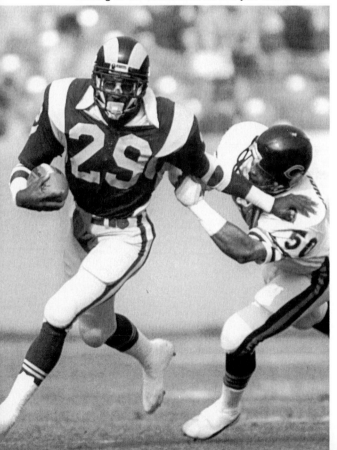

In 1986, Eric Dickerson of the L.A. Rams led the NFL in rushing for the third time in his four-year career.

the Western Division champion Los Angeles Rams, and the two wild-card teams, the San Francisco 49ers and the New York Giants.

The surprising Giants whipped the defending Super Bowl champion 49ers by the score of 17–3; but a week later, the Bears knocked off the Giants, 21–0. Meanwhile, Los Angeles dropped Dallas, 20–0, as the Rams' Eric Dickerson set a playoff record by rushing for 248 yards.

The superb Dickerson figured to be a tough challenge for the Bears' highly rated defense in the National Conference championship game. But it was no contest. Chicago demolished the Rams, 24–0. Never before had an NFL team recorded consecutive shutouts in playoff competition. Bear quarterback Jim McMahon ran for one touchdown and passed for another, and his defensive teammates held the Rams to only 130 yards in total offense. Next stop for the Bears: Super Bowl XX.

In the American Conference, the Los Angeles Raiders topped the Western Division, the Cleveland Browns led the Central Division, and the Miami Dolphins triumphed in the Eastern Division. The two wild-card teams were the New York Jets and the New England Patriots.

The Patriots took the measure of the favored Jets, 26–14, and a week later, New England scored an even bigger upset by besting the Raiders, 27–20. In the meantime, the Dolphins were coming from behind to sneak by the Browns, 24–21.

Again the underdog in the American Conference championship game, the Patriots refused to submit to the Dolphins. Instead, New England won convincingly, 31–14, as quarterback Tony Eason threw three touchdown passes. The Patriots were awarded a well-deserved trip to the Super Bowl.

But on January 26, 1986, in Super Bowl XX, the Patriots' dream ran afoul of the mighty Bears' juggernaut. Chicago overwhelmed New England, 46–10, before 73,818 fans in the Superdome in New Orleans, Louisiana. The Bears' defense held the Patriots to minus-19 yards in the first two quarters, as Chicago racked up a 23–3 halftime lead. They continued to pile it on in the second half, setting records for the most points scored and the widest margin of victory in a Super Bowl. Bear defensive end Richard Dent, who spent much of the afternoon in the Patriots' backfield, was named the game's most valuable player. Super Bowl XX wasn't suspenseful, but it brought plenty of excitement to the fans in Chicago, who celebrated their team's first NFL championship since 1963.

THE UNITED STATES FOOTBALL LEAGUE

In 1986, the United States Football League (USFL) faded into history. Unable to compete financially, the league folded. But the USFL's best players, most notably Herschel Walker, Kelvin Bryant, and Doug Flutie, continued their careers by signing with NFL teams.

THE 1986 NFL REGULAR SEASON

The Chicago Bears rolled on into the 1986 regular season, topping the National Conference Central Division with a 14–2 record. The Bears' Walter Payton, the NFL's career rushing leader, passed the 16,000-yard mark late in the season.

The other National Conference division titlists were the New York Giants (14–2) and the San Francisco 49ers (10–5–1); the wild-card teams were the Washington Redskins (12–4) and the Los Angeles Rams (10–6).

In the American Conference, the division titlists were the New England Patriots (11–5), the Cleveland Browns (12–4), and the Denver Broncos (11–5); the wild-card teams were the New York Jets (10–6) and the Kansas City Chiefs (10–6).

THE CANADIAN FOOTBALL LEAGUE

The Grey Cup, emblematic of the championship of the Canadian Football League, was won by the Hamilton Tiger-Cats. Hamilton had a mediocre 9–8–1 record during the regular season. But in a remarkable upset, they drubbed the Edmonton Eskimos, 39–15, in the Grey Cup game, played in Vancouver, British Columbia, in November. It was the Tiger-Cats' fourteenth Grey Cup victory, but only their first since 1972. Hamilton quarterback Mike Kerrigan completed 16 of 35 passes, including two for touchdowns, for a total of 309 yards. He was named the offensive player of the game.

New York Giants linebacker Lawrence Taylor was the most feared defensive player in the NFL.

COLLEGE FOOTBALL

The University of Miami (Florida) finished its regular season undefeated, with a record of 11–0, and was ranked number one in the country. But Pennsylvania State University (Penn State), ranked number two, was also 11–0. Since Miami and Penn State were to meet in the Fiesta Bowl, the final number-one ranking would have to await the outcome of that game. The University of Oklahoma, at 10–1, was ranked third.

Miami's Vinny Testaverde won the Heisman Trophy. During his senior year, the Hurricane quarterback completed 175 of 276 passes for 2,557 yards and 26 touchdowns.

Oklahoma tangled with Arkansas (9–2) in the Orange Bowl; Texas A&M (9–2) met Ohio State (9–3) in the Cotton Bowl; Nebraska (9–2) faced LSU (9–2) in the Sugar Bowl; and Michigan (10–1) vied with Arizona State (9–1–1) in the Rose Bowl.

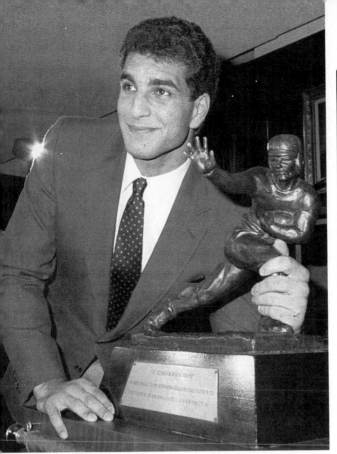

Miami Hurricane quarterback Vinny Testaverde was a landslide winner in voting for the 1986 Heisman Trophy.

NFL FINAL STANDINGS

AMERICAN CONFERENCE

Eastern Division

	W	L	T	Pct.	PF	PA
New England	11	5	0	.688	412	307
N.Y. Jets	10	6	0	.625	364	386
Miami	8	8	0	.500	430	405
Buffalo	4	12	0	.250	287	348
Indianapolis	3	13	0	.188	229	400

Central Division

	W	L	T	Pct.	PF	PA
Cleveland	12	4	0	.750	391	310
Cincinnati	10	6	0	.625	409	394
Pittsburgh	6	10	0	.375	307	336
Houston	5	11	0	.313	274	329

Western Division

	W	L	T	Pct.	PF	PA
Denver	11	5	0	.688	378	327
Kansas City	10	6	0	.625	358	326
Seattle	10	6	0	.625	366	293
L.A. Raiders	8	8	0	.500	323	346
San Diego	4	12	0	.250	335	396

NATIONAL CONFERENCE

Eastern Division

	W	L	T	Pct.	PF	PA
N.Y. Giants	14	2	0	.875	371	236
Washington	12	4	0	.750	368	296
Dallas	7	9	0	.438	346	337
Philadelphia	5	10	1	.344	256	312
St. Louis	4	11	1	.281	218	351

Central Division

	W	L	T	Pct.	PF	PA
Chicago	14	2	0	.875	352	187
Minnesota	9	7	0	.563	398	273
Detroit	5	11	0	.313	277	326
Green Bay	4	12	0	.250	254	418
Tampa Bay	2	14	0	.125	239	473

Western Division

	W	L	T	Pct.	PF	PA
San Francisco	10	5	1	.656	374	247
L.A. Rams	10	6	0	.625	309	267
Atlanta	7	8	1	.469	280	280
New Orleans	7	9	0	.438	288	287

COLLEGE FOOTBALL

Conference	Winner
Atlantic Coast	Clemson
Big Eight	Oklahoma
Big Ten	Michigan, Ohio State (tied)
Pacific Coast	San Jose State
Pacific Ten	Arizona
Southeastern	LSU
Southwest	Texas A&M
Western Athletic	San Diego State

Cotton Bowl: Ohio State 28, Texas A&M 12
Fiesta Bowl: Penn State 14, Miami 10
Orange Bowl: Oklahoma 42, Arkansas 8
Rose Bowl: Arizona State 22, Michigan 15
Sugar Bowl: Nebraska 30, Louisiana State 15

Heisman Trophy: Vinny Testaverde, University of Miami

In 1986, Jack Nicklaus won the Masters tournament for a record sixth time. Pat Bradley won the Ladies PGA and became the first player to win the four tournaments that make up the grand slam of women's golf.

GOLF

PROFESSIONAL		AMATEUR	
	Individual		**Individual**
Masters	Jack Nicklaus	**U.S. Amateur**	Buddy Alexander
U.S. Open	Raymond Floyd	**U.S. Women's Amateur**	Kay Cockerill
Canadian Open	Bob Murphy	**British Amateur**	David Curry
British Open	Greg Norman	**British Ladies Amateur**	Mernie McGuire
PGA	Bob Tway	**Canadian Amateur**	Brent Franklin
World Series of Golf	Danny Joe Pohl	**Canadian Ladies Amateur**	Marilyn O'Connor
U.S. Women's Open	Jane Geddes		
Ladies PGA	Pat Bradley		**Team**
		Curtis Cup	Britain/Ireland
	Team		
World Cup	not held in 1986		

HOCKEY

After a lapse of seven years, the Montreal Canadiens resumed one of the great dynasties in professional sports. In a year expected to belong once again to the powerful Edmonton Oilers, Montreal's "baby boomers" had been given little chance of recapturing the team's glory days. But after a series of playoff upsets unmatched in National Hockey League (NHL) history, the Canadiens won their 23rd Stanley Cup title. That gave them the most championships of any professional sports team in North America—one more even than baseball's New York Yankees.

The major upset was the defeat of the Oilers by the Calgary Flames. After winning two straight Stanley Cups, Edmonton had compiled the best record (56–17–7) and scored the most goals (426) during the 1985–1986 regular season. Entering the playoffs, the Oilers had lost only five games to Campbell Conference teams. Calgary, meanwhile, with only the sixth best record (40–31–9) in the league, finished a distant second to Edmonton in the Smythe Division race. In the second round of the playoffs, however, the Flames managed to oust the defending cham-

pions in a tight seven-game series. Calgary went on to defeat the St. Louis Blues in seven games for the Campbell Conference title and the team's first berth in the championship series.

Upsets were the order of the day in the Wales Conference playoffs as well. The Philadelphia Flyers, boasting the second best regular-season record (53–23–4) in the league, were eliminated by the surprising New York Rangers in the first round. The Rangers proceeded to defeat the Washington Capitals, the NHL's third best team (50–23–7), in the next round.

Montreal, with eight rookies on a roster guided by a freshman coach, finished the regular season with only the seventh best record (40–33–7) in the league. In the playoffs, however, the Canadiens advanced to the finals by defeating the Boston Bruins in three games, the Hartford Whalers in seven games, and the Rangers in five games.

Thus, for the first time ever, none of the top five teams in the regular-season standings reached the championship round. The Calgary-Montreal matchup was the first all-Canadian Stanley Cup final since 1967.

Anchored by 20-year-old goalie Patrick Roy, Montreal battled to its 23rd Stanley Cup championship.

NHL FINAL STANDINGS

WALES CONFERENCE

Patrick Division

	W	L	T	Pts.
Philadelphia	53	23	4	110
Washington	50	23	7	107
N.Y. Islanders	39	29	12	90
N.Y. Rangers	36	38	6	78
Pittsburgh	34	38	8	76
New Jersey	28	49	3	59

Adams Division

	W	L	T	Pts.
Quebec	43	31	6	92
Montreal	40	33	7	87
Boston	37	31	12	86
Hartford	40	36	4	84
Buffalo	37	37	6	80

CAMPBELL CONFERENCE

Norris Division

	W	L	T	Pts.
Chicago	39	33	8	86
Minnesota	38	33	9	85
St. Louis	37	34	9	83
Toronto	25	48	7	57
Detroit	17	57	6	40

Smythe Division

	W	L	T	Pts.
Edmonton	56	17	7	119
Calgary	40	31	9	89
Winnipeg	26	47	7	59
Vancouver	23	44	13	59
Los Angeles	23	49	8	54

Stanley Cup: Montreal Canadiens

OUTSTANDING PLAYERS

Hart Trophy (most valuable player)	Wayne Gretzky, Edmonton
Ross Trophy (scorer)	Wayne Gretzky, Edmonton
Vezina Trophy (goalie)	John Vanbiesbrouck, N.Y. Rangers
Norris Trophy (defenseman)	Paul Coffey, Edmonton
Selke Trophy (defensive forward)	Troy Murray, Chicago
Calder Trophy (rookie)	Gary Suter, Calgary
Lady Byng Trophy (sportsmanship)	Mike Bossy, N.Y. Islanders
Conn Smythe Trophy (Stanley Cup play)	Patrick Roy, Montreal

Calgary got off to a good start, winning the series opener, 5–2, on home ice. In the second game, however, the Canadiens bounced back in dramatic fashion. With the score tied 2–2, the game went into overtime. Then, only nine seconds into the extra period, Montreal rookie Brian Skrudland knocked the puck past the Calgary goaltender for the winning tally. It was the quickest overtime goal in NHL playoff history.

Boosted by that dramatic goal, the Canadiens raised their level of play and never lost again. In the third game, played before their home crowd, the "Habs" (a traditional nickname) scored four times in the first period and skated to an easy 5–3 victory. The fourth game was a hard-fought contest that remained 0–0 into the third period. Montreal's Claude Lemieux, another rookie, scored the game's only goal 11 minutes into the final frame. The fifth game was another nail-biter. The Canadiens took a 4–1 lead in the third period, but the Flames scored two quick goals to draw within one. With 14 seconds left on the clock, Montreal goalie Patrick Roy made a miraculous save to preserve the 4–3 victory—and bring home the Cup.

For his heroics throughout post-season play, Roy was awarded the Conn Smythe Trophy as the most valuable player (MVP) of the playoffs. At age 20, he was the youngest player ever to win that honor.

For the seventh year in a row, Edmonton center Wayne Gretzky won the Hart Trophy as the league's MVP. "The Great One" also won his sixth consecutive NHL scoring title. His 215 points (52 goals, 163 assists) broke his own single-season record of 212, set in 1981–82. Pittsburgh Penguin standout Mario Lemieux finished second in the scoring race with 141 points. Gretzky's teammate Paul Coffey was third with 138; Coffey also broke Bobby Orr's single-season record for most goals by a defenseman, hitting for 48. Yet another Oiler, Jari Kurri, was fourth with 131 points and led the league in goals with 68. Los Angeles center Marcel Dionne recorded his 1,599th career point, moving him into second place on the all-time scoring list. And John Vanbiesbrouck of the New York Rangers was named the winner of the Vezina Trophy as the year's top goalie.

ICE SKATING

FIGURE SKATING

World Championships

Men	Brian Boitano, U.S.
Women	Debi Thomas, U.S.
Pairs	Ekaterina Gordeeva/Sergei Grinkov, U.S.S.R.
Dance	Natalya Bestemianova/Andrei Bukin, U.S.S.R.

United States Championships

Men	Brian Boitano
Women	Debi Thomas
Pairs	Gillian Wachsman/Todd Waggoner
Dance	Renee Roca/Donald Adair

SPEED SKATING

World Championships

Men	Hein Vergeer, Netherlands
Women	Karin Kania, E. Germany

SKIING

WORLD CUP CHAMPIONSHIPS

Men	Marc Girardelli, Luxembourg
Women	Maria Walliser, Switzerland

U.S. ALPINE CHAMPIONSHIPS

Men

Downhill	Doug Lewis
Slalom	Henrik Smith-Meyer
Giant Slalom	Tiger Shaw
Combined	Tiger Shaw

Women

Downhill	Hilary Lindh
Slalom	Tamara McKinney
Giant Slalom	Beth Madsen
Combined	Beth Madsen

Marc Girardelli of Luxembourg—World Cup champion for the second straight year.

THE BUMPY RAINBOW

Debi Thomas is a special kind of figure skater. No, Debi Thomas is a special kind of person.

Her skating accomplishments speak for themselves. In February, 1986, at Uniondale, New York, the 18-year-old Californian turned in a dazzling performance to win the U.S. women's championship. The following month, in Geneva, Switzerland, she outleaped and out-scored the best of the rest and was crowned the new world champion.

But there are other things that make Debi Thomas special. For one, she is the first black skater ever to win a major individual title. For another, Thomas is a full-time college student. While her skating competitors devote themselves entirely to the sport, Thomas is a pre-med student at Stanford University. Her major is medical microbiology, and she plans to be an orthopedic surgeon when her skating days are over.

As for being the sport's first black champion, Thomas is matter-of-fact. "I never really thought about that too much," she said. But when it comes to studying and training, Thomas is far from matter-of-fact. She attends classes from 8 A.M. to lunch, hits the ice until early evening, and then hits the books—sometimes until 3 A.M. It's a difficult schedule, and success has been hard-won. Said Thomas after winning the U.S. championship: "I went through a lot to get here, and it feels good. This is like the pot of gold at the end of the rainbow, but it was a bumpy rainbow."

The rainbow began in Poughkeepsie, New York, where Debi was born. Her parents, both computer programmers, moved to California, and Debi was raised in San Jose. When she was 3½, her mother took her to see the Ice Follies. Debi was enchanted and begged for a pair of skates. She got them at 5, and at 9 she won her first figure-skating competition. The following year, her mother hired Alex McGowan to be her coach. (He's worked with Debi ever since.) To be near McGowan's ice rink, Debi enrolled in San Mateo High, about 45 minutes from home. Time was tight and so was money. Debi sewed her own skating dresses and usually competed in worn-out skates.

In addition to her perseverance and athletic ability, one quality that's helped Thomas rise to the top is her love of performance. "The more people the better," she says. "I get fired up and put more into it." A prime example was the U.S. championships. She had skated poorly in practice, unable to execute the five triple jumps in her program. Once in front of the crowd, however, Thomas was transformed. Her confidence grew as the cheering grew, and she landed every jump flawlessly. "When you kind of amaze yourself I think it helps the program," said the young champion.

Debi Thomas has amazed a lot of people.

In an action-packed, month-long tournament, 24 teams vied for soccer's most cherished prize—the World Cup. The championship match, which was played in Mexico City, pitted Argentina (striped shirts) against West Germany (green shirts). Argentina emerged victorious, 3–2.

THE 1986 WORLD SOCCER CUP

Soccer is the world's most popular sport, and the World Cup tournament is its crowning event. By comparison, the World Series and the Super Bowl are almost like backyard games. Held every four years, the soccer extravaganza is passionately followed in nearly every nation on the globe. In 1986 the 13th World Cup was held in Mexico, where 52 games were played in nine cities. According to estimates, a total of nine billion fans in 156 countries tuned in for the competition.

The road to Mexico had actually begun two years earlier with a worldwide elimination super-tournament. Teams representing 110 nations played qualifying matches to determine 22 of the 24 finalists. The defending champion, Italy, and the host country, Mex-

ico, received automatic berths in the final tournament. The ultimate winner would truly be the world champion—there is no greater source of national pride than winning the World Cup.

When all was said and done, it was Argentina that emerged as the best of the best. Led by superstar midfielder Diego Maradona, the Argentines compiled a record of 6 wins, 0 losses, and 1 tie in the Mexico tourney. They captured the cup with an exciting 3–2 victory over West Germany in the championship match. The triumph was their second in the last three tournaments; they had also won the trophy in 1978.

The final contest of the 1986 World Cup (or *Mundial*, in Spanish) was played in front of 114,500 fans at Mexico City's Azteca Stadium. Another two billion watched on television. Argentina took a 1–0 lead midway through the first half when defender José Luis Brown headed the ball into the net off a free kick. The Argentines struck again ten minutes into the second half as Jorge Valdano found a gap in the left side of the West German defense and slipped the ball past the lunging goaltender. With 35 minutes left to play, the 2–0 lead looked insurmountable.

But the tough, disciplined Germans wouldn't die easily. With just seventeen minutes on the clock, veteran star Karl-Heinz Rummenigge received a corner kick right in front of the Argentine goal and knocked it home. Then, seven minutes later, off another corner kick, teammate Rudi Voeller shocked everyone by heading in the tying goal.

The Germans' joy, however, was short-lived. Said Rummenigge after the game, "Our downfall was our happiness. We stopped concentrating after our second goal." Argentina, taking advantage of the lapse, struck back with lightning speed. Maradona, closely guarded all afternoon, picked up a loose ball and passed it with perfect precision past four German defenders. Fellow midfielder Jorge Burruchaga received the ball on the dead run and blasted in the winning tally.

The final whistle sounded seven minutes later. Argentine players fell to their knees and cried. Back home in Buenos Aires, hundreds of thousands of delirious fans poured into the streets.

The awarding of the World Cup to Argentina marked the end of an action-packed month of soccer in Mexico. The 24 teams had been divided into six groups (A–F), each of which played a round-robin schedule. The top 16 teams then advanced to a second-round elimination. Argentina reached the title match with a 2–0 victory over Belgium in the semifinals. Prior to that it defeated England 2–1, in a hotly contested quarterfinal; the match had political overtones because of the 1982 war between Argentina and Britain over the Falkland Islands. West Germany, meanwhile, advanced to the championship game with a 4–1 defeat of Mexico in the quarterfinals and a 2–0 triumph over France in the semifinals.

After Argentina and West Germany, France had the greatest tournament success. It defeated a surprisingly strong Belgian squad, 4–2 in overtime, to take third place. Earlier it ousted defending champion Italy, 2–0, and tournament favorite Brazil, 5–4 in an overtime penalty shootout. Lightly regarded Morocco also performed well, becoming the first African team ever to reach the second round.

Among individual performers, England's Gary Lineker was the top scorer with six goals. The great Maradona was second with five, and he set up many of his team's other scores. And Spain's Emilio Butragueño became the first World Cup performer in twenty years to notch four goals in one game, against Denmark.

The greatest honor, of course, went to the players on the winning team. The others went home already hoping for a chance to compete in the 1990 tournament, to be held in Italy. Meanwhile, for literally billions of soccer fans around the world, the 1986 Mundial in Mexico left enough memories to last those four years, and longer.

Gary Lineker was the leading scorer in the 1986 World Cup tournament. The English "striker" had six goals.

EL REY

His nickname was *Dieguito,* or "little Diego." Only 5'5" tall and weighing 152 pounds, Diego Armando Maradona of Argentina was already recognized as one of the biggest talents in international soccer. But by the end of the 1986 World Cup tournament in Mexico, followers of the sport everywhere agreed that he was simply *the* best player in the world. "He has to be the best," said Argentine Coach Carlos Bilardo. "He has the right age, the right physical condition, and the right technique. He is the World Cup. This is his world championship." After leading his team to the coveted title, *Dieguito* had earned a new nickname from his countrymen—*El Rey,* or "The King."

Maradona's soccer genius has stirred memories of the legendary Pelé, Brazil's star of an earlier generation. The 25-year-old Argentine team captain scored a total of five goals in the 1986 World Cup, one less than tournament leader Gary Lineker of England. However, unlike Lineker (as well as Pelé and other great scorers), Maradona doesn't play the front-line "striker" position. As a midfielder, he's also responsible for setting up plays and making the key passes to other attackers.

Most of all, it's Maradona's sheer speed and strength, dazzling skill with the ball, and uncanny sense of the game that leave fans and players alike in awe. Several times in Mexico, his darting, stutter-stepping bursts through the opponent's defense left four or five defenders dazed and embarrassed.

One of seven children, *Dieguito* first attracted international attention in 1979. At age 18, he captained the Argentine team that won the World Youth Championship. Then in both 1980 and 1981, playing for a team called the Boca Juniors, he was voted South American Player of the Year.

Maradona competed in his first World Cup in 1982, in Spain. Although he showed flashes of brilliance, that tournament was not the personal showcase that Mexico would prove to be. Still young and relatively inexperienced, he lost much of his effectiveness —and his temper—in the face of brutal fouling by the opposition.

After the 1982 World Cup, Maradona took his talents to Naples, Italy, where he was paid close to $1,000,000 a year to play in a league noted for roughness. (He still plays for this team.) Gaining maturity and learning to endure the kicks in his shins, he emerged as one of the world's great players. Fans idolized him, and the legend grew. By 1986, he was ready to be crowned *El Rey*.

Betsy Mitchell of the United States swam to a world record in the 200-meter backstroke.

SWIMMING

WORLD SWIMMING RECORDS SET IN 1986		
EVENT	**HOLDER**	**TIME**
	Men	
50-meter freestyle	Matt Biondi, U.S.	22.33
100-meter freestyle	Matt Biondi, U.S.	48.74
800-meter freestyle	Vladimir Salnikov, U.S.S.R.	7:50.64
100-meter butterfly	Pablo Morales, U.S.	52.84
200-meter butterfly	Michael Gross, W. Germany	1:56.24
	Women	
50-meter freestyle	Tamara Costache, Rumania	25.28
100-meter freestyle	Kristin Otto, E. Germany	54.73
200-meter freestyle	Heike Friedrich, E. Germany	1:57.55
100-meter breaststroke	Sylvia Gerasch, E. Germany	1:08.11
200-meter breaststroke	Silke Hoerner, E. Germany	2:27.40
200-meter backstroke	Betsy Mitchell, U.S.	2:08.60
400-meter freestyle relay	East Germany	3:40.57
800-meter freestyle relay	East Germany	7:59.33

In 1986, Ivan Lendl was the top men's tennis player.

TENNIS

For professional tennis fans, 1986 will be remembered as the year of the Czechs. Ivan Lendl and Martina Navratilova, both natives of Czechoslovakia, ranked as the number-one players in men's and women's competition. Each won two Grand Slam events and several other tournaments. Lendl took the French Open and U.S. Open men's singles titles; Navratilova (now a U.S. citizen) captured the Wimbledon and U.S. Open women's singles crowns. In addition, three other natives of Czechoslovakia—Hana Mandlikova, Helena Sukova, and Miloslav Mecir—reached the finals of major tournaments.

The dominance of the Czechs peaked at the U.S. Open. The two championship matches—Lendl vs. Mecir, and Navratilova vs. Sukova—marked the first time that four players born in the same European country reached the finals of the prestigious U.S. tournament. Both contests turned out pretty much as expected. Lendl defeated Mecir by scores of 6–4, 6–2, 6–0, to earn his second U.S. Open championship. Navratilova beat Sukova, 6–3 and 6–2, for her third U.S. title.

Earlier in the year, Navratilova had posted her seventh Wimbledon singles victory—one less than the record, held by American Helen Wills Moody. It was also Navratilova's fifth consecutive Wimbledon triumph, tying the record of France's Suzanne Lenglen (1919–23) and Sweden's Bjorn Borg (men's, 1976–1980). In the final, Navratilova recovered from a slow start to defeat Mandlikova, 7–6 and 6–3.

Not all the honors went to the Czechs, however. West Germany's Boris Becker, who in 1985 had become the youngest player (17) to win at Wimbledon, retained his title in 1986. With a booming serve, he managed to defeat Lendl in the championship match, 6–4, 6–3, 7–5. On the women's side, the ever popular American Chris Evert Lloyd remained a powerful force. At the French Open, she defeated archrival Navratilova, 2–6, 6–3, 6–3, winning a record seventh singles title. It was also Evert Lloyd's 18th Grand Slam victory, another record.

TOURNAMENT TENNIS

	French Open	Wimbledon	U.S. Open
Men's Singles	Ivan Lendl, Czechoslovakia	Boris Becker, West Germany	Ivan Lendl, Czechoslovakia
Women's Singles	Chris Evert Lloyd, U.S.	Martina Navratilova, U.S.	Martina Navratilova, U.S.
Men's Doubles	John Fitzgerald, Australia/ Tomas Smid, Czechoslovakia	Mats Wilander, Sweden/ Joakim Nystrom, Sweden	Andres Gomez, Ecuador/ Slobodan Zivojinovic, Yugoslavia
Women's Doubles	Martina Navratilova, U.S./ Andrea Temesvari, Hungary	Martina Navratilova, U.S./ Pam Shriver, U.S.	Martina Navratilova, U.S./ Pam Shriver, U.S.

Davis Cup Winner: Australia

TRACK AND FIELD

WORLD TRACK AND FIELD RECORDS SET IN 1986

EVENT	HOLDER	TIME, DISTANCE, OR POINTS
Men		
Pole vault	Sergei Bubka, U.S.S.R.	19'8½"
Shot put	Udo Beyer, E. Germany	74'3½"
Discus throw	Juergen Schult, E. Germany	243'0"
Hammer throw	Yuri Sedykh, U.S.S.R.	284'7"
Women		
200-meter run	Heike Drechsler, E. Germany	0:21.71
2,000-meter run	Maricica Puica, Rumania	5:28.69
5,000-meter run	Ingrid Kristiansen, Norway	14:37.33
10,000-meter run	Ingrid Kristiansen, Norway	30:13.74
100-meter hurdles	Yordanka Donkova, Bulgaria	12.26
400-meter hurdles	Marina Stepanova, U.S.S.R.	52.94
High jump	Stefka Kostadinova, Bulgaria	6' 9¾"
Long jump	Heike Drechsler, E. Germany	24' 5½"
Javelin throw	Fatima Whitbread, Britain	254' 1"
Heptathlon	Jackie Joyner, U.S.	7,161 pts.

Sergei Bubka of the Soviet Union pole vaults to a new world record of 19' 8½".

SPORTS BRIEFS

An American winning the Tour de France? *Sacrebleu!* A guy 5'7" tall winning the NBA slam-dunk contest? Incredible! A race with 20,000,000 runners? Impossible!

If anyone ever doubted that the world of sports could be wild and unpredictable, 1986 provided a whole year of surprises, amazements, and memorable events. And, from Moscow in the Soviet Union to Ouagadougou in the West African nation of Burkina Faso, there were also reminders that sports can play an important role in uniting people from all over the globe.

LE CHAMPION AMERICAIN

On July 4, 1986, while the rest of the United States was celebrating Independence Day and the 100th birthday of the Statue of Liberty, America's Greg LeMond was in a

Twenty-five-year-old American cyclist Greg LeMond said winning the Tour de France was "the dream of my career."

suburb of Paris, France. Along with 209 other cross-country cyclists, LeMond faced 2,500 miles and 23 days of arduous pedaling through the French countryside. The event was the Tour de France, the world's premier bike race. Never in the 83-year history of the race had a non-European cyclist been crowned *le champion*. LeMond was determined to be the first.

When he was growing up in Nevada, LeMond's first love was skiing. At age 14, he took up cycling just to build up his legs. He won the first official bike race he ever entered, and from then on he was hooked. Five years later, in 1980, he turned professional. Signing with a French team, he became one of the few Americans to ride full-time in Europe. In 1984 he finished third in the Tour de France. In 1985 he finished second behind his teammate, the legendary Bernard Hinault.

Nearing the end of his career, Hinault promised to help his American teammate win the Tour in 1986. He would do everything in his power to fend off and tire out the other racers. As it turned out, however, the Frenchman pushed LeMond himself to his very limit. The punishing course included 76 mountains and hills in the Pyrenees and Alps, and flat stretches of up to 160 miles in a single day. LeMond took the lead, then Hinault, then LeMond again. Millions of roadside spectators cheered on their favorites. One by one, 78 of the cyclists dropped out of competition.

By the final leg of the race, down the streets of Paris, it was clear that the 25-year-old LeMond would make cycling history. He crossed the finish line in a total elapsed time of 110 hours, 35 minutes, and 19 seconds. He later called it "the dream of my career." Hinault finished second, 3 minutes and 10 seconds behind.

Wearing the yellow jersey of the champion, LeMond mounted the victory stand and accepted the winner's trophy. For the first time in its long history, the Tour de France ended with the playing of the "Star-Spangled Banner"—even if it was 23 days after the Fourth of July.

At 5'7", Spud Webb was the shortest player in NBA history. At 7'7", Manute Bol was the tallest.

THE LONG AND THE SHORT OF IT

Manute Bol and Anthony "Spud" Webb would appear to have very little in common. Bol stands 7'7" tall. Webb is all of 5'7". Bol was born in the Sudan, Africa, into the Dinka tribe. Webb was born in Dallas, Texas, where his parents ran a food store.

Nevertheless, the two men have much in common. Overcoming great odds, Bol and Webb both found careers in the National Basketball Association (NBA) in 1986. As a member of the Washington Bullets, Bol became the tallest player in league history. As a member of the Atlanta Hawks, Webb became the shortest.

Bol faced two chief obstacles in making it to the pros. The first was his weight. Despite being a giant among giants, he was regarded by many scouts as too thin—a mere 190 pounds—to be an effective player. The other obstacle was his inexperience. Raised to be a herdsman, Bol never played basketball until he was 17 years old. After arriving in the United States in 1983, he spent only one year as a college player, at the University of Bridgeport, in Connecticut.

Working hard to gain weight and learn the finer points of the game, Bol gradually emerged as a force in the NBA. At 7'7", his specialty was blocking shots. By the end of the 1986 season, he led the NBA in blocks with an average of nearly five per game.

Spud Webb had only one obstacle—his lack of height. As far as Webb was concerned, however, the problem existed only in the minds of other people. Even in high school, the coach thought he was too short to play. But once given the chance, Webb showed that he packed a lot of heart—and talent—in his small frame. Nobody could stop him.

At Midland Junior College in Texas, and later at North Carolina State, Webb again had to prove himself to coaches and opposing players. With the quickness of a waterbug and an amazing leaping ability (he can jump 42 inches in the air from a standing position), Webb convinced everyone that he could play with the giants.

And so, despite all the skeptics, Spud Webb wasn't really surprised when he landed a job with the Atlanta Hawks of the NBA. Nor was he surprised to make a major contribution to that team as a scrappy guard, darting around the court to steal passes and lead the fast break. But what may have surprised even Webb was winning the NBA's annual slam-dunk contest against some of the league's best—and tallest—players. Said his former college coach after the high-flying performance, "What Spud Webb teaches us is to believe in our abilities."

THE GOODWILL GAMES

Not since the 1976 Olympics had athletes from all over the world—including both the United States and Soviet Union—taken part in a single international competition. The United States had boycotted the 1980 Moscow Olympics, and the Soviets had boycotted the 1984 Los Angeles Olympics. Not only had the athletes been unable to compete against each other, but the Olympic spirit of peace and friendship through athletic competition had been lost in the political shuffle.

To remedy that, American broad-casting executive Ted Turner had the idea of a major summer sports festival that would look like the Olympics but would be called the Goodwill Games. The event would be held every four years, midway between Olympics, and the site would alternate between the Soviet Union and the United States. Athletes from all over the world would take part, setting aside political differences.

With the help of Soviet sports officials, Turner's idea became a reality in the summer of 1986. The first Goodwill Games were held July 5–20 in Moscow, featuring nearly 5,000 athletes from some 70 countries.

Competitions were held in eighteen different sports, and there were many memorable performances. Sergei Bubka of the USSR, who was voted the outstanding athlete of the games, set a world record in the pole vault. Jackie Joyner of the United States set a

Some 5,000 athletes from 70 countries gathered in Moscow for the first Goodwill Games, held in July.

world record in the women's heptathlon (combining seven track-and-field events). When it was all over, the Soviet Union had won a total of 241 medals, 118 of them gold. U.S. athletes had won 142 medals, 42 gold. Bulgaria and East Germany also were strong.

But the importance of the Goodwill Games couldn't be measured in medals. The spirit and meaning of the event were summed up by Soviet leader Mikhail Gorbachev in the opening ceremonies. "The very name of these competitions is profoundly symbolic," he said. "It is goodwill that is needed in relations between people and nations, between states and governments, today more than ever before."

SPORT AID

It was in the same spirit of goodwill that another international sporting event was held in May, 1986. The week-long event was called Sport Aid, and its purpose was to raise money for starving people in Africa. The highlight of Sport Aid was a synchronized run called the Race Against Time. More than 20,000,000 participants in 76 countries set out on foot at 4 P.M. Greenwich Mean Time on May 25. In London alone, more than 200,000 runners took part. Tens of thousands ran in New York, Paris, Barcelona, Budapest, and other cities and towns throughout the world. In Ouagadougou, the capital of the West African nation of Burkina Faso, the entire government ran in 100-degree heat. It was billed as "the biggest mass sports participation in history."

Through individual donations, corporate sponsorships, and other contributions, Sport Aid was expected to raise up to $150 million for the victims of famine and drought. Said organizer Bob Geldof, the Irish rock musician who also organized the Band Aid benefit in 1984 and the Live Aid event in 1985, "Today means a lot of money, a lot of political conviction, and a lot of hope for Africa."

COMMONWEALTH GAMES

Unlike the Goodwill Games and Sport Aid, another major athletic event of 1986 was marred by political disharmony. The Commonwealth Games, which have also come to be known as the "friendly games," are held every four years for all the coun-

Sudanese runner Omar Khalifa carried the torch of Sport Aid on a three-continent tour that took him to twelve European cities—including Warsaw, Poland (*above*). In New York City, he lit a symbolic flame at the United Nations to mark the start of the Race Against Time.

tries, colonies, and territories that once made up the British Empire. In 1986, the 13th Commonwealth Games were held in Edinburgh, Scotland, from July 24 to August 2. Unfortunately, only 27 of the 58 eligible nations took part. Thirty-one nations boycotted the event to protest Britain's refusal to impose economic sanctions against South Africa and its racial policy of apartheid.

In the ten days of competition, England earned the most medals overall (137), followed by Australia (120), and Canada (115). In the gold medal race, England narrowly edged out Canada (52–51). One of the outstanding individual performers was 13-year-old Canadian swimmer Allison Higson, who won two gold medals. She became the youngest champion in the history of the Commonwealth Games.

LIVING HISTORY

Fireworks and fanfare welcomed the Statue of Liberty at its inauguration in New York Harbor in 1886. One hundred years later, in 1986, the United States marked the statue's birthday with an equally extravagant celebration. The reason for the excitement? The statue has long been an important symbol of American freedom.

LADY LIBERTY:
RADIANT AT 100

*Here at our sea-washed,
    sunset gates shall stand
A mighty woman with a torch . . .*
    Emma Lazarus
    "The New Colossus"

On July 4, 1986, hundreds of boats—from rubber rafts to Navy battleships—jammed New York Harbor. Thousands of people lined the shore. Above, blimps, helicopters, and jet fighters buzzed back and forth. As darkness fell, the sky exploded in the biggest fireworks display in U.S. history—40,000 skyrockets, bursting into showers of red, orange, yellow, blue, and green.

The reason for all this excitement? The country was celebrating the 100th birthday of the Statue of Liberty, the noble lady who towers more than 300 feet (90 meters) over the harbor. The statue, properly called *Liberty Enlightening the World,* had been given to the United States by France and dedicated in 1886. The hundred years that followed had brought a lot of wear and tear, and the statue had been given a multi-million-dollar face-lift in time for the anniversary.

All this money and attention wasn't showered on the statue just because it's one of the world's largest. Nor was the reason the fact that the statue represented an engineering triumph in its day. Those were important aspects—but much more important was what the statue stands for: the concept of freedom that has been central to the United States since the nation was founded. Standing at the entrance to New York Harbor, the statue was the first bit of America that millions of immigrants saw. Liberty, with her torch held high, welcomed them. She became a symbol of the hope they shared for a better life in a new land.

HOW THE STATUE WAS BUILT

The idea for the statue was first suggested at a dinner party in France, in 1865. The host, historian Édouard-René Lefebvre de Laboulaye, was a great admirer of the United States and its democratic form of government. At the same time, he chafed under the rule of France's emperor, Napoleon III. As de Laboulaye saw it, the statue would serve two purposes: It would be a magnificent gift marking French friendship and admiration of liberty; and it would be a subtle way of showing disapproval of the emperor's dictatorial regime. The sculptor Frédéric Auguste Bartholdi was among the dinner guests, and he was just the man for the job. Bartholdi, 31, had a taste for monumental works, and he took to the idea immediately.

Originally, the statue was to have been a gift for the United States' 100th birthday, in 1876. But for various reasons, building it took much longer than expected. De Laboulaye, in fact, never saw it—he died in 1883. But Bartholdi and others carried the project through.

In 1871, Bartholdi traveled to the United States to choose a site for the statue. He found it in New York, on Bedloe's Island (now Liberty Island), a small bit of land at the entrance to the harbor. "Here, my statue must rise," he said, "here where people get their first view of the New World." With a picture of the site clearly in his mind, he went home to work on the statue.

The first step was a plaster model 4 feet (1.2 meters) high, completed in 1875. It presented Liberty as a Greek goddess, dignified and stern. In her right hand, she held aloft a torch—symbolizing enlightenment and freedom. In her left, she held a tablet (inscribed with the date July 4, 1776), symbolizing the Declaration of Independence and the rule of law. On her head was a crown with seven spokes, standing for the seven continents and the seven seas. At her feet were broken shackles, symbolizing release from tyranny. The artist's mother is said to have been the model for Liberty's face.

What was most remarkable about the statue, though, was the scale Bartholdi planned for the work. It would stand 151 feet (46 meters) tall. The face was to be 10 feet (3 meters) wide; the waist, 35 feet (10 meters) around; the index finger, 8 feet (2 meters) long. For lightness, the completed statue would be hollow, made of thin copper sheeting. Even so, it would weigh 450,000 pounds (204,000 kilograms).

Holding this colossus together presented enormous problems in engineering—it would have to bear not only its own weight but also the forces of wind and weather. Nothing like it had been built before. Bartholdi turned to Alexandre Gustave Eiffel, the engineer who would later build the Eiffel Tower in Paris. Eiffel designed an interior iron framework for the statue. The copper exterior was to be attached to it by a system of iron struts and bars.

Bartholdi made progressively larger plaster models, refining the design as he went along. His final model was 36 feet (11 meters) high. He then cut this model into sections and carefully enlarged each one to full size. When the sections had been modeled in plaster, carpenters carved wood molds to fit over them. Then metalworkers hammered thin sheets of copper into the molds to form the final statue pieces.

Only the torch was ready in time for the U.S. centennial celebration in 1876. It was displayed in Philadelphia and caused quite a stir. When the head was completed in 1878, it was erected in Paris. For an admission fee, people could walk up and look through the 25 windows in the crown. In this way, Bartholdi helped raise money for his work; he also had models of the statue cast and sold to raise funds.

Piece by piece, the statue rose in Bartholdi's Paris work yard, looming over the city. By 1884, the last piece had been put in place. Then the statue was taken apart, packed into

The Statue of Liberty, before restoration. For 100 years, she has represented the "inner meaning" of America.

crates, and shipped across the Atlantic. It arrived in New York City in the spring of 1885.

In the United States, there were other problems. France was giving the statue, but America had to provide the pedestal for it to stand on. A committee had been formed to raise funds for the pedestal, which would be designed by Richard Morris Hunt. At first, there wasn't too much support. But after the newspaper publisher Joseph Pulitzer organized a major fund-raising campaign, the American public came up with the money. The granite pedestal, together with the eleven-pointed, star-shaped base, raised the statue to a total height of just over 305 feet (93 meters).

Finally, on October 28, 1886, the statue was ready to be dedicated. Ships and boats filled the harbor. President Grover Cleveland and officials from France and the United States gave speeches honoring U.S.–French relations. Bands played patriotic tunes. Then Bartholdi unveiled the statue, and Liberty's torch was lit.

A BEACON FOR IMMIGRANTS

From the start, the statue captured people's imaginations. Liberty holding her torch aloft appeared in paintings and stories, and poets wrote sonnets to her. The most famous of these poems, "The New Colossus," was written by Emma Lazarus in 1883, to help raise funds for the pedestal. Its words expressed the idea that the statue quickly came to symbolize:

"Give me your tired, your poor,
Your huddled masses yearning to breathe free,
The wretched refuse of your teeming shore.
Send these, the homeless, tempest-tost to me,
I lift my lamp beside the golden door!"

To thousands of immigrants, Liberty stood for refuge from poverty and oppression—a new chance in a new country. They came from every port in Europe, crossing the ocean in crowded ships. Many died on the way. But for those who made it to New York, the statue was their first sight.

One immigrant described what it was like: "Mothers and fathers lifted up the babies so that they too could see, off to the left, the Statue of Liberty. This symbol of America— this enormous expression of what we had all been taught was the inner meaning of this new country we were coming to—inspired awe. . . . Not until the last nightlight died out did these watchers—Armenian, Greek, Turk, Italian, French, what not—go below."

Beginning in 1892, many of these immigrants entered the United States at the U.S. Immigration Station on Ellis Island, also in New York Harbor. They passed through the station at a rate of 5,000 a day. The station's vast, white-tiled Great Hall echoed with the sounds of many languages. Most of the immigrants were on the island just a few hours, for medical and legal examinations. A few were detained, and about two percent were turned back because they were ill or because of legal difficulties.

By 1954, patterns of immigration had changed. People were more likely to arrive in the United States by plane than by ship, and more immigrants were arriving in the South (from Latin America) and the West (from Asia). Ellis Island was closed. But in

Over the years, some 12,000,000 immigrants, coming from every seaport in Europe, entered the United States by passing through Ellis Island. The Statue of Liberty was the first bit of America that they saw.

all, 12,000,000 people had passed through it —so many that today, more than half of all Americans have at least one ancestor who arrived there.

Emma Lazarus' poem, meanwhile, had achieved new stature. In 1903, it was placed on a plaque inside the statue's pedestal. And within a few years, its famous lines were permanently linked with the statue in people's minds.

MANY MEANINGS

Immigrants weren't the only people who found special meaning in the Statue of Liberty. Posters and songs about Liberty helped drum up patriotic feelings during World War I, and soldiers returning from the war were welcomed by the statue's beacon.

Over the years, various people and groups used Liberty to make statements, both personal and political. Bereaved families scattered the ashes of loved ones from the top of the statue. In 1956, the year of the Hungarian uprising against Communism, Hungarian demonstrators hung their flag below the statue's torch as a symbol of their desire for freedom. In 1971, demonstrators took control of the statue for two days to dramatize their opposition to the Vietnam War.

But a lot of people really took liberties with the statue. In 1883, Mrs. Cornelius Vanderbilt appeared at a costume ball dressed as the Lady. The next year, a laxative manufacturer offered $25,000 for the pedestal fund if its name could be placed on the pedestal for a year. The offer was turned down, but within a few years pictures of the statue were appearing regularly in advertisements for everything from matches to lemons. Liberty was shown dressed in the latest fashions to advertise fabrics, and pouring soap into the harbor to advertise cleaning products. A pig striking the statue pose advertised a hog remedy. Liberty also appeared on souvenir spoons, candlesticks, tie clips, and thimbles.

But all the commercial uses to which the statue was put never detracted from its most important message. The Statue of Liberty continued to be a much-loved symbol of the "inner meaning" of the United States. Over the years, millions of people climbed the 171-step spiral stairway that winds through the hollow statue to the crown, to pay tribute to Lady Liberty.

Restoration began, and towering scaffolds rose around the statue. The project was called "the job of the century."

RESTORING THE STATUE

Gradually, time took its toll on the statue. Parts of the framework were weakened by stress. The torch leaked. The right arm, which had originally been mounted incorrectly, shifted so that one point of Liberty's crown hit the arm and dented it. Insulation between the copper skin and the iron bars that held it in place crumbled away. Where the metal pieces came in contact with each other, they began to corrode. Salt air and pollution scored the surface of the statue and quickened the corrosion inside.

By 1982, the statue was in a sorry state. The U.S. government, looking ahead to the centennial, appointed a commission of private citizens and gave it the job of restoring the statue. The commission was also to restore the facilities on Ellis Island, which had fallen victim to weather and vandals.

The first step was to raise money for both projects, and the commission appealed to everyone from schoolchildren to major corporations to donate. Eventually, some 20,000,000 individuals and companies responded and sent more than $280,000,000.

Towering scaffolds rose around the statue, and hundreds of workers climbed up to begin the restoration. It was, as one worker put it, "the job of the century." Inside the statue, nearly every one of the almost 1,800 iron bars holding the copper skin was removed and replaced with a stainless steel bar. Warped struts were also replaced. Seven layers of paint and two layers of coal tar were stripped from the inside of the copper. The right shoulder was strengthened, the viewing area in the crown was improved and given new windows, and the stairway was widened.

Outside, the seven spokes of the crown were removed, refurbished, and set back in place. New copper pieces were made for parts of the nose and hair, where corrosion had destroyed the original. The new pieces were carefully colored to match the soft blue-green patina of the old copper. But many of the streaks on the statue couldn't be removed, so they were left in place.

The torch, which had undergone a number of renovations over the years, was removed completely. It was replaced with a new torch, made by a team of French artisans who traveled to the United States for the job. They worked with the same techniques that Bartholdi had used in his original design (which had been changed before the statue was dedicated in 1886). The flame of the old torch had windows and was lit from within. The new torch was made of copper, and its flame was covered with gold leaf—which in

The old torch, whose flame had windows and was lit from within, was completely replaced. The new torch has a flame covered with gold leaf and is illuminated by a ring of outside lights.

A fleet of tall ships from countries around the world paraded up and down the Hudson River—a highlight of the July 4, 1986, birthday celebrations.

the sun would gleam brightly, and at night would be illuminated by a ring of outside lights.

The pedestal was repaired and given a new elevator. Inside the base, an existing museum on immigration was expanded. And Liberty Island itself got a new docking area and pedestrian mall. Plans for Ellis Island included restoration of the old buildings to house a museum and exhibit areas. But this work was scheduled to be completed by 1992, in time for Ellis Island's anniversary. Meanwhile, everyone worked overtime to make sure that the statue was ready for its party in 1986.

THE CELEBRATION

The statue's birthday party lasted four days. On Thursday, July 3, Warren Burger, the chief justice of the U.S. Supreme Court, gave the oath of citizenship to several hundred immigrants on Ellis Island. Thousands more, in other cities, were sworn in at the same time. Then U.S. President Ronald Reagan, joined by French President François Mitterrand, relit the statue, bathing it in colored lights. A short time later, Reagan rekindled the torch.

The next day, July 4, President Reagan reviewed a flotilla of Navy warships in the harbor. Then a fleet of windjammers, tall ships from countries around the world, paraded up and down the Hudson River. In the evening came the spectacular fireworks show—ten tons of explosives let loose in less than half an hour. The bursting rockets were accompanied by a rousing concert broadcast on radio and television.

On July 5, the statue was reopened to the public, and hundreds of people lined up to see it. Others toured the tall ships and navy vessels in the harbor. Meanwhile, a harbor festival in lower Manhattan offered food and entertainment to the thousands of people who had come to New York City. The festival continued through Sunday, when the party ended with a huge show at Giants Stadium, across the Hudson River in New Jersey. The show featured thousands of performers.

Some people thought all the hoopla over the statue was too much—that with all the fun, people would forget what the statue stood for. But Liberty was no stranger to celebrations. Through it all, the statue gazed out toward the sea, the new torch shining as an unforgettable symbol of the ideals that are most important to Americans.

NOVEL VIEWS OF THE SOUTH

Harriet Beecher Stowe and Margaret Mitchell never knew each other. Stowe lived in the 19th century; Mitchell lived in the 20th century. Stowe was from Connecticut; Mitchell was from Georgia. Yet if the two women had ever met, they would have had a lot to talk about. Stowe's great novel *Uncle Tom's Cabin*, a powerful attack on the institution of slavery, helped push the United States toward the Civil War. Mitchell's enormously popular *Gone With the Wind*, a sweeping novel of the Old South, dramatized the effects of the same war.

In 1986—exactly 125 years after the Civil War began—the two great writers were remembered on special anniversaries. June 14 marked the 175th anniversary of Harriet Beecher Stowe's birth, and June 30 was the 50th anniversary of the publication of Margaret Mitchell's *Gone With the Wind*.

A LITTLE WOMAN AND A GREAT WAR

In 1863, two years into the Civil War, Harriet Beecher Stowe was taken to the White House to meet President Abraham Lincoln. The president strode toward her with outstretched hands and greeted her thus: ''So you're the little woman who wrote the book that made this great war!''

Uncle Tom's Cabin, the book Lincoln was talking about, had been published eleven years earlier, in 1852. It's the story of a faithful Kentucky slave named Uncle Tom, who is sold downriver to a new owner. When that owner dies, Tom becomes the property of a cruel plantation master named Simon Legree. Tom is whipped to death for refusing to reveal the whereabouts of two runaways.

A striking portrayal of good and evil, *Uncle Tom's Cabin* was an immediate success. It sold some 300,000 copies in the United States in one year, and more than 2,000,000 copies in other countries. It was one of the most widely read books of its time, stirring up strong antislavery sentiment. ''God wrote it,'' said Stowe. ''I merely did His dictation.''

Harriet Elizabeth Beecher came from a highly religious family. She was born on June 14, 1811, in Litchfield, Connecticut. Her father, Lyman Beecher, was a well-known clergyman and educator. She had a few years of schooling at Litchfield Academy and then attended a Christian school established by her older sister in Hartford. In 1832 she moved with her family to Cincinnati, Ohio, where her father became the head of a seminary (an institution for the training of clergymen). In 1836 she married Calvin Ellis Stowe, a professor at the seminary. She took up writing to supplement her husband's earnings.

During her years in Cincinnati, Stowe grew increasingly outraged at the violence

In her powerful novel *Uncle Tom's Cabin*, Harriet Beecher Stowe depicted the cruelty and evil of slavery.

and injustice of slavery. She met former slaves who had fled from neighboring Kentucky, and she had witnessed the evil of slavemasters on a visit to a Kentucky plantation. In 1849, when one of her children died, Stowe truly understood the anguish of slave mothers who were separated from their children. She vowed to do something.

The result was *Uncle Tom's Cabin,* Stowe's first book. Although she wrote many others—novels, poems, short stories, and nonfiction—none was as popular or as important as her story of Uncle Tom. Harriet Beecher Stowe died on July 1, 1896.

SCARLETT O'HARA AT 50

Margaret Mitchell wrote only one book, but it proved to be the best-selling novel of all time. Since it rolled off the presses in 1936, *Gone With the Wind* has sold more than 25,000,000 copies in 27 different languages. The 1939 movie version, starring Clark Gable and Vivien Leigh, may well be the most popular motion picture ever made.

Gone With the Wind provides a colorful panorama of Southern society before, during, and after the Civil War. Its celebrated heroine is the beautiful and willful Scarlett O'Hara of Tara plantation in Georgia. Scarlett spends most of the war years in Atlanta, Georgia, but bravely returns to Tara—a symbol of the order and grace of the Old South—to save it from doom. The vivid portrayal of Southern life, such dramatic events as the burning of Atlanta, and the romantic involvement between Scarlett O'Hara and the dashing Rhett Butler sweep the reader through the novel's 1,037 pages.

Born on November 8, 1900, in Atlanta, Margaret Mitchell was raised with a keen sense of local history. Her father was an attorney as well as the president of the Atlanta Historical Society. As a young girl, Mitchell developed a strong interest in the Civil War. She attended Smith College, in Massachusetts, for one year, but upon her mother's death she returned to Atlanta to keep house for her father and brother.

Mitchell began a career in journalism in 1922, writing columns for the Atlanta *Journal.* After her marriage to John R. Marsh in 1925, Mitchell resigned her position with the newspaper. She then began a project that would last ten years—putting down on paper

Gone With the Wind, the Civil War saga of Scarlett O'Hara and Rhett Butler, was the creation of Margaret Mitchell.

the stories of the Civil War and Reconstruction that she had heard in her childhood. Mitchell had constant doubts about her work, once telling a friend, "I don't know why I bother with it, but I've got to do something with my time." But the book was published on June 30, 1936, and it made publishing history. In 1937, Mitchell was awarded the Pulitzer Prize for fiction. She died on August 16, 1949.

In 1986, the 50th anniversary of *Gone With the Wind*'s publication was marked by a variety of special events and celebrations. The city of Atlanta offered an exhibition of Mitchell's papers and tours of her home. A commemorative U.S. postage stamp was issued. And a replica edition of her original book was published.

JEFFREY H. HACKER
Author, *Carl Sandburg*

TALES OF FAIRIES

Up the airy mountain,
Down the rushy glen,
We daren't go a-hunting,
For fear of little men.
William Allingham

The grass bends, and the leaves rustle with a soft sigh. A passing breeze, you say, and dismiss it without a second thought. But could it have been something else—something magical and mysterious?

In olden days, the rustling leaves might have been given a different explanation: A troop of fairies, invisible but real all the same, had passed by. Fairies, so it was believed, were magical beings of the woods and hills. They lived in a world that existed side by side with ours but wasn't the same. Sometimes the two worlds would cross. A lonely traveler might see a fairy castle rising from the mist, or catch a glimpse of a fairy ring—a lush green circle in a meadow or forest where the fairies danced. But when the traveler arrived at the scene, every trace of the sight would have vanished.

FAIRY FOLK

Stories of fairies are common in the British Isles and northern Europe. The word "fairy" can be traced back to the Old French word *feer*, to enchant, and to the Latin word *fatum*, or fate. And indeed, fairies had both the power of enchantment and the ability to see into the future.

Fairies were also known as elves, from the Scandinavian word *alfar*. The terms are confusing because both have been used for a great variety of strange and mythical beings—from tall, beautiful maidens who can enchant ordinary men with a mere glance to tiny blackened gnomes who inhabit hearths and play mischievous pranks around the house. But fairies and elves as we usually think of them can be divided into two groups.

The oldest tales tell of fairies who were tall and slender, graceful and fair. Their kingdoms were hidden—beneath lakes, inside the hollow hills (burial mounds left by early people), and on far-off magical islands shrouded in mist. Later tales describe fairies as little people—small enough to wear a flower for a cap or use a toadstool as a seat. A few, the tales say, even had wings and flitted about like insects. Some of the Scandinavian elves were said to be evil fairies whose realms were underground. But most stories present fairies as neither good nor evil. Fairies might use their powers to help humans. But they were quick to take offense, and once offended they were more likely to use their powers for harm.

For this reason, people who believed in these creatures seldom called them by name; to use a name without its owner's permission was, in times gone by, a great offense. Instead, it was safer to refer to them as the Fairy Folk, the Good People, the Gentry, the Blessed Court, the Mothers' Blessing.

STANDING TALL

How did tales of fairies arise? Some people think they began far back in history, when early inhabitants of an area were driven out by conquerors. The defeated people "went underground"—they lived hidden in caves and forests and went about secretly at night. The conquerors knew they were there, though. Every so often, one would be seen. Or a bit of food or a tool carelessly left lying around would disappear, taken by the silent folk.

The tall fairies of the stories were like humans in some ways. They were ruled by beautiful kings and queens, and they enjoyed dancing, hunting, feasting, and all the other things that people of the time enjoyed. Other people say that fairy tales began as stories of gods and goddesses who were worshipped in ancient times.

One thing is certain: The fairies of the stories were no ordinary mortals. They were said to live long—many, many times as long as the oldest person. Fairy time was not at all the same as human time. One Irish tale tells of a young boy who wandered into the forest and heard the sound of

196

beautiful singing. Enchanted, he leaned up against a tree to listen for a while. When he returned to his house, he found that his family had been dead for many years—a hundred years of human time had been just a few hours to the fairies.

Fairies could take the shapes of rocks, trees, or animals. They could appear and disappear at will. And, most of the time, they chose to be invisible to humans. A traveler once rounded a bend in the road and beheld a beautiful sight: a fairy market, with gaily colored tents and crowds of beautiful fairies around them. When he ran to the place, everything disappeared—but he knew his eyes hadn't deceived him because he could feel the pushing and shoving of the crowd!

The tall fairies of old tales had great magic powers, and it was dangerous to have dealings with them. One story tells of a village woman who was called to assist at the birth of a fairy baby. The fairies gave her some ointment to rub on the baby, and by accident she got some in her eye. After that, much to her surprise, she found that she could see the fairies anytime. But one day, when she greeted a passing fairy, he stopped and asked her which eye she saw him through. When she answered, he struck that eye and blinded it—so that she would never see fairies again.

The story of Sleeping Beauty (which has many different versions) shows the risks of insulting a fairy. In this tale, a king wanted to invite the fairies who lived in his realm to his baby daughter's christening. One fairy, however, wasn't invited. She was furious at having been left out, and appeared at the feast and laid a curse on the child—that she would prick her finger on a spindle at the age of 16 and die. One of the other fairies managed to soften the curse: The princess wouldn't die, but would sleep for a hundred years.

Other stories tell that fairies sometimes kidnapped people and held them captive in their magic kingdoms. And sometimes they stole human babies, putting a fairy baby in the crib instead. The parents would have to do something extraordinary to get this changeling, as the fairy baby was called, to reveal itself. It was said, for example, that if you brewed ale in an eggshell, the changeling would exclaim in surprise.

But fairies were by no means always evil. Some farmers believed that the fairies would bless their crops and ensure a good harvest. In a tale from Scotland, a young man was changed into a lizard by a witch. He lay by a tree, trapped in his ugly body, until a troop of fairies passed by. Their queen took pity on him and restored him to his human form.

In an Irish story, a chieftain named Teigue was sailing in pursuit of an enemy when a storm blew him across the invisible boundary between the real world and the fairy world. He landed on a fairy island, where the queen welcomed him warmly. She sent him on his way with a magic emerald cup that would protect him from harm, and a flock of enchanted birds that would guide him.

One of the most famous good fairies of legend was Cinderella's fairy godmother. In this well-known tale, the fairy steps in when Cinderella's wicked stepmother and stepsisters refuse to let her go to a royal ball. With a wave of her magic wand, the fairy produces a beautiful gown and a pair of glass slippers for Cinderella, and turns a pumpkin into a coach and mice into horses. Even if you didn't know the rest of the story, you could guess the ending: Cinderella marries the prince.

If you wonder why *you* never happen across a fairy gathering —or why no fairy godmother appears to make your dreams come true—the stories give a reason: The fairies left. Gradually, they became unhappy with the human world and had less and less contact with it. People reported seeing bands of fairies trooping to the sea, where they set sail for magic islands that are forever hidden from human eyes.

LITTLE PEOPLE

Not all storytellers agree that the fairies left the earth, however. Some say instead that they just diminished, growing smaller and smaller—until some were so small that they could hide behind leaves.

These fairies, the stories say, stayed with us, under many different names. They were blamed for all sorts of minor mischief. If you woke up with a snarl in your hair, you had an "elf lock" —fairies had tangled it overnight. If you had a bruise you couldn't explain, it was certain a fairy had pinched you. But like their larger ancestors, the little fairies also helped humans.

Brownies were house spirits, and it was lucky to have one around. They helped unseen with all sorts of chores, from spinning thread to sweeping the floor. But they could be mischievous, too. Sometimes a brownie would make a mess of a perfectly neat house, just because there was nothing else to do. To keep the house brownie happy, many people used to leave out a bowl of bread and milk.

Pixies sometimes helped around the house, too. But more often, they lived hidden in the woods. And like the tall fairies, they could sometimes be seen dancing on moonlit nights. The pixies' main form of mischief was to lead travelers astray until they were hopelessly lost.

The Little People of Ireland, sometimes called leprechauns, were much like the pixies. It was said that if you could catch one of them, he'd lead you to treasure buried at the end of a rainbow. But no one ever found out, because the Little People were fast talkers and always managed to trick anyone who tried to catch them.

Some Swedish elves began as tall fairies, but in later tales they were the smallest of the little fairies—less than a foot high, with gauzy wings. They were gentle nature spirits who could sit on flowers and talk to the birds, and it was thought that they helped flowers bloom and the seasons change.

Other stories depict elves as more like pixies and brownies. In the story of the shoemaker and the elves, for example, an old shoemaker finds that tiny elves are coming to his shop every night and doing his work for him. Delighted, he and his wife decide to reward the elves by making new suits of clothes for them. Unfortunately, the elves are so pleased with the new clothes that they put them on immediately and dance out the door, never to be seen again.

Do such creatures really exist? In 1917, two young girls in Cottingley, England, claimed to have seen a band of little fairies —and even to have danced with them. To prove their story, they borrowed a camera and took pictures of the little people. The pictures of the Cottingley Fairies caused quite a stir, and at the time many people thought they were genuine. Modern researchers, however, say that the pictures were faked.

So there is still no evidence that fairies exist, or that they ever did. But that hasn't stopped people from enjoying stories about them—or from making up new ones. Tinker Bell, in the story of Peter Pan, may be the best-known fairy of modern times. She is a tiny winged creature who can do both magic and mischief, and like many other fairies she's quick to take offense.

Modern authors have also drawn on some of the older fairy legends. J. R. R. Tolkien, in his book *The Hobbit* and his trilogy *The Lord of the Rings,* created a fantasy world where humans live side by side with all sorts of strange creatures. The elves in these books are very like the tall and beautiful fairies of old. And like them, they leave the earth, sailing west to a land where mortals cannot go.

Proof or no proof, the next time you see the leaves flutter, you just might want to take a closer look!

THE PEACE CORPS: AT 25

"How many of you are willing to spend ten years in Africa or Latin America working for the United States and working for freedom? How many of you who are going to be doctors are willing to spend your days in Ghana?"

With these words, presidential candidate John F. Kennedy challenged a group of Michigan college students in 1960. And his challenge was met the next year when, as president, he announced the formation of a new government agency—the Peace Corps. The idea behind the Peace Corps was to send thousands of young volunteers to developing countries around the world. There, they would help people meet their basic needs for health care, food, shelter, and education: Thus, they would help people help themselves.

In 1986, the Peace Corps celebrated its 25th anniversary. During those 25 years, more than 100,000 Americans served as volunteers in some 90 nations. And, although there were some difficult times, the agency has been mostly successful in meeting its three goals: to help developing countries meet their needs for skilled men and women; to promote understanding between the people of the United States and those of other countries; and to promote world peace and understanding.

The first Peace Corps volunteers were young men and women (with an average age of 23) who were inspired by the idea of helping others. They signed up for two-year tours of duty in Africa, Asia, and Latin America. The volunteers lived and worked side by side with their hosts, sharing the same rough living conditions. They helped families dig wells and build houses. They helped farmers set up irrigation systems for their crops. They taught in schools. And they tried to bring new standards of nutrition and health care to the remote villages where they often were stationed. In exchange, the volunteers received only a small allowance to cover their living expenses, plus a small amount set aside to help them get resettled when they returned to the United States.

The hard work and low pay didn't discourage young people from applying to the Peace Corps. By 1966 there were more than 15,000 volunteers. But in the late 1960's and early 1970's, the Peace Corps became less popular. Many young people who opposed U.S. involvement in the Vietnam War didn't want

Education is one of the main goals of the Peace Corps. Here, a volunteer in Costa Rica teaches methods of plant care to a group of young men.

to serve the U.S. government in any way. Others joined the Peace Corps not out of dedication but as a way to avoid being drafted into the army. Some became involved in anti-government politics in their host countries, and several were asked to leave. All this detracted from the agency's public image, and both the number of volunteers and the amount of funding the Peace Corps received declined.

Today, however, people are once again showing enthusiasm for the Peace Corps. In fact, when the agency made a special call for agriculture specialists to help in the famine-stricken areas of Africa, more than 20,000 people responded. And while the program has changed in some ways, its goals and working methods are mostly the same. Its main objective is still to help people survive today's problems and become self-sustaining in the future.

There are now more than 5,500 volunteers working on projects in some 60 countries, and the agency hopes to expand to 10,000 over the next few years. Volunteers (who must be at least 18 years old) are chosen carefully, for their dedication as well as for their skills. The hope is that they will represent the best qualities of the United States. And before they begin to serve, they receive extensive training in the language and culture of their host countries. The work is still hard, and the pay is still low—an average of $300 a month, plus $175 set aside for each month of service.

Most of the volunteers are still young. But more and more older people have joined, bringing the average age close to 29. Many of the volunteers have general skills, and they help people with basic living problems. Other volunteers are specialists in agriculture, the environment, and education. Still others specialize in such areas as banking, accounting, computers, and marketing, to help with business development. The kinds of projects the volunteers have been working on are varied:

• In Lesotho, a volunteer who is an eye doctor cares for 4,000 people a year.
• Another volunteer in Africa, a community organizer, helped a group of women set up an agency that makes loans to small businesses run by women.

As part of a cooperative farming project, this Peace Corps volunteer in Gambia helps a group of village women form their own savings society.

• Volunteers in Burundi are helping to set up vocational training programs.
• In Jamaica, a volunteer helped farmers develop a market for zucchini with the island's leading tourist hotels and restaurants.
• Volunteers in Costa Rica helped rural families build 270 homes.
• In Papua New Guinea, volunteers are helping with forest and timber management.

There are many other projects around the world. And volunteers say that they benefited as much by the experience as did the people they went to help: They expanded their horizons by living and working in another culture. As one volunteer put it, "Gradually, it will dawn on you that you're doing something for your country, for their country, and also for yourself."

BRINGING BACK THE WATERFRONTS

When towns and cities first began to grow up across North America, they were often located on natural harbors, rivers, and lakes. The reason was simple: Water provided a link with the rest of the world. Ships could bring goods, visitors, and news from outside and could carry the town's products to markets far away. Bustling waterfronts were often the busiest sections of cities in the 1800's. As rail and air travel became more important, however, many waterfronts fell into disrepair. Warehouses and factories became ramshackle, building lots stood empty, and piers rotted. People in the cities stayed away from the water.

But today, on the east and west coasts and on inland rivers and lakes, private groups and governments are getting together to bring the waterfronts back to life. Historic buildings are being restored. Boutiques and restaurants are being built. Parks are being carved out along the water's edge. Once again the waterfronts are bustling with activity—not as shipping depots but as places to shop, eat, live, and have fun.

San Francisco's Ghirardelli Square, housed in a building complex that was once a chocolate factory, was one of the first waterfront restorations in the United States. The work was done in the 1960's. Now the shops and restaurants in the 14 red brick buildings draw visitors day and night.

In Nova Scotia, Canada, a group of dilapidated historic warehouses on Halifax's harbor were saved from demolition. After a $10 million renovation project, the buildings are among the city's most fashionable addresses, with smart boutiques, offices, and restaurants.

Harborplace, built in the late 1970's, is part of a sweeping waterfront renovation project in Baltimore, Maryland. It includes 80 shops, 20 food markets, and 60 places to dine or snack—all housed in two airy, glass-enclosed pavilions overlooking the city's harbor. A famous ship, the U.S. frigate *Constellation*, is moored nearby and is open to the public as a museum. Elsewhere along Baltimore's harbor are a new world trade center, aquarium, and science center.

Entertainment especially for children and many other exciting events take place year-round—even in winter, on the ice—at Harbourfront, in Toronto, Canada. A broad promenade for strollers, joggers, and cyclists runs along the waterfront, past indoor and outdoor theaters, shops, restaurants, apartments, offices, marinas, hotels, and a museum.

Granville Island, on False Creek in Vancouver, Canada, was a decaying industrial area. Now it's home to theaters, an art college, shops, and restaurants. Shown is a popular shopping area: a public market for fresh meat, fish, and vegetables.

Faneuil Hall Marketplace, in Boston, celebrated its tenth anniversary in 1986. The centerpiece of the complex is Faneuil Hall (left), a historic colonial meeting house. Behind the meeting house are three long warehouse buildings packed with shops and restaurants. The center building, Quincy Market, has been restored to its original use as a food market, with stall after stall of tempting things to eat. Musicians, jugglers, clowns, and mimes entertain the crowds in the pedestrian malls between the buildings.

New York City's South Street Seaport is dwarfed by the sky-scrapers around it, but the renovation can't be called small. Its focal point is the Fulton Fish Market, once a wholesale market for fish and now a place to buy all kinds of food. There's a seaport museum and six historic ships, including the bark *Peking* and the *Ambrose* lightship. Shops and restaurants are found in historic row houses and in new buildings, including a huge glass-enclosed pavilion that juts out over the East River. And, like the other restorations, South Street gives city people and visitors a chance to stroll along the waterfront and enjoy an outdoor snack.

WHAT'S IN A NAME?

If you're like most people, you probably have several names: a first name, perhaps a middle name, and a last name (or surname). Your first name and your middle name were given to you at birth by your parents. Your surname is the same as theirs. But have you ever wondered how your family got its surname?

People didn't always have surnames. In fact, there are still a few places in the world where they don't. If there are only a few people in a village, first names are enough to tell them apart. But when there are more people, first names can be confusing—there may be ten, twenty, or two hundred Johns in a town. Surnames help distinguish one from the other.

Family names go back more than 2,000 years in China and in India. In many Western countries, however, surnames are more recent. In England, for example, surnames weren't used until after the Norman Conquest, in 1066. And in England and most other countries, people chose (or were given) their surnames in several different ways.

PATRONYMICS

One of the most common types of surnames is the patronymic—a name formed from the first name of a person's father or other male ancestor. For example, Peter the son of John became Peter Johnson. And the common surname Jones is an English-Welsh name that means "the son of Jone."

Patronymics are found in many countries and in many different languages. In Scotland and parts of Ireland, the prefixes *Mc* and *Mac* were used to mean "son of." McArthur, then, was the son of Arthur. Elsewhere in Ireland, *Fitz* was used in the same way, as in FitzGerald. The prefix *O'* had a looser meaning, "descendant of." In Germany, the suffix *sohn* was used—Mendelsohn, the son of Mendel. The Slavic languages also used suffixes—*vitch, off,* and *kin.* The son of Ivan might be Ivanovitch or Ivanoff.

You might wonder why you don't hear of names that mean "daughter of." The reason is that in most countries, women take their husbands' surnames when they marry. And the children carry the father's name, too. Thus a name that meant "daughter of" wouldn't survive even one generation. Although more women are choosing to keep their own names when they marry, the father's name is still the one carried by most children.

In some places, however, "daughter of"

John Swift   John Armstrong   John Merriman   John Lowe   John Beard

is used. In Iceland, all last names are formed from the father's first name—by adding *son* for a boy or *dottir* for a girl. Sveinn Asgeirsson's son Björn would be Björn Sveinnsson, and his daughter Vigdis would be Vigdis Sveinnsdottir. When Björn marries, his children would carry the last names Björnsson and Björnsdottir. When Vigdis marries, she would keep her surname. But her children's surname would be formed from her husband's first name. Icelanders usually call each other by their first names. And to avoid confusion, their telephone directories list people's occupations as well as names and addresses.

Hispanic names combine the father's and mother's names—Roberto Rodriguez López would be the son of a man named Rodriguez who married a woman named López. But when Roberto marries and has children, he will combine his father's name—Rodriguez—with his wife's name to form his children's names. López won't be carried on.

NAMES FROM TRADE

Some people carry names that show their ancestors' jobs or positions in society. If your name is Cooper, for example, you can bet that somewhere in your family history there was a man who made barrels for a living. In the same way, a man named Harold who made leather became Harold Tanner and passed on the name to his children. Some other common names that developed in this way are Baker, Barber, Carpenter, Carter, Clark (for clerk), Cook, Dyer, Hunter, Shepherd, Stewart (for steward), Taylor, Thatcher, and Weaver.

The most common English name of all— Smith—refers to the blacksmith, who forged tools and weapons and shod horses. This job was so essential that there was a blacksmith in every village. And because war and fighting were everyday occurrences during the Middle Ages, Archer, Fletcher (arrow maker), and Armour are common names today. Other names show the position an ancestor held in society—Baron, Knight, Chamberlain, Butler.

Similar names appear in many other languages. Smith, for example, is Schmidt in German, Ferrari in Italian, Herrera in Spanish, Kowalski in Polish, Kovar in Czech, and Seppanen in Finnish. Taylor is Schneider in German, Portnoy in Russian, and Kravitz in Polish. Some other common German names are Bauer (farmer) and Metzger (butcher). The Hebrew name Cohen originally referred to a prince or a priest.

NAMES FROM NICKNAMES

Suppose you've gone back in time to a medieval village to look for a man named John. There are five Johns in this village, so how will the villagers know which one you want? That's easy—you'll describe him. He's the John who has the beard, or the one who's so short. Perhaps he's always cheerful, or maybe he has strong arms or runs very fast.

Before surnames were common, people often went by nicknames that were based on physical or personality characteristics. And in many cases, these nicknames were shortened into real surnames that stuck with the people and their families. John with the beard became John Beard. The short John

Christopher Wren (architect)

Florence Nightingale (nurse)

John Jay (jurist)

Peter Finch (actor)

Thomas Love Peacock (poet)

Lynn Swann (football player)

became John Lowe. John who always smiled became John Merriman. John who ran fast became John Swift, while he of the strong arms became John Armstrong.

There are similar names in other languages. The Irish name Sullivan, for example, originally meant "black-eyed." The Russian name Tolstoy meant "fat." Today these names usually have nothing to do with the physical characteristics or personalities of their bearers. You may know a Sullivan with blue eyes, a Lowe who's six feet tall, or a Merriman who's always sad. But you can be certain that at sometime in their family histories, they had ancestors who lived up to their names.

NATURE NAMES

Many people took their surnames from the world around them—from the places where they lived or from some aspect of nature. Many English names, for example, were originally the names of towns and other

places in England: Bradford, Bristol, Chester, Lincoln, Sherwood. The ancestors of a person named Maynard probably lived in the duchy of Maine, a region of France.

Other names came from geographical features. Henry who lived on the hill became Henry Hill, while Walter who lived near a ford of a river became Walter Ford. Some other names formed the same way are Brook, Field, Grove, Lake, Rivers, Stiles, Wells, and Woods.

Common plants were also sources for names—Rice and Oates, for example. So were the names of birds and other animals—Dove, Finch, Fish, Partridge, and Woodcock in English; Adler (eagle) and Krebs (crabs) in German. Some people, however, took these names not because they were nature lovers, but for another reason: Before the 1800's, most people couldn't read. So every merchant put an easily recognized symbol (whether it had to do with his business or not) on the signboard in front of his shop. The merchants became known by their symbols (birds, flowers, angels), and the symbols became their surnames. In this way a German merchant who hung a picture of a star outside his shop acquired the name Stern—the German word for star.

NAMES BY CHANCE AND CHOICE

People didn't always acquire their surnames willingly. Sometimes the government ordered them to take names. In the mid-1400's, when England ruled Ireland, the English king Edward IV ordered all the Irish to take English surnames. They were allowed to choose the name of a place (such as Cork or Kinsale), the title of a job or occupation, or a color such as white, black, or brown.

In the early 1800's, the Russian czar Alexander I ordered all Russian Jews to take surnames. The officials in charge of assigning the new names saw a chance to make some money. They granted pleasant-sounding names only on payment of a big bribe; those who couldn't pay got less attractive names like Lumpe and Schmaltz.

Sometimes governments restricted what surnames could be used. In ancient China, the emperor decreed that all family names should be drawn from the text of a certain sacred poem. Because that limited the choice, many Chinese families have the same name. Among the most popular are Chang ("drawn bow"), Wang ("prince") and Li ("plum"). Unlike people in Western countries, the Chinese give their family names ahead of their individual names. A child named Wei born to the Chang family would be called Chang Wei.

Many surnames have changed over the centuries—either by accident or because their bearers wanted to change them. Spellings weren't set until the 1800's, when dictionaries became popular, so different spellings produced many variations in names. William Shakespeare's name, for example, was spelled 83 different ways.

In the United States, immigration produced many name changes. This happened in two ways. Sometimes immigrants changed their names by choice because having a foreign-sounding name made it harder to find a job and a place to live. And sometimes immigration officials were responsible for the changes—they couldn't understand or spell a newcomer's correct name, so they wrote down any English name that sounded similar.

Today there are over 1,000,000 different names in the United States, and they originated in countries all over the world. But there's still a lot of duplication—more than 2,000,000 Smiths, for example. So if you're looking for Mary Smith, you may have to add something to her name—"Mary Smith who lives on the hill," or "the smart Mary Smith," or "Mary Smith who runs fast."

ART NOUVEAU
ART DECO

Art Nouveau and Art Deco
are two styles of art design
that were very popular in
the early part of the 20th
century. Today they are in
demand once again.

The Victorian era, from the mid- to late 1800's, was a time of tradition and "proper" social values. Art, architecture, and the decorative arts (such as furnishings, fabrics, and jewelry) were traditional and proper, too. But by the end of the period, many people had decided that styles were too traditional —even stuffy.

And so something of a revolution swept through Europe and North America. But it wasn't a political revolution—it was a revolution in art design. Designers broke loose from the old styles, producing free, flowing, natural forms. The style known as art nouveau (from the French words for "new art") was born. At the height of its popularity, the art nouveau influence could be seen in everything from clothing to buildings.

By the 1920's, however, the curving lines that had at first seemed so free and new had become as old-hat as their Victorian predecessors. Designers reacted again, producing another new style—art deco—which relied on blocky, geometric forms.

Today neither style is the rage it once was, but both have undergone revivals in popularity. The art nouveau and art deco designs produced in the early part of the century are in demand again. And the two styles have also influenced contemporary designs.

ART NOUVEAU

France was the major center of the art nouveau movement. But the movement had actually begun in England and spread from there to the continent of Europe and the United States.

Several different influences came together to produce art nouveau. Earlier styles that also emphasized curving lines—such as the rococo, Gothic, and early Celtic styles— were revived and rediscovered in the late 1800's. There were also new influences. Japanese prints, for example, became popular in Western countries. Their flowing forms and flat (rather than three-dimensional) portrayals of objects affected many painters of the time.

In part, art nouveau was an outgrowth of these styles. But there was also something different about it: In art nouveau, for the first time, the most important aspect of a work of art was its design—not its subject matter or the emotions it produced.

This was the philosophy of William Morris, a leader in the English arts and crafts movement. Morris was dismayed by the ugliness of new products being produced by factories—a result of the Industrial Revolution. Morris wanted artisans to produce handmade items and stressed that beautiful designs should be part of everyday life. His designs and his philosophy had an important effect on art nouveau designers and artists.

Art nouveau designers preferred to start with forms from nature—especially anything that curved. Leaves and flowers, swans and peacocks, flowing water, and the human body were favorite subjects. But natural forms weren't simply copied. The artist would twist, bend, and distort them to make his design, sometimes until they were hardly recognizable. Some artists went a step further, working completely in geometric shapes and abstract patterns.

Art nouveau illustrators, such as Aubrey Beardsley of England and the Czech painter and decorator Alphonse Mucha, created works that were two-dimensional, with little background or sense of depth. Often figures were merely silhouettes, and often the pictures were created in simple, flat colors or in black and white. Lines were the most important features of these works—sweeping, swirling lines that suggested action and tension.

Architecture, of course, required three dimensions. But even here, the art nouveau style emphasized lines. Decorative swirls and curved windows covered the outsides of buildings. Entrances were outlined with twisting wrought-iron archways. Among the most famous of such designs are the entrances to the Métro (the Paris subway), designed by Hector Guimard around the turn of the century.

Despite the fanciful exteriors, however, the emphasis in an art nouveau building was on the inside. Everything from wall paneling and furniture to silverware and fabric was designed to harmonize with the new style. Glass in glowing colors—in stained-glass windows and lampshades and in hand-blown vases—was often featured. The glass designs of Louis Tiffany of the United States are among the most famous of the time.

Art nouveau designers achieved some of their wildest flights of fancy in jewelry. In

signers called the Glasgow School, who had used patterns of horizontal and vertical lines in their work, were especially influential.

Other sources for the new style were the arts and architecture of ancient Egypt and the Aztecs, which relied heavily on massive geometric forms such as the pyramid. Exotic, richly colored stage designs for the ballet and theater also had an effect. And so did the development of cubism and similar movements in art, which broke subjects down into basic geometric elements.

The new style was also influenced by a change in philosophy. Rather than glorifying handmade items, the designers of this time wanted to create things that could be mass-produced by machine—to join art and industry. The idea was to make good design available to everyone, not just the wealthy.

This new art style was called art deco—its name came from an exhibition of decorative

place of the traditional gold, silver, and diamonds of Victorian days, jewelers made use of pearls, coral, opals, and even glass, set in bronze, brass, and aluminum. With these gems and settings, jewelers created glittering serpents and peacocks and twisting leaves and flowers. French designer René Lalique was particularly renowned for his exotic work in jewelry and glassware.

In time, however, the once-fresh lines of art nouveau became excessive, as though each design were trying to outdo the one before. One critic termed the movement a "strange decorative disease." People were ready for a change.

ART DECO

For a while, people went back to earlier styles, those that had been popular in the 1700's. But after World War I, a new style began to develop. Like art nouveau, it grew out of many different sources.

One source was art nouveau itself, especially in its more restrained and geometric forms. A turn-of-the-century group of de-

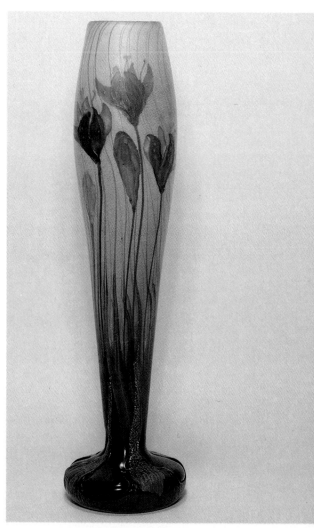

Art Nouveau: flowing, curving lines; natural forms—leaves and flowers, butterflies and peacocks; decorative and ornate objects; fine woods, semiprecious gems, and bronze and brass; hand-blown vases and brilliantly colored stained-glass lamps.

arts in Paris in 1925. Art deco designs were symmetrical (balanced) and solid-looking. They used rectangles and similar shapes in preference to curves and twisting lines. And they made use of the materials of mass-production—plastic, glass, concrete, and chrome.

Like the illustrations in the art nouveau style, those of art deco were often two-dimensional, in black and white or simple but vibrant colors. They were also highly stylized. But there the similarities ended. The forms in art deco pictures seem massive and solid. Lines are bold and straight, joining at sharp angles. Often the pictures have a dark, brooding atmosphere; they show man in the machine age.

In architecture, art deco could be given full play. Blocklike concrete buildings and towering skyscrapers, such as the Chrysler Building in New York City, echoed the forms of ancient buildings. The top of a skyscraper, for example, might stair-step to a point like an Aztec pyramid. The outsides of art deco buildings were vastly simpler than those of art nouveau buildings. Still, they were often decorated with geometric carvings and sculpture.

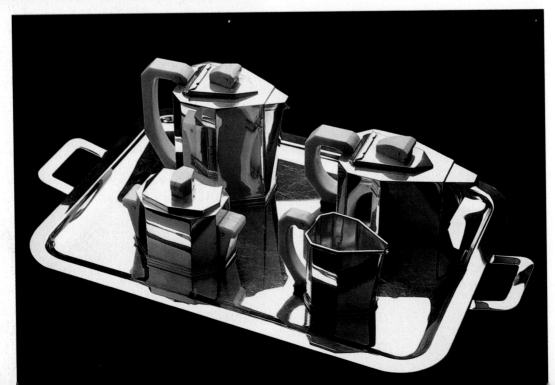

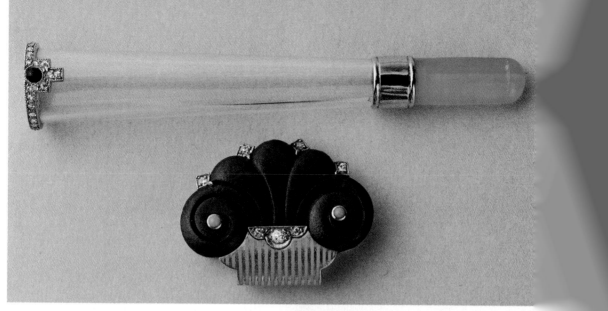

Inside, the decoration echoed the geometric forms and blocklike shapes. Like art nouveau, art deco stressed the importance of design. But a principle important to art deco designers was that objects should be functional—that is, they should look like what they were, and they should be designed so that they would be easy to use. Thus most chairs, tables, teapots, and other household objects were simple. Tubular steel was often used in the making of furniture, and chrome and plastic were used for smaller objects.

At the height of its popularity, in the 1930's, the art deco style could be seen everywhere. Jewelry was designed in blocky shapes or in patterns that reflected the art of ancient Egypt. Pottery and glassware stressed geometric forms and bright, vibrant colors. Even plastic radios were styled in the stair-step shape of Aztec pyramids.

As was the case with art nouveau, however, many people found that the art deco style had gone too far. Much of what was produced didn't reflect good design. Gradually, art deco was discarded in favor of newer styles.

Today people have come to appreciate both art nouveau and art deco once again. And they recognize the important step these styles took in breaking with the traditional designs of the past. By developing new, bold ways of presenting lines and shapes and by stressing the importance of good design, art nouveau and art deco laid the groundwork for contemporary design.

YOUTH

A bunch of brightly colored balloons seems to capture what being young is all about. When you are young, the sky's the limit, and bright hopes and dreams take you floating toward the future.

MIND GAMES

It's an odd silver-painted contraption decorated with screws, thumbtacks, ice-cream sticks, discarded spark plugs, and other odds and ends. It comes packaged in a papier-mâché "meteorite," and it brings messages of friendship from Mars.

You won't find this product in stores, however. The "Friendship Machine" was invented by a group of "Martians" from Schroeder Elementary School in Troy, Michigan, for an unusual competition: OM, or Odyssey of the Mind. Their task—to design, develop, and mass-produce an entirely new product within strict limits of time and cost—was just one of several challenges set by OM in 1985–86.

The OM competitions were begun in the 1970's by a group of educators who believed that creative problem solving could open new doors for students. By working on problems, these educators felt, students would learn more than the basic facts of school subjects such as science, mathematics, history, and literature. They would learn to think more creatively. And in the process, they would have fun.

THE 1986 COMPETITIONS

By 1986, OM competitions were drawing entries from about 4,000 elementary, middle, and high schools in the United States and Canada. Teams from these schools worked through the school year to solve any of five long-term problems. They presented their solutions at local and regional competitions, where they were also faced with new, "spontaneous" problems that had to be solved by individual team members on the spot. Winners of the regional competitions went on to the World Finals, held in May, 1986, in Flagstaff, Arizona.

The teams were divided into three divisions: I (kindergarten through fifth grades), II (sixth through eighth grades), and III (ninth through twelfth grades). At all levels of competition, scores were determined by three factors: the team's solution to the long-term problem, their style—including the costumes and songs used, and the solution to the spontaneous problem.

Each team had an adult adviser—but, under the competition rules, no adult suggestions were allowed. Instead, team members had to work together to find their own solutions to the problems. And some of their solutions were creative indeed.

In the problem called **Bridging the Gap**, teams in Divisions I, II, and III built weight-bearing structures out of thin strips of balsa wood. This took some creative engineering because the requirements were exacting. Each team had to construct two structures that, together, would stand 8 to 8.5 inches (20 to 21.5 centimeters) high and would weigh no more than 25 grams. The balsa-wood strips had to be just an eighth of an inch (3 millimeters) thick.

In competition, the teams—dressed in

Bridging the Gap, Division I: Cedar Park and Edgewood Schools, Selma, Alabama

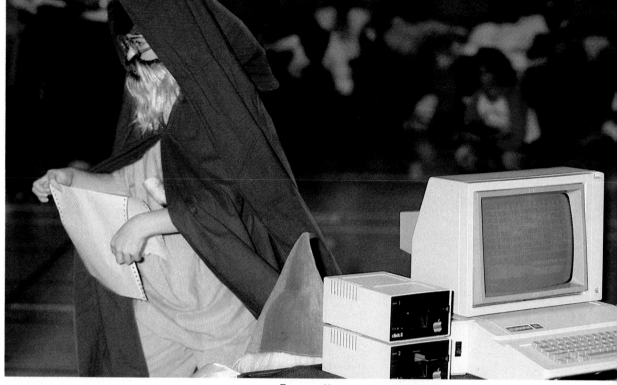

Treasure Hunters, Division II: Cook Elementary School, Richmond, British Columbia, Canada

History—The Way It Was, Division I (Joan of Arc): Star Hill School, Camden, Delaware

wild and fanciful costumes to show style—carefully piled weights on top of their creations, to see which could hold the most. A Division II team had the top weight in the eight minutes allowed for the test: an amazing 398 pounds (180 kilograms).

Teams in Divisions II and III tackled a computer problem called **Treasure Hunters**. Their task was to design a computer program that would guide team members through a 49-square grid laid out on the competition floor. Various items of ''treasure'' and a hazard were placed in different squares on the grid, but their exact locations weren't known until competition day.

On that day, each team was given ten minutes to modify its program and then, using information from the computer, send two treasure hunters through the grid to pick up or move the items. Each square on the grid could be entered only once, diagonal moves were forbidden, and each hunter could make only 25 moves. The other team members couldn't speak to the hunters or touch them. Instead, they used codes—such as flashing lights or flag signals—to tell them where to move next.

Imagination ran wild when it came to solving the problem **History—The Way It Was**.

Great Art Lives, Division I (*The Millinery Shop*): Hackensack Elementary School, Hackensack, New Jersey

Teams in all divisions chose from a list of ten famous historical incidents. Then, in a skit lasting ten minutes or less, they told both the standard story and their own humorous interpretation of what really happened.

For example, a Division II team from Fincastle, Virginia, showed Benjamin Franklin returning from the grave to give the "true story" of how electricity was discovered. Franklin said that he hadn't been conducting a scientific experiment—he'd actually made the discovery by accident as a child.

A team from Camden, Delaware, presented the story of Joan of Arc—as told by her dog. Naturally, it was the dog, not Joan, who was responsible for saving France during the Hundred Years War. In this version, the war was settled by a singing contest.

Great Art Lives made use of both artistic and dramatic talents. In this problem, teams painted or sculpted three works of art: two copies of works by a famous master (chosen from a list) and one in the style of that master. Then they brought one of the copied works to life in a skit, beginning or ending in the positions of the subjects in the painting.

For example, a Division I team from Hackensack, New Jersey, developed a story to fit Edgar Degas' painting *The Millinery Shop*. In their skit, the shopkeeper contemplated selling the shop, and the hats came to life one by one to convince her not to. Each turned out to have been worn by a famous person, and each sang a song. Another team, from Livingston, Montana, showed Paul Cezanne's *The Card Players*. In their version, Cezanne was painting the scene when an argument broke out among the players over whether a woman could join the game.

The "Friendship Machine" was one of the ingenious solutions to the problem called **Technocrats**. The Division I students who tackled this problem designed their products and production lines in advance. In competition, they were given ten minutes to produce ten reasonably identical products, package them, and place them on a shipping dock. Besides being new, the products had to work. Extra points were offered for finishing the products in less than the time limit and for using multiple components and a variety of materials. The teams also produced

222

jingles and commercials for their products, and they dressed in costumes for the work.

"Teacher's Pet" was invented by students from Dagsboro, Delaware. And it was a pet no teacher should be without—an odd mechanical contraption that looked something like a dog. Equipped with chalk, foam and felt rollers, and a squirt gun, it could write on, erase, and wash chalkboards. It came packaged in a cage, with a piece of chalk for food.

A Division III team from Mendham, New Jersey, dressed in duck costumes to produce "Mr. Duck's Teach & Play," a toy for toddlers. It had a clock for a stomach, eyes that lit up, and a cloth covering with zippers and shoelaces to help young children learn how to dress. And a Division II team from Shorewood, Wisconsin, turned out the "Soggy Doggy Sanitizer." This product was an automated dog-washing machine assembled from a Styrofoam cooler. Each machine was packed with instructions and an order form for accessories (including goggles, earplugs, and a hairdryer for the dog). Commer-

cials included testimonials from celebrities and a jingle, the "Soggy Doggy Shuffle."

TAKE UP THE CHALLENGE

OM has come up with five more puzzlers for 1986–87. Students who take up the challenge will be asked to:

• Design and construct a vehicle that will fit into two suitcases, and then complete a set of tasks with it.

• Perform a set of tasks using energy from a chain reaction triggered by mousetraps.

• Design and construct a balsa-wood structure 9 to 11½ inches (23 to 29 centimeters) tall that weighs just 15 grams.

• Present a parody, satire, or analogy of a famous poem in the form of a skit.

• Create a performance of a scene that takes place in a cave in prehistoric times, showing an important discovery.

Whatever solutions the teams come up with, one thing is certain: Their answers will be creative, and they'll have lots of fun. Perhaps you and your classmates might like to take up the challenge too!

Technocrats, Division I (Friendship Machine): Schroeder Elementary School, Troy, Michigan

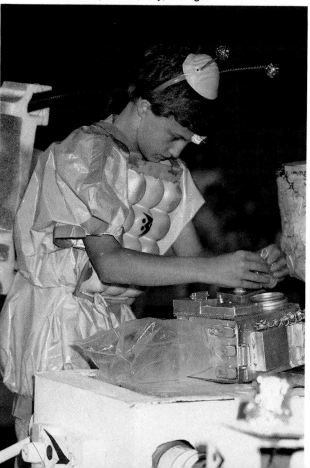

Technocrats, Division III (Mr. Duck's Teach & Play): West Morris Mendham High School, Mendham, New Jersey

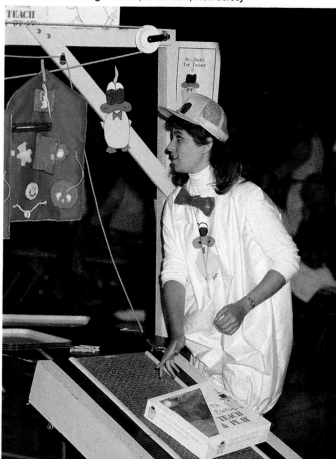

YOUNG PLAYWRIGHTS

The Young Playwrights Festival celebrated its fifth anniversary in 1986, proving once again that there is no lack of young talent when it comes to writing for the theater.

The goal of the festival, which is sponsored by the prestigious Dramatists Guild, is to give young playwrights a chance to present their works in high-quality stage performances. Each year the festival judges receive up to 1,000 scripts from young people aged 18 and under. Every play is read twice and then returned to the author with a written commentary.

The best of the student plays are given full stage productions by professional actors and directors in New York City. In 1986, there were three winners:

• *Remedial English,* by 18-year-old Evan Smith of Savannah, Georgia, is set in a Catholic school for boys and spoofs students and teachers alike. The hero is a daydreaming student who learns a hard lesson when he is asked to tutor a classmate he admires—and finds out that his hero is a dolt.

• *Coup d'Etat,* by 18-year-old Carolyn Jones of San Rafael, California, is a political satire set in a small island country. The island is ruled by an unpopular king and is beset by revolution.

• *A Delicate Situation,* by 17-year-old Eve Goldfarb of New York City, is the most serious play of the 1986 winners. Its central character is a 17-year-old girl whose parents are divorced. Unable to deal with family problems, she becomes rebellious and self-destructive.

Three runners-up were also presented, in staged readings. They were *Once Upon a Time There Was a Family,* by Kenn Adams, 18, of New York City; *Dinner at Eight,* by Isa-Jill Gordon, 15, of Hartsdale, New York; and *Waning Crescent Moon,* by Stephen Serpas, 18, of Baton Rouge, Louisiana.

Remedial English, by Evan Smith, 18: A student learns a hard lesson about his hero.

Coup d'Etat, by Carolyn Jones, 18: A fictitious Caribbean island country is beset by revolution in this political farce.

A Delicate Situation, by Eva Goldfarb, 17: A teenager becomes rebellious and self-destructive when she is unable to deal with her parents' marital problems.

Legoland—a miniature land where everything is made from little plastic building blocks.

IT'S A SMALL WORLD

In these days of jet travel, people have gotten used to the idea of flying across oceans in a matter of hours. But did you know that there's a place where you can tour the entire world in just an afternoon?

The place is Legoland, a theme park built by a Danish toy manufacturer in Billund, a town in the western part of Denmark. At this park, the saying "It's a small world" has taken on new meaning—small is what Legoland is all about.

The centerpiece of the park is Miniland, a world where everything is shrunk down to one twentieth of its normal size. There are scenes from all over Europe—the Dutch countryside, with windmills; Denmark's capital, Copenhagen; medieval buildings from Britain; the Austrian alps; and the Rhine valley of West Germany, to name just a few. From the United States, there's a space shuttle launching pad and even a min-iature replica of Mount Rushmore, the famous U.S. presidential monument.

All the buildings, monuments, and figures in Miniland are made from Lego bricks, the little plastic building blocks that snap together. Electric power operates mini cranes, drawbridges, and trains that move through the exhibit area. There are little lakes and rivers, and little trees and shrubs that have been specially grown to match the Miniland scale.

But Miniland is only one area of the park. When you've completed your tour, you can move on to lots of other attractions, both inside and out.

To get your bearings, ride up to the top of Legotop, a 100-foot (30-meter) tower with an observation deck. Or whisk around the park on the monorail train. Then, if you like, you can go on a safari, in a remote-controlled electric car that will carry you to Africa.

There you'll see elephants, giraffes, monkeys, and other exotic animals. (There's no need to be afraid of the animals—all are made of Lego bricks.) There's also a mini-boat ride that will take you to some of the world's most famous sights, including the Acropolis in Athens and the Egyptian temples of Abu Simbel.

In the park's amusement area, there are rides and a playground for younger children. (Of course, there's also a special area where you can build your own creations with the little bricks.) Older children can try their hands at piloting small, rubber-bumpered cars in the Driving School. After twenty minutes of practice, you'll receive a Legoland driving license that bears your picture.

Legoredo Town gives visitors a taste of the U.S. Wild West. In this full-size replica of an old Western town, you can get your name printed on a "wanted" poster, pan for "gold" dust, and go splashing down the long chute of the Timber ride. An Indian chief will show you how to bake bread over a campfire, and a mining train will carry you through a replica of a working mine.

The outdoor sections of the park close in winter, but indoors there are exhibits that draw weekend visitors all year. One of the most fascinating is Titania's Palace, a fifteen-room miniature fairy castle built by the British painter Sir Nevile Wilkinson around 1900. Wilkinson began the palace at the request of his young daughter, who thought she had seen tiny fairies in the garden and wanted a house for them. The building took fifteen years to complete. Each room is beautifully furnished—there are more than 3,000 items inside, and many are made of gold, silver, and precious stones.

Antique toys and dolls are also on display. The doll collection consists of about 450 dolls and dollhouses. The oldest doll is more than 400 years old. The toy collection consists of 1,200 antique toys, many of them the mechanical tin toys that were popular with children from the early 1800's to the 1950's.

There are other exhibits, too—and entertainment, including a puppet theater and a children's marching band. Altogether, there's a lot to see and do in this very small world.

Take an around-the-world cruise on a miniboat and see such exotic sights as this temple in Thailand.

YOUNG HEADLINERS

Eleven-year-old **Katerina Lycheva** of Moscow (above, left) toured the United States to promote world peace in 1986, making stops in five cities. The trip commemorated the visit of an American girl, Samantha Smith, to the Soviet Union in 1983. Samantha was 10 when she made her trip; in 1985 she died in a plane crash. In the Soviet Union, Katya (as her friends call her) has appeared in five peace-promoting films. She's seen here with her U.S. traveling companion, Star Rowe, 10, of San Francisco, California.

"Absolutely extraordinary" and "near perfect" are words that have been applied to the violin playing of **Midori**, a 14-year-old Japanese girl who is studying in New York City. In 1986, Midori won rave reviews for a performance as guest soloist with the Boston Symphony. She also made her first recording, featuring pieces by Bach and Vivaldi. Besides playing the violin, Midori's favorite pastimes are reading and outdoor games.

Wei-Jing Zhu of New York City (right) and **Wendy Kay Chung** of Miami (below) tied for first place in the 1986 Westinghouse Talent Search. Each won a $20,000 scholarship in the contest, which is open to high school seniors and is the most prestigious science contest in the United States. Wei-Jing's project dealt with algebraic number theory. He was born in China, moved to the United States in 1980, and plans a career in scientific research. Wendy studied the behavior of the Caribbean fruit fly, collecting specimens with a portable vacuum cleaner. She plans a career in biochemistry or medicine. This was only the second time that there had been a tie for first place since the contest began in 1942.

When it comes to chess, **the Polgar sisters** of Hungary don't play around. At the 1986 New York Open Chess Tournament in April, Susan, 16, finished 25th in the toughest section, defeating top adult players. Sophia, 11, won second place in the expert division. And Judith, 9, finished first among 1,000 unranked players. All have studied chess from an early age and practice for hours each day. In 1985, when Susan was just 15, she was the world's top-rated female player.

Five-year-old **Brent Meldrum** of Lynn, Massachusetts, gets a grateful kiss from 6-year-old **Tanya Branden**, after his quick thinking saved her life in 1986. The two were playing when Tanya choked on a piece of candy. Brent immediately remembered the Heimlich maneuver, a method of saving choking victims that he had seen on TV. He locked his arms around her waist, squeezed, and then banged her feet on the floor. Out popped the candy, and Tanya could breathe. Brent's action drew a flurry of awards and other honors.

GARBAGE PAIL KIDS

"Ugly," "nasty," and "cruel" are some of the words adults use to describe the bubble-gum cards called Garbage Pail Kids. Some parents and even some schools have banned them. But that didn't stop the cards from being all the rage with kids in 1986. The characters on the cards look something like the popular Cabbage Patch dolls. But they're quite different in that each, in its own way, is—well, revolting!

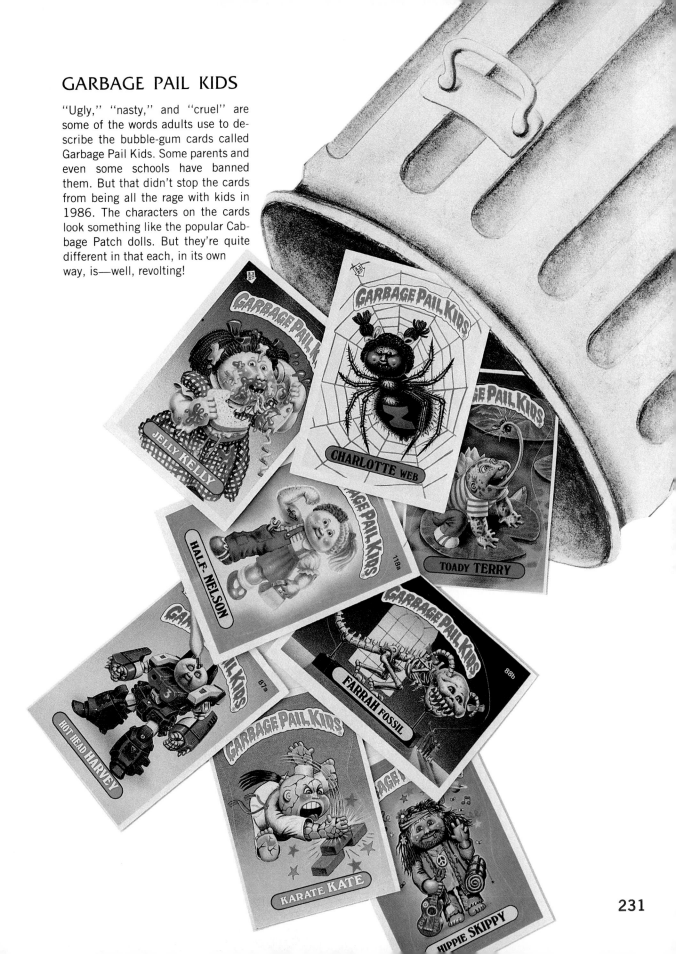

231

CAREERS IN FASHION

The fashion industry: Outsiders see it as a world of glamour, talent, and constant change—a world that thrives on new ideas and creativity. It is these things . . . and more. It's also an unpredictable world, with crazy schedules, frenzied activity, and intense competition. In short, it's one of the most exciting and challenging industries around.

The most glamorous fashion careers—the ones most people think of right away—are designing and modeling. Each of these careers includes many specialties, and each requires certain talents and skills. But there are hundreds of different kinds of jobs in fashion, each with its own responsibilities and educational requirements. That's because fashion is such a broad field—it includes everything from designing fabrics to selling clothes in stores.

FIRST COME THE FABRICS

There are two basic elements in any item of clothing: the fabric and the design. Fabrics, or textiles, are a very important part of the world of fashion. The kinds of fabrics available help determine the kinds of clothes that designers will create—and, therefore, the kinds of clothes that you will find in stores in the coming season.

In textile companies, the people responsible for creating fabric designs include stylists, designers, and colorists. They have a technical knowledge of fibers and dyes and a good sense of color. Most of them attended college or technical school, where they studied art and textiles. They usually began their careers as apprentices to more experienced people.

These people are always on the lookout for ideas—when reading books, going to museums, watching movies, even lying on the beach watching bathers walk past. And they pay great attention to what's happening in the world—to important news events, economic trends, fads among teenagers, and changing styles of music. All these may be sources of ideas. Equally important, all may affect what consumers want to buy.

Stylists oversee the design department, coordinating the work of fabric designers and colorists. In addition to having a good knowledge of design and textiles, they have a knowledge of marketing—they understand what will sell. This is extremely important. You can create the most beautiful fabric or the most stunning garment, but that doesn't mean much if no one buys it.

Stylists play a major role in deciding what designs and colors will be used in the fabrics made by their company. They have to be able to convince the company's management that what they have chosen is what the clothing designers will want to buy—and, eventually, what people will want to wear. Thus,

Fabric design and clothing design are the two basic elements of fashion. Above: One way of getting a design on fabric is by silk-screening. Below: Many clothing designers specialize, some creating only sportswear.

The runway model takes part in the fashion industry's most important event—the fashion show, at which a designer's latest line of clothing is introduced.

decide what colors will appeal to customers. This isn't as simple as it sounds—textile manufacturers usually make such decisions two years before garments incorporating the fabrics actually reach the stores!

Colorists generally work under the direction of a fabric designer or a stylist. The job is often a stepping stone to becoming a designer and, eventually, a stylist.

CLOTHING DESIGNERS

Clothing designers have many of the same skills as textile designers. They're creative people with artistic talent and a good knowledge of colors and fabrics. They're always studying trends and looking for ideas. They have good communication skills and often spend a lot of time in meetings with their bosses, deciding what the company's new line of clothing will consist of. They must also be able to explain their ideas to pattern-makers, models, and others with whom they work.

Clothing designers also need to understand consumers. They have to create clothes that people want to buy, at prices they can afford. They must always consider the use and cost of the items they create. On a very simple level, this means that a good designer won't use cheap fabric for an expensive evening gown or put gold buttons on an inexpensive house dress.

Once a designer gets an idea for a garment, he or she makes a sketch—and another, and another. Dozens, perhaps hundreds, of sketches may be made before the garment is completed. The first sketches are rough. Gradually, details are added—a collar, cuffs, buttons, stitching. There is a lot of experimentation, a lot of trial and error. A collar may be drawn and redrawn many times until the designer decides it's right. Pleats may be added, then removed, then added again. And all the time, the designer keeps asking a very unartistic question: Can this garment be manufactured and priced to make a profit?

Many designers specialize. Some create only sportswear, some only coats and suits, and some only junior clothing. Others work on expensive clothes sold only in exclusive stores. Still others create clothes for the mass market. Each of these markets has dif-

they also need good writing and speaking skills. And later, after the fabrics have been manufactured, stylists often help to promote and advertise the fabrics, too.

Fabric Designers are artists who draw the designs that will be printed on the fabrics. In addition to their artistic talents, they must have a strong knowledge of colors and fabrics. They work within guidelines established by the stylist, and they must often draw designs over and over until they produce exactly what the company wants.

Colorists use paints or dyes to color in the designs created by the fabric designers. They may also help forecast colors—that is, help

ferent requirements: Secretaries and movie stars have different clothing needs; so do lawyers and farmers, or teenagers and senior citizens.

Some people have careers as **accessories designers.** They design shoes, belts, scarves, gloves, hats, and jewelry. Sometimes they work closely with clothing designers to create and coordinate fashions.

Many successful designers followed a liberal arts or business program in college. Most also had specialized training in design, either at a design school or while working in the clothing industry. It's important for a designer to understand fabrics and to know all the steps in the manufacturing process. An accessories designer must be familiar with all the materials used in accessories, from leather to metals to gems.

MANY TYPES OF MODELS

When people hear the word "model" they often think of a tall, thin, beautiful woman.

But one need not have these attributes to be a fashion model. And even men, children, and senior citizens can have successful modeling careers.

Clothing models work side-by-side with designers. After a designer has completed drawings for a garment, a sample is made, and the clothing model tries it on. The designer sees how the garment looks, and the model tells how it feels—whether it's comfortable and easy to move in. Many changes may have to be made in the design before it's satisfactory.

To be a successful clothing model, a person must have a good figure. Many women's designers look for clothing models who are a perfect size eight.

Runway models take part in the most important events in the fashion industry—fashion shows, at which the designers' latest lines of clothing are introduced to the public. At the shows, models walk, twirl, and dance down long runways. With the poise and

GETTING STARTED IN FASHION

People who enter the fashion industry should be prepared to start in low-level, low-paying jobs. Those who want to be designers usually start as trainees and apprentices. Those who want to be models may start by volunteering to take part in fashion shows put on by local stores. It's very rare for someone to be an "instant success." In general, the most successful people in the fashion industry have gone through years of learning, practice, and hard work.

If you're interested in a career in fashion, there are several ways to begin investigating the industry. Discuss the subject with school guidance counselors, and read books about it. Take a part-time job in a local clothing store, to study people's buying habits. Make clothes for yourself and members of your family. Or take a summer job in a sewing factory—to learn how fabrics are cut and what goes into the manufacture of clothes. Volunteer to model in fashion shows held by local charitable organizations. This will help you learn how to display clothes.

Additional information on careers, their educational requirements, and student financial aid can be obtained from professional organizations and from colleges and universities that offer design, textile, and art programs. Here are a few organizations that can supply you with career information:

The Fashion Group, Inc.—9 Rockefeller Plaza, New York, NY 10020

Fashion Canada—c/o Department of Industry, Trade and Commerce, 235 Queen Street, Ottawa, Ont. K1A 0H5

American Apparel Manufacturers Association—1611 North Kent Street, Suite 8000, Arlington, VA 22209

Canadian Manufacturers Institute—116 Albert Street, Suite 803, Ottawa, Ont. K1P 5G3

American Textile Manufacturers Institute—400 South Tryon Street, Charlotte, NC 28285

Canadian Textiles Institute—1080 Beaver Hall Hill, Suite 1002, Montreal, Quebec H2Z 1T6

World Modeling Association—P.O. Box 100, Croton-on-Hudson, NY 10520

The retail end of the fashion industry: Buyers select the merchandise that will be sold in their stores.

drama of actors and actresses, they show off the new clothes, making each garment seem more glamorous than the last.

Runway models don't have to be physically perfect. But they must be graceful, with an excellent sense of how to move. They must be able to make clothes look attractive, exciting . . . and desirable.

The best-known and often best-paid models are **photographic models**. They appear on the covers of magazines, in catalogs, even on billboards. These people are tall, slim, and attractive. But that's not enough. They are also photogenic—that is, they photograph well. Some photographic models have looks that consumers think of as "nice" or "average." Such models can be convincing whether they are modeling tennis clothes or business suits or prom dresses.

Open almost any newspaper or fashion magazine and you'll see sketches of models wearing the latest fashions offered by a designer or a store. The models who posed for the artists who drew the sketches are called **illustration models**. Here again, the models' looks aren't particularly important. But they must have excellent figures, so that they make the clothes look terrific.

There are other kinds of models, too.

Some designers specialize in creating clothes for people who are larger than average. **Large-size models** are needed to show off these clothes. Successful large-size models must be photogenic and well proportioned. **Foot and leg models** are needed to advertise socks, shoes, and pantyhose. These people have well-shaped feet and legs. **Hand models** are needed to hold pocketbooks and display rings and bracelets. They have attractive hands, with long, slender fingers and beautifully groomed nails.

All models have certain characteristics in common, however. They take good care of their hair and skin. They eat good, balanced diets and exercise regularly. And they know how to use makeup. This is true for male models as well as female models.

Modeling is a very competitive field. If you wish to become a model, it's important to analyze your features. This will help you determine which type of modeling you're best suited for. If you're very short, you probably would have difficulty getting work as a photographic model. But you might be able to work as a foot or hand model. If you don't photograph well but have a great figure, you might try to get a job as a clothing model or an illustrator's model.

The wholesale end of the fashion industry: Skilled sewers put the fabric pieces together to produce the garment.

WHOLESALE AND RETAIL

The fashion industry is roughly divided into two branches: the wholesale industry, which makes the clothes, and the retail industry, which buys the clothes from manufacturers and sells them to the public. Most people who enter retailing begin by selling in a store. In this way, they learn what customers are looking for when they shop.

A salesclerk may go on to become a **buyer**, who selects the merchandise that will be sold. A large store may also have a **fashion director**, who is responsible for coordinating the fashions sold in different departments. Buyers and fashion directors need a keen fashion sense, so that they can judge which styles will be popular with the customers who shop in their stores. They also need good business sense, so that the store can make a profit when it resells the clothes they buy to customers. Many people in retailing study general business courses in college or attend schools that specialize in fashion merchandising.

Clothing manufacturers have salespeople and fashion directors, too—they present the clothes to the store buyers. But there are specialized careers in the wholesale industry. And some of these require special skills.

Patternmakers, for example, take apart the sample garments made by the designer and use the pieces to make paper patterns. Each piece must be scaled, or graded, to the different sizes that will be produced in the factory. **Cutters** take the patterns and use them to cut out fabric for the garment. **Sewers** put the pieces together. These skills are generally learned at specialized fashion schools or through apprenticeships with experts in the business.

Manufacturers also have **production managers**, who coordinate the various steps in the manufacturing process. **Costing clerks** are responsible for figuring out how much it will cost to produce each garment—an important consideration if the manufacturer is to make a profit. These people generally have business backgrounds.

One group of fashion specialists—**fashion publicists, photographers, writers**, and **illustrators**—may work in both the retail and wholesale fields. They may be involved in advertising for a store or a manufacturer, or in reporting on the latest styles to the public. These people have the skills and talents needed for their specialties plus a knowledge of fashion that comes from years of watching trends.

YOUNG PHOTOGRAPHERS

Spots on a giraffe . . . stripes on a shirt . . . a delicate tracery of leaves. Line and pattern can be captured by the camera so we can see them in new ways. Sometimes all it takes is an eye for composition and a little thought. Sometimes darkroom wizardry—hand-coloring and other techniques—turns an everyday photograph into a work of art. Either way, the results can be extraordinary. A photograph can evoke the gentler time of a bygone era or the neon vibrancy of today's hectic world.

The young people who took the pictures shown on these pages were among the winners in the 1986 Scholastic/Kodak Photo Awards Program. The program offers scholarships and other awards to high school juniors and seniors in the United States and Canada.

Face Splash,
by Jennelle Marcereau, 17,
Mt. Clemens, Michigan

Stretch,
by William Fornwalt, 18,
Chesterfield, Missouri

Reticulation, by Ann Laienski, 16, Elk Grove, California

Electric Ghosts, by Jennifer Laskin, 18, Mayfield, Ohio

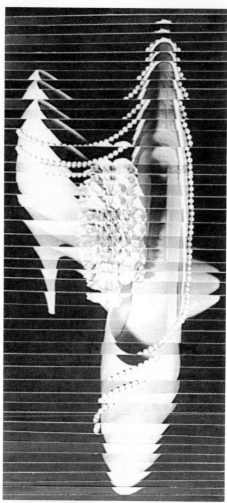

String Along,
by Lisa McDonald, 17,
Chesterfield, Missouri

Balloonrise,
by Eric Thun, 17,
DeWitt, New York

240

Studying,
by Lurline Tau'a, 14,
Waianae, Hawaii

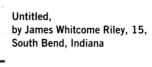

Untitled,
by James Whitcome Riley, 15,
South Bend, Indiana

241

CREATIVITY

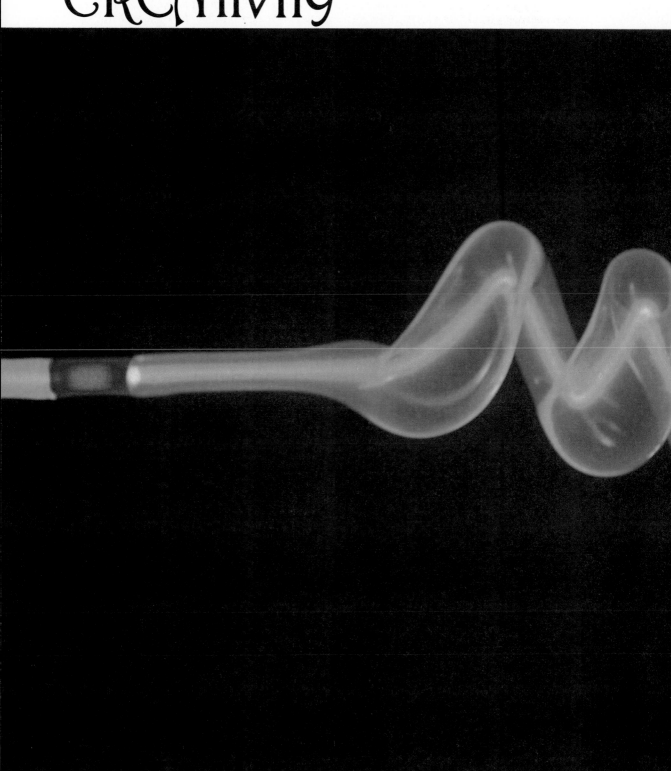

Like a jagged streak of lightning, a vivid neon light corkscrews through the darkness. Formed of hand-shaped glass tubes filled with glowing neon gas, lights like this have become an art form.

Neon is glowing again, in advertising signs . . .

NEON—NEW AND NIFTY

Streaks of hot pink and electric blue light up the night sky, pulsing and blinking in rhythmic patterns. It's not an invasion from outer space—it's neon. Once looked down upon as the ultimate in poor taste, neon signs are enjoying a dazzling revival today.

Neon signs first made their appearance about 1910, when a French inventor perfected a technique for making them. The basic element in a neon sign is a long, thin glass tube, carefully heated and bent by hand to whatever shape the sign maker wants. All the air is sucked out of the tube, to create a vacuum. Then the tube is filled with neon, a colorless and odorless gas. (The name "neon" is from the Greek word meaning "new." It was given to the gas in 1898 by its discoverers, the British chemists Sir William Ramsay and Morris W. Travers.)

Neon has a remarkable property: When electricity is passed through the tube, the gas glows in brilliant colors. Pure neon glows a bright red. By adding other gases or by coloring the tube, the sign maker can produce other colors. A few drops of mercury, for example, produce a vivid blue.

From the 1920's on, neon signs popped up all over North America and around the world. They advertised theaters, restaurants, nightclubs and casinos, car dealers, hotels, and countless individual products. At night, downtown shopping areas glowed with unearthly light as neon signs flashed and blinked to attract people's attention. Many signs even showed animated figures that seemed to move as different neon tubes went on and off.

By the 1950's, neon signs were becoming less popular. Many people thought the bright colors and flashing lights were in poor taste.

Neon signs were also expensive to maintain, and they were easily damaged by the weather. Businesses turned to other ways of making signs that would light up at night—fluorescent bulbs placed behind sheets of plastic, for example.

Some businesses, however, continued to use neon signs. And some areas remained famous for their signs. The casinos in Las Vegas, Nevada, for example, have huge and elaborate neon signs that turn night into day. New York City's Times Square and Tokyo's famous shopping district, the Ginza, are other areas that are well known for their nighttime signs.

But today people are looking at neon signs in a new way—as an art form. The brilliant colors and bent glass tubes of a neon sign can create striking forms and patterns that just can't be duplicated in other ways. Neon advertising signs are being displayed in art galleries. And artists are also using neon tubing to create works that have nothing to do with advertising.

Neon has become the subject of books and of articles in art magazines. It's been used in

. . . as decorative accents in "in" restaurants . . .

. . . and in art studios.

stage productions, such as the Broadway show *Sophisticated Ladies,* to create the feeling of past eras. It's been used to present the future, too: In science fiction films, neon lights are often used to represent lasers and other space-age weapons.

With improved materials and computers to synchronize the flashing of the signs, businesses are also returning to neon. Some restaurants and stores are bringing the glowing advertising tubes indoors, where they serve as decorative accents.

All this has created a lot of work for sign-making companies. Since neon signs can't be mass produced, the companies have had to train new workers in the delicate art of forming the glass tubes. Also, while vibrant new neon works are being created, some people are trying to save and preserve the best and most famous of the neon signs of the past—so that they can keep glowing right into the future.

A CELEBRATION OF INDIA

A land of tigers and elephants, maharajahs and holy men, temples and fabulous jewels —India calls up exotic and mysterious images to many people in the West. And in 1985–86, people in the United States fell in love with India. The reason was the Festival of India, a dazzling celebration that brought to America hundreds of exhibitions and performances depicting India's rich cultural traditions—both classic and folk.

The festival was sponsored by the U.S. and Indian governments. Their hope was that by bringing India's culture to cities and towns across the United States, they would help people better understand that Asian country, both as it was in the past and as it is today.

THE FESTIVAL

Works of art, many never before seen in the United States, were a major part of the festival. Museums in several cities hosted exhibits, concentrating on different styles and periods. One of the largest, at the Metropolitan Museum of Art in New York City, covered the period from 1300 to 1900. In addition to paintings and sculpture, this exhibit featured decorative arts—jade cups, a fabulous jeweled carpet, and a prince's luxurious silk tent. A companion exhibit featured the legendary jewel-covered costumes worn by India's royalty in the 1800's.

In Washington, D.C., the Smithsonian Institution staged an Indian folk festival. Outdoors, there were acrobats, scroll painters, fire jugglers, basket sellers, and a miniature Hindu temple. Inside, Indian handicrafts were displayed in a setting that duplicated an Indian village. Folk art, including mud-wall paintings and intricate embroidery, was also shown in Washington and several other cities.

Traditional dance and music were spotlighted in the Festival of India, a celebration of Indian culture that took place throughout the United States in 1985–86. Here, fabulously costumed Indian dancers act out legends from the Hindu epic *Mahabharata . . .*

Music, drama, and dance were represented with performances that toured many U.S. cities and towns. In India, these art forms are closely related. And, like India's painting and sculpture, they are often linked to religion. There were groups of musicians, representing both folk and classical music. They played drums, flutes, and traditional Indian stringed instruments such as the sitar. And people in the United States had a chance to see traditional Indian dances, such as the Krishnattam, in which elaborately masked and costumed dancers portray scenes from the life of the Hindu god Krishna. This dance has been performed outside of India only once in 300 years.

There was even a stage performance of India's great mythical epic, the *Mahabharata*. This 12,000-page book is the longest in the world, and it took 1,000 years to write. It tells how a quarrel between two families grows into a battle that includes gods, magicians, and monsters. Episodes from it are often sung and danced in India.

A more modern view of the country was presented in special exhibits of films and photographs. And there were special events for children. For example, a museum in Madison, Wisconsin, set up exhibits where children could try on Indian costumes and hear stories of Indian legends.

Above all, the festival focused on the visual arts, especially painting and sculpture. To many people in the West, Indian painting and sculpture are unfamiliar and exotic. But these art forms are among the oldest and richest in the world, reaching back more than 4,000 years. They combine three great religious influences: Buddhist, Hindu, and Muslim.

THE CLASSICAL ART OF INDIA

The earliest Indian art we know of was created by ancient civilizations that flourished along the Indus River from 2500 to 1500 B.C. Little is known about these people because, to this day, their writing cannot be deciphered. But they built advanced cities,

... and a father and son play a one-stringed instrument, the *ektara*, traditionally used by wandering minstrels. But while performing arts like these were an important part of the festival, its main focus was on India's fascinating visual arts.

Various religions influenced Indian art. A stone carving from about A.D. 200 (*above*) shows scenes from the life of the Buddha. Stone sculpture from about the year 1000 (*below*) depicts the Hindu elephant god, Ganesa.

laid out in grid plans and served by drainage systems. And they left many small sculptures of people and animals in stone, terra cotta, and copper. With their rounded forms and soft, flowing lines, these sculptures show many of the qualities of later Indian sculpture.

Around 1500 B.C., the Indus region was invaded by Aryan tribes from the north. They brought an end to the Indus civilization and left no distinctive art of their own. Indian art didn't emerge again until after 300 B.C. At that time, two major trends were changing society: Tribes were organizing into kingdoms and republics, and Buddhism, the first great world religion, was founded.

Most of the art that remains from this time is from Buddhist temples—some of which were carved out of rock, like caves, right into the sides of hills. To help draw converts, these temples were often decorated inside and out with sculptures and wall paintings showing popular scenes and stories from the Buddha's life. Among the most famous of these works are the wall paintings in the caves of Ajanta, done between 100 B.C. and A.D. 600. The story panels are packed with action and figures, many in poses similar to those in traditional Indian dance. As well as illustrating the Buddha's life, they tell much about what Indian life was like at that time in history.

Classical Buddhist art reached a peak about A.D. 320–540, in a time called the Gupta period. It was at this time that the famous, serene image of the sitting Buddha was perfected. It became a model for Buddhist artists throughout Asia, all the way to Japan. The Buddha and other figures were shown in specific postures, with their hands in certain positions, each of which had a meaning to worshippers.

By this time India's other major religious group, the Hindus, were also producing great sculpture. At their simplest, Hindu temples were simply houses for the gods—small buildings with a niche where statues of the gods were placed. But gradually they became more elaborate. And like the Buddhist temples, they were covered with carvings showing stories from the lives of Shiva, Vishnu, and other Hindu gods. To illustrate the various forms and aspects that these gods had, they were shown in different ways. Shiva, for example, might appear as the god of destruction or the god of restoration. The goddess Devi was sometimes shown with many arms, indicating her many powers.

In southern India, the tradition of elaborate temple sculptures continued unbroken for many centuries. But in northern India, the Muslim influence was felt when Arabs began to invade the Indus valley in the 700's. By 1200 they had defeated the Hindu kingdoms of the north. The Muslim religion forbade the making of images of humans and animals. Instead, Muslim art focused on architecture—building mosques and palaces with beautiful domes and arches and towering minarets. These buildings were decorated chiefly with abstract forms, both flowing and geometric, and with lacelike cut stonework.

This miniature watercolor dates from the early 1600's and depicts a court lady strolling in a garden. It shows the influence of many earlier painting traditions, including Muslim and Persian styles.

MOGUL AND LATER ART

Indian art traditions, however, didn't die out. In fact, they combined with Muslim influences to produce one of the great periods of Indian art, during the Mogul dynasty (1526–1757).

The Mogul dynasty was founded by Babur, a descendant of Turkish and Mongol rulers. He conquered northern India in 1526. Babur and the Mogul rulers who followed him preferred Persian culture to Arab culture, and they brought such innovations as formal gardens, fountains, courtly etiquette, and polo to India. They were also great patrons of the arts. Many people consider the Taj Mahal, built by the ruler Shah Jahan as a tomb for his wife in the mid-1600's, to be the finest example of Mogul architecture. But painting also flourished. Although the

Moguls were Muslims, they interpreted religious law loosely when it came to art and allowed a full range of subjects to be painted.

The Mogul ruler Akbar (1542–1605) assembled an artists' studio at his court. There, beautiful miniatures the size of book pages were painted. They illustrated famous stories and showed scenes of court life. Miniature painting had existed in India for many centuries. But the early Mogul miniatures were based on Persian traditions in line and in their jewel-like colors.

As time went on, however, Mogul painting became less and less Persian. Figures were shown with more rounded, natural forms, and individual faces were portrayed with

This delicate cup was made in the mid-1600's at the court of an Indian ruler. Shaped like a flower, it is formed of jade with rubies and emeralds set in gold.

A miniature from the early 1800's depicts a scene from a favorite Hindu myth: the story of the romance between the god Krishna and Radna, a mortal woman.

250

After the British came to India, first to trade and then to rule, Western influences were seen in Indian art. In this photograph, an Indian prince wearing traditional clothes poses against a background of European-style furniture. The picture was taken about 1890 by Lala Din Dayal, India's first major professional photographer.

great accuracy. It became fashionable for rulers and courtiers alike to have their portraits painted. The Moguls were also fascinated by art from around the world, and some paintings done at their courts show European influences. A few even seem to be copied from the works of European Renaissance masters.

Mogul arts began to decline in the late 1600's, as the empire began to lose its power. But the tradition of miniature painting was carried on by the Rajput artists. The Rajputs were Hindu rulers of small Indian kingdoms, mostly under Mogul rule but still retaining their independent nature. Like the Moguls, they supported the arts.

In Rajput paintings (and in those produced in other small Indian states at this time), Hindu gods and goddesses once again appear in scenes from Hindu mythology. But, rather than being large and awesome as they were in earlier Hindu sculptures, the gods in these paintings seem almost human—handsome people strolling through gardens, wearing beautiful clothes. One of the favorite subjects was a love story involving the god Krishna and Radna, a human woman.

Starting in the late 1700's, another new influence made its mark on Indian art. The British came, first to trade and then to rule. Indian artists were trained in Western techniques of drawing and painting, and these techniques can be seen in their works. Buildings showed Western influences, too. Today many Indian artists continue to blend styles from the West with India's artistic traditions, producing works that are modern but distinctly their own.

Gwen Verdon and Don Ameche (best supporting actor) in *Cocoon.*

1986 ACADEMY AWARDS

CATEGORY	WINNER
Motion Picture	*Out of Africa*
Actor	William Hurt (*Kiss of the Spider Woman*)
Actress	Geraldine Page (*The Trip to Bountiful*)
Supporting Actor	Don Ameche (*Cocoon*)
Supporting Actress	Anjelica Huston (*Prizzi's Honor*)
Director	Sydney Pollack (*Out of Africa*)
Cinematography	David Watkin (*Out of Africa*)
Song	"Say You, Say Me" (*White Knights*)
Foreign Language Film	*The Official Story* (Argentina)
Documentary Feature	*Broken Rainbow*
Documentary Short	*Witness to War: Dr. Charlie Clements*

Rebecca DeMornay and Geraldine Page (best actress) in *The Trip to Bountiful.*

Meryl Streep in *Out of Africa* (best motion picture).

THE MUSIC SCENE

On the popular music scene, 1986 was the year of the woman artist. Soul singers, in particular, made news on the best-seller charts, in music videos, and in the media. Whitney Houston, Janet Jackson, Patti LaBelle, Tina Turner, and Aretha Franklin were just a few of the performers who were the talk of the industry.

Twenty-three-year-old Whitney Houston was the hottest artist of the year. The daughter of gospel singer Cissy Houston, Whitney attracted as much attention in the media as she did in record sales and air play. Her 1985 debut album, *Whitney Houston*, sold over 10,000,000 copies and was acclaimed as the most successful solo debut album—male or female—of all time. The hit album also pro-

It was the year of the woman artist: Whitney Houston's album was the most successful debut album of all time . . .

duced three number-one singles—"Greatest Love of All," "How Will I Know?," and "Saving All My Love for You." Houston's year wouldn't have been complete without winning a few awards, and these included a Grammy, an MTV Video Award, and two American Music Awards.

Janet Jackson, a member of the famous Jackson clan, spent the year making it on her own. Her third album, *Control*, was her first big hit. On its journey to the top of the charts, it yielded two smash singles, "Nasty," and "When I Think of You."

Several of the more established female stars were also extremely popular. Patti LaBelle hit it big with her album *Winner in You* and her love ballad duet with Michael McDonald, "On My Own." Tina Turner continued her winning ways with successful follow-ups to 1984's award-winning *Private Dancer*. She won a Grammy as Best Rock Female Vocalist with "One of the Living," and scored on the album charts with *Break Every Rule*. Her best-selling single from that album, "Typical Male," proved to be yet another hit with her fans.

Aretha Franklin made the charts with her new album *Aretha*, which included a new version of The Rolling Stones' "Jumpin' Jack Flash." She made bigger news, however, by becoming the first female artist to be inducted into the recently established Rock and Roll Hall of Fame.

The "Women of Soul" weren't alone on the charts. Some of the other female singers who commanded large audiences were Madonna, Sade, Amy Grant, Cyndi Lauper, and Heart. Madonna followed up her best-selling albums *Like a Virgin* and *Madonna* with *True Blue*. This latest release included two hit singles, "Papa Don't Preach" and "Live to Tell."

Sade, working with British jazz musicians and samba-flavored rhythms, recorded the hit album *Promise*, which in turn created another smash single, "The Sweetest Taboo." Amy Grant, whose spiritual songs have a rock and roll beat, won a Grammy as Best Female Gospel Performer with her album *Unguarded*.

After a year-long absence from the recording studio, Cyndi Lauper climbed the charts once again with *True Colors*. And Heart, the group led by the sister team of Ann and Nancy Wilson, scored its first number-one single with "These Dreams."

Linda Ronstadt continued recording standards of the pre-Rock years. Her first two albums in this series, *What's New* and *Lush Life*, were big hits with the record-buying public. In 1986 she released her third "oldies but goodies" album, *For Sentimental Reasons*, and it, too, found its audience. All three albums were superbly arranged by award-winning arranger/conductor Nelson Riddle, who helped create hits for Frank Sinatra and Nat "King" Cole in the 1950's. (Riddle died in late 1985, at the age of 64, just before *For Sentimental Reasons* was completed.)

Barbra Streisand also looked to the past for her latest recording. In *The Broadway Album*, Barbra returned to her theatrical roots, singing fifteen classic show tunes. The selections spanned more than fifty years of the American musical theater, from Jerome Kern's *Show Boat* to Stephen Sondheim's *Sunday in the Park With George*. "I've always thought of myself not as a singer," Streisand said, "but as an actress who sings. It was time for me to do something I truly believed in." Her dedication to the album was so great that she filmed a video special, "Putting It Together: The Making of the Broadway Album."

THE MALE CONTINGENT

In 1986, no male singer captured the imagination of fans as Bruce Springsteen had done in 1985. But the men were well represented on the charts, nevertheless.

Billy Joel scaled the charts with *The Bridge*. Bob Dylan created what some described as a masterpiece in *Biograph*, a five-record retrospective of his career. John Cougar Mellencamp made the Top 10 list with *Scarecrow*. Billy Ocean continued crossing over with big ballads like "Love Zone" and "There'll Be Sad Songs." Huey Lewis and the News hit number-one with "Stuck With You" and had a top album in *Fore!*. And Lionel Richie and his mellow baritone once again entertained his legion of followers with the romantic "Say You, Say Me" and the high-flying album *Dancing on the Ceiling*.

. . . Patti LaBelle had a winner in *Winner in You* . . .

. . . and Sade, working with British jazz musicians, hit it big with *Promise* and "The Sweetest Taboo."

Peter Gabriel made the Top 10 charts with "Sledgehammer," from his rhythm and blues-oriented *So* album.

Like ex-Commodore Lionel Richie, a number of new solo artists came from successful rock groups. Peter Cetera, formerly of Chicago, had a best-seller with "Glory of Love," the love theme from the hit film *Karate Kid II*. David Lee Roth, who left the top-rated Van Halen, produced a Top 10 LP in *Eat 'Em and Smile*. Daryl Hall, working without his partner John Oates, displayed his considerable talent as a soloist in his second album, *Three Hearts in the Happy Ending Machine*. Hall also had a hit single with "Dreamtime."

Actor Don Johnson's status as a superstar on the "Miami Vice" TV series opened the door to a recording session. While Johnson's likeable tenor voice helped give him the hit single "Heartbeat," his recording debut lacked the impact of his work as an actor.

Members of the British group Genesis continued recording solo with great success. Guitarist Mike Rutherford (performing as Mike & the Mechanics) had hit singles in "Silent Running" and "All I Need Is a Miracle"; Peter Gabriel made the Top 10 charts with "Sledgehammer," from his rhythm and blues-oriented *So* album; and Phil Collins, Genesis' drummer/singer, continued his popularity with *No Jacket Required*.

The Pet Shop Boys (Britain's Neil Tennant and Chris Lowe) recorded a best-selling hit single, "West End Girls." The duo demonstrated that you don't need to play concert dates to have a hit record. Without a concert tour, but with the help of programmed synthesizers and MTV, "West End Girls" went straight to the top of the charts.

SOMETHING UNUSUAL

"Rock Me Amadeus" was probably the strangest hit of the year. Written and recorded by 29-year-old Austrian Hans Holzel, the song was inspired by the film *Amadeus*, which traced the career and tragic life of 18th-century composer Wolfgang Amadeus Mozart. Holzel, who records under the name Falco, first introduced "Rock Me Amadeus" to European audiences. It became a disco favorite in Europe and then swept across the best-selling charts in the United States, Brazil, Israel, and India. The huge success of this single created an audience for Falco's third album, *Falco 3,* which climbed to number five on American album charts.

Exotic sounds were also produced by American artists in 1986. Paul Simon's *Graceland* album was recorded mostly in South Africa with the help of local musicians, in a style known as mbaqanga, or "township jive." But the album actually represented a union of several musical cultures, since two of the tracks were recorded with a New Orleans zydeco band (Good Rockin' Dopsie and the Twisters) and an East Los Angeles Tex-Mex rock band (Los Lobos). The album also contained "Under African Skies," a Simon duet with Linda Ronstadt; and the Everly Brothers were backup performers on the album's title song. While Simon's prior album, *Hearts and Bones,* wasn't the success his fans had hoped for, *Graceland* made the Top 20 on album charts. A single from the album, "You Can Call Me Al," also found a large audience.

Paul McCartney also tried something a little unusual this time around the recording studio. The result was *Press to Play,* which departed from the simplistic romantic verse that characterized his earlier recordings with Wings.

Still another exotic sound was heard in *Brothers in Arms,* the number-one hit album by the veteran British group Dire Straits. Dire Straits also won a Grammy as Best Rock Vocal Group for their single "Money for Nothing."

EVERYTHING OLD IS NEW AGAIN

Songs composed between 1900 and 1950 made a big revival during 1986. The Ronstadt/Riddle albums were in great demand. So, too, was *The Complete Sarah Vaughan,* a new seventeen-record compilation. Two male singers of yesteryear also found their way back into the record stores. Tony Bennett recorded *The Art of Excellence,* his first album in many years. And a six-record an-

thology of long-unavailable recordings by Frank Sinatra, recorded between 1943 and 1952, was released to an eager public—young and old alike.

Nostalgia was also seen in new releases of not-quite-so-oldies. The Beach Boys revived the Mamas and the Papas' "California Dreaming"; the Beatles (in a re-issue) were back on the charts with their 1964 hit "Twist and Shout"; and Ben E. King's 1961 soul classic "Stand By Me" enjoyed success all over again. A new group, the Far Corporation, offered a remake of Led Zeppelin's 1971 hit, "Stairway to Heaven." New Edition returned to the charts with the Penguins' hit of 1954, "Earth Angel." And Run-D.M.C.'s "Walk This Way," a hit for Aerosmith in 1976, made the Top 10 list.

RANDOM MUSICAL NOTES

Rap music became a national phenomenon in 1986. Its widespread popularity seemed to have been generated by Run-D.M.C.'s album *Raising Hell* and the hit single "Walk This Way." The success of Rap artists The Fat Boys *(Big & Beautiful),* Whodini, and Doug E. Fresh indicated that this unusual

Aided by computerized synthesizers and MTV, Britain's Pet Shop Boys had a hit with "West End Girls."

Paul Simon's *Graceland* was recorded mostly in South Africa with the help of local musicians, in a style known as "township jive." It made the Top 20 on album charts.

form of musical entertainment was popular among both black and white audiences. The style made a teenage sensation of disk jockey James Todd Smith (who records under the name L. L. Cool J). His debut Rap album, *Radio,* went Gold, and produced the hit single "Rock the Bells."

Although a number of heavy-metal groups continued to be criticized for their songs of violence and destruction, heavy-metal stars continued to shine in 1986. Ozzy Osbourne's *The Ultimate Sin* made the Top 10 lists, while *Afterburner* by the Texas power trio ZZ Top also went to number-one on the charts. Van Halen (with new lead singer Sammy Hagar replacing David Lee Roth) made music news with their new album *5150.* Other heavy-metal groups who delighted their fans with concerts and new albums included AC/DC with *Who Made Who;* B-52's *Bouncing Off the Satellites;* and Metallica, whose third album, *Master of Puppets,* sold nearly 1,000,000 copies worldwide.

One movie soundtrack was responsible for several single hits during the year. The successful film *Top Gun* produced four big discs: "Danger Zone" and "Playing With the Boys," by Kenny Loggins; "Heaven in Your Eyes," by Canada's Loverboy; and Berlin's synth-rock "Take My Breath Away." *Top Gun*'s soundtrack album alone sold more than 1,000,000 copies.

It came as no surprise that "We Are the World" gathered many of the 1986 Grammy Awards. This 1985 anthem of help for starving Africans won honors as Record of the Year, Song of the Year, and Best Performance by a Vocal Group.

Humanitarianism continued as rock impressario Bill Graham promoted a series of concerts for Amnesty International, an organization whose purpose is to free political prisoners throughout the world. Sting, U2, Joan Baez, Lou Reed, Bryan Adams, the Hooters, and Peter Gabriel were just a few of the artists who performed in the series.

1986 GRAMMY AWARDS

Record of the Year	"We Are the World"	USA for Africa, artists
Album of the Year	*No Jacket Required*	Phil Collins, artist
Song of the Year	"We Are the World"	Michael Jackson, Lionel Richie, songwriters
New Artist of the Year		Sade
Pop Vocal Performance—female	"Saving All My Love for You"	Whitney Houston, artist
Pop Vocal Performance—male	*No Jacket Required*	Phil Collins, artist
Pop Vocal Performance—group	"We Are the World"	USA for Africa, artists
Rock Vocal Performance—female	"One of the Living"	Tina Turner, artist
Rock Vocal Performance—male	"The Boys of Summer"	Don Henley, artist
Rock Vocal Performance—group	"Money for Nothing"	Dire Straits, artists
Country Vocal Performance—female	"I Don't Know Why You Don't Want Me"	Rosanne Cash, artist
Country Vocal Performance—male	"Lost in the Fifties Tonight (In the Still of the Night)"	Ronnie Milsap, artist
Country Vocal Performance—group	*Why Not Me*	The Judds, artists
Rhythm and Blues Vocal Performance—female	"Freeway of Love"	Aretha Franklin, artist
Rhythm and Blues Vocal Performance—male	*In Square Circle*	Stevie Wonder, artist
Rhythm and Blues Vocal Performance—group	"Nightshift"	Commodores, artists
Original Score for a Motion Picture	*Beverly Hills Cop*	Various composers and songwriters
Score for an Original Cast Show	*West Side Story*	John McClure, producer
Classical Album	*Berlioz: Requiem*	Robert Shaw conducting the Atlanta Symphony Orchestra
Recording for Children	*Follow That Bird*	Jim Henson, Muppets creator; Steve Buckingham, producer

A NEW HALL OF FAME

During 1986, eight cities were being considered as the home for the soon-to-be-built Rock and Roll Hall of Fame. Cleveland, Ohio, was the site finally selected. The plans call for the construction of a theater and of a museum to house rock and roll memorabilia. In the meantime, 200 record executives, composers, critics, music historians, and performers voted for the first sixteen pioneer artists to be inducted into the Hall of Fame. These performers, who were honored at a fund-raising dinner in New York City, included Chuck Berry, Ray Charles, Fats Domino, the Everly Brothers, Buddy Holly, Elvis Presley, and Little Richard. Fifteen more music pioneers were announced for induction into the Hall of Fame in 1987, including Bo Diddley, Bill Haley, Ricky Nelson, Carl Perkins, B. B. King—and the sole female inductee, Aretha Franklin.

ARNOLD SHAW
Author, *A Dictionary of American Pop/Rock*
and *Black Popular Music in America*

Dire Straits won a 1986 Grammy Award as Best Rock Vocal Group for their single "Money for Nothing."

A DELICATE ART

Lush flowers, an ancient emperor, a watchful cat—these are examples of one of the most beautiful and delicate folk crafts: Chinese paper cutting.

Scissors or sharp knives are used to cut the paper. The artist doesn't sketch or mark the paper in advance but simply starts cutting, carefully moving the scissors until the cut lines have formed a flower, an animal, or a human being. The artist may then paint the designs.

This craft is centuries old and is popular among people of all ages and all walks of life. The Chinese use papercuts to decorate their homes or as stencil designs for fabrics and ceramics.

This appliquéd marriage quilt from the early 1800's is filled with hearts, a universal symbol of love. The heart was a traditional design in the folk art of colonial America.

HEART TO HEART

The folk art of America from the 1700's to the late 1800's depicts a variety of traditional designs. The heart—a universal symbol of love, courage, friendship, hospitality, and fidelity—is one of the most enchanting.

Traveling artists painted hearts on dower chests and birth and baptismal certificates. Young girls stitched and embroidered hearts on samplers and quilts. Tinsmiths pierced hearts in foot warmers. Potters etched them on presentation plates. Puritan stonecutters carved hearts on gravestones, and carpenters and craftsmen carved out and drew hearts on furniture, including chests and chairs. Ironmongers wrought heart shapes on kitchen utensils, and sailors carved hearts

on whales' teeth during their long voyages in search of the great sperm whales. Hearts were glazed onto stoneware, woven into coverlets, and cut out from paper.

All these products of brush, kiln, loom, needle, and scissors were necessary objects. But they were decorated to please the eye of the maker and to kindle feelings in the beholder. They were the personal expressions of men and women—folk artists who were by nature, rather than by training, masters of their craft.

The heart was a traditional, symbolic design. Most often, it was used in folk art connected with the major events of life: birth, marriage, and death. Most of the decorated objects were found in the home. Many were used for "best" or for "company." They became family heirlooms, carefully saved generation after generation. All these objects now provide us with a record of a design form and of an entire way of life.

HEART HISTORY

The simple heart, with its bold form and appealing grace, is an ancient design with hazy origins and a fascinating history. It has roots reaching back 20,000 years: A great heart was found on a painting of a mammoth in the caves of Cro-Magnon man. Almost every ancient religion and culture throughout the world has given the heart important symbolic meaning. Chinese, Hindu, Judaic, Christian, and Islamic religions all viewed the heart as the center of life, the soul or spirit of a person. Thus the heart became a symbol related to the worship of God.

The heart shape as we know it today can be found in Egyptian art dating from the 14th century B.C. It was part of the distinctive decoration painted on Egyptian coffins. Later, hearts appeared on Coptic (Egyptian Christian) embroidery—possibly as religious symbols. It is the Egyptians who have been credited with bringing the heart form to Europe, in the A.D. 500's.

The Middle Ages (from the 500's to the mid-1400's) witnessed a dramatic evolution of culture, art, and language throughout Europe. From this period there are scattered clues as to the directions that the heart design would take in later folk art.

The heart representing the love of God was used in the ornamentation and architecture of cathedrals and in paintings and sculpture. When Parisian cardmakers, at the end of the 1300's, introduced the first set of playing cards using the now familiar suits—hearts, diamonds, spades, and clubs—each suit was thought to represent one class of medieval French society. The hearts were associated with the church.

Germans and other northern Europeans adopted the heart on their cards but chose

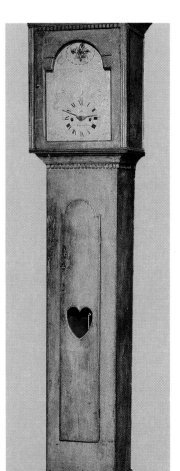

Everyday items for the home were decorated with hearts by tinsmiths, potters, stonecutters, quilters, ironmongers, carpenters, and weavers. They carved hearts out on furniture, glazed them onto stoneware, and fashioned them into kitchen utensils.

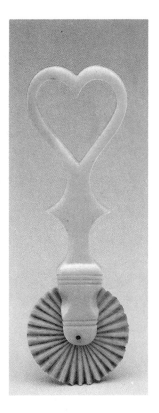

bells, leaves, and acorns for the remaining suits. Their selection reflects a different tradition, in which the heart is one of several symbols associated with growth, fertility, and regeneration. The heart, the source from which all things grow, became in later folk art a symbol of Mother Earth.

The romantic medieval tradition of courtly and chivalric love began using the heart as a symbol by the 1100's. In the 1100's and 1200's, the heart was associated with romantic love in French ballads that told of troubadours offering their hearts to fair maidens. The red heart appears in a 15th-century French illuminated manuscript called *The Book of Love*. The heart was also found on woven carpets, on carvings in ivory, and on jewelry boxes of this period.

In the Renaissance, philosophers and scientists focused on the brain as the center of thinking and reasoning, and on the heart as the center of the emotions. Martin Luther

The Pennsylvania Dutch often used hearts in their Frakturs —documents in ink and watercolor that combined decorative lettering and ornamental designs.

and John Calvin, leaders of the Protestant Reformation, both adopted the heart in their seals.

By the 1700's, people had gained a new degree of independence and wealth, allowing them to decorate their homes and objects of daily use more richly. And they adopted familiar and traditional designs, perhaps copying without understanding the meaning of the religious symbols of the past. Thus the heart became as much associated with love between people as with God's love. It appeared on painted furniture, textiles, embroidery, and other objects. In many European countries, it became associated with the traditions and customs surrounding courtship and marriage.

HEARTS IN AMERICA

In America, the early settlers carried on the traditional use of this design. As early as 1674, a gravestone cutter carved a heart on a tombstone in Charlestown, Massachusetts. A blacksmith cut out a heart, a cloverleaf, and the date 1682 on a banner weather vane that stood on the roof of the second meetinghouse in Lynn, Massachusetts. But America's folk art—and the heart design— flowered after the Revolutionary War. And particularly after 1820, the heart became an increasingly sentimental design, associated with romance and friendship.

To the immigrants from Switzerland and Germany who settled in Pennsylvania, the heart was an image of love with faint overtones of religious meaning. The Pennsylvania Germans (or Pennsylvania Dutch, as these settlers were sometimes called) developed the tradition of Fraktur—documents in ink and watercolor with decorative lettering and ornamental designs. The most common type of Fraktur was the birth and baptismal certificate, but other examples include rewards of merit, house blessings, bookplates, religious texts, and valentines. The heart was often drawn on the borders of certificates, and used as a central design surrounding vital statistics or a religious text. Many of the unknown Fraktur artists were rural schoolmasters. But there were also important Fraktur artists, known for their distinctive handling of the heart design.

Large and small hearts appeared in embroidered samplers (done to show mastery of various stitches) from many parts of the country. Quilts, especially bridal quilts, were often decorated with hearts. Paired or intertwining hearts, representing marriage, were a common design, as were combinations of a heart with paired birds and a single or double heart pierced by an arrow. Heart-shaped wreaths of vines or flowers signified a blessing and protection of the home. The "heart and hand" was another popular design in textiles, particularly in quilts. It was associated with "giving one's hand in marriage" and also with friendship.

Country furniture was often enlivened with paint or simple carving. Thus the heart appears on the chests, chairs, beds, and tables of that time. And even country homes would have appeared empty without pictures on the walls. Watercolor-and-ink family records were a popular art form in the late 1700's and early 1800's, and a number of artists incorporated hearts in their basic designs for these works. One such artist, who became known as the "heart and hand" artist, drew family records decorated with hearts and hands in the borders framing them.

Boxes were made from materials at hand —wood, tin, whalebone, cardboard, and papier-mâché—and came in every size and shape. Their broad, flat sides provided superb surfaces for decorations, which often included hearts. Little hand-whittled and carved heart-shaped boxes, small enough to fit in the palm of a hand, were made as love tokens. Heart-shaped key plates surrounded the keyholes of boxes. And heart-shaped bandboxes carried the "theater caps" of fashionable women to an evening at the opera or theater. At the theater, the woman would remove her tall bonnet and replace it with the smaller cap.

Many kitchen utensils had hearts wrought, carved, or incised into the patterns that decorated them. In some cases the hearts were purely decorative; in others, the heart was featured as a symbol of love and pride. It was customary in Pennsylvania German families for the parents to give their daughter for her dowry a fork, spatula, and taster, each decorated with a heart. Tin cookie cutters with the heart-and-hand design and the simple heart mold were used mainly at

This cutwork love letter, filled with endearments, was created by folding a piece of paper and scissor-cutting the hearts-and-flowers design on the folded edges.

Christmas and Easter by these families, and strung together and hung in the attic when not in use.

The custom of giving hand-decorated love letters replete with hearts and lovingly written verse was introduced in America by the Pennsylvania Germans around 1750. If sent on February 14, these letters were considered valentines. The most common were circular, cutwork love letters, created by folding a piece of paper and then skillfully scissor-cutting a design on the folded edges. The true lover's knot—a continuous labyrinth forming intertwining hearts—was introduced in the first decade of the 1800's.

Early valentines and love letters are also found outside Pennsylvania. Small, intricately designed hearts, hearts and hands, or heart and key designs were often created by young girls and boys to be given as tokens of love and esteem to friends and teachers. Whether on love letters, valentines, or love tokens, the heart symbolized true feeling, the most treasured of human emotions.

from *Folk Hearts*
Cynthia V. A. Schaffner and Susan Klein

FACES, PLACES, EVENTS

With 175,000,000 copies of his books in print, **Louis L'Amour**, 78, is the third best-selling U.S. novelist of all time (after Harold Robbins and Irving Wallace). Most of his books—such as *Kid Rodelo* and a 14-volume saga of the Sackett family—are set in the West. And while Westerns are out of style at the movies, they seem to be "in" with readers. Some critics dismiss L'Amour's works, but others praise his lean writing style and his careful attention to accurate detail. And he has been awarded both the Congressional Medal of Honor and the Presidential Medal of Freedom for his work.

Bathed in rainbow-colored lights, a fairy-tale building rose against the skyline of St. Paul, Minnesota, in February, 1986. Two weeks later, it was gone. The building was an **ice palace**, built for the city's 100th anniversary of its famous Winter Carnival. Made of 10,000 massive blocks of ice, it towered 12 stories high and was guarded by lions and eagles carved from ice. Inside the whimsical wonder, more than 1,000 computer-controlled lights blinked on and off in an ever-changing play of color.

An actress known for one-woman shows in which she portrays an enormous range of characters, **Whoopi Goldberg** won acclaim in 1986 as the star of the film *The Color Purple*. Goldberg, whose real name is Caryn Johnson, was born about 1949 in New York City and grew up in a housing project there. From an early age, she was fascinated by films, and she says she has always considered herself an actress rather than a comedian in her stage performances. During 1986, Goldberg also appeared in a second film, *Jumpin' Jack Flash*, and began work on a third film, *Burglar*.

In 1986, **Robert Penn Warren**, 80, was named the first U.S. poet laureate. He had previously won three Pulitzer prizes and many other honors for his poetry and fiction. Britain has been appointing poet laureates for life since the 1600's, when the job entailed writing poems that royalty wanted to hear. The U.S. poet won't write on command, however, and the job is to last just one or two years. The main purpose of creating the post was to give greater prestige to poetry. Warren (shown here with his wife) was born in Kentucky and has taught at Yale University. He lives in Connecticut.

The art world was taken by storm in 1986 when the existence of 240 previously unknown paintings by **Andrew Wyeth** was revealed. Wyeth, 69, is one of the most popular living American artists. He is known for his realistic drawings and paintings, which often convey a feeling of sadness or mystery. The 240 newly discovered works had been done over a 15-year period and were kept secret by the artist. All featured the same model, named Helga, who was believed to be a neighbor of Wyeth's in Chadds Ford, Pennsylvania.

The blowout of the year was held in San Francisco's Exploratorium in April, 1986. It was billed as the **2nd Ever Bubble Festival**, and it featured bubble magic, bubble movies, bubbly drinks, and bubbles of all shapes and sizes—including some big enough to blow bubbles in!

Lionel Richie's song "Say You, Say Me" hit the top of the charts in 1986—the ninth year in a row that the 36-year-old singer and songwriter has had a number-one hit. Richie, who was born in Alabama, got his start with the pop group the Commodores. He released his first solo album in 1982 and since then has won armfuls of awards.

With four hit movies behind her—*Tempest, Sixteen Candles, The Breakfast Club,* and *Pretty in Pink*—**Molly Ringwald** had star status in 1986. But the 18-year-old California actress had been working toward that success for a long time. She sang before audiences as a 3-year-old, acted in local theater at 4, recorded an album at 6, and soon began appearing in professional theater and on TV. More movies are in the works.

The Soviet Union's **Kirov Ballet** toured Canada and the United States in 1986—for the first time in 22 years. One of the greatest dance companies in the world, the Kirov is known for the grace and classicism of its performances. It has produced some of the world's most famous ballet dancers, including Anna Pavlova and George Balanchine. During the 1960's, several top Kirov stars defected to the West while on tour, leading the company to cancel its North American visits for many years.

Actor **Clint Eastwood** made a name for himself in "tough guy" roles. In Westerns like *A Fistful of Dollars* and *Pale Rider,* and in detective movies like *Dirty Harry,* he played cowboys and lawmen who battled City Hall to end injustice. But in April, 1986, he took on a new role—*inside* City Hall, as mayor of Carmel-by-the-Sea, California. Eastwood, 55, won the job after a heated campaign in which he proposed that the tiny town of 4,700 people loosen some of its strict regulations against development.

In April, 1986, 81-year-old pianist **Vladimir Horowitz** made a triumphant return to the Soviet Union. Born in Kiev, he had left the country permanently as a 21-year-old and, eventually, made his home in the United States. Horowitz won cheers from audiences and raves from critics on his Soviet tour. In July, back in America, he received the Presidential Medal of Freedom.

The city is a carnival in the works of U.S. artist **Red Grooms**, many of which poke subtle fun at ordinary life. In his *Ruckus Manhattan* (right), viewers move through the sculpture, a wildly painted subway car with larger-than-life papier-mâché figures. This and many other works of the 49-year-old artist—including paintings, lithographs, and films—traveled around the United States in a retrospective exhibition in 1985–86.

THE WAY THEY WERE

Michelangelo's paintings on the ceiling of the Sistine Chapel, done in the early 1500's, are counted among the masterpieces of Western art. For centuries, people have flocked to this chapel in the Vatican to admire the flowing forms and muted colors created by the master. Stories of the paintings are famous: how Michelangelo lay on his back on a tall scaffold, cramped for space, and worked painstakingly from sketches he had made for each section of the ceiling.

The paintings have survived partly because they are frescoes; that is, the paint was applied to wet lime plaster on the ceiling, and it bonded chemically with the plaster. Now the famous paintings are being cleaned and restored—an enormous project that began in 1980 and won't be finished until 1992.

Already, however, the restorers have learned some surprising things about the chapel ceiling. For one thing, Michelangelo didn't lie down to paint it. When workers reconstructed his scaffold, they found there was plenty of room to stand up.

Second, the colors Michelangelo used weren't muted at all—centuries of dirt and smoke from oil lamps had just made them look dull. The master chose vivid reds and greens, bright blues and yellows. And he used colors in unusual ways: To show a fold in a green robe, for example, he used purple rather than a deeper shade of green. And he applied paint in thin layers, for a transparent effect never before seen in frescoes.

Third, Michelangelo painted the ceiling even more carefully than had been supposed, often painting over and correcting mistakes. But on the lunettes—wall panels above the chapel windows—he worked faster. In some cases he didn't bother with preliminary sketches. In his haste he left paintbrush hairs in the paintings. And there are gaps between different painted areas, left when the painter moved his scaffold.

These and other surprises are giving new insights into Michelangelo's work and his importance as an artist. But this isn't the first time that the restoration of a work of art has brought new information to light.

Art restoration has become a science. It makes use of X-ray and infrared photography, laboratory analyses, and a whole battery of chemicals. Experts in this field can find traces of an artist's original sketch beneath an oil painting—or even an earlier work that was painted over. And with new techniques, they can repair damage and preserve great works of art for the future.

ASSESSING THE DAMAGE

The first step in restoring a painting is to assess the damage. A painting may have been scratched or chipped. Air pollution may have faded the colors, or dirt or an old coat of varnish may have darkened them. Moisture may have caused the varnish over an oil painting to "bloom" (turn a cloudy, milky white), made the paint come loose, or set the stage for mildew and fungus to grow

One of Michelangelo's lunettes: Before restoration . . .

on the paint. Dryness may have cracked or flaked the paint, and heat may have blistered it. If the artist used poor quality oil paints, the surface of the painting may have wrinkled. In some old paintings, the top layers of paint have become transparent over time, so that the artist's background brushwork is visible.

The support of a painting—the substance it was painted on—can also be damaged. Canvas can sag and rot. Wood can warp and crack, and plaster can crack and chip.

Previous restorations may have done damage, too. In times past, oil paintings were often dunked in water and scrubbed or stored folded, so that the paint cracked. At one point, Vatican restorers attempted to clean the Sistine Chapel ceiling with wine. Later workers brushed a coat of glue over the ceiling—which only attracted more dirt.

Restorers use several methods to assess damage. First, they look the painting over in strong natural light, perhaps with a magnify-ing glass. Then they shine a beam of strong light across the surface of the painting from the side. In this side light, called a *raking light,* ridges and cracks in the paint show up like the craters and mountains of the moon. The artist's brushstrokes can be seen clearly, so the experts learn about his or her painting style.

Ultraviolet light helps the restorer spot areas where the varnish has cracked or peeled away or where a painting has been retouched. Under this light, different materials glow with different colors. Varnished areas show up yellow-green; unvarnished areas, a dark purple-brown; and recently applied paint, purple.

Computer imaging is a new technique that allows restorers to peer below the top surface of the painting. Section by section, the painting is scanned by a camera and converted to a computer image, which is displayed on a screen. Once the image is in the computer, blurry areas can be sharpened to

. . . and after restoration. His famous Sistine Chapel frescoes are undergoing a major cleaning.

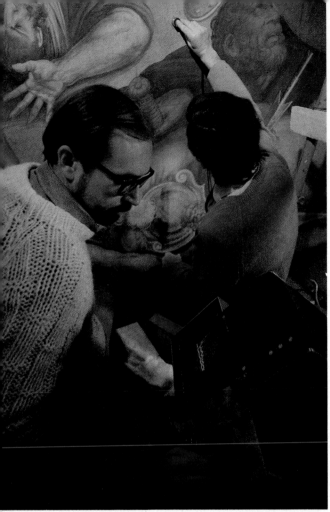

Today ultrasonic scanning and other sophisticated techniques are used to assess damage to works of art.

ors. Beyond the layers of paint, the structure of the painting's support will show up on an X ray as well. *Ultrasonic scanning* is a newer technique that will also peer beneath the paint and reveal damage.

Finally, *microscopic examination* and *chemical analyses* give information about the paint the artist used and about its condition. Experts often rely on chemical analyses when they are trying to find out if the painting is genuine or fake or whether it has been touched up. For example, they may find that a painting supposedly from the 1500's contains pigments that weren't invented until the 1700's. A new technique, *laser analysis,* gives even more information about paints. Lasers scan the painting layer by layer. The laser heats the paint slightly, and by recording the paint's response, restorers can learn about the qualities of the pigments the artist used. The laser can even reveal how well the paint has adhered to the surface.

CONSOLIDATION

The next step in restoring a painting may be to clean it. But if the paint is loose, the restorer will first want to reattach it to the support, a process called consolidation.

Flaking paint can be reattached by dripping a wax-resin compound onto the surface and carefully working it under the loose paint, using an electric heating iron that looks something like a spatula. To flatten blisters, they are first injected with a special type of glue. Then the restorer puts a tissue over the paint to protect it, heats it carefully with the heating iron, and gently pushes the blister down. Wrinkles can also be smoothed out with heat.

Holes and tears in canvas are filled and patched from behind, using canvas that matches the original and plastic adhesives. When the canvas is badly deteriorated, the restorer may add a new canvas lining. The painting is put face down on a work table, and the back is coated with a wax-resin mixture. Then a new canvas lining is placed over the wax and simply ironed on. (Some restorers use special lining tables, in which the work surface heats up to melt the wax and pressure is applied with vacuum suction rather than an iron.)

Paintings on wooden panels may warp or

reveal details. And some colors can be filtered out, to reveal more about what lies underneath the paint. When this technique was used on Leonardo da Vinci's famous *Mona Lisa,* traces of a pearl necklace, later painted over, were found on the subject's neck.

Infrared light also penetrates through the upper layers of paint to show the underlying foundation of an artist's composition. Sometimes it reveals details and objects that were lost in shadow; sometimes, an artist's signature or the original sketch beneath the paint. One of the newest methods combines infrared light and computer imaging.

X rays can penetrate still farther. They record only white pigments containing lead. If these pigments were used in the painting, they will appear on the X ray even if the artist later painted over them with dark col-

crack when the wood dries out. To correct warping, restorers put the panels in a humid area and gradually add weights to flatten them out. Cracks are fixed with glue, and chips and holes are filled in with putty or another material. Wooden braces, or cradles, are often attached to the backs of the panels to keep these problems from developing again.

When a painting's support is very badly damaged, restorers can even transfer the paint onto a completely new backing. First, the paint is protected with layers of paper and fabric, held in place with soluble glue. Then, bit by bit, the old backing is scraped, peeled, or sanded away. Even the ground—the coating the artist used to prepare the painting surface—can be almost entirely removed if it is damaged. Then a new ground is brushed on, and a lightweight fabric support is embedded in it. Finally the painting is attached to a new canvas lining or a new wooden panel, and the protective paper on the front is removed.

CLEANING AND RETOUCHING

Restorers use many different special compounds to clean paintings, depending on the type of paint and support. Some are designed to remove grime, and others to remove old layers of varnish as well. (When the varnish is removed from an oil painting, a new coat is usually put on to protect the paint and to bring out its colors.) Generally the restorers work on one small area at a time. On the Sistine Chapel ceiling, for example, workers clean areas 12 inches (30 centimeters) square with a solvent, quickly wiping the solvent off before it can damage the paint.

Cleaning may reveal new colors and details that were hidden under centuries of dirt. It may also reveal clumsy attempts at retouching, or painting over, damaged areas. An earlier restorer may have been fooled by the dirt and used the wrong colors. Or the touch-up job may have been sloppy.

Skilled restorers can carefully scrape these mistakes away or remove them with solvents. Then the painting can be retouched again. This takes great artistic skill—the paint in the touched-up area must be built up to the level of the surrounding paint, and the pigments and brushstrokes must match the original. It's also important not to let the new paint overlap the original paint at any point.

Cleaning and restoring famous works of art has often produced controversy. People aren't always happy when their favorite paintings suddenly have new colors and details that were never noticeable before. But more often, the process brings greater understanding of art. For example, when a work by the 17th-century Spanish painter Diego Velázquez was cleaned several years ago, art historians were amazed to find brushstrokes similar to those of the French impressionists, who painted 300 years later.

The techniques of art restoration are being used to save many other major works. They range from Leonardo da Vinci's famous fresco *The Last Supper* in Milan, Italy (which began to peel soon after it was painted in 1495) to ancient Buddhist wall paintings in Indian caves. And the scientific approach taken in these restorations has also shed new light on how to preserve works of art—with filtered air and controls on temperature and humidity. In this way, they can be enjoyed for centuries to come.

Restorers must have great artistic skills. They often work many months repairing the damage to a work of art.

Rue McClanahan, Bea Arthur, and Betty White (best actress, comedy series) in "The Golden Girls" (best comedy series).

1986 EMMY AWARDS

CATEGORY	WINNER
Comedy Series	"The Golden Girls"
Actor—comedy series	Michael J. Fox, "Family Ties"
Actress—comedy series	Betty White, "The Golden Girls"
Supporting Actor—comedy series	John Larroquette, "Night Court"
Supporting Actress—comedy series	Rhea Perlman, "Cheers"
Drama Series	"Cagney & Lacey"
Actor—drama series	William Daniels, "St. Elsewhere"
Actress—drama series	Sharon Gless, "Cagney & Lacey"
Supporting Actor—drama series	John Karlen, "Cagney & Lacey"
Supporting Actress—drama series	Bonnie Bartlett, "St. Elsewhere"
Special—drama	"Love Is Never Silent"
Special—variety, music, or comedy	"The Kennedy Center Honors: A Celebration of the Performing Arts"

Tyne Daly and Sharon Gless
(best actress, drama series)
in "Cagney & Lacey."

Michael J. Fox (best actor,
comedy series) in "Family Ties."

FUN
TO
READ

Milton, Rupert, and Lydia are the stars of It's Mine!, *a charming fable about three frogs who live on an island in the middle of Rainbow Pond. The three quarrel and quibble from dawn to dusk until an emergency—a storm that floods the island—teaches them the importance of cooperation. Leo Lionni wrote this picture book and did the cheerful collage illustrations that accompany the story.*

The Pied Piper of Hamelin

The West German town of Hameln is probably one of the few places on Earth to become famous for its rats. Actually, it wasn't the rats themselves that brought renown to this town on the banks of the Weser River—it was a strange legend that grew up about them in the Middle Ages.

The legend is the story of the Pied Piper of Hamelin (as the town's name was spelled in earlier times), and it has been told in many forms. One of the most famous versions, a poem by Robert Browning, is reproduced here. According to the tale, to get rid of the town's hordes of rats, the town council hired a piper (called "pied" for his multicolored clothes) with magical powers. When he played, all the rats came tumbling out and followed him to the river, where they drowned. But the town refused to pay the piper, and he took a terrible revenge. He played his pipe and lured all the town's children away. They were never seen again.

No one is sure when these events took place. Some town records give 1284 as the year. Browning gives 1376. Most historians say, however, that these events most likely never took place at all. Instead, they say, the story of the rats and the piper grew up around some other event that involved the disappearance of many children from the town. Some think the event was a crusade to the Holy Land, although the last children's crusade took place many years earlier. Others think the children were sent to colonize vacant lands.

All the same, the story made Hameln famous. Today it's a quaint town, with many old buildings. If you visit, you'll see a clock on which figures of the piper, the rats, and the children come out to chime the hour. And once a week, local children re-enact the tale, following a piper who dances through the streets. Of course, when the show is over, the children go home!

Hamelin Town's in Brunswick
By famous Hanover city;
  The river Weser, deep and wide,
  Washes its wall on the southern side;
  A pleasanter spot you never spied;

But, when begins my ditty,
  Almost five hundred years ago,
  To see the townsfolk suffer so
    From vermin was a pity.
                              Rats!

They fought the dogs, and killed the cats,
  And bit the babies in the cradles,
And ate the cheeses out of the vats,
  And licked the soup from the cook's own ladles,
Split open the kegs of salted sprats,
Made nests inside men's Sunday hats,
And even spoiled the women's chats,
  By drowning their speaking
  With shrieking and squeaking
In fifty different sharps and flats.

At last the people in a body
  To the Town Hall came flocking:
" 'Tis clear," cried they, "our Mayor's a noddy;
  And as for our Corporation—shocking
To think that we buy gowns lined with ermine
For dolts that can't or won't determine
What's best to rid us of our vermin!
You hope, because you're old and obese,
To find in the furry civic robe ease?
Rouse up, sirs! Give your brain a racking
To find the remedy we're lacking,
Or, sure as fate, we'll send you packing!"
At this the Mayor and Corporation
Quaked with a mighty consternation.

An hour they sat in council,
  At length the Mayor broke silence:
"For a guilder I'd my ermine gown sell;
  I wish I were a mile hence!
It's easy to bid one rack one's brain—
I'm sure my poor head aches again
I've scratched it so, and all in vain,
  Oh for a trap, a trap, a trap!"
Just as he said this, what should hap
At the chamber door but a gentle tap?
  "Bless us," cried the Mayor, "what's that?"

(With the Corporation as he sat,
Looking little though wondrous fat;
Nor brighter was his eye, nor moister,

Than a too-long-opened oyster,
Save when at noon his paunch grew mutinous
For a plate of turtle green and glutinous),
  "Only a scraping of shoes on the mat?
  Anything like the sound of a rat
  Makes my heart go pit-a-pat!"

"Come in!"—the Mayor cried, looking bigger:
And in did come the strangest figure.
His queer long coat from heel to head
Was half of yellow and half of red;
And he himself was tall and thin,
With sharp blue eyes, each like a pin,
And light loose hair, yet swarthy skin,
No tuft on cheek nor beard on chin,
But lips where smiles went out and in—
There was no guessing his kith and kin!
And nobody could enough admire
The tall man and his quaint attire.
Quoth one: "It's as my great grandsire,
Starting up at the Trump of Doom's tone,
Had walked this way from his painted tombstone."

He advanced to the council-table:
And, "Please, your honours," said he, "I'm able,
  By means of a secret charm, to draw
  All creatures living beneath the sun,
  That creep, or swim, or fly, or run,
  After me so as you never saw!
  And I chiefly use my charm
  On creatures that do people harm,
  The mole, and toad, and newt, and viper;
  And people call me the Pied Piper."
(And there they noticed round his neck

A scarf of red and yellow stripe,
To match with his coat of the selfsame cheque;
  And at the scarf's end hung a pipe;
And his fingers, they noticed, were ever straying
As if impatient to be playing
Upon this pipe, as low it dangled
Over his vesture so old-fangled.)
  "Yet," said he, "poor piper as I am,
  In Tartary I freed the Cham,
  Last June, from his huge swarms of gnats;
  I eased in Asia the Nizam
  Of a monstrous brood of vampire bats:
  And, as for what your brain bewilders,
  If I can rid your town of rats
  Will you give me a thousand guilders?"
  "One? fifty thousand!"—was the exclamation
Of the astonished Mayor and Corporation.

Into the street the Piper stept,
  Smiling first a little smile,
As if he knew what magic slept
  In his quiet pipe the while;
Then, like a musical adept,
To blow the pipe his lips he wrinkled,
And green and blue his sharp eyes twinkled
Like a candle-flame where salt is sprinkled;
And ere three shrill notes the pipe uttered,
You heard as if an army muttered;
And the muttering grew to a grumbling;
And the grumbling grew to a mighty rumbling;
And out of the house the rats came tumbling.
Great rats, small rats, lean rats, brawny rats,
Brown rats, black rats, gray rats, tawny rats,

Grave old plodders, gay young friskers,
  Fathers, mothers, uncles, cousins,
Cocking tails and pricking whiskers,
  Families by tens and dozens,
Brothers, sisters, husbands, wives—
Followed the Piper for their lives.
From street to street he piped advancing,
And step by step they followed dancing,
Until they came to the river Weser
Wherein all plunged and perished
—Save one, who, stout as Julius Caesar,
Swam across and lived to carry
(As he the manuscript he cherished)
To Rat-land home his commentary,
Which was, "At the first shrill notes of the pipe,
I heard a sound as of scraping tripe,
And putting apples, wondrous ripe,
Into a cider press's gripe;
And a moving away of pickle-tubboards,
And a leaving ajar of conserve cupboards,
And a drawing the corks of train-oil-flasks,
And a breaking the hoops of butter casks;
And it seemed as if a voice
(Sweeter far than by harp or by psaltery
Is breathed) called out, Oh, rats! rejoice!
The world is grown to one vast drysaltery!
To munch on, crunch on, take your nuncheon,
Breakfast, supper, dinner, luncheon!
And just as a bulky sugar puncheon,
All ready staved, like a great sun shone
Glorious scarce an inch before me,
Just as methought it said, come, bore me!
—I found the Weser rolling o'er me."

You should have heard the Hamelin people
Ringing the bells till they rocked the steeple.
  ''Go,'' cried the Mayor, ''and get long poles!
  Poke out the nests and block up the holes!
  Consult with carpenters and builders,
  And leave in our town not even a trace
  Of the rats!''—when suddenly up the face
  Of the Piper perked in the market-place,
With a, ''First, if you please, my thousand guilders!''

A thousand guilders! The Mayor looked blue;
So did the Corporation too.
For council dinners made rare havoc
With Claret, Moselle, Vin-de-Grave, Hock;
And half the money would replenish
Their cellar's biggest butt with Rhenish.
To pay this sum to a wandering fellow
With a gipsy coat of red and yellow!
  ''Beside,'' quoth the Mayor, with a knowing wink,
  ''Our business was done at the river's brink;
  We saw with our eyes the vermin sink,
  And what's dead can't come to life, I think.
  So, friend, we're not the folks to shrink
  From the duty of giving you something to drink,

And a matter of money to put in your poke,
But, as for the guilders, what we spoke
Of them, as you very well know, was in joke.
Besides, our losses have made us thrifty;
A thousand guilders! Come, take fifty!''

The Piper's face fell, and he cried,
''No trifling! I can't wait, beside!
I've promised to visit by dinnertime
Bagdad, and accepted the prime
Of the Head Cook's pottage, all he's rich in,
For having left the Caliph's kitchen,
Of a nest of scorpions no survivor—
With him I proved no bargain-driver,
With you, don't think I'll bate a stiver!
And folks who put me in a passion
May find me pipe to another fashion.''
''How?'' cried the Mayor, ''d'ye think I'll brook
Being worse treated than a Cook?
Insulted by a lazy ribald
With idle pipe and vesture piebald?
You threaten us, fellow? Do your worst,
Blow your pipe there till you burst!''

Once more he stept into the street;
  And to his lips again
Laid his long pipe of smooth straight cane;
  And ere he blew three notes (such sweet
Soft notes as yet musicians cunning
  Never gave the enraptured air),

There was a rustling, that seemed like a bustling
Of merry crowds justling, at pitching and hustling,
Small feet were pattering, wooden shoes clattering,
Little hands clapping, and little tongues chattering,
And, like fowls in a farmyard when barley is scattering,
Out came the children running.
All the little boys and girls,
With rosy cheeks and flaxen curls,
And sparkling eyes and teeth like pearls,
Tripping and skipping, ran merrily after
The wonderful music with shouting and laughter.
The Mayor was dumb, and the Council stood
As if they were changed into blocks of wood,
Unable to move a step, or cry
To the children merrily skipping by—
And could only follow with the eye
That joyous crowd at the Piper's back.
But how the Mayor was on the rack,
And the wretched Council's bosoms beat,
As the Piper turned from the High Street
To where the Weser rolled its waters
Right in the way of their sons and daughters!
However, he turned from South to West,
And to Koppelberg Hill his steps addressed,
And after him the children pressed;
Great was the joy in every breast.
   "He never can cross that mighty top!
   He's forced to let the piping drop,
   And we shall see our children stop!"
When lo! as they reached the mountain's side,
A wondrous portal opened wide,
As if a cavern was suddenly hollowed;
And the Piper advanced and the children followed,

And when all were in to the very last,
The door in the mountain-side shut fast.
Did I say all? No! one was lame,
And could not dance the whole of the way;
And in after years, if you would blame
His sadness, he was used to say:
   "It's dull in our town since my playmates left;
   I can't forget that I'm bereft
   Of all the pleasant sights they see,
   Which the Piper also promised me;
   For he led us, he said, to a joyous land,
   Joining the town and just at hand,
Where waters gushed and fruit trees grew,
And flowers put forth a fairer hue,
And everything was strange and new.
The sparrows were brighter than peacocks here,
And their dogs outran our fallow deer,
And honey-bees had lost their stings;
And horses were born with eagle's wings;
And just as I became assured
My lame foot would be speedily cured,
The music stopped, and I stood still,
And found myself outside the Hill,
Left alone against my will,
To go now limping as before,
And never hear of that country more!"

Alas, alas for Hamelin!
   There came into many a burgher's pate
   A text which says, that Heaven's Gate
   Opes to the Rich at as easy rate
As the needle's eye takes a camel in!

The Mayor sent East, West, North and South,
To offer the Piper by word of mouth,
    Wherever it was men's lot to find him,
Silver and gold to his heart's content,
If he'd only return the way he went,
    And bring the children all behind him.
But when they saw 'twas a lost endeavour,
And Piper and dancers were gone forever
They made a decree that lawyers never
    Should think their records dated duly
If, after the day of the month and year,
These words did not as well appear,
    "And so long after what happened here
    On the twenty-second of July,
    Thirteen hundred and seventy-six:"
And the better in memory to fix
The place of the Children's last retreat,
They called it, the Pied Piper's street—
Where any one playing on pipe or tabor,
Was sure for the future to lose his labour.
Nor suffered they hostelry or tavern
    To shock with mirth a street so solemn;
But opposite the place of the cavern
    They wrote the story on a column,

And on the great church window painted
The same, to make the world acquainted
How their children were stolen away;
And there it stands to this very day.
And I must not omit to say
That in Transylvania there's a tribe
Of alien people that ascribe
The outlandish ways and dress,
On which their neighbours lay such stress,
To their fathers and mothers having risen
Out of some subterraneous prison,
Into which they were trepanned
Long time ago in a mighty band
Out of Hamelin town in Brunswick land,
But how or why they don't understand.

So, Willy, let you and me be wipers
Of scores out with all men—especially pipers;
And, whether they pipe us free from rats or from mice,
If we've promised them aught, let us keep our promise.

Haiku: Poetry In Miniature

All the rains of June:
and then one evening, secretly,
through the pines, the moon!
Ōshima Ryōta (1718–87)

In just a few words, the poet who wrote these few lines captured the image of a late spring night. You can almost feel the soft

Haiku have long been very popular with the Japanese. In times past, master poets spent their whole lives composing haiku.

Frost on the Country Side,
by Honda Tojo

breeze that clears away the clouds after the rain, see the moon peeking through, and smell the damp pine needles on the ground.

The poem is a haiku, a traditional Japanese verse. Like many Japanese art forms, the haiku at its best is a perfectly crafted miniature, giving readers new insight into its subject. These poems have a set form and usually take some aspect of nature as their subject.

Today the haiku is appreciated all around the world. People read the poems of ancient Japanese masters in translation, and they write haiku in their own languages.

THE HAIKU FORM

Haiku developed from a form of ancient Japanese verse called *tanka,* which means "short poem." The *tanka* has five lines: a three-line opening, and a couplet that is linked to the opening and completes the thought of the poem. Thousands of these poems were written over the centuries. Often they were written by two poets in collaboration—one composed the opening three lines (or *hokku*), and the other produced the linking couplet.

Later, chains of these linked poems were strung together, forming longer works called *renga*. The stanzas often seemed to skip from subject to subject, but each was linked

The three lines of a haiku have seventeen syllables—usually five in the first line, seven in the second, and five in the third. But the rhyme and meter typical of Western poems don't appear in haiku. Instead, the Japanese poet relies on such literary devices as assonance (the repetition of vowel sounds) and alliteration (the repetition of consonants). In a short verse form like this, the poet must choose words carefully—every one must be lively and add something to the picture.

Walking Alone in Spring,
by Okuno Sakae

to the one before by the feeling it produced. By the 1600's, writing *renga* had become a popular entertainment. Such verses were frequently composed on the spur of the moment, at poetry-making parties.

The first haiku, then, were simple *hokku* that stood alone. (The name "haiku" means "game verse" and was first applied to these poems in the 1800's.) And as the haiku form developed, so did elaborate rules.

In traditional haiku, subject as well as form is restricted. The poet chooses some detail of nature (including human nature) and selects words that will convey its image. The Japanese love of nature and close observation of its details are understandable—with its mountains and rugged coasts, flowering trees and gardens, Japan is a country of great natural beauty.

Many of the images presented in traditional Japanese haiku are also connected in some way with Buddhist philosophy. But, even without knowledge of the philosophy, the poems can be appreciated as gemlike images of the natural world. And at their best, haiku are more than word pictures. They convey meaning and perhaps reveal the inner nature of their subjects. Often the last line of the poem contains a little twist or surprise—a contrasting image that helps the reader see the subject in a new way.

Each haiku is also supposed to contain a word or a phrase that will tell the reader what season is being described. The poet need not name the season, but there are stock words that are used. Spring, for example, may be evoked by nightingales and swallows, cherry and plum blossoms, spring rain and haze. Cuckoos, fireflies, poppies,

Song of a Summer Shower,
by Yuki Somei

and morning glories refer to summer. Fall is suggested by the harvest moon and wild geese; winter, by frost and snow.

In its ability to call up a powerful image in just a few words, the haiku is like Japanese and Chinese ink paintings. These paintings present their subjects with a few simple brushstrokes, leaving the rest of the picture to the imagination. In fact, haiku are often accompanied by *haiga*, rough sketches done with the writing brush. A *haiga* doesn't always illustrate the same scene that is evoked by the haiku it accompanies. But, in their own way, these drawings are designed to produce the same feelings in the reader.

MASTERS OF THE HAIKU

Many poets have written great haiku, but four Japanese have been considered masters of the form. The first of these was Matsuo Bashō (1644–94). Bashō lived when the linked-verse form *renga* was at the height of its popularity. And he earned his living by traveling from place to place, teaching the craft of writing these poems.

Bashō felt that much of the poetry being written in his time was superficial and common. He told his students that just looking at an object wasn't enough—the poet had to study the subject and learn its inner nature. "Learn of the pine from the pine; learn of the bamboo from the bamboo," he wrote. Then, he said, the words of the poem should make the inner nature of the object plain.

> *Into the darkness*
> *which a lightning-streak has slashed,*
> *recedes the wild night-heron's shriek.*

The second haiku master, Yosa Buson (1716–84), was much influenced by Bashō's work. Like Bashō, he felt the poetry of his day had become stale and superficial, and he urged a return to the first master's principles. Buson was primarily a painter, and he illustrated both his own and Bashō's work. He brought his painter's eye to his poetry, observing fine details in nature.

> *Without a sound, the white camellia fell,*
> *To sound the darkness*
> *of the deep stone well.*

Kobayashi Issa (1763–1823) was less worldly and sophisticated than Bashō and

Buson. But his poems are among the most popular of all haiku. Issa often chose commonplace subjects—grasshoppers, flies, a beggar by the side of the road—that few people appreciated. His poems showed the humor, gentleness, and beauty these subjects contained. This poem was written when he was 6.

Oh, ragged sparrow without any mother,
When we are lonely,
let's play with each other!

By the time of Masaoka Shiki (1867–1902), the last of the four great masters, few *renga* were being written. Most poets concentrated on producing individual verses, and Shiki was the first to give the name "haiku" to the three-line stanzas that had once been part of *tanka* and *renga*. Staying within the traditional form, he chose new subjects and took a fresh look at many old ones. For this, he is credited with bringing haiku into the modern age.

White with hoarfrost
lies the garden bed,
On which one berry drops, a lively red.

Many other poets have continued the tradition of the masters, each making his or her own contribution to the haiku form. And many of the most famous haiku have been translated into other languages.

TRANSLATING HAIKU

Haiku can be written in any language, fitting the words into the proper three lines and seventeen syllables. But translating Japanese works into English poses problems: It's rarely possible to find English words that evoke the same feelings as the Japanese words and still fit the strict haiku form. Thus translators must also be poets—interpreting the haiku and writing it anew. Notice, for example, the haiku used in this article. All were translated from the Japanese. They don't fit the strict haiku seventeen-syllable form, but they contain the essence of the masters' poems.

Sometimes several poets may translate the same haiku, and it will appear in different versions. Here is a haiku by Bashō (one that he said was a model of his style) and three different translations:

Autumn in a Mountain Village,
by Ishikawa Kinichiro

furuike ya
kawazu tobikomu
mizu no oto

old pond . . .	the old pond!
a frog leaps in	A frog jumps in:
water's sound	the sound of the water!

The old green pond is silent; here the hop
Of a frog plumbs the evening stillness: plop!

In each of these versions, the translator has chosen the words and form that seem to best convey the feeling of the original. The results, however, are quite different from each other. Nevertheless, through translations the beauty of Japanese haiku can be appreciated by everyone.

The world that the English writer Rudyard Kipling created for children is a magical one. It's a world where animals speak and have spine-tingling adventures in far-off, exotic lands. Although Kipling's stories were written nearly a hundred years ago, they remain favorites with young people today.

Kipling was a product of the British Empire. He was born in India in 1865 and learned the language and culture of that country as a young boy. (India was a British colony at that time.) At 5, he was sent to live in England, where he attended school. There, he first began to write, and he later recalled his school days in the book Stalky and Co. (1899). He returned to India in 1882 and began a career as a newspaper reporter. He also wrote short stories and poems. By the time Kipling went back to England, in 1889, he was already a well-known author. He published a novel, The Light That Failed, two years later.

Kipling traveled widely, visiting America, South Africa, New Zealand, and Australia as well as India. In 1892 he married Carrie (Caroline Starr) Balestier and moved with her to Vermont. There, after their first child was born, he wrote The Jungle Books (1894–95). These stories tell mostly of Mowgli, an Indian boy raised by animals. During his Vermont years he also wrote Captains Courageous (which was published in 1897). Kipling continued to write for children as well as for adults after returning to England in 1896, producing Kim (1901), the Just So Stories (1902), and other works. And he continued to travel, often to South Africa.

In 1907, Kipling was awarded the Nobel Prize for Literature. He also received many other awards, and at his death in 1936 he was one of Britain's most honored writers. Today some of his works seem out of date. They reflect the British colonial view that whites had an obligation to bring "civilization" to the other peoples of the world. But many of the tales he wrote are just as wonderful today as they were when they first appeared. Here is one of them—the story of the Indian mongoose Rikki-tikki-tavi, adapted from the first Jungle Book.

Rikki-tikki-tavi

This is the story of the great war that Rikki-tikki-tavi fought single-handed. Darzee, the tailorbird, helped him, and Chuchundra, the muskrat, who never comes out into the middle of the floor, but always creeps by the wall, gave him advice. But Rikki-tikki did the real fighting.

He was a mongoose, rather like a little cat in his fur and his tail, but quite like a weasel in his head and his habits. His eyes and the end of his restless nose were pink. He could scratch himself anywhere he pleased, with any leg, front or back, that he chose to use. He could fluff up his tail till it looked like a bottle-brush, and his war cry as he scuttled through the long grass was "*Rikk-tikk-tikki-tikki-tchk!*"

One day, a high summer flood washed him out of the burrow where he lived with his father and mother, and carried him, kicking and clucking, down a roadside ditch. He found a little wisp of grass floating there and clung to it till he lost his senses. When he revived, he was lying in the hot sun in the middle of a garden path, very draggled indeed, and a small boy was saying: "Here's a dead mongoose. Let's have a funeral."

"No," said his mother. "Let's take him in and dry him. Perhaps he isn't really dead."

They took him into the house, and a big man picked him up between his finger and thumb and said he was not dead but half choked. So they wrapped him in cotton-wool and warmed him, and he opened his eyes and sneezed.

"Now," said the big man (he was an Englishman who had just moved into the bungalow), "don't frighten him, and we'll see what he'll do."

It is the hardest thing in the world to frighten a mongoose because he is eaten up from nose to tail with curiosity. The motto of all the mongoose family is "Run and find out"; and Rikki-tikki was a true mongoose. He looked up, ran around the table, sat up and put his fur in order, scratched himself, and jumped on the small boy's shoulder.

"Don't be frightened, Teddy," said his father. "That's his way of making friends."

"Ouch! He's tickling under my chin," said Teddy.

Rikki-tikki looked down between the boy's collar and neck, snuffed at his ear, and climbed down to the floor.

"Good gracious," said Teddy's mother, "and that's a wild creature! I suppose he's so tame because we've been kind to him."

"All mongooses are like that," said her husband. "If Teddy doesn't pick him up by the tail or try to put him in a cage, he'll run in and out of the house all day long. Let's give him something to eat."

They gave him a little piece of raw meat. Rikki-tikki liked it immensely, and when it was finished he went out onto the veranda and sat in the sunshine and fluffed up his fur to make it dry to the roots. Then he felt better.

"There are more things to find out about in this house," he said to himself, "than all my family could find out in all their lives. I shall certainly stay and find out."

He spent all that day roaming over the house. He nearly drowned himself in the bathtub, put his nose into the ink on a

writing table, and burned it on the end of the big man's cigar, for he climbed up in the big man's lap to see how writing was done. At nightfall he ran into Teddy's nursery to watch how kerosene lamps were lighted, and when Teddy went to bed Rikki-tikki climbed up too. But he was a restless companion because he had to get up and attend to every noise all through the night and find out what made it. Teddy's mother and father came in, the last thing, to look at their boy, and Rikki-tikki was awake on the pillow. "I don't like that," said Teddy's mother. "He may bite the child." "He'll do no such thing," said the father. "Teddy's safer with that little beast than if he had a bloodhound to watch him. If a snake came into the nursery now . . ."

But Teddy's mother wouldn't think of anything so awful.

Early in the morning Rikki-tikki came to breakfast on the veranda riding on Teddy's shoulder, and they gave him a banana and some boiled egg.

Then Rikki-tikki went out into the garden to see what was to be seen. It was a large garden, only half cultivated, with rose bushes as big as summer houses, lime and orange trees, clumps of bamboo, and thickets of high grass. Rikki-tikki licked his lips. "This is a splendid hunting-ground," he said, and he scuttled up and down the garden, snuffing here and there till he heard very sorrowful voices in a thornbush.

It was Darzee, the tailorbird, and his wife. They had made a beautiful nest by pulling two big leaves together and stitching them up the edges with fibers, and had filled the hollow with cotton and downy fluff. The nest swayed to and fro, as they sat on the rim and cried.

"What is the matter?" asked Rikki-tikki.

"We are very miserable," said Darzee. "One of our babies fell out of the nest yesterday and Nag ate him."

"H'm!" said Rikki-tikki, "that is very sad—but I am a stranger here. Who is Nag?"

Darzee and his wife only cowered down in the nest without answering, for from the thick grass at the foot of the bush there came a low hiss—a horrid cold sound that made Rikki-tikki jump back two feet. Then inch by inch out of the grass rose up the head and spread hood of Nag, the big black cobra, and he was five feet long from tongue to tail. When he had lifted one-third of himself clear of the ground, he stayed balancing to and fro exactly as a dandelion tuft balances in the wind, and he looked at Rikki-tikki with the wicked snake's eyes that never change their expression, whatever the snake may be thinking of.

"Who is Nag?" he said. "*I* am Nag. The great god Brahm put his mark upon all our people when the first cobra spread his hood to keep the sun off Brahm as he slept. Look, and be afraid!"

He spread out his hood even more, and Rikki-tikki saw the spectacle-mark on the back of it that looks exactly like the eye part of a hook-and-eye fastening. He was afraid for a minute. But it is impossible for a mongoose to stay frightened for long, and though Rikki-tikki had never met a cobra before, he knew that a mongoose's purpose in life was to fight and eat snakes. Nag knew that too, and at the bottom of his cold heart he was afraid.

"Well," said Rikki-tikki, and his tail began to fluff up again, "marks or no marks, do you think it is right for you to eat fledglings out of a nest?"

Nag was thinking to himself and watching a little movement in the grass behind Rikki-tikki. He knew that mongooses in the garden meant death sooner or later for him and his family. But he wanted to get Rikki-tikki off his guard. So he dropped his head a little and put it on one side.

"Let us talk," he said. "You eat eggs. Why should I not eat birds?"

"Behind you! Look behind you!" sang Darzee.

Rikki-tikki jumped up in the air as high as he could go, and just under him whizzed by the head of Nagaina, Nag's wicked wife. She had crept up behind him as he was talking, to make an end of him, and he heard her savage hiss as the stroke missed. He came down almost across her back, and if he had been an older mongoose he would have known that then was the time to break her back with one bite. But he was afraid of the terrible lashing return-stroke of the cobra. He bit, indeed, but did not bite long enough, and he jumped clear of the whisking tail, leaving Nagaina torn and angry.

"Wicked Darzee!" said Nag, lashing up as high as he could reach toward the nest in the thornbush. But Darzee had built it out of reach of snakes, and it only swayed to and fro.

Rikki-tikki felt his eyes growing red and hot (when a mongoose's eyes grow red, he is angry), and he sat back on his tail and hind legs like a little kangaroo and looked all around him, and chattered with rage. But Nag and Nagaina had disappeared into the grass. So he trotted off to the gravel path near the house and sat down to think. Just then, Teddy came running down the path, and Rikki-tikki was ready to be petted.

But just as Teddy was stooping, something flinched a little in the dust, and a tiny voice said: "Be careful. I am death!"

It was Karait, the dusty brown snakeling whose bite is as dangerous as the cobra's. But he is so small that nobody thinks of him, and so he does more harm to people.

Rikki-tikki's eyes grew red again, and he danced up to Karait with the peculiar rocking, swaying motion that he had inherited from his family. It looks very funny, but it is so perfectly balanced a gait that you can fly off from it at any angle you please, and in dealing with snakes this is an advantage. If Rikki-tikki had only known, he was doing a much more dangerous thing than fighting Nag, for Karait is so small, and can turn so quickly, that unless Rikki bit him close to the back of the head, he would get the return-stroke in his eye or lip. But Rikki did not know. His eyes were all red and he rocked back and forth, looking for a good place to hold. Karait struck out. Rikki jumped sideways and tried to run in, but the wicked little dusty gray head lashed within a fraction of his shoulder, and he had to jump over the body, and the head followed his heels close.

Teddy shouted to the house: "Oh, look here! Our mongoose is killing a snake." And Rikki-tikki heard a scream from Teddy's mother. His father ran out with a stick, but by the time he came up, Karait had lunged out once too far, and Rikki-tikki had sprung, jumped on the snake's back, bitten as high up the back as he could get hold, and rolled away. That bite paralyzed Karait, and Rikki-tikki was just going to eat him when he remembered that a full meal makes a slow mongoose. If he wanted all his strength and quickness, he must keep himself thin.

Then Teddy's mother picked him up and hugged him, and Teddy's father said that he had saved Teddy from death, and Teddy looked on with big scared eyes. Rikki-tikki was amused at the fuss.

That night, at dinner, he could have stuffed himself with nice things. But he remembered Nag and Nagaina, and though it was pleasant to be petted by Teddy's mother, and to sit on Teddy's shoulder, his eyes would get red from time to time, and he would chant his long war cry of "*Rikk-tikk-tikki-tikki-tchk!*"

Teddy carried him off to bed and insisted on Rikki-tikki sleeping under his chin. Rikki-tikki was too well bred to bite or scratch, but as soon as Teddy was alseep he went off for his nightly walk around the house. In the dark he ran up against Chuchundra, the muskrat, creeping round by the wall. Chuchundra is a broken-hearted little beast. He whimpers and cheeps all night, trying to make up his mind to run into the middle of the room, but he never gets there.

"Don't kill me," said Chuchundra, almost weeping. "Rikki-tikki, don't kill me."

"Do you think a snake-killer kills muskrats?" said Rikki-tikki scornfully.

"Those who kill snakes get killed by snakes," said Chuchundra, more sorrowfully than ever. "And how am I to be sure that Nag won't mistake me for you some dark night?"

"There's not the least danger," said Rikki-tikki. "But Nag is in the garden, and I know you don't go there."

"My cousin Chua, the rat, told me . . ." said Chuchundra, and then he stopped.

"Told you what?"

"Hush! Nag is everywhere, Rikki-tikki. You should have talked to Chua in the garden."

"I didn't—so you must tell me. Quick, Chuchundra, or I'll bite you!"

Chuchundra cried till the tears rolled off his whiskers. "I never had spirit enough to run out into the middle of the room! I mustn't tell you anything! Can't you *hear*, Rikki-tikki?"

Rikki-tikki listened. The house was as still as still, but he thought he could just catch the faintest scratch-scratch—a noise as faint as that of a wasp walking on a windowpane—the dry scratch of a snake's scales on brickwork.

"That's Nag or Nagaina," he said to himself. "And he is crawling into the bathroom sluice."

Rikki stole off to the bathroom. At the bottom of the smooth plaster wall there was a brick pulled out to make a sluice for the bathwater. And as Rikki-tikki crept in, he heard Nag and Nagaina whispering together outside in the moonlight.

"When the house is emptied of people," said Nagaina to her husband, "*he* will have to go away, and then the garden will be our own again. Now, go in quietly."

"But are you sure that there is anything to be gained by killing the people?" said Nag.

"Everything. When there were no people in the bungalow, did we have any mongoose in the garden? So long as the bungalow is empty, we are king and queen of the garden. And remember that as soon as our eggs in the melon patch hatch (which may be tomorrow), our children will need room and quiet."

"I had not thought of that," said Nag. "I will go and kill the big man and his wife, and the child if I can, and come away."

Rikki-tikki tingled all over with rage and hatred at this, and then Nag's head came through the sluice, and his five feet of cold body followed it. Angry as he was, Rikki-tikki was very frightened as he saw the size of the big cobra. Nag coiled himself up, raised his head, and looked into the bathroom in the dark, and Rikki could see his eyes glitter.

"Now, if I kill him here, Nagaina will know. And if I fight him on the open floor, the odds are in his favor. What am I to do?" said Rikki-tikki-tavi.

Nag waved to and fro, and then Rikki-tikki heard him drinking from the big water jar that was used to fill the bath. "That is good," said the snake. "Now, I shall wait here until the big man comes in to bathe in the morning."

Nag coiled himself down, coil by coil, round the bulge at the bottom of the water jar, and Rikki-tikki stayed still as death. After an hour he began to move, muscle by muscle, toward the jar. Nag was asleep, and Rikki-tikki looked at his big back, wondering which would be the best place for a good hold. "If I don't break his back at the first jump," said Rikki, "he can still fight. And if he fights—Oh, Rikki!" He looked at the thickness of the neck below the hood, but that was too much for him. And a bite near the tail would only make Nag savage.

"It must be the head," he said at last. "The head above the hood, and, when I am once there, I must not let go."

Rikki-tikki jumped. He had just one second's time, and he made the most of it. Then he was battered to and fro as a rat is shaken by a dog—to and fro on the floor, up and down, and round in great circles. But his eyes were red, and he held on as the body cartwhipped over the floor, upsetting the tin dipper and the soap dish, and banged against the tin side of the bath. As he held he closed his jaws tighter and tighter. He was dizzy, aching, and felt shaken to pieces when something went off like a thunderclap just behind him. A hot wind knocked him senseless and red fire singed his fur. The big man had been wakened by the noise, and had fired both barrels of a shotgun into Nag.

Rikki-tikki held on with his eyes shut, but the head did not move. The big man picked him up and said: "It's the mongoose again, Alice. The little chap has saved *our* lives now." Then Teddy's mother came in and saw what was left of Nag, and Rikki-tikki dragged himself to Teddy's bedroom and spent half the rest of the night shaking himself tenderly to find out whether he really was broken into forty pieces, as he fancied.

When morning came he was very stiff, but well pleased with his doings. "Now I have Nagaina to settle with, and she will be worse than five Nags. And there's no knowing when her eggs will hatch. Goodness! I must go and see Darzee," he said.

Rikki-tikki ran to the thornbush where Darzee was singing a song of triumph at the top of his voice. The news of Nag's death was all over the garden, for the sweeper had thrown the body on the rubbish heap.

"Oh, you stupid tuft of feathers!" said Rikki-tikki angrily. "Is this the time to sing? Where is Nagaina?"

"Nag is dead—is dead—is dead!" sang Darzee. "The valiant Rikki-tikki caught him by the head and held fast. The big man brought the bang-stick and Nag fell in two pieces! He will never eat my babies again."

"All that's true enough. But where's Nagaina?" said Rikki-tikki, looking carefully around him. "You don't know when to do the right thing at the right time, Darzee. You're safe enough in your nest there, but it's war for me down here. Stop singing a minute!"

"For the great, the beautiful Rikki-tikki's sake I will stop," said Darzee. "What is it, Oh killer of the terrible Nag?"

"Where is Nagaina, for the third time?"

"On the rubbish heap, mourning for Nag. Great is Rikki-tikki with the white teeth."

"Bother my white teeth! Have you ever heard where she keeps her eggs?"

"In the melon patch, on the end nearest the wall, where the sun strikes nearly all day. She had them three weeks ago."

"And you never thought it worthwhile to tell me?"

"Rikki-tikki, you are not going to eat her eggs?"

"Not eat exactly, no. Darzee, if you have a grain of sense, you will fly off to the rubbish heap and pretend that your wing is broken and let Nagaina chase you away. I must get to the melon patch, and if I went there now, she'd see me."

Darzee was a feather-brained little fellow who could never hold more than one idea at a time in his head. And just because he knew that Nagaina's children were born in eggs like his own, he didn't think at first that it was fair to kill them. But his wife was a sensible bird, and she knew that cobras' eggs meant young cobras later on. So she flew off from her nest and left Darzee to keep the babies warm and continue his song about the death of Nag. Darzee was very like a man in some ways.

She fluttered in front of Nagaina by the rubbish heap and cried out, "Oh, my wing is broken!"

Nagaina lifted up her head and hissed, "You warned Rikki-tikki when I would have killed him. Indeed and truly, you've chosen a bad place to be lame in. What is the use of running away? I am sure to catch you. Little fool, look at me!"

Darzee's wife knew better than to do *that*, for a bird who looks at a snake's eyes gets so frightened that she cannot move. Darzee's wife fluttered on, piping sorrowfully, and never leaving the ground, and Nagaina quickened her pace.

Rikki-tikki heard them going up the path, and he raced for the melon patch. There, in the warm litter about the melons, he found twenty-five eggs, each with a whitish skin instead of a shell.

"I was not a day too soon," he said, for he could see the baby cobras curled up inside the skin, and he knew that the minute they were hatched they could each kill a man or a mongoose. He bit off the tops of the eggs as fast as he could, until there was only one left. But as he started to destroy it, he heard Darzee's wife screaming: "Rikki-tikki, I led Nagaina toward the house, and she has gone onto the veranda, and she means killing!"

Rikki-tikki tumbled backward down the melon bed with the last egg in his mouth, and scuttled to the veranda as hard as he could put foot to ground. Teddy and his mother and father were there at breakfast, but Rikki-tikki saw that they were not eating. They sat stone-still, and their faces were white. Nagaina was coiled up on the matting by Teddy's chair, within easy striking distance of Teddy's bare leg, and she was swaying to and fro.

Teddy's eyes were fixed on his father, and all his father could do was whisper, "Sit still, Teddy. You mustn't move."

Then Rikki-tikki came up and cried: "Turn around, Nagaina. Turn and fight!"

"All in good time," said she, without moving her eyes. "I will settle my account with *you* presently. Look at your friends, Rikki-tikki. They are still and white. They are afraid. They dare not move, and if you come a step nearer I strike."

"Look at your eggs," said Rikki-tikki, "in the melon patch near the wall. Go and look, Nagaina."

The big snake turned half around and saw the egg on the veranda. "Ah-h! Give it to me," she said.

Rikki-tikki put his paws one on each side of the egg, and his
eyes were blood-red. "What price for a snake's egg? For a young
cobra? For the last—the very last—of the brood?"

Nagaina spun clear around, forgetting everything for the sake
of the one egg. And Rikki-tikki saw Teddy's father shoot out a
big hand, catch Teddy by the shoulder, and drag him across the
little table, safe and out of reach of Nagaina.

"Tricked! Tricked! Tricked! *Rikk-tck-tck!*" chuckled Rikki-
tikki. "The boy is safe." Then he began to jump up and down,
all four feet together, his head close to the floor. "Come then,
Nagaina. Come and fight with me."

Nagaina saw that she had lost her chance of killing Teddy, and
the egg lay between Rikki-tikki's paws. "Give me the egg, Rikki-
tikki. Give me the last of my eggs, and I will go away and never
come back," she said, lowering her hood.

"Yes, you will go away and never come back, for you will go
to join Nag. Fight, widow!"

Rikki-tikki was bounding all around Nagaina, keeping just out
of reach of her stroke, his little eyes like hot coals. Nagaina
gathered herself together and flung out at him. Rikki-tikki jumped
up and backward. Again and again she struck, and each time her
head came with a whack on the matting of the veranda, and she
gathered herself together like a watch spring.

He had forgotten the egg. It still lay on the veranda, and Nagaina came nearer and nearer to it till at last, while Rikki-tikki
was drawing breath, she caught it in her mouth, turned to the
veranda steps, and flew like an arrow down the path.

Rikki-tikki knew that he must catch her or all the trouble would
begin again. She headed straight for the long grass, and as he was
running, Rikki-tikki heard Darzee still singing his foolish little
song of triumph. But Darzee's wife was wiser. She flew off her
nest as Nagaina came along and flapped her wings about Nagaina's head. That instant's delay brought Rikki-tikki up to her,
and as she plunged into the rat hole where she and Nag used to
live, his little teeth were clenched on her tail, and he went down
with her—and very few mongooses, however wise and old they

may be, care to follow a cobra into its hole. It was dark in the hole, and Rikki-tikki never knew when it might open out and give Nagaina room to turn and strike at him. He held on savagely, and struck out his feet to act as brakes on the dark slope of the hot, moist earth.

Then the grass by the mouth of the hole began to quiver, and Rikki-tikki, covered with dirt, dragged himself out of the hole leg by leg, licked his whiskers, shook some of the dust out of his fur, and sneezed. "It is all over," he said. "The widow will never come out again."

Rikki-tikki curled himself up in the grass and slept till it was late in the afternoon. "Now," he said, when he awoke, "I will go back to the house. Tell the coppersmith, Darzee, and he will tell the garden that Nagaina's dead."

The coppersmith is a bird who makes a noise exactly like the beating of a little hammer on a copper pot. And the reason he is always making it is because he is the town crier to every Indian garden, and tells all the news to everybody who cares to listen. As Rikki-tikki went up the path, he heard his "attention" notes like a tiny dinner gong, and then the steady "*Ding-dong-tock! Nagaina is dead—dong!*" That set all the birds in the garden singing, and the frogs croaking, for Nag and Nagaina used to eat frogs as well as little birds.

When Rikki got to the house, Teddy and his mother and father came out and almost cried over him. That night he ate all that was given him till he could eat no more, and he went to bed on Teddy's shoulder, where Teddy's mother saw him when she came to look late at night.

"He saved our lives," she said to her husband.

Rikki-tikki woke with a jump, for all mongooses are light sleepers. "Oh, it's you," said he. "What are you bothering for? All the cobras are dead. And if they weren't, I'm here."

Rikki-tikki had a right to be proud of himself, but he did not grow too proud. And he kept that garden as a mongoose should keep it, with tooth and jump and spring and bite, till never a cobra dared show its head inside the walls.

LOOKING AT BOOKS

The Magic Horse

In ancient Persia lives a powerful King . . . and a wicked Wizard. The Wizard has a beautiful life-size horse carved of ebony and inlaid with gold and jewels. Whoever mounts the horse can fly high into the sky and travel anywhere in the world. The King's son gets on the horse and travels to a distant land, where he falls in love with a beautiful princess. He brings the princess home, and the King announces that the two young people will marry. But the evil Wizard tricks the princess and uses the magic horse to take her away. More adventures follow, but finally the princess is reunited with her prince. This fairy tale, retold and charmingly illustrated by Sally Scott, is from *The Arabian Nights*.

300

Berry Woman's Children

Raven made the Earth. Then he made animals and birds. He told Berry Woman to look after the animals and birds, to treat them as her children. This striking book, written and illustrated by Dale De Armond, is based on ancient Eskimo myths and folklore. It tells about Berry Woman's children: sea otter, polar bear, walrus, seal, and other animals that live in the North. There's a fable about a woman who had a crab child. Another fable describes what happened to a little girl who turned into a porcupine. Still another tells how Raven escaped after he flew into a whale's mouth and down its throat.

Sarah, Plain and Tall

In the rolling plains of the West, a pioneer family is without a wife and mother. Papa places an ad in a newspaper for a bride. His children wonder if Sarah, the woman who answers the ad, can make stew and braid hair. And most important: Can she sing like their mother used to sing? This poignant story tells about happiness and hope and what it is that makes a family. Written by Patricia MacLachlan, it is based on a true incident from her family history. The book received the 1986 John Newbery Medal, the highest American award for a book for young people.

THE POLAR EXPRESS

It's Christmas Eve, and the town is quiet. A young boy lies in bed listening for—yet not believing he'll *really* hear—the bells of Santa's sleigh. Suddenly the sounds of hissing steam and squeaking metal fill his room. The boy looks out the window and sees a long, black train. He tiptoes downstairs and goes outdoors just as the train conductor calls ''All Aboard!'' And so begins a mysterious journey to the North Pole, which turns out to be a huge city filled with toy factories and elves. There, Santa gives the boy any gift he desires. Only when the boy is back home does he learn what a very special gift he has, a gift valued only by someone who truly believes in the magic of Christmas. Written and illustrated by Chris Van Allsburg, this book won the 1986 Randolph Caldecott Medal as the best American picture book for children.

MURDO'S STORY

Long ago, according to an Indian legend, summer lasted all year long in half the world. The other half spent the year in continual winter. How the animals of the winter world found the secret of summer (which was guarded by the frog and the crane) is the story told in this book. *Murdo's Story* was written by Murdo Scribe, who lived in Manitoba, Canada, and wrote down many such Indian tales during his life. Terry Gallagher did the illustrations, which were awarded a 1986 children's literature prize by the Canada Council.

THE WITCH'S HANDBOOK

If you've ever wanted to be a witch (a good witch, of course!), this book by Malcolm Bird is the one for you. It's filled with a witty collection of things to make and do in order to become a successful witch. You'll learn how to tell fortunes, cast spells, and make batty party decorations. You'll discover how witches stay so beautiful and fashionable, and find out which witches get which jobs. And in your own kitchen, you'll be able to create such witchy treats as dustbread biscuits and worm soup—although you may have to substitute ground ginger for dust, and spaghetti for worms. You'll also be brought up to date on the latest old wives' tales for witches, such as "Pigs running about with straws in their mouth foretell the coming of windy weather."

POETRY

TOADSTOOLS

I found a ring of toadstools,
  Yellow, pink and white,
But not a single toad or frog
  Was anywhere in sight.

Perhaps the toads sit on them
  And so keep their feet dry;
But I should think that toads would find
  The footstools rather high.

Maybe when playing leapfrog
  The toads jump up and stop,
Or Mother Frog helps baby
  To climb upon the top.

But when it's misty weather
  Or rain falls from the sky,
The stools make fine umbrellas
  To keep toads nice and dry.

RUPERT SARGENT HOLLAND (1878–1952)

THE STARGAZER

A stargazer out late at night,
With eyes and thoughts turned both upright,
Tumbled by chance into a well
(A dismal story this to tell);
He roared and sobbed, and roared again,
And cursed the ''Bear'' and ''Charles's Wain.''

His woeful cries a neighbour brought,
Less learned, but wiser far in thought:
''My friend,'' quoth he, ''you're much misled,
With stars to trouble thus your head;
Since you with these misfortunes meet,
For want of looking to your feet.''

UNKNOWN

THE HAG

The hag is astride,
  This night for a ride,
Her wild steed and she together;
  Through thick and through thin,
  Now out, and then in,
Though ne'er so foul be the weather.

  A thorn or a burr
  She takes for a spur;
With a last of a bramble she rides now,
  Through brakes and through briars,
  O'er ditches and mires,
She follows the spirit that guides now.

  No beast for his food
  Dares now range the wood,
But hush'd in his lair he lies lurking;
  While mischief by these,
  On land and on seas,
At noon of night are found working.

  The storm will arise
  And trouble the skies,
This night; and, more for the wonder,
  The ghost from the tomb
  Affrightened shall come,
Called out by the clap of the thunder.

ROBERT HERRICK (1591–1674)

AN EGG

In marble walls as white as milk,
Lined with a skin as soft as silk,
Within a fountain crystal clear,
A golden apple doth appear.
No doors there are to this stronghold,
Yet thieves break in and steal the gold.

UNKNOWN

THE MOUNTAIN AND THE SQUIRREL

The mountain and the squirrel
Had a quarrel,
And the former called the latter "Little prig;"
Bun replied,
"You are doubtless very big;
But all sorts of things and weather
Must be taken in together
To make up a year,
And a sphere.
And I think it no disgrace
To occupy my place.
If I'm not so large as you,
You are not so small as I,
And not half so spry:
I'll not deny you make
A very pretty squirrel track.
Talents differ; all is well and wisely put;
If I cannot carry forests on my back,
Neither can you crack a nut."

RALPH WALDO EMERSON (1803–1882)

UNTITLED

The Grass so little has to do—
A Sphere of simple Green—
With only Butterflies to brood
And Bees to entertain—

And stir all day to pretty Tunes
The Breezes fetch along—
And hold the Sunshine in its lap
And bow to everything—

And thread the Dews, all night, like Pearls—
And make itself so fine
A Duchess were too common
For such a noticing—

And even when it dies—to pass
In Odors so divine—
Like Lowly spices, lain to sleep—
Or Spikenards, perishing—

And then, in Sovereign Barns to dwell—
And dream the Days away,
The Grass so little has to do
I wish I were a Hay—

EMILY DICKINSON (1830–1886)

THE BUTTERFLY'S BALL

Come take up your hats, and away let us haste,
To the Butterfly's Ball, and the Grasshopper's Feast.
The trumpeter Gadfly has summoned the crew,
And the revels are now only waiting for you.

On the smooth-shaven grass by the side of a wood,
Beneath a broad oak which for ages has stood,
See the children of earth and the tenants of air,
For an evening's amusement together repair.

And there came the Beetle, so blind and so black,
Who carried the Emmet, his friend, on his back.
And there came the Gnat, and the Dragonfly too,
And all their relations, green, orange, and blue.

And there came the Moth, with her plumage of down,
And the Hornet, with jacket of yellow and brown;
Who with him the Wasp, his companion, did bring,
But they promised that evening, to lay by their sting.

Then the sly little Dormouse crept out of his hole,
And led to the feast his blind cousin the Mole.
And the Snail, with his horns peeping out of his shell,
Came, fatigued with the distance, the length of an ell.

A mushroom their table, and on it was laid
A water-dock leaf, which a tablecloth made.
The viands were various, to each of their taste,
And the Bee brought the honey to sweeten the feast.

With steps most majestic the Snail did advance,
And he promised the gazers a minuet to dance;
But they all laughed so loud that he drew in his head,
And went in his own little chamber to bed.

Then, as evening gave way to the shadows of night,
Their watchman, the Glow-worm, came out with his light.
So home let us hasten, while yet we can see;
For no watchman is waiting for you and for me.

WILLIAM ROSCOE (1753–1831)

Incident at the Haymarket

On July 4, 1986, America celebrated the 100th birthday of its most recognized, most cherished, and most richly symbolic monument—the Statue of Liberty. Americans everywhere recalled stories, passed on through generations, of downtrodden immigrants who sighted Liberty's beacon from the crowded deck of a steamship and saw in it the promise of a better life. The message of freedom and compassion was given voice in Emma Lazarus' well-known poem of 1883, "The New Colossus." Inscribed on a bronze plaque inside the statue's pedestal, her tribute contains these famous lines:

"Give me your tired, your poor,
Your huddled masses yearning to breathe free,
The wretched refuse of your teeming shore.
Send these, the homeless, tempest-tost to me,
I lift my lamp beside the golden door!"

But her poetic words of welcome weren't inscribed on the statue until 1903. On October 28, 1886, when President Grover Cleveland dedicated the statue, immigration was still a sensitive issue. Foreigners had been streaming in for decades, and America was struggling with a new identity. Its image as a "melting pot"—a place in which all peoples could live together, preserving and blending their native cultures—was yet to come. Indeed, there were many Americans who did *not* open their arms to the "huddled masses" arriving at the nation's door.

The anti-immigration sentiments of the late-1800's were rooted in a variety of circumstances. A tremendous influx of foreigners in 1882—nearly 800,000—had been followed by four years of economic decline. Many U.S. workers viewed the immigrants, who were willing to work for lower wages, as a threat to their livelihood. At the same time, U.S. cities were reeling under the weight of the Industrial Revolution, as laborers poured in from the countryside to work in the factories. Overcrowding gave birth to slums and other social ills, and these, too, were blamed on immigration.

Finally, some foreigners were regarded as radicals seeking to undermine the American way of life. Although many immigrants were willing to accept low pay and grim working conditions, others sought improvements through the rapidly growing labor movement. At that time, however, much of American society still viewed labor unions as a threat to the capitalist system and traditional American values. To the dismay of industrialists and the wealthier class, the year 1886 witnessed vigorous efforts by the labor movement to improve conditions. That spring, for example, hundreds of thousands of workers went on strike to demand an eight-hour workday. Because of the fear of unions, many immigrants who took part in such activities were unfairly accused of being "socialists" and "anarchists" (people who reject authority and advocate public disorder). There were, in fact, radicals in the labor movement, but most of the immigrants only wanted better working conditions.

Nowhere was the mood of the times more evident than in the city of Chicago. A port on Lake Michigan and the hub of the nation's railroad, Chicago was at the forefront of the Industrial Revolution. It was a center of industry, commerce, and finance. Immigrants came from everywhere seeking jobs. Ethnic neighborhoods were carved out. Slums spread. The labor movement was growing ever larger and more active, and many native Chicagoans felt threatened.

Tensions in the "Windy City" came to a head on May 4, 1886. To protest police violence against striking workers, a rally was held at downtown Haymarket Square that evening. The atmosphere was highly charged, and city officials were nervous. Finally the police marched on the crowd to break it up. A bomb went off. Nobody ever learned who threw the bomb or exactly how many died. Of the police, however, seven lay dead and about 60 were injured. The incident, which became known as the Haymarket Affair, set off a furious public reaction against "foreign anarchists." Eight men, several of them German, were brought to trial. Four eventually were hanged.

The story that follows is set in Chicago during that spring of 1886. While it is a fictional account, the backdrop of events is real, and the plight of the immigrant family is typical of the times.

Chicago came to life like an awakening giant. Trolleys rumbled through the streets, scattering pedestrians and pushcarts. Chimneys huffed thick clouds of smoke and steam. Streams of shoppers pulsed through the doors of Marshall Field's department store. At the new Board of Trade Building, stockbrokers and futures dealers shouted their first bids of the day.

In the attic apartment at 1731 Halsted Street, 12-year-old Anton Tripp awoke to the smell of freshly baked bread and pastry. As the boy's eyes fluttered open, he pushed away his mop of blond hair and squinted through the thin curtain that divided the room. Mama moved about the kitchen quietly, setting things on the table. Papa sat reading a newspaper, the *Arbeiter Zeitung*.

"Goot morning," chimed Mrs. Tripp as the boy peeked around the curtain.

A look of disappointment passed across Anton's face. Every morning the warm smell from the bakery downstairs reached his nostrils as he lay on the tattered mattress. With the windows left open to let in the spring air, the aroma was so strong that Anton was sure a fresh loaf of soft American white bread was waiting on the kitchen table. And maybe a few strawberry tarts. Or one of those rich, creamy pies he saw in the bakery window. But again he was mistaken. Breakfast would be the same as always —a cup of tea and a chunk of heavy, dry black bread. No butter, only lard.

Anton's father folded his newspaper and got up from the table. He was a tall, burly, sandy-haired man with dark, deep-set eyes. His hands were thick and strong, the palms toughened from swinging a hammer ten hours a day at Union Depot. Konrad Tripp was luckier than most other immigrant laborers. Two dollars a day hardly made him a rich man, but it was enough to pay a modest rent and put some food on the table. Even when times were bad, like now, he could count on working four days a week. Every evening when he got home, Anton watched him scrub the grime from his hands, sometimes for fifteen minutes.

As Konrad put on his cap, Mama stuffed a thick slice of the black bread into his coat pocket. Gertie Tripp was a stout, ruddy-cheeked woman with light hair turning to gray. As she pulled her husband aside, her soft, pleasant eyes were narrow with worry.

"Please," she whispered in German. "Don't go tonight. Come home for supper. I'll make a fresh cabbage."

"Don't worry," said Konrad softly. "Nothing will happen. Keep the cabbage warm."

"But why you must go?" she pleaded.

"Because it is the right thing to do," he said placing his big hands on her shoulders. "I must."

Konrad planted a kiss on her cheek and turned to Anton. He spoke in English, smiling gently.

"Make quickly, Tony. You have papers to deliver before school. I see you tonight."

"Yes, Papa," said the boy. "Good-bye, Papa."

The early edition of the newspaper carried a banner headline

that stretched full across the front page. Anton normally didn't have time to read the paper, what with 42 copies to deliver and 20 blocks to walk to school. But that morning there was no ignoring the big, bold letters on page one: POLICE FIRE ON STRIKERS; PROTEST SLATED FOR HAYMARKET. Stopping between each house along his route, Anton read the article from top to bottom:

> Chicago, May 4—In an ongoing series of incidents between police and striking workers, violence broke out yesterday afternoon at the McCormick Harvester Company plant in downtown Chicago. Four strikers were reported killed and several others injured.
>
> The skirmish took place as nonstriking laborers were leaving the plant at the end of the 4 o'clock shift. According to a police spokesman, the strikers taunted and then attacked the laborers with rocks and sticks. Police guards, who had been stationed at the plant since the strike began, moved in quickly with Gatling guns and clubs.
>
> In the aftermath of the incident, leaders of the Eight-Hour League and other labor groups called for a rally at Haymarket Square tonight at 7:30 to protest "the senseless and brutal act" of the police.
>
> Mayor Carter Harrison immediately issued a statement calling on the unionists to postpone the action "until tempers cool." Police Inspector John Bonfield, known in unionist circles as "Black Jack," gave a blunt warning at a press conference last night. "Call it off," he said. "The city of Chicago will not tolerate socialist hooliganism."

All day at school, Anton thought about the article and Papa's words that morning: "It is the right thing to do. I must." When the bell sounded at 2 o'clock, he bounded out of the building and ran all the way home.

"Mama! Mama!" he heaved, bursting through the door.

Gertie Tripp looked up from peeling potatoes and answered calmly. "Ah, hello Tony. What is the matter?"

"Where is Papa going tonight? I read an article and, and. . . ."

Gertie went back to peeling. "Nowhere, Tony. He is just meeting friends."

"But, Mama," he cried. "I heard you talking this morning. Police will be there. I read it in today's newspaper."

"Never mind that," she said sternly. "Why don't you go to the park and play baseball with your friends?"

"I hate baseball!" he screamed. "I don't like those American boys! If I say anything they laugh at me. They call me Sauerkraut and Blondie and, and . . . and I just don't like them!"

He stomped out of the kitchen and buried his face in his pillow.

When he finished crying, Anton went to the closet and pulled out a big egg crate with two boxes inside. He picked up one of them and gently lifted out his prize possession—the new Kilburn stereoscope his Onkel Klaus had sent for Christmas. Anton had never seen a stereoscope before the package arrived, but he was immediately enthralled. Each view, a double photograph, slid into the viewer and created a three-dimensional image through the two eyepieces. It was like looking through binoculars and seeing whole scenes come to life.

The second box contained a thick stack of the view cards—landscapes, still lifes, portraits, comics. Every week, with the money he earned from delivering papers, Anton bought three new cards. He had a big collection by now, but his favorites were still the twenty of Germany that Onkel Klaus had sent with the viewer.

One by one, he slipped the cards into the stereoscope and gazed at the scenes. Each one had a label, and he knew them by heart—*The Black Forest, Neuschwanstein Castle in Bavaria, Oktoberfest in Munich, The Rhine Valley*. Anton lost himself in every one . . .

He remembered when the man with the pocketwatch had come to their village and Papa had signed the papers. They all boarded a ship, and it was cold and everybody was hungry, but finally they saw America and they took a train to Chicago, and the man with the pocketwatch met them again, and it was all so different. Soon Papa went to work and . . .

Papa!

Anton dropped the viewer and bolted to his feet. Mama was just about to call him to supper, but he flew out the door and was halfway down the stairs before she could say a word. She stuck her head out the window to call after him, but it was too late. Already Anton was racing down Halsted Street, lost in the crowd of bicycles, pushcarts, and horse-drawn wagons.

It was a hot, muggy night with dark clouds hanging low in the sky. Not a star was showing.

In Haymarket Square, on Randolph Street between Halsted and Desplaines, a crowd began to gather. The men arrived in clusters, each one holding an upraised torch. The bright, oily flames lit their faces in stark relief. Gaunt and somber, they carried the expressions of hungry, mostly jobless men who clung to the hope of a fairer shake in life. It was more a look of desperation than of anger. The only sound was of worn shoe leather shuffling over cobblestone.

At the south end of the square, in a narrow alley between two warehouses, Anton Tripp crouched in the dark. Looking out to his left, he could see the men turning into Haymarket from Halsted Street. Across the square to his right, others came in from Desplaines. He strained to see every face, and several times he thought he saw Papa.

By now there were a thousand, maybe two thousand, men milling toward the center of the square. It was a quiet, peaceable scene, but there was a growing nervousness in the air. The pamphlets and posters had promised speeches and an organized demonstration. "Good speakers will be present to denounce the latest atrocious acts of the police!" they announced. Still no voices could be heard, only faint whispers and the crackling of torchlights. Policemen and Pinkerton detectives paced the shadowy fringes of the square, carrying long billy clubs.

Suddenly the boy's view was blocked by the silhouette of two men. He shifted deeper into the darkness and held his breath as they spoke. Both wore sleeveless gray undershirts and flat wool caps tilted to the side. The man with the cigar spoke first.

"Ol' Black Jack's just itchin' to break heads on this one," he muttered.

"Yeah, I know," the second one answered. "But I'm afraid it looks quiet so far."

"Too bad," the first man grumbled.

"Yeah, too bad," the other one answered.

The two men were quiet for a moment. Then the one with the cigar took the stub from his teeth and blew out a stream of smoke.

"Well," he said finally. "Let's see if we can't get the boys to do something about that."

He dropped the stub to the cobblestone and scrunched it under his shoe. The two men parted ways and headed toward the crowd.

Anton let out his breath and moved slowly to the front of the alley. "I have to find Papa!" he thought. "I have to!"

Inching out of the darkness, the boy pressed his back to the wall and made his way around the square. Several times he had to duck out of the view of policemen. Every step of the way he peered into the crowd, desperately hoping for a glimpse of his father. No sign.

At the corner of Desplaines, Anton hid behind a stack of baled hay, watching and waiting. The crowd seemed to be getting restless, and then there was pushing somewhere in the middle of the pack.

"Those two men are hired goons!" a voice cried out.

"Don't start trouble!" came another.

As abruptly as it started, the pushing stopped.

It was around 8:30 that Anton noticed the crowd moving slowly toward the north end of the square. The throng of men and torchlights packed in close around the entrance of a large factory. Then a cheer went up as a tall, black-haired man climbed onto a wagon by the front gate. He raised his hands for quiet and smiled faintly as he scanned the scene. His voice was deep and clear, and it carried well in the damp night air. He spoke slowly, with a harsh, throaty accent.

"Welcome fellow workers," he began, rolling up the sleeves of his collared white shirt. "My name is August Spies. I am the editor and publisher of *Arbeiter Zeitung*."

Another cheer rose from the crowd, and torches bobbed up and down.

"Yesterday," he went on, "they killed one of your brothers at the McCormick plant. It was a senseless and brutal act, and now it is time to defend your rights and resist the scabs and capitalist tycoons. It is time to demand the eight-hour workday. It is time. . . ."

It was a familiar speech, full of slogans and rallying cries worn smooth from overuse. Yet it struck a chord with the Haymarket crowd, raising their spirits and strengthening their resolve. Many had heard the speech before or had read the slogans on handbills, but every word fanned a faint spark of hope in each man.

The next speaker was a man named Albert Parsons, a short, slim Southerner with jet-black hair and a flowing mustache. Parsons and Spies were best friends, as well as co-leaders of Chicago's Eight-Hour League. Parsons gave a speech very much like that of his comrade—impassioned, animated, and filled with urgency.

"There is nothing in the eight-hour movement to excite the capitalists. Then why is the military under arms? Is this Germany or Russia or Spain? Whenever you make a demand for an increase in pay, the militia and the deputy sheriff and the Pinkerton men are called out and you are shot and clubbed in the streets. But I am not here for the purpose of inciting anybody, just to speak out to tell the facts as they exist."

A light drizzle began to fall, and the torchlights flickered. Parsons spoke on, criticizing "cops and capitalists," but he was careful not to say anything that was too inflammatory. It was a powder-keg atmosphere, and the wrong word might touch off an ugly scene. Fuses were short.

From behind the bales of hay, Anton heard the faint staccato of hoofbeats coming up Desplaines. Two men on horseback made their way up the dim, gaslit street and halted at the corner of Haymarket. The horses whinnied as the men climbed down, not twenty feet from where the boy hid. One of the men was wearing a bowler hat, black waistcoat, and brocade vest. The other wore a long blue jacket with two rows of brass buttons, a wide leather belt, and a large gold star just below the shoulder. Both men took off their hats, giving Anton a clear view of their faces. He recognized them immediately. Their pictures had been on the front page of the paper. It was Mayor Harrison and Police Inspector Black Jack Bonfield!

"You wait here, Jack," said the mayor.

Bonfield clenched his jaw and gave a perfunctory "Yes, sir."

Mayor Harrison clasped his hands behind his back and strode slowly toward the crowd. Heads turned as he passed, but no one spoke a word. About ten minutes later he emerged from the throng and made his way back to the corner of Desplaines, where Bonfield squeezed the horses' reins in a tight fist.

"I have no right to interfere with any peaceable meeting of the people," said Mayor Harrison in an official tone. "So long as they are orderly I won't interfere."

Bonfield turned red with frustration. "But, sir," he sputtered.

"No buts, Jack. Now I'm going home, and I trust there will be no incidents. I leave you in charge."

Mayor Harrison climbed back on his horse, tugged on the reins, and clip-clopped slowly down Desplaines. Bonfield lingered a moment, then tied his horse to a lamppost and swaggered toward the factory entrance.

Now it was 10 o'clock, and Parsons had been talking for nearly an hour. Finally he introduced the last speaker, a Lancaster Englishman named Samuel Fielden. The crowd pressed closer as Fielden mounted the wagon. They knew him as a radical and a fiery speaker.

"The law is your enemy," he told the crowd. "We are rebels against it. The law is framed only for those who are your enslavers. The law must be throttled, killed, and stabbed!"

Black Jack Bonfield pounded his fist in his hand. "That's it!" he said through his teeth, and rushed off. A chill wind swept in a curtain of rain, and Anton shivered behind the bales of hay.

Many in the crowd scrambled for shelter, but Fielden kept on talking, growing louder and more vehement as the rain got heavier. Then Bonfield reappeared, pushing his way to the front of the crowd. Two lines of police stood ready at the entrance to the square. Shiny new revolvers and long hickory clubs hung at their sides.

"In conclusion," Fielden said—and stopped dead.

"In the name of the people of the State of Illinois," shouted Bonfield, "I command this meeting immediately and peaceably to disperse!"

Much of the soggy crowd had already begun to drift away. The ones that remained huddled closer together.

Again Bonfield shouted the order. "I command you in the name of the law to desist and disperse!"

When no one moved, Bonfield raised his right arm and waved the signal. The police began moving forward, reaching for guns and clubs.

Fielden stared straight into Bonfield's eyes and spoke calmly. "But inspector," he said, "we are peaceable."

Suddenly, an object carrying a slender tail of fire rose in the air above the advancing line of police. Anton covered his head, and a tremendous explosion shook the brick walls of Haymarket Square. It echoed like a round of cannonfire.

Rubble showered down on the boy for what seemed an eternity. When it finally stopped, he slowly opened his eyes and peeked out from behind the haystack. In the dust and smoke, several police lay dead on the cobblestone. Flashes of light and

the crackling of revolvers burst from the rear. The protestors fired back. People ran, screamed, moaned, cursed. More bodies fell. Then the shots died down, and soon all was quiet.

Anton lay motionless, afraid to budge. Tears streamed down his face, and his heart pounded like sledgehammers.

The first thought that crossed his mind was whether Papa lay out on the cobblestone with all the others. Ambulance wagons began rolling into the square, and scores of injured policemen were carried off on stretchers. Bloodied protestors staggered away from the grim scene. Others ministered to their fallen comrades. Anton wobbled to his feet and, looking over his shoulder, disappeared into the fog of gunpowder.

It was after midnight before Gertie heard footsteps coming up the stairs. She flung open the door and took her son in her arms.

"Thank God," she cried, stroking his hair. "Where did you go, Tony? Where have you been?"

The boy shuddered, still in shock. "I could not find Papa," he stammered.

"Oh, Tony, Tony," she whispered. "Everything is OK. Papa is here."

It was dark where Papa lay, and Anton was afraid to go behind the curtain.

"Go ahead," said his mother softly. "He wants to see you."

Anton could barely make out his father's figure lying on the bed.

"Is that you, son?" came a hoarse voice.

"Yes, Papa," he whispered.

Anton's eyes adjusted to the dark, and he found the edge of the mattress. Papa was still in clothes, but his shirt was open and his head and ribs were wrapped in bandages. He reached out a hand, and Anton could see that it was still covered with grime.

"Where have you been, Tony?" he said, clutching the boy close to him.

"I saw everything, Papa. At Haymarket. I looked for you, but. . . ."

"Shhh," his father whispered. "I will be OK. We will talk tomorrow."

"But Papa," Anton said. "Can we go home?"

"No," he answered. "This *is* our home."

"But people are always fighting with us, Papa."

Konrad Tripp scanned the bare room. His head throbbed, and a sharp pain stabbed his chest with every breath. He held the boy tighter.

"Listen to me, Tony," he said finally. "You must learn how to forgive people. Some day you will be a professor, or an engineer, or maybe a baseball player. If you forgive people enough, you will belong to them. They will belong to you. Life is very hard for us here, but we must have faith. America is a place where we can make things better for ourselves."

"What is faith, Papa?"

"Well, Tony," he said. "Faith is believing we will get all the good things we wish for. That is faith."

"Papa?" the boy said.

"Yes, son?"

"I have faith you will be all better tomorrow."

Konrad smiled. "It will take a few days, Tony. In the meantime, I want you to help your mother. Until I am back on my feet, you are the man of the house."

That night, Anton lay awake thinking about the day's events. The newspaper headlines. The torchlit faces. The man with the cigar. Mayor Harrison and Black Jack Bonfield. The slender tail of fire. As he drifted into sleep, he imagined all the scenes through the double lens of a stereoscope, far away and disjointed, yet somehow alive. And then he dreamed about Neuschwanstein Castle and the Black Forest, the man with the pocketwatch, the ship. "What is faith, Papa?". . .

It was still dark when he awoke. Mama and Papa were sleeping, and the first faint smell of baking dough drifted through the window. Slowly Anton drew away the covers and swung his feet to the floor. The boards creaked as he tiptoed to the closet and squatted at the door. Reaching into the darkness, he took hold of the wooden egg crate and found the box of cards inside. He counted his favorite twenty from the top of the stack and stuffed them in his nightshirt. Careful not to cause a stir, he pulled on a pair of pants and padded silently out of the room.

Old Mr. Gormley was just opening up when Anton arrived at the shop. The boy followed him in.

"I want to sell some stereo cards," said Anton nervously.

Mr. Gormley looked at the cards, then at Anton. "You sure, son? If I buy them from you, I'll have to sell them to someone else."

"Yes, sir," said the boy. "I'm sure."

"How many you got there, anyway?" asked Gormley.

"Twenty," the boy said. "Twenty nice ones."

Old Mr. Gormley rubbed his chin. "Well," he said finally, "twenty cents fair?"

"Yes, sir," the boy said quickly and held out his hand.

Squeezing the two dimes, Anton ran back down Halsted. The sun was coming up, and the street was filling with people. Dodging pedestrians and bicycles, the boy made his way past the stockyards, factories, and Union Depot. He had one last stop before going home . . .

Clamboring up the stairs, a small package under each arm, Anton prayed that Mama and Papa were still asleep. When he reached the top landing, he paused to catch his breath and squeaked open the door. All was still.

Quietly he unwrapped the packages and set them on the table. Then he crept back to bed and breathed in the warm smell of fresh bread and pastry—coming from his own kitchen. He closed his eyes and smiled. Outside, a trolley rumbled past.

EPILOGUE

The day after the Haymarket bombing, newspapers around the country called for swift revenge against "foreign radicals." In Chicago, the police invaded working-class neighborhoods and arrested every suspected radical they could find. Eight men eventually went on trial for conspiracy to commit murder. There was no evidence that identified any of them as the actual bomb thrower, but all eight were found guilty. Seven were sentenced to hang, and one drew fifteen years in prison. Later, two of the death sentences were reduced to life in prison. On November 11, 1887, four of the Haymarket conspirators were hanged; another was found to have committed suicide in his cell.

There were some people who felt that the trial had been unfair and that the men had been executed unjustly. For years these people petitioned state officials to release the remaining Haymarket prisoners. Finally, in 1892, Governor John Altgeld agreed to re-view the case. After many months, he ruled that the trial had indeed been unfair. The evidence was inconclusive, he determined, and the men had been found guilty only because of the fear, hatred, and prejudice against so-called "anarchists." Governor Altgeld issued a statement that officially pardoned all eight Haymarket defendants.

In the spring of 1986, as New York was preparing for the Statue of Liberty centennial, Chicago remembered the men—immigrants, U.S. citizens, and public servants—who had died at the Haymarket. Mayor Harold Washington proclaimed May as "Labor History Month." The police union held a parade to commemorate the seven officers who had lost their lives. And outside the Chicago Historical Society, where a special exhibit was being shown, a young man carried a sign that read: "Tell the Truth about Haymarket." For some people, the case was still being debated.

JEFFREY H. HACKER
Author, *Carl Sandburg*

THE NEW BOOK OF KNOWLEDGE
1987

The following articles are from the 1987 edition of *The New Book of Knowledge*. They are included here to help you keep your encyclopedia up to date.

DEFOE, DANIEL (1660?–1731)

Daniel Defoe, famed as the author of *Robinson Crusoe*, was born in London, probably in 1660. Little is known of his early life. His parents were "dissenters"—people who did not support the established Church of England. At 14, Daniel was sent to a school run by dissenters. He studied to be a minister, but in 1685 he decided to go into business.

Throughout his life, Defoe was active as both a businessman and a journalist. He not only wrote about business, but he was himself an investor, wholesaler, and manufacturer. He had his own periodical called *The Review* from 1704 to 1713, and he wrote many books and articles on political and social issues.

Defoe took an active part in many of the major political events of his time. These events often were related to religious strug- gles. In 1685 he joined in an unsuccessful revolt against the Catholic king of England, James II. In 1688 he supported the Protestant William of Orange, who became king after James II was deposed.

In 1702, Defoe wrote a satiric pamphlet called *The Shortest Way with Dissenters,* in which he pretended to be a prejudiced member of the Church of England who wished to destroy all dissenters. This pamphlet was Defoe's way of mocking the extreme supporters of the Church of England. He was punished publicly for the satire by having to stand in the pillory (a wooden device that locked around the head and hands). But even after this, Defoe continued to write about politics.

The works of fiction for which Daniel Defoe is remembered today were not written until late in his life. *The Life and Strange Surprising Adventures of Robinson Crusoe* was published in 1719. It tells of a young man who travels to distant lands. When he finally returns home, he is a wealthy man. The major part of the book is an account of Crusoe's shipwreck on a deserted island. Through this story, Defoe raises questions about a human being's ability to survive apart from society.

Another of Defoe's best-known works was *Moll Flanders,* which appeared in 1722. This is the story of a poor girl, born in prison, who eventually becomes a rich landowner in Virginia.

One of Defoe's most remarkable books is *A Journal of the Plague Year* (1722). From writings about the terrible London plague of 1665, Defoe put together what seems to be a vivid eyewitness account. For such achievements, Defoe is now ranked as one of the first great realistic novelists.

Daniel Defoe died in London on April 26, 1731.

EVERETT ZIMMERMAN
Author, *Defoe and the Novel*

▶ ROBINSON CRUSOE

Robinson Crusoe has spent many years learning to survive on the remote island where he has been shipwrecked. One day he is astonished to discover the footprint of another human being in the sand. But it is not until much later, when a group of cannibals comes to the island for their feasts, that he finds a companion. In the following episode, Robinson Crusoe rescues one of their prisoners, whom he later names Friday, after his day of rescue.

It came now very warmly upon my thoughts, and indeed irresistibly, that now was my time to get me a servant, and perhaps a companion or assistant, and that I was called plainly by Providence to save this poor creature's life. I immediately ran down the ladders with all possible expedition, fetched my two guns, for they were both but at the foot of the ladders, as I observed above, and getting up again, with the same haste, to the top of the hill, I crossed toward the sea, and having a very short cut, and all down hill, clapped myself in the way between the pursuers and the pursued, hallooing aloud to him that fled, who, looking back, was at first perhaps as much frightened at me as at them; and I beckoned with my hand to him to come back; and, in the meantime, I slowly advanced towards the two that followed; then rushing at once upon the foremost, I knocked him down with the stock of my piece. I was loth to fire, because I would not have the rest hear; though, at that distance, it would not have been easily heard, and being out of sight of the smoke too, they would not have easily known what to make of it. Having knocked this fellow down, the other who pursued with him stopped, as if he had been frightened, and I advanced apace towards him; but as I came nearer, I perceived presently he had a bow and arrow, and was fitting it to shoot at me; so I was then necessitated to shoot at him first, which I did, and killed him at the first shot.

The poor savage who fled, but had stopped, though he saw both his enemies falled and killed, as he thought, yet was so frightened with the fire and noise of my piece, that he stood stock-still, and neither came forward nor went backward, though he seemed rather inclined to fly still, than to come on.

I hallooed again to him, and made signs to come forward, which he easily understood, and came a little way, then stopped again, and then a little farther, and stopped again; and I could then perceive that he stood trembling, as if he had been taken prisoner, and had just been to be killed, as his two enemies were. I beckoned him again to come to me, and gave him all the signs of encouragement that I could think of; and he came nearer and nearer, kneeling down every ten or

Robinson Crusoe finds a single mysterious footprint in the sand of his desert island: "I stood like one thunderstruck, or as if I had seen an apparition."

twelve steps, in token of acknowledgment for my saving his life. I smiled at him, and looked pleasantly, and beckoned to him to come still nearer. At length he came close to me, and then he kneeled down again, kissed the ground, and laid his head upon the ground, and taking me by the foot, set my foot upon his head. This, it seems, was in token of swearing to be my slave for ever. I took him up, and made much of him, and encouraged him all I could. But there was more work to do yet, for I perceived the savage whom I knocked down was not killed, but stunned with the blow, and began to come to himself; so I pointed to him, and showing him the savage, that he was not dead, upon this he spoke some words to me; and though I could not understand them, yet I thought they were pleasant to hear; for they were the first sound of a man's voice that I had heard, my own excepted, for above twenty-five years.

ARCTIC

Surrounding the geographic North Pole is a deep, ice-covered ocean, the Arctic Ocean, which is bordered by the northern parts of the continents of North America, Europe, and Asia. This is the Arctic region. Here, periods of daylight lasting for months at a time alternate with periods of darkness lasting just as long. Cold pervades the region. But unlike the southern polar region of Antarctica, which has no native human inhabitants, people have lived in the Arctic for thousands of years. Because of its location, geography, climate, and wealth of natural resources, the Arctic region is politically, scientifically, and economically important.

The boundaries of the Arctic region are measured in different ways. The Arctic is sometimes defined as the area north of the Arctic Circle, an imaginary line around the globe at 66° 30′ (66 degrees, 30 minutes) north latitude. Other ways of determining the region's limits include the tree line, the most northerly point at which trees will grow, and the extent of polar sea ice and of permafrost—land that is forever frozen.

▶ **GEOGRAPHY OF THE ARCTIC**

The Arctic is dominated by the Arctic Ocean and a vast treeless plain called the tundra. Unlike Antarctica, which is an ice-covered continent, much of the Arctic consists of ice-covered seas.

The Arctic Ocean. The Arctic Ocean, which covers approximately 5,000,000 square miles (13,000,000 square kilometers), makes up about two thirds of the Arctic region. East of the island of Greenland, the Arctic Ocean connects with the Atlantic Ocean. West of Greenland the Arctic flows through Baffin Bay, Davis Strait, and shallow outlets between the northern islands of Canada. The Arctic Ocean joins the Pacific Ocean through the Bering Strait, which separates Soviet Siberia from Alaska. Although its extent varies from summer to winter, ice covers the Arctic Ocean year-round, making navigation frequently difficult and dangerous. From October to June the ocean is completely ice-locked. Only submarines can cross it completely, by passing under the ice.

At times, icebergs break off the glaciers in Greenland and Canada. Many float south into the shipping lanes of the Atlantic Ocean and create hazards to navigation.

The Tundra. The tundra begins on the land areas of the Arctic at the tree line, where the forests end. When the summer sun melts the ice and snow cover, the Arctic tundra becomes a rich green living carpet of plants. But beneath a thin layer of soil lies ground

The frozen Arctic Ocean (*far left*) dominates the Arctic region. The people of the Arctic have survived in their harsh environment by developing simple but useful equipment, such as the dogsled (*center*). When the summer sun melts its covering of ice, the tundra (*left*) blooms with plants and flowers.

that is always frozen. This permafrost forms whenever the ground temperatures remain continuously below the freezing point, 32°F (0°C), for two or more years. Most of Greenland, much of Alaska, half of Canada and the Soviet Union, and parts of Scandinavia, Mongolia, and Northeast China are affected by permafrost. Its greatest thickness—4,900 feet (1,500 meters)—is in Siberia.

Not all the land in the Arctic region is covered by the flat tundra. Rocky, mountainous islands are scattered around the Arctic Ocean. Greenland, with mountains ringing its coast, is almost completely covered by a large ice sheet, second in size only to the ice sheet of Antarctica.

▶ CLIMATE

Although low temperatures are the major characteristic of its climate, the Arctic is not always bitterly cold. During the summer, temperatures over the Arctic Ocean are near 32°F (0°C). Winter temperatures, however, average between −22° and −31°F (−30° to −35°C). It is colder over land areas, especially over the Greenland ice sheet, where a winter temperature of −87°F (−66°C) has been recorded. In the subarctic, a region just south of the Arctic, winters are colder but summers are warmer. The lowest temperature ever recorded here was −90°F (about −68°C) in Siberia.

Like Antarctica, the Arctic receives little precipitation (rain or snow). The generally low temperatures limit the amount of moisture that can be held in the air and consequently the amount of snow that will fall. In March and April, when the greatest amount of snow covers the ground, the average depth in the Arctic is 8 to 20 inches (20 to 50 centimeters). The snow, however, remains for 10 months of the year.

The Arctic year is divided into a long, cold winter and a short, cool summer. Because of its geographical position, the Arctic is marked by long periods of darkness and daylight. At the North Pole the sun remains above the horizon for six months at a time and below the horizon for another six months, giving six months of daylight followed by six months of darkness.

▶ PLANT AND ANIMAL LIFE

Plants and animals are plentiful in the Arctic. More than 90 types of plants grow not far from the North Pole. Closer to the Arctic Circle scientists have identified 450 varieties of plant life. In summer the tundra is covered with flowers and various plants, including lichens, mosses, grasses, and small shrubs. More than a hundred types of birds live in the Arctic. Musk oxen, caribou, reindeer, foxes, wolves, bears (including polar bears), valuable fur-bearing animals such as ermine and sable, snowshoe hares, and lemmings (small, mouselike animals) thrive in the region. The Arctic waters are rich in fish, including salmon, cod, and rockfish, and many kinds of seals, whales, and porpoises.

▶ ARCTIC PEOPLES

The Arctic has been populated by small groups of people for thousands of years. They probably followed herds of reindeer, caribou, and musk oxen from Central Asia northward and eventually adapted to the environment. One of the most widespread peoples native to the region are the Inuit, commonly called Eskimos. They are found in Alaska and Canada, as well as Greenland and Siberia. Indians also live in some areas of the North American Arctic region, especially in Alaska and Canada.

Perhaps the best-known people of the European Arctic region are the Lapps, who live in the northern areas of Finland, Norway, and Sweden and in parts of the Soviet Union. Many Lapps still follow their traditional ways of life as hunters and reindeer herders. But as the Arctic is increasingly exploited for its natural resources, they are being trained for more settled occupations, such as farming and mining.

In Siberia, in the Asian Arctic region of the Soviet Union, the native peoples include the Chukchi, Koyaki, and Yakuts, as well as some Inuit and Lapps. Most continue to follow their traditional occupations—herding reindeer, hunting, fishing, and fur trapping.

All the native Arctic peoples have developed a unique ability to survive in their harsh environment by skillfully using the few materials available to them. From snow, ice, and animal skins and bones they have fashioned a simple technology that enables them to build shelters, weapons, and such forms of transportation as sleds and kayaks (small, skin-covered boats). Land and sea animals and fish provide their main source of food.

NATURAL RESOURCES

The natural resources of the Arctic can be divided into four main groups—furs, whale products, fish, and minerals. In the early days of Arctic exploration, seals attracted fur traders. Because of the region's large whale population, a booming industry soon developed in whale oil, whalebone, and other products from these great creatures. Today, because many marine animals are in danger of being wiped out, their hunting is limited by international agreements.

The Arctic seas provide some of the oldest and most productive fishing areas in the world. The amount that can be caught by any country, however, is controlled by national territorial limits and by other internationally recognized agreements.

The Arctic's mineral resources include coal, copper, diamonds, gold, iron, lead, zinc, nickel, and tin. Large petroleum and natural gas deposits exist in the northern areas of Alaska, Canada, and the Soviet Union. Petroleum from Alaska and Canada is transported south by pipelines.

EXPLORATION AND DISCOVERY

The first recorded explorers of the Arctic were the Norsemen who sailed from Norway to Iceland, Greenland, and North America. By the mid-16th century, British and Dutch merchants and sailors began exploring the Arctic in search of a northeast passage to China and India. Although these explorers did not find the passage, they did learn more about the Arctic. These searches also opened up sea trade with Russia and led to the development of the whaling and sealing industries.

About the same time, other British explorers were searching for a northwest passage to Asia around the North American continent. In 1576, Martin Frobisher sailed for the first time to Canada's Baffin Island. Within the next 40 years, Davis Strait, Baffin Bay, and Hudson Bay had been explored. Between the early 17th and 19th centuries the attention of merchants and explorers focused on developing land routes to support the fur trade. As a result of these explorations, two British explorers, Samuel Hearne and Alexander Mackenzie, followed Canadian rivers northwest to the Arctic Ocean.

During the 18th and 19th centuries explorers continued to search the Arctic for the elusive Northwest Passage. This route was not found until the early years of the 20th century, when Norway's Roald Amundsen became the first person to sail northwest from the Atlantic Ocean through the Arctic to the Pacific Ocean. His voyage lasted from 1903 to 1906. (Amundsen later led the first expedition to reach the South Pole.)

Once the Northwest Passage was discovered, explorers turned their attention to the North Pole. During these expeditions much scientific information was obtained, including data on sea ice and the Arctic Ocean collected by the Norwegian explorer Fridtjof Nansen. In 1909 an American expedition led by Robert E. Peary successfully reached the North Pole for the first time.

Since the beginning of the 20th century, advances in technology have expanded Arctic exploration. The first flight over the North Pole was accomplished by the American Richard E. Byrd in 1926. In 1958 the U.S. nuclear-powered submarine *Nautilus* became the first ship to reach the North Pole, by traveling under the Arctic ice. In 1977 the nuclear-powered Soviet icebreaker *Arktika* was used to explore the frozen Arctic Ocean. Scientists completed a seven-year exploration project on the ecology of the Bering Sea in 1983.

▶ THE ARCTIC TODAY

Political and Strategic Importance. National territorial rights are recognized for all Arctic land areas. But the extent to which nations can control Arctic coastal waters is still unresolved. With the growth of the offshore oil industry in the Arctic, control of its waters will become more important. The Arctic's strategic importance lies in its central position between North America, Europe, and Asia. Both the United States and the Soviet Union maintain air and missile defense systems in the region and radar installations to provide early warning against attack.

Research and Environmental Protection. Most scientific research in the Arctic concentrates on its climate and its unusual geographical and physical characteristics. In addition, environmental research and protection have become increasingly important as new technology enables us to tap the mineral resources of the region. This is vital because the ecology of the Arctic can be easily disrupted or damaged and recovers very slowly, sometimes not at all. As a result, the United States, Canada, and many European nations have established strict measures to protect this unique, fascinating, and invaluable region of the world.

WINIFRED REUNING
Division of Polar Programs
National Science Foundation

The strategic importance of the Arctic region lies in its central location between the continents of North America, Europe, and Asia.

DROUGHT

A drought is a condition of significantly below-normal water levels in the ground, lakes, reservoirs, and rivers. The most obvious effect of drought is crop failure. In less-developed nations—where local agriculture is barely enough to feed the population—drought-caused crop failure may result in the deaths of many people from starvation and malnutrition. In any area stricken by drought, the possibility of forest fires and grass fires is greatly increased; soils dry out and may be blown away by winds; and animals may die of thirst.

▶ THE OCCURRENCE OF DROUGHT

Drought occurs when the major forces involved in the earth's water-balance cycle take more water away from the ground than precipitation adds. (Precipitation is rain, snow, sleet and hail.) Groundwater is lost mostly through evaporation and transpiration, which is the use of groundwater by plants in their food-making process. When there is not enough rain (or other precipitation) to balance the loss, a drought occurs.

Drought is a shortage of water caused by abnormally dry climate conditions. During the recent long drought in Africa, famine and thirst forced people to migrate.

Drought often occurs when periods of extreme heat totally dry out the land. Or drought can occur when temperatures are cooler but there is very little rain.

The most important cause of drought is a change in the regular weather pattern. When the normal storm track moves away from an area, there are fewer storms to bring rain, and drought becomes possible. Forecasting droughts is very difficult, though, because scientists are not sure why these storm tracks move from year to year.

While drought is a condition of below-normal water levels, different parts of the world can have greatly different "normal" conditions. For example, Seattle, Washington, has a normal rainfall of 38.6 inches (980 millimeters) per year, while Cairo, Egypt, has a normal rainfall of 1.1 inches (27.9 millimeters) per year. So, an amount of rain that is well below normal in Seattle can easily be much above normal in Cairo.

What people consider a drought can change depending on how people use water. An abnormally dry period of one month may not even be noticed by someone who lives in a city. But the same abnormally dry month can have severe effects on a farmer's livelihood if it happens during the crop-growing season.

Dry periods that are part of an area's normal weather pattern are not considered droughts. For example, Seattle does not get a steady stream of rain during the year. The city usually has warm, dry summers and rainy or snowy winters. Even though summers are dry, the dry period is not considered to be a drought because that is part of Seattle's normal weather pattern.

▶ THE DURATION OF DROUGHTS

Droughts can be short and last only a few weeks. Or they can drag on for years.

An example of a long drought occurred in the Sahel region of north central Africa. Rainfall was below normal in this area from 1968 through 1984. Many people were forced to leave the Sahel in search of food and water. It became so dry there that some parts of the area, which used to be farmland, have now become part of the Sahara desert.

Crops wither and die during a drought, and farmers often face severe economic hardship.

A much shorter drought happened in the summer of 1980 in the United States. This drought started in June in Texas and moved eastward all summer until it reached the East Coast in early September. Much of the southern United States quickly dried out, even though the South had had a very wet spring. The drought was marked by extremely hot temperatures. From late June through early August, temperatures near Dallas, Texas, reached 100°F (38°C) or higher for 42 consecutive days. Throughout the drought-stricken area, crops, livestock, and nearly 1,300 people died because of the heat.

Another type of drought hit New York City during the summer of 1985. There was enough rain to keep the grass green and crops growing on nearby farms. But the city's reservoirs were at dangerously low levels because there had been very little snow or rain during the previous winter. Winter precipitation is very important for keeping reservoirs full. This is because the loss of water to evaporation and transpiration is lowest during the cold season. So, during the winter, relatively more precipitation winds up in reservoirs than during the summer.

▶ HUMAN ACTIVITY AND DROUGHT

People can do things that make drought worse. In the Sahel region of Africa, people cut down many trees. Trees absorb some of the sun's heat. Without the trees, some scientists think, temperatures were hotter in north central Africa than they were when the trees were still there. Thus, human actions —in this case, the cutting of trees—probably worsened the effects of drought.

Some scientists also believe that the residents of New York City made their drought worse by using much more water than residents of other cities normally use. The city's reservoirs were drained very quickly. Finally, city authorities had to order people to stop watering lawns, washing cars, and otherwise using water unnecessarily. These steps were taken so that the half-filled reservoirs would have enough water to last through the summer.

Careful conservation of the water supply is perhaps the best way that people can prepare for the possibility of drought. However, during periods of good rainfall, people tend to forget that drought can occur quickly and can quite rapidly reduce the water supply.

ROBERT A. WEISMAN
State University of New York at Albany

327

DISNEY, WALT (1901–1966)

When people think of animated cartoons, one name immediately comes to mind—Walt Disney. While he did not invent animated cartoons, Disney was responsible for improving their quality and making them into an art form. Out of his work came what is probably the world's best known cartoon character—Mickey Mouse.

Walt Disney began by making a mouse the world could love—and then went on to create a family entertainment empire.

Walter Elias Disney was born in Chicago, Illinois, on December 5, 1901, the fourth of five children of Elias· and Flora Disney. When he was a baby, the family moved to a farm near Marceline, Missouri. It was here that Walt spent his early years and developed his interest in drawing. In 1910 the family moved again—this time to Kansas City. There, Walt delivered newspapers and went to school. When he was 14, he enrolled in art classes at the Kansas City Art Institute.

Mickey Mouse, Disney's most famous creation, first appeared in *Steamboat Willie*, in 1928. Mickey soon became a movie "star" around the world.

The Disney family moved back to Chicago in 1917. Walt attended one year of high school there before joining a Red Cross unit and spending nine months as an ambulance driver in France at the end of World War I.

When Disney returned from France in 1919, he decided to make art his career. He soon joined the staff of the Kansas City Film Ad Company, which was producing a simple type of animation. He and a colleague, Ubbe Iwerks, learned enough about animation to try doing some of their own. They formed a company called Laugh-O-Gram Films, where they made crude animated cartoons.

Disneyland, in Anaheim, California, was a dream of Walt Disney's for many years. The dream came true in 1955. Millions of people flock to Disneyland and its sister park, Disney World in Orlando, Florida, each year.

In 1923, Disney moved to California, and in partnership with his brother Roy he began Walt Disney Productions. After five years of making silent cartoons, he produced *Steamboat Willie,* the first cartoon to use synchronized sound (sound that matches what is going on in the film). Walt Disney's cartoon creation, Mickey Mouse, appeared in that 1928 cartoon, using Disney's own voice. Disney's success led to the film series *Silly Symphonies,* which was introduced in 1929 and first used color in 1932. Soon full-color Disney cartoons, such as *Three Little Pigs* and *The Tortoise and the Hare,* were winning Academy Awards. The 1930's brought fame to Walt Disney as Mickey Mouse and his pals Donald Duck, Pluto, Minnie Mouse, and Goofy appeared not only in cartoons but on merchandise items licensed by Disney.

Mickey Mouse cartoons featured a supporting cast of such popular characters as Minnie Mouse, Donald Duck, Goofy, and Pluto.

Two of Disney's earliest, and still most popular, feature-length cartoons were *Snow White and the Seven Dwarfs* (*below*), made in 1937, and *Bambi* (*left*), made in 1942. *Fantasia*, made in 1940, combined cartoons with classical music.

Disney's *The Mickey Mouse Club*, a weekly television series of the 1950's, featured teenage singers and puppeteers.

Epcot Center opened at Disney World in 1982. The Center features displays of new technology and exhibits from many countries.

In 1937 the Disney studio produced the world's first animated feature film, *Snow White and the Seven Dwarfs.* Then came *Pinocchio* and *Fantasia* in 1940, *Dumbo* in 1941, and *Bambi* in 1942. *Song of the South,* in 1946, used cartoon characters with live actors.

During World War II the Disney organization designed military insignia and made training films for the United States armed forces. After the war Disney continued to make animated films, such as *Alice in Wonderland* (1951), *Peter Pan* (1953), and *The Jungle Book* (1967). He also turned to live-action films such as *Treasure Island* (1950) and *20,000 Leagues Under the Sea.*

Moving into a totally new area, Walt Disney opened Disneyland in Anaheim, California, in 1955. He had wanted to design an amusement park where families could have fun together. Disneyland had exciting rides and attractions, and the park eventually came to be one of the most popular tourist attractions in the United States.

During the next decade, Disney added new attractions to Disneyland while continuing to make films the whole family could enjoy. *Mary Poppins,* in 1964, is considered by many to be the pinnacle of his filmmaking career. Disney won a record 32 Academy Awards for his technical innovations in film.

Walt Disney also pioneered the production of feature films for television. Some of these appeared on his weekly series ''The Mickey Mouse Club'' (1955–59) and on ''Walt Disney's Wonderful World of Color,'' which aired, under several titles, for 29 seasons.

Shows prepared for the New York World's Fair in 1964 enabled Disney to show off his innovative Audio-Animatronics figures in such attractions as *It's a Small World* and *Great Moments with Mr. Lincoln.* The lifelike figure of Abraham Lincoln, which stood and recited passages from some of Lincoln's speeches, amazed fairgoers.

Walt Disney never rested. Before he died, on December 15, 1966, he was planning a new Walt Disney World vacation kingdom in Florida, and Epcot, an experimental prototype community of tomorrow. Both parks came into being after his death, Walt Disney World opening in 1971 and Epcot Center in 1982.

SHARON DISNEY LUND

DIGESTIVE SYSTEM

Biting into an apple, sniffing the aroma of a cake baking, or even thinking about your favorite food is enough to start your mouth watering. That is the first step in a process called digestion, by which the foods you eat are changed into forms that the body can use for energy and building materials.

During digestion, food passes through the body along a sort of assembly line, which is equipped with work stations where foods are chopped up, churned around, and soaked in chemical baths. These treatments gradually reduce the solid lumps of food to a soupy semi-liquid and finally to individual chemicals small enough to pass into the bloodstream. From there, they are carried as nourishment to the body's cells.

▶ ORGANS OF THE DIGESTIVE SYSTEM

The digestive tract is one long, continuous tube running from the mouth down through the neck and into the trunk of the body, finally ending at the opening called the anus. Along the way, the tube curves and loops repeatedly. In an adult, about 30 feet (9 meters) of digestive tract are packed into the area of the body between the mouth and the anus.

The mouth is the receiving chamber for food. It is equipped with 32 teeth, which are specialized for cutting, tearing, and grinding all kinds of foods. The **esophagus,** a muscular tube, acts like a conveyor belt for chewed food. It carries food from the mouth down to the **stomach** for further processing.

In the stomach, food is churned around and mixed with digestive chemicals to help break it into smaller particles that the body can use.

The stomach leads into the **small intestine,** a tube about 20 feet (6 meters) long that is looped and coiled to take up most of the space inside the abdomen. The inner wall of the intestine is covered with microscopic fingerlike projections, called **villi.** There are hundreds of villi in 1 square inch (6 square centimeters) of intestinal wall. They provide a large surface area for nutrients to be absorbed into the body. The three main parts of the small intestine are the **duodenum,** the C-shaped first part; the **jejunum,** the coiling

middle section; and the **ileum,** the final section that empties into the **large intestine.**

The last organ of the digestive tract is the large intestine. It is made up of two parts: the **colon,** which passes up, across, and down the abdomen; and the **rectum,** which leads out of the body through the anus.

In addition to the organs of the digestive tract itself, the pancreas and liver are also part of the digestive process. They produce chemicals that aid digestion in the small intestine. Bile, a product of the liver used in digestion, is stored temporarily in the gall bladder.

▶ A TRIP THROUGH THE DIGESTIVE SYSTEM

It is lunchtime, and you are sitting down to a tempting meal: a hamburger on a bun, a glass of milk, and a juicy apple for dessert. What happens when you eat this food? How does your body get the nutrients it needs?

This sample lunch provides plenty of all the main kinds of food substances. There are proteins in the hamburger, bun, and milk; carbohydrates in the bun, milk, and apple; and fats in the hamburger and milk. These foods also contain water, vitamins, and minerals; but they will not need to be digested—the body can absorb them just as they are.

Your mouth is starting to water as you bite into the hamburger. Your teeth grind the bread and meat as they are mixed with a watery fluid, **saliva,** produced by salivary glands in the mouth. An enzyme (a substance that speeds up a chemical reaction) in the saliva begins the digestive process already. It starts to break down the carbohydrates from the bun into sugars. (If you chewed long enough, the bread would start to taste sweet.)

After a big swallow, the food slips down your throat. Passing through the **pharynx,** a shared passageway for food and air, it travels down into the esophagus. There, waves of muscle contraction, known as **peristalsis,** carry it to the stomach. Gravity helps move the food, but it is not essential. Astronauts in space can eat normally even when they are in weightless environments.

In the Stomach. Some substances are absorbed directly through the stomach wall.

If the human digestive tract were stretched out in a line, it would be 30 feet long—more than five times taller than an average adult.

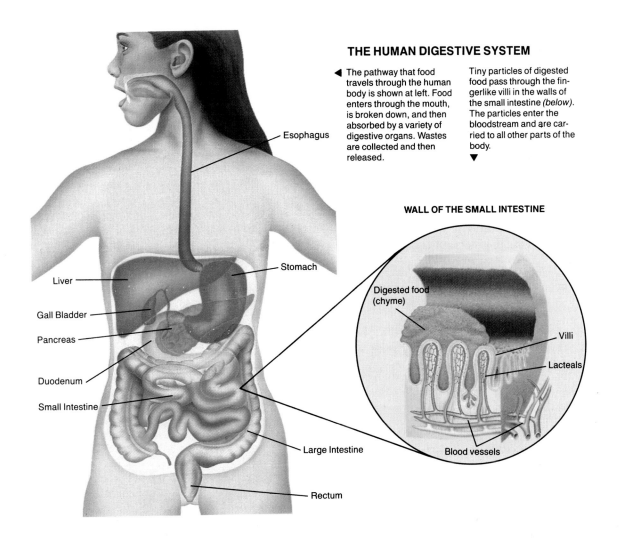

THE HUMAN DIGESTIVE SYSTEM

◄ The pathway that food travels through the human body is shown at left. Food enters through the mouth, is broken down, and then absorbed by a variety of digestive organs. Wastes are collected and then released.

Tiny particles of digested food pass through the fingerlike villi in the walls of the small intestine *(below)*. The particles enter the bloodstream and are carried to all other parts of the body.
▼

Esophagus

Stomach

Liver

Gall Bladder

Pancreas

Duodenum

Small Intestine

Large Intestine

Rectum

WALL OF THE SMALL INTESTINE

Digested food (chyme)

Villi

Lacteals

Blood vessels

These are generally small molecules, such as water, salt, and simple sugars. Some of the sugar from your apple will pass into the bloodstream directly from the stomach.

Most other food must undergo further digestion, however. Contractions of the muscular stomach wall produce a churning motion that mixes the food with strong chemicals produced in special glands in the stomach lining. One of these chemicals, hydrochloric acid, is strong enough to curdle milk, changing it into soft lumps. An enzyme called pepsin helps to digest the proteins from the hamburger bun and meat by breaking them down into chemically simpler substances. (The proteins are not completely broken down here. They must travel to the small intestine for further digestion.)

Through the Small Intestine. By the time the food is ready to leave the stomach, it has turned into a soupy semi-liquid called **chyme.** This is squirted down into the duodenum part of the small intestine. Here, muscular contractions move the chyme along as a number of digestive chemicals work on it.

The pancreas contributes a salt, sodium bicarbonate, that neutralizes the acid from the stomach. This creates the alkaline conditions that are best for the work of the digestive enzymes in the intestines. Some of these enzymes also come from the pancreas. They are amylase, which breaks down carbohydrates into sugars; lipase, which breaks down fats into fatty acids and glycerol; and trypsin, which breaks down proteins into the building blocks—the amino acids.

Glands in the walls of the intestines also produce digestive enzymes. Some of these are sucrase and lactase, which change complex sugar molecules into simple sugars; and aminopeptidase, which breaks down partially digested proteins into amino acids. Bile, made by the liver, breaks down large fat globules (droplets) into tiny ones so lipases from the intestines can digest them more readily.

The products of digestion are absorbed through the villi in the lining of the small intestine. These villi contain tiny blood vessels that carry most of the nutrients into the bloodstream. The sugars from digested carbohydrates and the amino acids from digested proteins pass into these tiny blood vessels. Minerals, such as iron from the hamburger meat and calcium from the milk, also pass into these blood vessels. Vitamins are also absorbed into the bloodstream. The blood vessels from the villi lead to the liver, where some of the food materials are stored for later use.

Something different, however, happens to the products of fat digestion. They are absorbed into **lacteals,** which are structures in the villi that are connected to the lymphatic system. This system eventually empties into the bloodstream.

Through the Large Intestine. By the time the remains of the meal reach the large intestine, the process of digestion is basically complete. The main job of the large intestine is to remove water from the undigested food matter and form this matter into solid masses, called **feces,** which are eliminated from the body. Bacteria live in the large intestines and feed on the undigested matter, helping to break it down further.

▶ DISORDERS OF THE DIGESTIVE SYSTEM

Nearly everyone suffers now and then from a digestive system problem. Some disorders are due to poor eating habits, but others can be serious and must be treated by a doctor.

Stomachache is a rather vague term that most people use for discomfort in the abdomen, where the intestines are, rather than in the stomach. Eating spoiled food or drinking water contaminated by bacteria can cause painful muscle cramps in the intestines; an emotional upset also can have this effect.

Heartburn is a painful burning sensation in the middle of the chest that actually does not involve the heart. It occurs when acidic digestive fluids in the stomach squirt up into the esophagus and cause irritation.

The stomach lining is normally protected from these acids by a coating of gooey mucus. But sometimes the acid gets through to the delicate cells of the stomach or duodenum and produces a painful sore called an **ulcer.**

In diarrhea, muscle contractions move the contents of the intestines along too quickly. There is not enough time for the water to be absorbed, and the feces are soft or even liquid instead of solid. Infection in the digestive tract is a common cause of diarrhea. If diarrhea continues, the body may lose too much water and become dangerously dehydrated.

In constipation, the contents of the intestines do not move along fast enough. Waste materials stay in the large intestine so long that too much water is removed and the feces become hard. When the feces become hard, elimination may be painful, which adds to the problem.

▶ DIGESTION IN THE LIVING WORLD

All animals, from single-celled creatures such as the amoeba to human beings with trillions of body cells, must digest the foods they take in. Even plants have to digest some of the stored food materials that they have manufactured themselves during the process of photosynthesis.

Digestion in a single-celled amoeba is a simple matter. A bit of food is enclosed in a bubble called a **vacuole,** and digestive enzymes flow in. As the food is broken down, the usable chemicals pass through the membrane that surrounds the vacuole and are absorbed by the cell. When only waste products remain, the vacuole moves to the surface of the cell, opens up, and releases its contents.

All complex organisms, beginning with the earthworm, have a tube-type digestive system in which food moves through a long tube in the body, starting with the mouth and ending at the anus. Such a system permits an efficient assembly-line arrangement where specialized work stations along the digestive tract handle various kinds of food materials.

ALVIN SILVERSTEIN
VIRGINIA SILVERSTEIN
Co-authors, *The Digestive System*

BABYLONIA

In Babylonia (a region in what is now southern Iraq), a talented people built a great civilization almost 4,000 years ago. Among their accomplishments, the Babylonians developed the exact sciences, especially mathematics and astronomy. Because the Babylonians sought to use their science to predict the future, their astronomy gave way to astrology, a belief that the motion of the heavenly bodies affects the course of human events. Thus, while the Babylonians laid a foundation for modern science, it remained for the later Greeks to separate science from superstition.

The Babylonians were a Semitic people whose language was related to Hebrew and Arabic. They were influenced by a people who lived in the region earlier, the Sumerians. Like the Sumerians, they used a style of writing called cuneiform ("wedge-shaped") and developed a culture built around large cities.

The capital of Babylonia was the city of Babylon, situated near the Euphrates River where it approaches the Tigris River. It was not far from present-day Baghdad, the capital of Iraq.

The Tower of Babel. The most distinctive type of Babylonian building was the ziggurat, a towerlike temple, built in stages and topped by a religious shrine. Although the ziggurat was first developed by the Sumerians, the Babylonians carried on the tradition. The most famous ziggurat is the Tower of Babel mentioned in the Bible. The chief god of the Babylonians was Marduk, whose cult spread with the growth of the Babylonian Empire.

The Code of Hammurabi. Babylon became important after 1800 B.C. under a succession of kings known as the First Dynasty of Babylon. The most famous monarch in that line was Hammurabi (Hammurapi), who ruled from about 1792 to 1750 B.C. By the use of shrewd diplomacy and strong armies, he defeated his rivals, the kings of other city-states, and carved out the most powerful empire of his day. Hammurabi also established a code of laws that regulated society strictly, with justice but little mercy. Although harsh, Hammurabi's laws protected his subjects from injustice.

Hammurabi's Code, one of the world's oldest sets of laws, was inscribed about 4,000 years ago on this tablet. The seated figure is that of Hammurabi, king of Babylon.

Nebuchadnezzar II. The next great king of Babylon lived a thousand years later. Nebuchadnezzar II, who reigned from 605 to 562 B.C., made Babylon the greatest city of its day. He beautified its capital with structures such as the Hanging Gardens, famed as one of the Seven Wonders of the Ancient World. Nebuchadnezzar conquered many nations, including the Jews, whose Temple in Jerusalem he destroyed in 586 B.C.

The long rule of Babylon ended with its capture by the Persians under Cyrus the Great, in 539 B.C. At least one great monument of the Babylonians survives, however. The development of modern Iraq is due in large measure to its restoration of the ancient irrigation canal system built by the Babylonians. This ancient system made the region between the Tigris and Euphrates rivers the most fertile in the world.

CYRUS H. GORDON
New York University
Author, *Hammurapi's Code*

ALPHABET

An alphabet is a group of signs that are used to write a language. The signs—called letters—express all the individual sounds that people use when they speak.

We think of the letters of our alphabet as having a fixed order—beginning with A and ending with Z—only because that is how we learned it. The letters originally were made up as they were needed, rather than in any logical pattern. We could easily change the order of the letters in our alphabet, and it would not affect the way we write or speak.

The ancestor of the alphabet we use for writing English was created more than 3,000 years ago. Our alphabet is called the Latin or Roman alphabet because it is taken directly from the alphabet used by the ancient Romans. The Romans adapted this alphabet from the one used by the Etruscans, another people who lived in Italy, who in turn had borrowed it from the Greeks. The Greeks had taken the alphabet from the Phoenicians, a Semitic people who lived along the eastern end of the Mediterranean Sea. Which Semitic people actually originated the concept of the alphabet remains a mystery. But by about 1000 B.C., several groups of people speaking related languages—including the Arameans, the Phoenicians, and the Hebrews—were all using this same basic system for writing their languages.

▶ FORERUNNERS OF THE ALPHABET

An alphabet is a writing system that expresses the sounds of language. This kind of writing system is called phonetic ("by sounds"). An alphabet has signs for the smallest individual speech sounds. We call these individual sounds **phonemes** ("sound units"). Another type of writing system is also phonetic, but it is not considered an alphabet. It uses signs to stand for **syllables.** Syllables are speech units that are made up of phonemes. A syllable can be a complete word or part of a word, but it must contain a vowel sound.

A third type of writing system has signs that stand for complete words regardless of how many syllables the word has. Even though we have an alphabet, we sometimes use signs for complete words in order to save time and space. For example, all of our numerals are word signs. It is much easier to write 1945 than to use our alphabet to spell out "one thousand nine hundred forty-five." Other common word signs that we use include & for "and," + for "plus," and $ for "dollar."

Word Writing Systems. The earliest writing systems, which came into use about 3000 B.C., used almost all word signs. These were the hieroglyphic writing of ancient Egypt and the cuneiform writing of the ancient Sumerians. The main disadvantage to a writing system that uses only word signs is that it needs a large number of signs because there are many words in a language. Look at the size of the dictionary. Imagine having to learn a different sign for every word in the dictionary in order to be able to read and write.

Actually, in a word writing system the same sign often stands for several related words. The reader must decide which of the words the writer meant with the sign that was used. Such a system still needs about 1,000 signs. Chinese is one of the only modern languages to use a word writing system.

Word-Syllabic Writing Systems. Because of the drawbacks of using only word signs, the Sumerians and Egyptians quickly developed signs for syllables, which they used in combination with word signs. This was a tremendous improvement over using word signs by themselves because the exact word the writer intended to use could be expressed more accurately.

The Sumerians indicated vowel sounds in their syllabic signs. This meant that they needed a sign for each consonant/vowel combination. (In English, for example, different signs would be needed to express the syllables ba, be, bi, bo, bu, da, de, di, do,

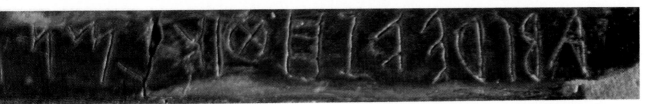

The Etruscan alphabet, which reads from right to left, is one of the ancestors of our alphabet. This carving, made about 700 B.C., was probably used for teaching.

du, and so on.) The Egyptian signs were simpler. They stood for the consonant plus any vowel. In this system the reader had to supply the correct vowel, which caused some confusion. It would be like writing "ht" in English and leaving it to the reader to decide whether the letters meant hot, hat, hit, or hut. The advantage of the system was that the number of syllabic signs needed was reduced to the number of consonants in the language.

Syllabic Writing Systems. The Semitic peoples of Syria and Palestine developed purely syllabic writing systems. Their systems were very simple because they eliminated word signs completely and, like the Egyptians, their signs expressed consonants plus any vowel. This simplification was an important step in the development of the alphabet.

Because vowels were not expressed by the writing, these syllabic systems—called **syllabaries**—were not true alphabets. Alphabets have a sign for each phoneme in the language. But the Semitic syllabaries developed into the alphabets used today. The most important of the Semitic syllabaries were the Phoenician, from which the Greeks developed their alphabet, and the Aramaic.

The Phoenician Writing System. The earliest example of Phoenician writing that we have is from the city of Byblos and dates from about 1000 B.C., but the writing system was surely in use before this. Byblos was a major center of commerce. It was so important in the trade in papyrus, a paperlike material used for writing, that its name gave the Greeks their word for "book" (*biblos*) and the English language its "Bible." Some scholars think that Byblos may have been the place where the Semitic writing system was first created, but there is no direct evidence of this.

The Phoenician writing system had 22 signs. Each sign had a name, the first sound of which was the sound that the sign represented. In many cases the signs can be recognized as pictures of the object that forms the name of the sign. The first sign was called *aleph,* which was the Phoenician word for "bull," and the sign looked like a bull's head.

The second sign, called *beth,* represented the sound "b." It was the Phoenician word for "house," and the letter looked something like the plan of a simple house. You can go all the way through the Phoenician script in this manner, finding meanings for almost all the names of the signs and relating the signs to the names. The last sign was *taw,* which meant "sign" or "mark." It was in the shape of a simple cross.

This, then, was the writing system that the Greeks adapted to write their own language.

▶ THE DEVELOPMENT OF THE ROMAN ALPHABET

Greeks. When the Greeks adapted the Phoenician writing system to their own language, some time before the 8th century B.C., they made a very significant change. They created signs for vowels and used them each time a vowel occurred. Simple as this sounds, it was the last important step in the development of writing systems that had been going on for more than 2,000 years. The Greek writing system was truly an alphabet, because each sound in the language now had its own sign. Every word could be written accurately with a system that used a very small number of signs.

The Greeks did not invent new signs for the vowels but simply converted some of the Phoenician signs that they did not need for their own language into vowel symbols. They also added some letters and later dropped others to create the 24-letter Greek alphabet. When the Greeks borrowed signs from the Phoenicians, they kept the names for the signs, although they had no meaning in Greek. Thus *aleph* became *alpha,* and *beth* became *beta.* It is from the names of these two letters that our word "alphabet" comes.

Etruscans. The next step in the alphabet's journey was to the Etruscans. They were a people of northern Italy who were influential from the 11th to the 6th century B.C. The Etruscans wrote their language using an early Greek alphabet, with some modifications. The most important offshoot of the Etruscan alphabet was the Roman alphabet.

Romans. The Romans adapted the Etruscan alphabet, probably beginning in the 6th century B.C. Of the 26 letters of the original Etruscan alphabet, the Romans accepted 20.

By the 3rd century B.C. the Roman alphabet consisted of 21 letters: A, B, C, D, E, F, G, H, I, K, L, M, N, O, P, Q, R, S, T, V, and X. Only J, U, W, Y, and Z remained to be added to the alphabet. When the Romans conquered Greece in the 1st century B.C., a large number of Greek words were taken into the Latin language. The Romans found it necessary to borrow some Greek letters in order to write these new words. The Greek letter *upsilon* had developed into a sound between *u* and *e,* and the Romans gave it the

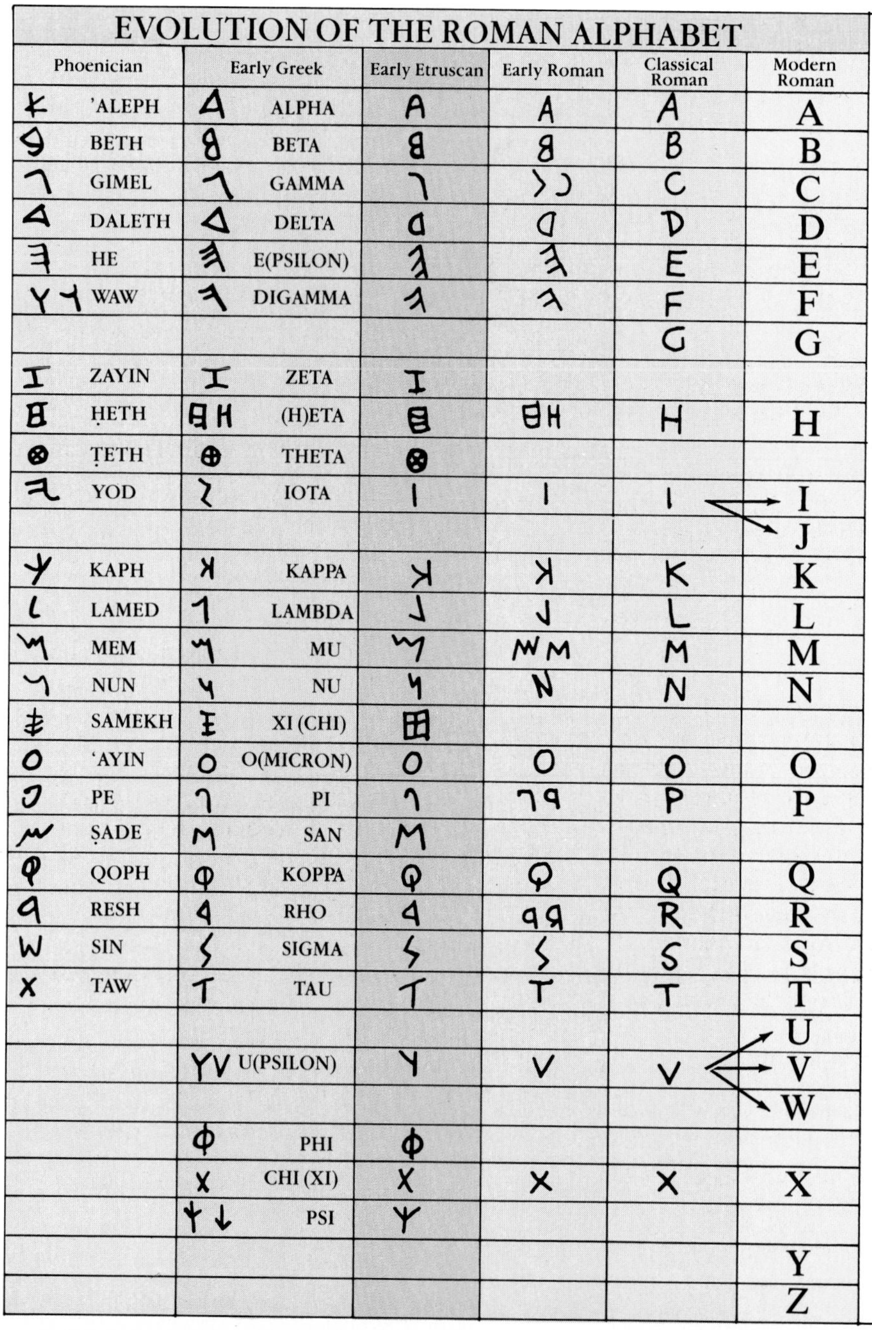

EVOLUTION OF THE ROMAN ALPHABET

Phoenician		Early Greek		Early Etruscan	Early Roman	Classical Roman	Modern Roman
𐤀	'ALEPH	A	ALPHA	A	A	A	A
𐤁	BETH	8	BETA	8	8	B	B
𐤂	GIMEL	⌐	GAMMA	⌐	)	C	C
𐤃	DALETH	△	DELTA	◁	◁	D	D
𐤄	HE	ᴈ	E(PSILON)	ᴈ	ᴈ	E	E
𐤅	WAW	ᚴ	DIGAMMA	ᚴ	ᚴ	F	F
						G	G
𐤆	ZAYIN	I	ZETA	I			
𐤇	ḤETH	日 H	(H)ETA	日	日H	H	H
𐤈	ṬETH	⊕	THETA	⊗			
𐤉	YOD	۵	IOTA	I	I	I	I / J
𐤊	KAPH	ʞ	KAPPA	ʞ	ʞ	K	K
𐤋	LAMED	٦	LAMBDA	٦	٦	L	L
𐤌	MEM	ᙢ	MU	ᙢ	MM	M	M
𐤍	NUN	�	NU	�	N	N	N
𐤎	SAMEKH	王	XI (CHI)	田			
𐤏	'AYIN	O	O(MICRON)	O	O	O	O
𐤐	PE	ᒋ	PI	ᒋ	ᒋ9	P	P
𐤑	ṢADE	M	SAN	M			
𐤒	QOPH	Φ	KOPPA	Q	Q	Q	Q
𐤓	RESH	◁	RHO	◁	99	R	R
𐤔	SIN	⟨	SIGMA	⟨	⟨	S	S
𐤕	TAW	T	TAU	T	T	T	T
							U
		Y V	U(PSILON)	Y	V	V	V
							W
		Φ	PHI	Φ			
		X	CHI (XI)	X	X	X	X
		Y ↓	PSI	Y			
							Y
							Z

The Roman alphabet, which is used to write English and many other modern languages, developed over thousands of years. From left: The Phoenician syllabary was an important early writing system. From it the Greeks developed their alphabet, which spread to the Etruscans. The Romans adapted the Etruscan alphabet. By the 3rd century B.C., 21 of the capital letters that we use today had been perfected by the Romans.

name *wye*. The letter *zeta* had been rejected five centuries earlier and its place in the order taken by G, but it was now accepted and along with Y placed at the end of the alphabet after X. This brought the total number of letters to 23. This was the alphabet that was used during the time of the Roman Empire. J, U, and W were added at a much later time.

Capital and Small Letters. In ancient times, all writing was done in what we call capital (or uppercase) letters. Small (or lowercase) letters developed later.

The Roman letters were perfected by the 1st and 2nd centuries A.D. The form known as square capitals was written with great precision, especially on stone, and the letters were symmetrical and well proportioned. These forms are what we still use for our capital letters today.

The small letters of our modern alphabet developed more gradually. While square capitals were fine for stone inscriptions, everyday writing, done with a pen or brush on papyrus or parchment, required more flexibility and speed. The everyday script, which used much rounder forms of the letters (still capitals), was called cursive. Writing materials were expensive, so the scribes who copied books tried to fit as much lettering as possible on a page and in the process created a number of "book hands." These two factors—the need to write quickly and the need to save space—led to the development of our small letters.

▶ **TODAY'S ALPHABETS**

Many different alphabets are used in the world today, but with the possible exception of the Korean alphabet all of them developed in one way or another from the Semitic writing system.

The Cyrillic Alphabet. We have already seen how the Greek alphabet developed from the Phoenician and how the Roman alphabet developed from the Greek. Two other alphabets also developed from the Greek but at a much later date. In the 9th century A.D., the Glagolitic and the Cyrillic alphabets were devised to write the Slavic languages. Both were based on the Greek alphabet then in use. Glagolitic was more popular at first but eventually was replaced by Cyrillic, which is not as complicated. Cyrillic in various forms is used today in Bulgaria, parts of Yugoslavia, and the Soviet Union.

Other Alphabets. Except for those areas that use the Greek and Cyrillic alphabets, some form of the Roman alphabet is used throughout Europe. Almost all the rest of the world's alphabets developed from the Semitic syllabary known as Aramaic. The alphabets derived from the Aramaic include those used to write the modern Semitic languages—Arabic, Hebrew, and Syriac. Alphabets used in India and Southeast Asia and the Mongol script are also derived from the Aramaic.

In the 3,000 years since its invention, the alphabet has proved to be a very durable and flexible tool for expressing language. It has been adapted successfully to many languages. Apparently it is here to stay.

ROBERT M. WHITING
The Oriental Institute
The University of Chicago

POTTER, HELEN BEATRIX
(1866–1943)

Helen Beatrix Potter was born in London on July 28, 1866. Unlike her younger brother, who was sent off to school, Beatrix was educated at home by governesses. She had no playmates her own age, so she turned for friendship to the stuffed animals she played with in the nursery of her family's large house.

In the summer her parents took Beatrix and her brother to Scotland. These vacations opened her eyes to the wonders of the countryside. She made sketches of the animals, birds, and insects that she saw. Back in London she would entertain herself with her pet snails, mice, rabbits, and a hedgehog named Mrs. Tiggy-Winkle, which drank out of a doll's teacup.

As Beatrix grew older, she wrote many letters to her younger friends. These letters were filled with drawings and stories she made up to entertain them. One series of letters to the sick child of her former governess tells the original tale of the naughty Peter Rabbit. Her stories became so popular among her friends that, in 1900, she decided to publish *The Tale of Peter Rabbit* in a private edition. Her publisher was soon bringing out her stories as quickly as she could write and illustrate them.

The following years saw the publication of *The Tailor of Gloucester* (1902), *The Tale of Squirrel Nutkin* (1903), and *The Tale of Benjamin Bunny* (1904). Beatrix Potter believed that a small child's book should be small itself, so all of her tales appeared in little books, with only one or two sentences and a watercolor illustration on each page.

In 1905 she purchased Hill Top Farm in the village of Sawrey in northern England and began to raise sheep. Many of the scenes and animals in her most famous books were drawn from Hill Top Farm. The next eight years were Beatrix Potter's most creative period. She published her finest work, including the tales of Jeremy Fisher, Jemima Puddle-duck, Tom Kitten, the Flopsy Bunnies, Mrs. Tittlemouse, and Pigling Bland.

In 1913, Beatrix Potter married William Heelis, a lawyer. In her later years she dedicated herself to buying tracts of land in the

BEATRIX POTTER'S BEST LOVED CHARACTERS

PETER RABBIT, who is naughty and careless and disobeys his mother, nearly gets put into a pie by Mr. McGregor when he steals into the farmer's garden to eat lettuce.

THE TAILOR OF GLOUCESTER works cross-legged on a table from morning till dark, making himself ill, so that his friends the mice must finish the Mayor's new coat.

SQUIRREL NUTKIN, his brother Twinkleberry, and their many cousins go to pick nuts on Old Brown's island, where naughty Nutkin teases the old owl once too often.

BENJAMIN BUNNY, Peter Rabbit's clever cousin, who has no opinion of cats, visits Flopsy, Mopsy, Cottontail, and Peter and rescues Peter's clothes from Mr. McGregor.

JEREMY FISHER, who likes getting his feet wet and never catches cold, goes out on his round green boat and has an adventure fishing in the middle of the pond.

MRS. TITTLEMOUSE, the wood mouse who lives in a barn, is terribly tidy but has a few too many uninvited visitors, including the very messy Mr. Jackson.

MRS. TIGGY-WINKLE, who is scrupulously clean, helps Lucie find her lost pocket handkerchief — all clean and starched and ironed — and gives her a friendly cup of tea.

Lake District in order to preserve the area from commercial development. In her will she turned over her vast holdings to the National Trust for future preservation.

Beatrix Potter died in Sawrey on December 22, 1943. Her home, now part of the National Trust, is open to the public.

RICHARD KELLY
University of Tennessee

338

▶ THE TALE OF JEMIMA PUDDLE-DUCK

Jemima Puddle-duck sets off to find a secret place to hatch her eggs. She meets an elegant gentleman with black ears and a long bushy tail, who offers her the use of his cozy wood-shed. But Jemima is such a foolish duck that she does not recognize her benefactor as—a fox!

He was so polite, that he seemed almost sorry to let Jemima go home for the night. He promised to take great care of her nest until she came back again the next day.

He said he loved eggs and ducklings; he should be proud to see a fine nestful in his wood-shed.

Jemima Puddle-duck came every afternoon; she laid nine eggs in the nest. They were greeny white and very large. The foxy gentleman admired them immensely. He used to turn them over and count them when Jemima was not there.

At last Jemima told him that she intended to begin to sit next day—"and I will bring a bag of corn with me, so that I need never leave my nest until the eggs are hatched. They might catch cold," said the conscientious Jemima.

"Madam, I beg you not to trouble yourself with a bag; I will provide oats. But before you commence your tedious sitting, I intend to give you a treat. Let us have a dinner-party all to ourselves!

"May I ask you to bring up some herbs from the farm-garden to make a savoury omelette? Sage and thyme, and mint and two onions, and some parsley. I will provide lard for the stuff—lard for the omelette," said the hospitable gentleman with sandy whiskers.

Jemima Puddle-duck was a simpleton: not even the mention of sage and onions made her suspicious.

She went round the farm-garden, nibbling off snippets of all the different sorts of herbs that are used for stuffing roast duck.

And she waddled into the kitchen, and got two onions out of the basket.

The collie-dog Kep met her coming out, "What are you doing with those onions? Where do you go every afternoon by yourself, Jemima Puddle-duck?"

Jemima was rather in awe of the collie; she told him the whole story.

The collie listened, with his wise head on one side; he grinned when she described the polite gentleman with sandy whiskers.

He asked several questions about the wood, and about the exact position of the house and shed.

Then he went out, and trotted down the village. He went to look for two fox-hound puppies who were out at walk with the butcher.

Jemima Puddle-duck went up the cart-road for the last time, on a sunny afternoon. She was rather burdened with bunches of herbs and two onions in a bag.

She flew over the wood, and alighted opposite the house of the bushy long-tailed gentleman.

He was sitting on a log; he sniffed the air, and kept glancing uneasily round the wood. When Jemima alighted he quite jumped.

"Come into the house as soon as you have looked at your eggs. Give me the herbs for the omelette. Be sharp!"

He was rather abrupt. Jemima Puddle-duck had never heard him speak like that.

She felt surprised, and uncomfortable.

While she was inside she heard pattering feet round the back of the shed. Some one with a black nose sniffed at the bottom of the door, and then locked it.

Jemima became much alarmed.

A moment afterwards there were most awful noises—barking, baying, growls and howls, squealing and groans.

And nothing more was ever seen of that foxy-whiskered gentleman.

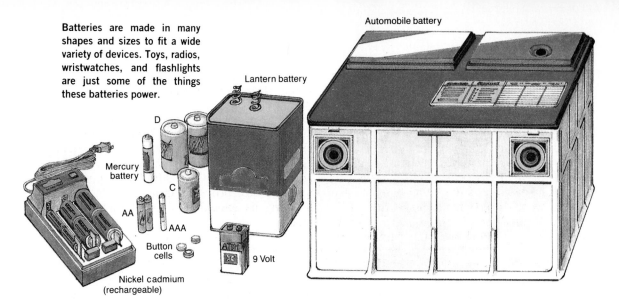

Batteries are made in many shapes and sizes to fit a wide variety of devices. Toys, radios, wristwatches, and flashlights are just some of the things these batteries power.

Automobile battery

Lantern battery

D

Mercury battery

C

AA

AAA

Button cells

9 Volt

Nickel cadmium (rechargeable)

BATTERIES

When you enjoy music from a portable radio or find your way in the dark with a flashlight, you are using the most common portable power source known—the battery.

Batteries are very much a part of our lives. Without them many toys would not work, automobiles would not start, and digital wristwatches would not tell time. Even satellites in orbit would stop relaying their signals to Earth.

▶ WHAT IS A BATTERY?

A battery is a device that produces electrical energy, usually by means of a chemical reaction. This chemical reaction takes place in the part of the battery known as the **cell.** Cells are the battery's building blocks. Each battery contains one or more cells. The common transistor radio battery, for example, is made up of six cells. The common "D" battery is just a single cell.

Batteries can be either **primary** or **secondary** devices. Primary batteries are those that can be used only as long as the supply of chemicals inside them lasts. (The process of producing electricity uses up the chemicals.) When a primary battery stops producing power, it is thrown away.

Secondary batteries, on the other hand, can be recharged. When these batteries are exhausted, an electrical current can be applied to the battery to reverse the chemical reaction that took place inside the cells. The result is a battery with a new supply of energy; it can be used until it runs down again.

▶ HOW PRIMARY BATTERIES WORK

The most common primary battery is the "D" battery, also known as the flashlight battery or the dry cell. The dry cell is not really dry. It contains a central carbon rod surrounded by a damp chemical paste. These are enclosed in a container made of zinc. When the battery is being used, the carbon and zinc react with each other to produce electricity.

To start the chemical reaction, the battery must be in an electrical circuit. Only when there is a demand for power will the battery produce electricity. When the "on" switch is moved—on a flashlight, for example—a complete path, or electrical circuit, is formed that includes the battery, switch, connecting wires, and bulb. Electricity can now flow through the circuit, and the flashlight bulb lights.

Often more than one battery is needed to provide sufficient power to run a device. Several batteries can be used together if they are lined up in a certain way. In a **series connection,** the positive end of one battery must be in contact with the negative end of another battery. This type of arrangement multiplies the force that pushes the electricity (like a pump pushing water) through the device being powered.

Sometimes cells can be wired in a **parallel connection,** that is, positive end to positive end and negative end to negative end. When this is done, the "push" available is the same as from a single battery, but the amount of electricity is multiplied. This type of connection is used where heavy loads, such as electrical motors, must be powered.

Types of Primary Batteries

The flashlight battery is just one of many kinds of primary batteries. Another common type of dry cell, also based on a carbon-zinc chemical reaction, is the 9-volt battery, also known as the transistor radio battery. This device is made up of six flat, 1.5-volt cells stacked one upon the other in a package that will easily fit the small spaces in pocket-size transistor radios and calculators. (These devices do not all use 9-volt batteries. Some take "A" or "AA" cells.) The battery's connecting posts, called **terminals,** are made into clips, and both are located on the top of the package. This helps avoid the problem of putting the battery into a device upside down or backward.

Another type of primary battery is the alkaline battery, which is becoming more popular because of its longer life. Its operation is similar to that of the carbon-zinc dry cell —the only difference is the chemicals used. The basic package is almost identical.

Other types of primary batteries are the mercury battery, the silver-oxide battery used in electronic wristwatches, and the new, very long-life lithium battery. These batteries are named for the chemicals they contain.

Because all primary batteries will, in time, run down and have to be replaced, they are most widely used in products where low cost is important or where recharging is not practical, such as in a wristwatch.

► HOW SECONDARY BATTERIES WORK

Secondary batteries are often referred to as "wet cells" since many contain liquids (unlike the dry or damp chemicals in primary batteries). Secondary batteries are also often called storage batteries because when they are being recharged, they can be thought of as storing energy.

The most common secondary battery is the lead-acid automobile battery. This device is made up of six cells, each of which contains metal plates made of lead and lead dioxide. The plates are immersed in a weak solution of sulfuric acid and water. On the outside of the battery, positive and negative terminals are used to make the electrical connection to the metal plates and acid solution inside.

The automobile battery is turned on by the ignition switch in the car. This action forms a completed electrical circuit. As the battery is being used, or discharged, the lead plates chemically change into different compounds of lead. This process can provide electricity as long as enough lead is present on the plates.

When the battery runs low, however, it can be recharged by forcing electricity to flow into it in the reverse direction. This is the process called charging. It is carried out in a car by a device called an alternator, which is a small electrical generator run by the automobile engine. During charging, the chemical compounds change back into the original lead and lead dioxide. The life of such a battery is measured in years, because it can be charged thousands of times as it runs down.

A Primary Battery

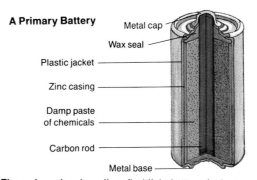

The carbon-zinc dry cell, or flashlight battery, is the most common type of primary battery. A chemical reaction between the carbon, zinc, and damp chemical paste causes an electrical current to be produced.

A Secondary Battery

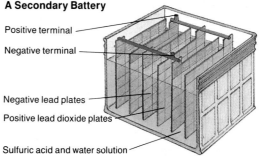

The lead-acid automobile battery, a type of secondary battery, contains lead and lead-oxide plates set in a solution of sulfuric acid and water. This kind of battery can be charged and used over and over again.

Types of Secondary Batteries

Other types of secondary batteries are the nickel cadmium and silver cadmium batteries, which are named for the chemicals they contain. Like the lead-acid automobile battery, they can be charged many times. This is done with a charging device that plugs into an electrical outlet. These batteries can be used in the same applications as primary batteries. They also are used to power rechargeable flashlights, portable two-way radios, and a variety of other battery-operated household appliances that are supplied with their own chargers.

In general, secondary batteries are used where large amounts of power are needed or where charging is practical to carry out. Though they initially cost more than primary batteries, secondary batteries can be very economical because they are not discarded and replaced every time they run down.

▶ HOW POWERFUL ARE BATTERIES?

The amount of power that a battery can deliver is directly related to the amount and type of chemicals it contains. This power is measured in both amperes and volts. An ampere is the amount of electricity the battery can produce in 1 second. Volts are a measure of the "push" the battery can give to electricity flowing through a wire.

The amount of chemicals in a battery also influences the battery's size, so a large battery is more powerful than a small one. Small "AAA" penlight batteries (1.5 volts and ⅛ ampere) will run a penlight for an hour or so. An automobile battery (12 volts and 50 amperes) will provide enough power to start a car or run an electric golf cart.

The life of a battery also depends on the amount of power it must deliver to the device it is running. An automobile battery can start a car and keep it running for a short while, but it will very quickly run down if the car's alternator (turned by the engine) does not begin to charge it. On the other hand, tiny button-size batteries will operate a digital wristwatch for a year or more. This is because the power requirements of a wristwatch are extremely small.

▶ NEW TYPES OF BATTERIES

All of the batteries described ultimately will run down and have to be replaced. Even rechargeable units will reach a point where they will not respond to charging. As a result, scientists are constantly trying to develop the ideal battery that will last for years (when not in use) and will deliver maximum power for long periods of time when needed. Two candidates are the solar cell and the fuel cell.

Solar Cells

Solar cells are unique because no chemical reaction occurs to use up material. Electricity is produced when light, particularly sunlight, strikes the surface of the cell. This surface is a thin wafer of specially treated, pure silicon.

The power produced by such cells is directly related to the amount of light present. In darkness, nothing is produced. In the presence of light, a 3-inch (8-centimeter) solar cell will produce about one third the amount of electrical energy of a "AAA" penlight battery. It will do so, however, as long as light falls on the cell—even for years.

Individual solar cells are almost always connected together to form solar batteries. They are used in applications where it is impractical or even impossible to replace worn-out batteries. The power source for most satellites circling the earth consists of large solar batteries made up of hundreds of individual cells. Solar batteries may one day be used as inexpensive power sources for our homes.

Fuel Cells

Another candidate for the ideal battery is the fuel cell. This device produces electricity from the interaction of two gases—typically hydrogen and oxygen. This battery works by passing hydrogen and oxygen gas over a heated substance in a specially constructed chamber. A complex chemical process combines the two gases and produces electricity as a result.

An interesting by-product of the operation of the fuel cell is pure water. Because the gases are obtained easily and inexpensively and the by-product is useful, large fuel cells someday may become a major source of power for our cities.

IRWIN MATH
Author, *Wires and Watts:
Understanding and Using Electricity*

DAY CARE

Day care is the care of children by paid adults during part of the day when parents are away from home. Day care is provided mainly for infants and preschoolers but also for elementary school children before and after school and during school vacations.

▶ REASONS FOR DAY CARE

Day care for children is necessary for several reasons. In many families both parents or the single parent works outside the home. In the past, other relatives often lived with or near the family and could provide some child care. Today fewer grandparents or other family members are able to care for children whose parents work. Therefore working parents must depend more than ever before on the availability of day care.

▶ TYPES OF DAY CARE

Day care can be provided in two main ways. **Day care centers** typically care for large groups of children in settings resembling nursery schools. They may be run by commercial chains or by nonprofit organizations such as churches or civic groups. Some employers provide day care centers for children of employees.

Day care homes provide care for smaller numbers of children in family settings. This type of care, also called **family day care**, is preferred for very young children, who need a great deal of individual attention. Children over three may benefit more from the group activities in day care centers.

▶ ACTIVITIES

High-quality day care centers and homes offer a variety of activities for children. During the day, children play indoors and outdoors with toys and other play materials. They meet in groups for storytelling, puppet shows, and music. Children receive individual help with a wide variety of projects, such as cooking, science experiments, woodworking, and artwork.

Play materials in centers and homes should encourage both independent play and social play. They should include books, puzzles, blocks, costumes, household objects, dolls, stuffed animals, puppets, clay, paints, crayons, and musical instruments.

A day care center is a place where children are cared for while their parents work outside the home. Supervised by adults, children play together and learn new skills.

▶ CHOOSING DAY CARE

The best way to choose good day care is to interview the adults taking care of the children and to observe the children in the day care settings.

Five important questions should be asked when observing the day care facility. First, are children separated into small groups according to their ages and learning abilities? Second, are there enough adults to supervise the groups and give children individual attention? As a rule of thumb, look for at least one adult for every five preschoolers and at least one adult for every three infants. Third, do the adults know enough about child development to provide appropriate care? Fourth, is the day care setting safe, attractive, comfortable, and clean? Fifth, do the children in the day care setting appear to be happy and engaged in activities?

Accreditation standards for day care programs in the United States are provided by the Academy of Early Childhood programs of the National Association for the Education of Young Children. For more information, write to NAEYC, 1834 Connecticut Avenue, N.W., Washington, D.C. 20009.

ELIZABETH J. HRNCIR
University of Virginia

The writer Kenneth Grahame called on childhood memories of the English countryside to create the setting for his beloved children's book *The Wind in the Willows*.

GRAHAME, KENNETH
(1859–1932)

Kenneth Grahame lived two lives. He was one of the most important bankers in Europe and also one of the greatest writers of children's literature. He was born in Edinburgh, Scotland, on March 8, 1859, the third of four children. When he was 5, his mother died and the children were sent to live with their grandmother, in England.

Although "Granny Ingles" showed little affection for the children, her comfortable old house with its oak beams, its gardens, and the river Thames nearby all made a lifelong impression on young Kenneth. Years later he would bring the river and woods to life again by populating them with Rat, Mole, Toad, Badger, and the other remarkable characters in *The Wind in the Willows*.

Grahame was too poor to be able to attend the university, so in 1879 he went to work as a clerk in the Bank of England. He also began to write essays and sketches. In 1893 he published his first book, *Pagan Papers,* a collection of essays. Between 1894 and 1897 he also wrote for *The Yellow Book,* a well-known literary magazine.

Grahame won fame as a writer of children's books with *The Golden Age* (1895) and *Dream Days* (1898). Both books reflect the rich imaginative life he created to make up for the unhappiness of his childhood. They tell the story of five orphaned children living in a country house with unloving relatives. The children separate themselves from their adult caretakers by acting out stories from their books.

In 1898, Grahame became the secretary of the Bank of England. The next year he married Elspeth Thomson. Their only child, Alastair (nicknamed "Mouse"), was born in 1900. Grahame's most famous book, *The Wind in the Willows* (1908), began as stories told to 4-year-old Alastair. It is a story of friendship, home, and exploration.

The character of Mole is like a child investigating the world for the first time. He has a friendly tutor in the person of Rat, who lives on the edge of the river in a wonderfully cozy home. Badger is a philosopher who lives deep in the Wild Woods. He hates society but becomes friends with Mole and Rat. Another friend is Toad, a reckless fellow who lives in Toad Hall when he is not in jail as the result of some prank. Mole and Rat come to understand that the song of the wind in the willows is one of life and death and the peace that nature offers.

Kenneth Grahame retired from banking in 1908. He wrote little in his later years and died on July 6, 1932, at his home in the village of Pangbourne, on the Thames River.

RICHARD KELLY
University of Tennessee

▶ **THE WIND IN THE WILLOWS**

In this episode from *The Wind in the Willows,* Toad has persuaded Rat and Mole to take to the Open Road with him in a gypsy caravan. But Toad unexpectedly discovers an even more exciting mode of travel.

They were strolling along the highroad easily, the Mole by the horse's head, talking to him, since the horse had complained that he was being frightfully left out of it, and nobody considered him in the least; the Toad and the Water Rat walking behind the cart talking together—at least Toad was talking, and Rat was saying at intervals, "Yes, precisely; and what did *you* say to *him?*" —and thinking all the time of something very different, when far behind them they heard a faint warning hum, like the drone of a distant bee. Glancing back, they saw a small cloud of dust, with a dark centre of energy, advancing on them at incredible speed, while from out of the dust a faint "Poop-poop!" wailed like an uneasy animal in pain. Hardly regarding it, they turned to resume their conversation, when in an instant (as it seemed) the peaceful scene was changed, and with a blast of wind and a whirl of sound that made them jump for the nearest ditch, It was on them! The "poop-poop" rang with a brazen shout in their ears, they had a moment's glimpse of an interior of glittering plate glass and rich morocco, and the magnificent motorcar, immense, breath-snatching, passionate, with its pilot tense and hugging his wheel, possessed all earth and air for the fraction of a second, flung an enveloping cloud of dust that blinded and enwrapped them utterly, and then dwindled to a speck in the far distance, changed back into a droning bee once more.

The old grey horse, dreaming, as he plodded along, of his quiet paddock, in a new raw situation such as this simply abandoned himself to his natural emotions. Rearing, plunging, backing steadily, in spite of all the Mole's efforts at his head, and all the Mole's lively language directed at his better feelings, he drove the cart backwards towards the deep ditch at the side of the road. It wavered an instant—then there was a heart-rending crash—and the canary-coloured cart, their pride and their joy, lay on its side in the ditch, an irredeemable wreck.

The Rat danced up and down in the road, simply transported with passion. "You villains!" he shouted, shaking both fists. "You scoundrels, you highwaymen, you—you—road hogs!—I'll have the law on you! I'll report you! I'll take you

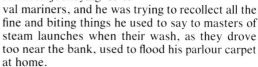

through all the courts!" His homesickness had quite slipped away from him, and for the moment he was the skipper of the canary-coloured vessel driven on a shoal by the reckless jockeying of rival mariners, and he was trying to recollect all the fine and biting things he used to say to masters of steam launches when their wash, as they drove too near the bank, used to flood his parlour carpet at home.

Toad sat straight down in the middle of the dusty road, his legs stretched out before him, and stared fixedly in the direction of the disappearing motorcar. He breathed short, his face wore a placid, satisfied expression, and at intervals he faintly murmured "Poop-poop!"

The Mole was busy trying to quiet the horse, which he succeeded in doing after a time. Then he went to look at the cart, on its side in the ditch. It was indeed a sorry sight. Panels and windows smashed, axles hopelessly bent, one wheel off, sardine tins scattered over the wide world, and the bird in the birdcage sobbing pitifully and calling to be let out.

The Rat came to help him, but their united efforts were not sufficient to right the cart. "Hi, Toad!" they cried. "Come and bear a hand, can't you!"

The Toad never answered a word, or budged from his seat in the road; so they went to see what was the matter with him. They found him in a sort of trance, a happy smile on his face, his eyes still fixed on the dusty wake of their destroyer. At intervals he was still heard to murmur "Poop-poop!"

The Rat shook him by the shoulder. "Are you coming to help us, Toad?" he demanded sternly.

"Glorious, stirring sight!" murmured Toad, never offering to move. "The poetry of motion! Here to-day—in next week to-morrow! Villages skipped, towns and cities jumped—always somebody else's horizon! O bliss! O poop-poop! O my! O my!"

DOLLAR

A dollar is a unit of currency. The United States, Canada, Australia, Hong Kong, and several other countries all call their basic currency unit the dollar. The United States and Canadian dollars are paper bills or coins that equal 100 cents.

"Dollar" comes from the German word *thaler.* In 1519, a large silver coin called the *Joachimsthaler* was minted in Joachimsthal (the Valley of St. Joachim) in Bohemia. The coin was used throughout Europe. The name of the coin became shortened to *thaler,* and English-speaking people gradually changed the pronunciation to "dollar."

With the Coinage Act of 1792, the new government of the United States selected the dollar as the basic unit of currency. At the time, the most familiar currency in use was the Spanish peso, which Americans called a Spanish dollar. Since most people were familiar with prices in terms of Spanish dollars, Thomas Jefferson suggested that the least confusing currency system for the United States would be one based on dollars.

▶ **THE DECIMAL SYSTEM**

Jefferson also suggested a decimal system of coinage, by which a dollar is divided into 100 cents (from the Latin word *centum,* meaning "100"). This system permitted prices to be listed in multiples of 10.

The decimal system of coinage was unusual at that time. Most major currencies had irregular methods for breaking down, or making change from, the basic currency. For example, a Spanish peso was valued at eight *reals* (the term "piece of eight" is familiar from pirate tales). American colonists were accustomed to cutting the Spanish pesos into four pieces in order to make change. Each piece, or bit, was called a "two-real." Even today, the slang for a quarter of a dollar is "two bits." But Thomas Jefferson believed that it was too difficult to use a multiple of four every time someone needed to figure out change or set prices. So the decimal system of coinage was adopted.

The decimal system of coinage was not immediately adopted by other countries. It

U.S. paper money now in circulation

Federal Reserve Notes make up over 99% of the total dollar amount of paper money in general circulation in the United States. They are now issued only in the denominations shown here, although they were formerly available in denominations of $500, $1,000, $5,000 and $10,000. The printing of notes for amounts of $500 or more was discontinued in 1945.

Face: George Washington
Reverse: "One" and Great Seal of the United States

Face: Thomas Jefferson
Reverse: Signing of the Declaration of Independence

Face: Abraham Lincoln
Reverse: Lincoln Memorial

Face: Alexander Hamilton
Reverse: U.S. Treasury

Face: Andrew Jackson
Reverse: White House

Face: Ulysses S. Grant
Reverse: U.S. Capitol

Face: Benjamin Franklin
Reverse: Independence Hall

was not until 1971, for example, that Britain changed to a decimal system.

▶ PRINTING DOLLAR BILLS

Maintaining the supply of dollars is a big job. The Bureau of Engraving and Printing, a division of the United States Treasury Department, produces paper money with a face value of some $50,000,000,000 (billion) every year. The bills roll off the presses in large sheets containing 32 bills and are cut up for distribution. In its two buildings in Washington, D.C., the bureau produces nearly 20,000,000 individual bills a day.

The basic design of today's paper money was set in 1929, when the United States Government decided that existing paper bills were too big. The current size is 6.14 by 2.61 inches (15.6 by 6.6 centimeters).

The bills printed today are only in denominations of $1, $5, $10, $20, $50, and $100. More than half the bills printed are $1 bills,

---

How can you tell if a bill is counterfeit?

The best way to tell if a bill is counterfeit is to compare it with a real bill of the same value. The detail of the features on a counterfeit is likely to be irregular and smudged. Look especially for these differences:

Real bill:	Counterfeit bill:
1. Small red and blue fibers are **in** the paper. (These fibers may not be visible if the bill is old or worn.)	1. Small red and blue fibers are printed **on** the paper.
2. The portrait appears lifelike and stands out clearly from the background. Hair lines are distinct.	2. The portrait is lifeless and merges into the background. The background is too dark. Hair lines are indistinct.
3. The saw-tooth points around the rim of the Treasury Seal are clear and sharp.	3. The saw-tooth points around the rim of the Treasury Seal may be uneven, broken, or blunt.
4. Serial numbers are evenly spaced and lined up perfectly. Ink color should be the same as that of the Treasury Seal.	4. Serial numbers may be unevenly spaced, out of line, or poorly printed. Ink color may be different from that of the Treasury Seal.
5. All ornamental work should be clear and distinct with unbroken lines.	5. Ornamental work may be blurred and broken.

New models of photocopying machines may be able to make very accurate and real-looking counterfeit bills. Because of this, the United States Treasury is planning small, subtle changes in paper money so that counterfeit bills made by photocopying machines will be easier to detect. One suggested change is to add a "security thread" — a thin strip of small printed letters — to all new bills. These letters will be readable to the eye, but if copied on a photocopying machine, the letters will look like a thin line. Thus a "thin line," rather than readable letters, will indicate that the bill is counterfeit.

Another idea is to use a hologram — a three-dimensional picture — on new bills. Holograms cannot be copied correctly by photocopying machines.

The best defense, however, against counterfeiting is careful examination of bills by anyone who handles money.

The United States Secret Service is the division of the Treasury that enforces the laws against counterfeiting. If you receive a counterfeit bill, the Secret Service advises that you:

1. Do not return the bill to the person who gave it to you.

2. Contact the police or the nearest office of the United States Secret Service. Be ready to provide a description of the person who gave you the bill.

3. Write your initials and the date on the bill and give it only to the police or the Secret Service.

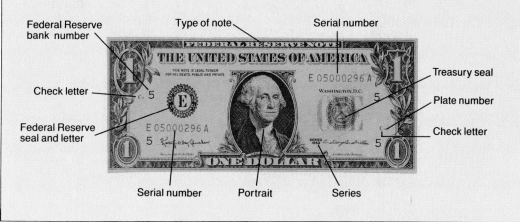

Federal Reserve bank number
Type of note
Serial number
Check letter
Federal Reserve seal and letter
Treasury seal
Plate number
Check letter
Serial number
Portrait
Series

At the Bureau of Engraving and Printing, in Washington, D.C., a worker adjusts the press that prints serial numbers and the government seal on dollar bills.

$100,000 bill printed in 1934. President Woodrow Wilson was pictured on the bill.

Bills are printed from intricately engraved plates designed to stop counterfeiters (people who illegally make copies of bills). In a further effort to combat counterfeiting, the government bans the manufacture—except for sale to the Treasury—of the special paper on which money is printed. Even though the paper is especially durable, bills last an average of only 22 months before they are returned to Federal Reserve Banks for replacement. There the worn bills are shredded into confetti-sized pieces and burned.

Paper money shows its ancestry. Small letter-number combinations identify the metal plates used to print the bills as well as the quadrant, or corner, of the large sheet from which the bill came. The particular Federal Reserve Bank that distributed the bill is identified by both the bank's seal on the left-hand side of the face of the bill and a number in each corner. Each bill has its own serial number.

Paper dollars were printed as early as 1775, even before the dollar was established as the basic unit of currency. Otherwise, the earliest dollars were coins.

▶ **DOLLAR COINS**

Coins are produced by the United States Mint, at factories in Philadelphia and Denver. A silver dollar was issued at various times from 1794 until 1935. Minting of a dollar coin was resumed in 1971. In 1979 and 1980, a smaller dollar coin, bearing the head of Susan B. Anthony, was issued.

Canada has a $1 coin and also issues paper bills in the amounts of $1, $2, $5, $10, $20, $50, $100, $500, and $1,000.

G. DAVID WALLACE
Author, *Money Basics*

and the second most numerous denomination printed is the $20 bill. As of 1982, a total of some $156,000,000,000 (billion) in cash was in circulation, an average of $670 for every person in the United States.

Some $2 bills printed in honor of the 200th anniversary of the Declaration of Independence are still in circulation. Other denominations printed in the past but no longer in circulation are the $500, $1,000, $5,000, and $10,000 bills. The largest denomination of U.S. paper currency ever printed was a

Various silver dollars, such as the Liberty Head, were issued by the United States between 1794 and 1935, when production of dollar coins stopped. The 1971 Eisenhower dollar marked the reintroduction of the dollar coin, with a silver version for collectors and a nonsilver version for general circulation. The Statue of Liberty dollar, minted in 1986, was enormously popular with collectors. Some dollar coins, such as the Canadian gold piece below, are minted for collectors rather than circulation.

Liberty Head   **Dwight Eisenhower**   **Statue of Liberty**   **Canadian $100 (gold)**

INTERNATIONAL STATISTICAL SUPPLEMENT

Independent Nations of the World

The United States

    Senate

    House of Representatives

    Cabinet

    Supreme Court

    State Governors

Canada and Its Provinces and Territories

INDEPENDENT NATIONS OF THE WORLD

NATION	CAPITAL	AREA (in sq mi)	POPULATION (estimate)	GOVERNMENT
Afghanistan	Kabul	250,000	18,200,000	Najibullah—communist party secretary
Albania	Tirana	11,100	3,000,000	Ramiz Alia—communist party secretary and president Adil Carcani—premier
Algeria	Algiers	919,595	21,700,000	Chadli Benjedid—president
Angola	Luanda	481,354	8,800,000	José Eduardo dos Santos—president
Antigua and Barbuda	St. John's	171	80,000	Vere Bird—prime minister
Argentina	Buenos Aires	1,068,297	30,600,000	Raúl Alfonsín—president
Australia	Canberra	2,967,895	15,800,000	Robert Hawke—prime minister
Austria	Vienna	32,374	7,600,000	Kurt Waldheim—president Franz Vranitzky—chancellor
Bahamas	Nassau	5,380	231,000	Lynden O. Pindling—prime minister
Bahrain	Manama	240	420,000	Isa ibn Sulman al-Khalifa—head of government
Bangladesh	Dhaka	55,598	99,000,000	Hussain Mohammed Ershad—president
Barbados	Bridgetown	168	254,000	Errol Barrow—prime minister
Belgium	Brussels	11,781	9,900,000	Baudouin I—king Wilfried Martens—premier
Belize	Belmopan	8,867	166,000	Manuel Esquivel—prime minister
Benin (Dahomey)	Porto-Novo	43,484	4,000,000	Mathieu Kerekou—president
Bhutan	Thimbu	18,147	1,400,000	Jigme Singye Wangchuk—king
Bolivia	La Paz Sucre	424,165	6,500,000	Victor Paz Estenssoro—president
Botswana	Gaborone	231,804	1,100,000	Quett Masire—president
Brazil	Brasília	3,286,478	136,000,000	José Sarney—president
Brunei Darussalam	Bandar Seri Begawan	2,226	270,000	Sultan Muda Hassanal Bolkiah—head of state
Bulgaria	Sofia	42,823	9,000,000	Todor Zhivkov—communist party secretary Georgi Atanasov—premier
Burkina Faso (Upper Volta)	Ouagadougou	105,869	7,900,000	Thomas Sankara—head of government
Burma	Rangoon	261,218	37,600,000	U San Yu—president U Maung Maung Kha—prime minister
Burundi	Bujumbura	10,747	4,700,000	Jean-Baptiste Bagaza—president
Cambodia (Kampuchea)	Pnompenh	69,898	7,300,000	Heng Samrin—communist party secretary
Cameroon	Yaoundé	183,569	10,100,000	Paul Biya—president

NATION	CAPITAL	AREA (in sq mi)	POPULATION (estimate)	GOVERNMENT
Canada	Ottawa	3,851,809	25,550,000	Martin Brian Mulroney—prime minister
Cape Verde	Praia	1,557	340,000	Aristides Pereira—president
Central African Republic	Bangui	240,535	2,600,000	André Kolingba—head of state
Chad	N'Djemena	495,754	5,000,000	Hissen Habré—president
Chile	Santiago	292,257	12,200,000	Augusto Pinochet Ugarte—president
China	Peking	3,705,390	1,060,000,000	Deng Xiaoping—paramount leader Hu Yaobang—communist party secretary Zhao Ziyang—premier
Colombia	Bogotá	439,736	26,600,000	Virgilio Barco Vargas—president
Comoros	Moroni	838	450,000	Ahmed Abdallah—president
Congo	Brazzaville	132,047	1,800,000	Denis Sassou-Nguessou—president
Costa Rica	San José	19,575	2,600,000	Oscar Arias Sánchez—president
Cuba	Havana	44,218	10,100,000	Fidel Castro—president
Cyprus	Nicosia	3,572	670,000	Spyros Kyprianou—president
Czechoslovakia	Prague	49,370	15,500,000	Gustáv Husák—communist party secretary and president Lubomir Štrougal—premier
Denmark	Copenhagen	16,629	5,100,000	Margrethe II—queen Poul Schlüter—premier
Djibouti	Djibouti	8,494	330,000	Hassan Gouled Aptidon—president
Dominica	Roseau	290	85,000	Mary Eugenia Charles—prime minister
Dominican Republic	Santo Domingo	18,816	6,200,000	Joaquín Balaguer—president
Ecuador	Quito	109,483	9,400,000	León Febres Cordero Rivadeneira—president
Egypt	Cairo	386,660	49,800,000	Muhammad Hosni Mubarak—president Atef Sedki—premier
El Salvador	San Salvador	8,124	4,900,000	José Napoleón Duarte—president
Equatorial Guinea	Malabo	10,831	400,000	Obiang Nguema Mbasogo—president
Ethiopia	Addis Ababa	471,777	44,000,000	Mengistu Haile Mariam—head of state
Fiji	Suva	7,055	700,000	Ratu Sir Kamisese Mara—prime minister
Finland	Helsinki	130,120	4,900,000	Mauno Koivisto—president Kalevi Sorsa—premier
France	Paris	211,207	55,200,000	François Mitterrand—president Jacques Chirac—premier
Gabon	Libreville	103,346	1,200,000	Omar Bongo—president
Gambia	Banjul	4,361	700,000	Sir Dauda K. Jawara—president
Germany (East)	East Berlin	41,768	16,600,000	Erich Honecker—communist party secretary Willi Stoph—premier
Germany (West)	Bonn	95,976	61,000,000	Richard von Weizsäcker—president Helmut Kohl—chancellor

NATION	CAPITAL	AREA (in sq mi)	POPULATION (estimate)	GOVERNMENT
Ghana	Accra	92,099	13,600,000	Jerry Rawlings—head of state
Greece	Athens	50,944	9,900,000	Christos Sartzetakis—president Andreas Papandreou—premier
Grenada	St. George's	133	110,000	Herbert A. Blaize—prime minister
Guatemala	Guatemala City	42,042	8,000,000	Marco Vinicio Cerezo Arévalo—president
Guinea	Conakry	94,926	6,000,000	Lansana Conté—president
Guinea-Bissau	Bissau	13,948	900,000	João Bernardo Vieira—head of government
Guyana	Georgetown	83,000	800,000	Desmond Hoyte—president
Haiti	Port-au-Prince	10,714	5,200,000	Henri Namphy—head of government
Honduras	Tegucigalpa	43,277	4,400,000	José Azcona Hoyo—president
Hungary	Budapest	35,919	10,700,000	János Kádár—communist party secretary György Lazar—premier
Iceland	Reykjavik	39,768	240,000	Vigdis Finnbogadottir—president Steingrimur Hermannsson—prime minister
India	New Delhi	1,269,340	751,000,000	Zail Singh—president Rajiv Gandhi—prime minister
Indonesia	Jakarta	735,358	165,000,000	Suharto—president
Iran	Teheran	636,294	44,600,000	Ruhollah Khomeini—religious leader Hojatolislam Ali Khamenei—president Mir Hussein Moussavi—premier
Iraq	Baghdad	167,925	15,900,000	Saddam Hussein—president
Ireland	Dublin	27,136	3,600,000	Patrick Hillery—president Garret FitzGerald—prime minister
Israel	Jerusalem	8,019	4,300,000	Chaim Herzog—president Yitzhak Shamir—prime minister
Italy	Rome	116,303	57,200,000	Francesco Cossiga—president Bettino Craxi—premier
Ivory Coast	Yamoussoukro	124,503	9,800,000	Félix Houphouët-Boigny—president
Jamaica	Kingston	4,244	2,300,000	Edward P. G. Seaga—prime minister
Japan	Tokyo	143,751	121,000,000	Hirohito—emperor Yasuhiro Nakasone—premier
Jordan	Amman	37,738	3,500,000	Hussein I—king Zaid Rifai—premier
Kenya	Nairobi	224,959	20,400,000	Daniel arap Moi—president
Kiribati	Tarawa	264	64,000	Ieremia Tabai—president
Korea (North)	Pyongyang	46,540	20,400,000	Kim Il Sung—president Kang Sang-san—premier
Korea (South)	Seoul	38,025	41,200,000	Chun Doo Hwan—president Lho Shin Yong—premier
Kuwait	Kuwait	6,880	1,700,000	Jabir al-Ahmad al-Sabah—head of state
Laos	Vientiane	91,429	4,000,000	Phoumi Vongvichit—president Kaysone Phomvihan—premier

NATION	CAPITAL	AREA (in sq mi)	POPULATION (estimate)	GOVERNMENT
Lebanon	Beirut	4,015	2,700,000	Amin Gemayel—president Rashid Karami—premier
Lesotho	Maseru	11,720	1,600,000	Moshoeshoe II—king Justin Lekhanya—prime minister
Liberia	Monrovia	43,000	2,200,000	Samuel K. Doe—president
Libya	Tripoli	679,362	3,600,000	Muammar el-Qaddafi—head of state
Liechtenstein	Vaduz	61	27,000	Francis Joseph II—prince
Luxembourg	Luxembourg	999	370,000	Jean—grand duke Jacques Santer—premier
Madagascar	Antananarivo	226,657	10,000,000	Didier Ratsiraka—president
Malawi	Lilongwe	45,747	7,100,000	H. Kamuzu Banda—president
Malaysia	Kuala Lumpur	127,317	15,600,000	Sultan Mahmood Iskandar—king Mahathir Mohammad—prime minister
Maldives	Male	115	181,000	Maumoon Abdul Gayoom—president
Mali	Bamako	478,765	8,200,000	Moussa Traoré—president
Malta	Valletta	122	380,000	Agatha Barbara—president Carmelo Mifsud Bonnici—prime minister
Mauritania	Nouakchott	397,954	1,900,000	Maouya Ould Sidi Ahmed Taya—president
Mauritius	Port Louis	790	1,100,000	Aneerood Jugnauth—prime minister
Mexico	Mexico City	761,602	79,000,000	Miguel de la Madrid Hurtado—president
Monaco	Monaco-Ville	0.6	27,000	Rainier III—prince
Mongolia	Ulan Bator	604,248	1,900,000	Dzhambiin Batmunkh—communist party secretary
Morocco	Rabat	172,413	22,000,000	Hassan II—king Mohammad Karim Lamrani—premier
Mozambique	Maputo	309,494	14,000,000	Joaquím A. Chissano—president
Nauru	Yaren District	8	8,000	Hammer DeRoburt—president
Nepal	Katmandu	54,362	16,600,000	Birendra Bir Bikram Shah Deva—king Nagendra Prasad Rijal—prime minister
Netherlands	Amsterdam	15,770	14,500,000	Beatrix—queen Ruud Lubbers—premier
New Zealand	Wellington	103,736	3,300,000	David Lange—prime minister
Nicaragua	Managua	50,193	3,300,000	Daniel Ortega Saavedra—president
Niger	Niamey	489,190	6,100,000	Seyni Kountche—head of government
Nigeria	Lagos	356,667	95,200,000	Ibrahim Babangida—president
Norway	Oslo	125,181	4,200,000	Olav V—king Gro Harlem Brundtland—premier
Oman	Muscat	82,030	1,200,000	Qabus ibn Said—sultan
Pakistan	Islamabad	310,404	96,200,000	Mohammed Zia ul-Haq—president
Panama	Panama City	29,761	2,200,000	Eric Arturo Delvalle—president

NATION	CAPITAL	AREA (in sq mi)	POPULATION (estimate)	GOVERNMENT
Papua New Guinea	Port Moresby	178,260	3,300,000	Paias Wingti—prime minister
Paraguay	Asunción	157,047	3,700,000	Alfredo Stroessner—president
Peru	Lima	496,222	19,700,000	Alan García Pérez—president
Philippines	Manila	115,830	54,400,000	Corazon C. Aquino—president Salvador H. Laurel—vice-president
Poland	Warsaw	120,725	37,400,000	Wojciech Jaruzelski—communist party secretary and president Zbigniew Messner—premier
Portugal	Lisbon	35,553	10,200,000	Mário Soares—president Anibal Cavaço Silva—premier
Qatar	Doha	4,247	300,000	Khalifa ibn Hamad al-Thani—head of government
Rumania	Bucharest	91,700	23,000,000	Nicolae Ceauşescu—communist party secretary Constantin Dascalescu—premier
Rwanda	Kigali	10,169	6,300,000	Juvénal Habyarimana—president
St. Christopher and Nevis	Basseterre	105	45,000	Kennedy Simmonds—prime minister
St. Lucia	Castries	238	134,000	John Compton—prime minister
St. Vincent and the Grenadines	Kingstown	150	125,000	James Mitchell—prime minister
São Tomé and Príncipe	São Tomé	372	110,000	Manuel Pinto da Costa—president
Saudi Arabia	Riyadh	830,000	11,500,000	Fahd ibn Abdul-Aziz—king
Senegal	Dakar	75,750	6,500,000	Abdou Diouf—president
Seychelles	Victoria	107	65,000	France Albert René—president
Sierra Leone	Freetown	27,700	3,700,000	Joseph Saidu Momoh—president
Singapore	Singapore	224	2,600,000	Wee Kim Wee—president Lee Kuan Yew—prime minister
Solomon Islands	Honiara	10,983	270,000	Solomon Mamaloni—prime minister
Somalia	Mogadishu	246,200	5,400,000	Mohammed Siad Barre—president
South Africa	Pretoria Cape Town Bloemfontein	471,444	32,400,000	Pieter W. Botha—president
Spain	Madrid	194,897	38,800,000	Juan Carlos I—king Felipe González Márquez—premier
Sri Lanka (Ceylon)	Colombo	25,332	15,800,000	Junius R. Jayewardene—president Ranasinghe Premadasa—prime minister
Sudan	Khartoum	967,500	21,600,000	Sadiq al-Mahdi—prime minister
Suriname	Paramaribo	63,037	400,000	Désiré Bouterse—military leader
Swaziland	Mbabane	6,704	650,000	Mswati III—king
Sweden	Stockholm	173,731	8,400,000	Carl XVI Gustaf—king Ingvar Carlsson—premier

NATION	CAPITAL	AREA (in sq mi)	POPULATION (estimate)	GOVERNMENT
Switzerland	Bern	15,941	6,500,000	Pierre Aubert—president
Syria	Damascus	71,498	10,300,000	Hafez al-Assad—president Abdel Raouf al-Kassem—premier
Taiwan	Taipei	13,885	19,000,000	Chiang Ching-kwo—president Yu Kuo-hwa—premier
Tanzania	Dar es Salaam	364,898	21,700,000	Ali Hassan Mwinyi—president
Thailand	Bangkok	198,457	51,300,000	Bhumibol Adulyadej—king Prem Tinsulanonda—premier
Togo	Lomé	21,622	3,000,000	Gnassingbe Eyadema—president
Tonga	Nuku'alofa	270	100,000	Taufa'ahau Tupou IV—king Prince Tu'ipelehake—prime minister
Trinidad & Tobago	Port of Spain	1,980	1,200,000	Sir Ellis Clarke—president A.N.R. Robinson—prime minister
Tunisia	Tunis	63,170	7,100,000	Habib Bourguiba—president
Turkey	Ankara	301,381	49,300,000	Kenan Evren—president Turgut Ozal—prime minister
Tuvalu	Funafuti	10	8,000	Tomasi Puapua—prime minister
Uganda	Kampala	91,134	15,500,000	Yoweri Museveni—president
U.S.S.R.	Moscow	8,649,512	279,000,000	Mikhail S. Gorbachev—communist party secretary Andrei A. Gromyko—president Nikolai I. Ryzhkov—premier
United Arab Emirates	Abu Dhabi	32,278	1,300,000	Zayd ibn Sultan al-Nuhayan—president
United Kingdom	London	94,226	56,500,000	Elizabeth II—queen Margaret Thatcher—prime minister
United States	Washington, D.C.	3,618,467	241,300,000	Ronald W. Reagan—president George H. Bush—vice-president
Uruguay	Montevideo	68,037	3,000,000	Julio María Sanguinetti—president
Vanuatu	Vila	5,700	142,000	Walter Lini—prime minister
Venezuela	Caracas	352,143	17,300,000	Jaime Lusinchi—president
Vietnam	Hanoi	128,402	59,700,000	Nguyen Van Linh—communist party secretary
Western Samoa	Apia	1,097	163,000	Malietoa Tanumafili II—head of state
Yemen (Aden)	Madinat al-Shaab	128,559	2,300,000	Haider Abu Bakr al-Attas—president
Yemen (Sana)	Sana	75,290	6,500,000	Ali Abdullah Saleh al-Hasani—president
Yugoslavia	Belgrade	98,766	23,200,000	Sinan Hasani—president Branko Mikulic—premier
Zaïre	Kinshasa	905,565	30,400,000	Mobutu Sese Seko—president
Zambia	Lusaka	290,585	6,700,000	Kenneth D. Kaunda—president
Zimbabwe	Harare	150,333	8,300,000	Canaan Banana—president Robert Mugabe—prime minister

THE CONGRESS OF THE UNITED STATES

UNITED STATES SENATE

(55 Democrats, 45 Republicans)

Alabama
Howell T. Heflin (D)
Richard C. Shelby (D)*

Alaska
Ted Stevens (R)
Frank H. Murkowski (R)**

Arizona
Dennis DeConcini (D)
John McCain (R)*

Arkansas
Dale Bumpers (D)**
David H. Pryor (D)

California
Alan Cranston (D)**
Pete Wilson (R)

Colorado
William L. Armstrong (R)
Timothy E. Wirth (D)*

Connecticut
Lowell P. Weicker, Jr. (R)
Christopher J. Dodd (D)**

Delaware
William V. Roth, Jr. (R)
Joseph R. Biden, Jr. (D)

Florida
Lawton Chiles, Jr. (D)
Bob Graham (D)*

Georgia
Sam Nunn (D)
Wyche Fowler, Jr. (D)*

Hawaii
Daniel K. Inouye (D)**
Spark M. Matsunaga (D)

Idaho
James A. McClure (R)
Steve Symms (R)**

Illinois
Alan J. Dixon (D)**
Paul Simon (D)

Indiana
Richard G. Lugar (R)
Dan Quayle (R)**

Iowa
Charles E. Grassley (R)**
Thomas R. Harkin (D)

Kansas
Robert J. Dole (R)**
Nancy Landon Kassebaum (R)

Kentucky
Wendell H. Ford (D)**
Mitch McConnell (R)

Louisiana
J. Bennett Johnston (D)
John B. Breaux (D)*

Maine
William S. Cohen (R)
George J. Mitchell (D)

Maryland
Paul S. Sarbanes (D)
Barbara A. Mikulski (D)*

Massachusetts
Edward M. Kennedy (D)
John F. Kerry (D)

Michigan
Donald W. Riegle, Jr. (D)
Carl Levin (D)

Minnesota
David F. Durenberger (R)
Rudy Boschwitz (R)

Mississippi
John C. Stennis (D)
Thad Cochran (R)

Missouri
John C. Danforth (R)
Christopher S. Bond (R)*

Montana
John Melcher (D)
Max Baucus (D)

Nebraska
Edward Zorinsky (D)
J. James Exon, Jr. (D)

Nevada
Chic Hecht (R)
Harry Reid (D)*

New Hampshire
Gordon J. Humphrey (R)
Warren B. Rudman (R)**

New Jersey
Bill Bradley (D)
Frank R. Lautenberg (D)

New Mexico
Pete V. Domenici (R)
Jeff Bingaman (D)

New York
Daniel P. Moynihan (D)
Alfonse M. D'Amato (R)**

North Carolina
Jesse Helms (R)
Terry Sanford (D)*

North Dakota
Quentin N. Burdick (D)
Kent Conrad (D)*

Ohio
John H. Glenn, Jr. (D)**
Howard M. Metzenbaum (D)

Oklahoma
David L. Boren (D)
Donald L. Nickles (R)**

Oregon
Mark O. Hatfield (R)
Bob Packwood (R)**

Pennsylvania
John Heinz (R)
Arlen Specter (R)**

Rhode Island
Claiborne Pell (D)
John H. Chafee (R)

South Carolina
Strom Thurmond (R)
Ernest F. Hollings (D)**

South Dakota
Larry Pressler (R)
Thomas A. Daschle (D)*

Tennessee
James R. Sasser (D)
Albert Gore, Jr. (D)

Texas
Lloyd Bentsen (D)
Phil Gramm (R)

Utah
Jake Garn (R)**
Orrin G. Hatch (R)

Vermont
Robert T. Stafford (R)
Patrick J. Leahy (D)**

Virginia
John W. Warner (R)
Paul S. Trible, Jr. (R)

Washington
Daniel J. Evans (R)
Brock Adams (D)*

West Virginia
Robert C. Byrd (D)
John D. Rockefeller IV (D)

Wisconsin
William Proxmire (D)
Robert W. Kasten, Jr. (R)**

Wyoming
Malcolm Wallop (R)
Alan K. Simpson (R)

(D) Democrat
(R) Republican

* elected in 1986
** re-elected in 1986

UNITED STATES HOUSE OF REPRESENTATIVES

(258 Democrats, 177 Republicans)

Alabama
1. H. L. Callahan (R)
2. W. L. Dickinson (R)
3. W. Nichols (D)
4. T. Bevill (D)
5. R. G. Flippo (D)
6. B. Erdreich (D)
7. C. Harris (D)*

Alaska
D. Young (R)

Arizona
1. J. J. Rhodes III (R)*
2. M. K. Udall (D)
3. B. Stump (R)
4. J. Kyl (R)*
5. J. Kolbe (R)

Arkansas
1. W. V. Alexander, Jr. (D)
2. T. F. Robinson (D)
3. J. P. Hammerschmidt (R)
4. B. F. Anthony, Jr. (D)

California
1. D. H. Bosco (D)
2. W. Herger (R)*
3. R. T. Matsui (D)
4. V. Fazio (D)
5. S. G. Burton (D)
6. B. Boxer (D)
7. G. Miller (D)
8. R. V. Dellums (D)
9. F. H. Stark, Jr. (D)
10. D. Edwards (D)
11. T. P. Lantos (D)
12. E. L. Konnyu (R)*
13. N. Y. Mineta (D)
14. N. D. Shumway (R)
15. T. Coelho (D)
16. L. E. Panetta (D)
17. C. Pashayan, Jr. (R)
18. R. H. Lehman (D)
19. R. J. Lagomarsino (R)
20. W. M. Thomas (R)
21. E. Gallegly (R)*
22. C. J. Moorhead (R)
23. A. C. Beilenson (D)
24. H. A. Waxman (D)
25. E. R. Roybal (D)
26. H. L. Berman (D)
27. M. Levine (D)
28. J. C. Dixon (D)
29. A. F. Hawkins (D)
30. M. G. Martinez, Jr. (D)
31. M. M. Dymally (D)
32. G. M. Anderson (D)
33. D. Dreier (R)
34. E. E. Torres (D)
35. J. Lewis (R)
36. G. E. Brown, Jr. (D)
37. A. A. McCandless (R)
38. R. K. Dornan (R)
39. W. E. Dannemeyer (R)
40. R. E. Badham (R)
41. W. D. Lowery (R)

42. D. E. Lungren (R)
43. R. Packard (R)
44. J. Bates (D)
45. D. L. Hunter (R)

Colorado
1. P. Schroeder (D)
2. D. Skaggs (D)*
3. B. N. Campbell (D)*
4. H. Brown (R)
5. J. Hefley (R)*
6. D. Schaefer (R)

Connecticut
1. B. B. Kennelly (D)
2. S. Gejdenson (D)
3. B. A. Morrison (D)
4. S. B. McKinney (R)
5. J. G. Rowland (R)
6. N. L. Johnson (R)

Delaware
T. R. Carper (D)

Florida
1. E. Hutto (D)
2. B. Grant (D)*
3. C. E. Bennett (D)
4. W. V. Chappell, Jr. (D)
5. B. McCollum, Jr. (R)
6. K. H. MacKay (D)
7. S. M. Gibbons (D)
8. C. W. B. Young (R)
9. M. Bilirakis (R)
10. A. Ireland (R)
11. B. Nelson (D)
12. T. Lewis (R)
13. C. Mack III (R)
14. D. A. Mica (D)
15. E. C. Shaw, Jr. (R)
16. L. J. Smith (D)
17. W. Lehman (D)
18. C. D. Pepper (D)
19. D. B. Fascell (D)

Georgia
1. R. L. Thomas (D)
2. C. F. Hatcher (D)
3. R. B. Ray (D)
4. P. L. Swindall (R)
5. J. Lewis (D)*
6. N. Gingrich (R)
7. G. B. Darden (D)
8. J. R. Rowland, Jr. (D)
9. E. L. Jenkins (D)
10. D. Barnard, Jr. (D)

Hawaii
1. P. Saiki (R)*
2. D. K. Akaka (D)

Idaho
1. L. E. Craig (R)
2. R. H. Stallings (D)

Illinois
1. C. A. Hayes (D)
2. G. Savage (D)
3. M. Russo (D)
4. J. Davis (R)*
5. W. O. Lipinski (D)
6. H. J. Hyde (R)
7. C. Collins (D)
8. D. Rostenkowski (D)
9. S. R. Yates (D)
10. J. E. Porter (R)
11. F. Annunzio (D)
12. P. M. Crane (R)
13. H. W. Fawell (R)
14. J. D. Hastert (R)*
15. E. R. Madigan (R)
16. L. M. Martin (R)
17. L. Evans (D)
18. R. H. Michel (R)
19. T. L. Bruce (D)
20. R. Durbin (D)
21. C. M. Price (D)
22. K. J. Gray (D)

Indiana
1. P. J. Visclosky (D)
2. P. R. Sharp (D)
3. J. P. Hiler (R)
4. D. R. Coats (R)
5. J. Jontz (D)*
6. D. L. Burton (R)
7. J. T. Myers (R)
8. F. McCloskey (D)
9. L. H. Hamilton (D)
10. A. Jacobs, Jr. (D)

Iowa
1. J. Leach (R)
2. T. J. Tauke (R)
3. D. R. Nagle (D)*
4. N. Smith (D)
5. J. R. Lightfoot (R)
6. F. Grandy (R)*

Kansas
1. C. P. Roberts (R)
2. J. C. Slattery (D)
3. J. Meyers (R)
4. D. Glickman (D)
5. B. Whittaker (R)

Kentucky
1. C. Hubbard, Jr. (D)
2. W. H. Natcher (D)
3. R. L. Mazzoli (D)
4. J. Bunning (R)*
5. H. D. Rogers (R)
6. L. J. Hopkins (R)
7. C. C. Perkins (D)

Louisiana
1. R. L. Livingston, Jr. (R)
2. C. C. Boggs (D)
3. W. J. Tauzin (D)
4. C. E. Roemer III (D)
5. T. J. Huckaby (D)

6. R. Baker (R)*
7. J. Hayes (D)*
8. C. Holloway (R)*

Maine
1. J. Brennan (D)*
2. O. J. Snowe (R)

Maryland
1. R. P. Dyson (D)
2. H. Delich Bentley (R)
3. B. L. Cardin (D)*
4. T. McMillen (D)*
5. S. H. Hoyer (D)
6. B. Butcher Byron (D)
7. K. Mfume (D)*
8. C. A. Morella (R)*

Massachusetts
1. S. O. Conte (R)
2. E. P. Boland (D)
3. J. D. Early (D)
4. B. Frank (D)
5. C. G. Atkins (D)
6. N. Mavroules (D)
7. E. J. Markey (D)
8. J. P. Kennedy II (D)*
9. J. J. Moakley (D)
10. G. E. Studds (D)
11. B. J. Donnelly (D)

Michigan
1. J. Conyers, Jr. (D)
2. C. D. Pursell (R)
3. H. E. Wolpe (D)
4. F. Upton (R)*
5. P. B. Henry (R)
6. B. Carr (D)
7. D. E. Kildee (D)
8. B. Traxler (D)
9. G. Vander Jagt (R)
10. B. Schuette (R)
11. R. W. Davis (R)
12. D. E. Bonior (D)
13. G. W. Crockett, Jr. (D)
14. D. M. Hertel (D)
15. W. D. Ford (D)
16. J. D. Dingell (D)
17. S. M. Levin (D)
18. W. S. Broomfield (R)

Minnesota
1. T. J. Penny (D)
2. V. Weber (R)
3. B. Frenzel (R)
4. B. F. Vento (D)
5. M. O. Sabo (D)
6. G. Sikorski (D)
7. A. Stangeland (R)
8. J. L. Oberstar (D)

Mississippi
1. J. L. Whitten (D)
2. M. Espy (D)*
3. G. V. Montgomery (D)

4. W. Dowdy (D)
5. T. Lott (R)

Missouri
1. W. L. Clay (D)
2. J. Buechner (R)*
3. R. A. Gephardt (D)
4. I. Skelton (D)
5. A. D. Wheat (D)
6. E. T. Coleman (R)
7. G. Taylor (R)
8. W. Emerson (R)
9. H. L. Volkmer (D)

Montana
1. P. Williams (D)
2. R. C. Marlenee (R)

Nebraska
1. D. Bereuter (R)
2. H. Daub (R)
3. V. Smith (R)

Nevada
1. J. Bilbray (D)*
2. B. Farrell Vucanovich (R)

New Hampshire
1. R. C. Smith (R)
2. J. Gregg (R)

New Jersey
1. J. J. Florio (D)
2. W. J. Hughes (D)
3. J. J. Howard (D)
4. C. H. Smith (R)
5. M. S. Roukema (R)
6. B. J. Dwyer (D)
7. M. J. Rinaldo (R)
8. R. A. Roe (D)
9. R. G. Torricelli (D)
10. P. W. Rodino, Jr. (D)
11. D. A. Gallo (R)
12. J. Courter (R)
13. H. J. Saxton (R)
14. F. J. Guarini (D)

New Mexico
1. M. Lujan, Jr. (R)
2. J. R. Skeen (R)
3. W. B. Richardson (D)

New York
1. G. J. Hochbrueckner (D)*
2. T. J. Downey (D)
3. R. J. Mrazek (D)
4. N. F. Lent (R)
5. R. J. McGrath (R)
6. F. H. Flake (D)*
7. G. L. Ackerman (D)
8. J. H. Scheuer (D)
9. T. J. Manton (D)
10. C. E. Schumer (D)
11. E. Towns (D)
12. M. R. O. Owens (D)
13. S. J. Solarz (D)
14. G. V. Molinari (R)
15. B. Green (R)
16. C. B. Rangel (D)
17. T. Weiss (D)
18. R. Garcia (D)
19. M. Biaggi (D)
20. J. J. DioGuardi (R)
21. H. Fish, Jr. (R)
22. B. A. Gilman (R)
23. S. S. Stratton (D)
24. G. B. Solomon (R)
25. S. L. Boehlert (R)
26. D. O. Martin (R)
27. G. C. Wortley (R)
28. M. F. McHugh (D)
29. F. Horton (R)
30. L. M. Slaughter (D)*
31. J. Kemp (R)
32. J. J. LaFalce (D)
33. H. J. Nowak (D)
34. A. Houghton, Jr. (R)*

North Carolina
1. W. B. Jones (D)
2. T. Valentine (D)
3. M. Lancaster (D)*
4. D. E. Price (D)*
5. S. L. Neal (D)
6. H. Coble (R)
7. C. Rose (D)
8. W. G. Hefner (D)
9. J. A. McMillan III (R)
10. C. Ballenger (R)*
11. J. McC. Clarke (D)*

North Dakota
B. L. Dorgan (D)

Ohio
1. T. A. Luken (D)
2. W. D. Gradison, Jr. (R)
3. T. P. Hall (D)
4. M. G. Oxley (R)
5. D. L. Latta (R)
6. B. McEwen (R)
7. M. DeWine (R)
8. D. Lukens (R)*
9. M. C. Kaptur (D)
10. C. E. Miller (R)
11. D. E. Eckart (D)
12. J. R. Kasich (R)
13. D. J. Pease (D)
14. T. C. Sawyer (D)*
15. C. P. Wylie (R)
16. R. Regula (R)
17. J. A. Traficant, Jr. (D)
18. D. Applegate (D)
19. E. F. Feighan (D)
20. M. R. Oakar (D)
21. L. Stokes (D)

Oklahoma
1. J. M. Inhofe (R)*
2. M. Synar (D)
3. W. W. Watkins (D)
4. D. McCurdy (D)
5. M. H. Edwards (R)
6. G. English (D)

Oregon
1. L. AuCoin (D)
2. R. F. Smith (R)
3. R. L. Wyden (D)
4. P. A. DeFazio (D)*
5. D. Smith (R)

Pennsylvania
1. T. M. Foglietta (D)
2. W. H. Gray III (D)
3. R. A. Borski, Jr. (D)
4. J. P. Kolter (D)
5. R. T. Schulze (R)
6. G. Yatron (D)
7. C. Weldon (R)*
8. P. H. Kostmayer (D)
9. B. Shuster (R)
10. J. M. McDade (R)
11. P. E. Kanjorski (D)
12. J. P. Murtha (D)
13. L. Coughlin (R)
14. W. J. Coyne (D)
15. D. L. Ritter (R)
16. R. S. Walker (R)
17. G. W. Gekas (R)
18. D. Walgren (D)
19. W. F. Goodling (R)
20. J. M. Gaydos (D)
21. T. J. Ridge (R)
22. A. J. Murphy (D)
23. W. F. Clinger, Jr. (R)

Rhode Island
1. F. J. St. Germain (D)
2. C. Schneider (R)

South Carolina
1. A. Ravenel, Jr. (R)*
2. F. D. Spence (R)
3. B. C. Derrick, Jr. (D)
4. L. J. Patterson (D)
5. J. M. Spratt, Jr. (D)
6. R. M. Tallon (D)

South Dakota
T. Johnson (D)*

Tennessee
1. J. H. Quillen (R)
2. J. J. Duncan (R)
3. M. Lloyd (D)
4. J. H. S. Cooper (D)
5. W. H. Boner (D)
6. B. J. Gordon (D)
7. D. K. Sundquist (R)
8. E. Jones (D)
9. H. Ford (D)

Texas
1. J. Chapman (D)
2. C. Wilson (D)
3. S. Bartlett (R)
4. R. M. Hall (D)
5. J. W. Bryant (D)
6. J. L. Barton (R)
7. B. Archer (R)
8. J. M. Fields (R)
9. J. Brooks (D)
10. J. J. Pickle (D)
11. J. M. Leath (D)
12. J. C. Wright, Jr. (D)
13. E. B. Boulter (R)
14. D. McC. Sweeney (R)
15. E. de la Garza (D)
16. R. D. Coleman (D)
17. C. W. Stenholm (D)
18. M. Leland (D)
19. L. E. Combest (R)

20. H. B. Gonzalez (D)
21. L. Smith (R)*
22. T. D. DeLay (R)
23. A. G. Bustamante (D)
24. M. Frost (D)
25. M. A. Andrews (D)
26. R. K. Armey (R)
27. S. P. Ortiz (D)

Utah
1. J. V. Hansen (R)
2. W. Owens (D)*
3. H. C. Nielson (R)

Vermont
J. M. Jeffords (R)

Virginia
1. H. H. Bateman (R)
2. O. B. Pickett (D)*
3. T. J. Bliley, Jr. (R)
4. N. Sisisky (D)
5. D. Daniel (D)
6. J. R. Olin (D)
7. D. F. Slaughter, Jr. (R)
8. S. Parris (R)
9. F. C. Boucher (D)
10. F. R. Wolf (R)

Washington
1. J. R. Miller (R)
2. A. Swift (D)
3. D. L. Bonker (D)
4. S. W. Morrison (R)
5. T. S. Foley (D)
6. N. D. Dicks (D)
7. M. Lowry (D)
8. R. Chandler (R)

West Virginia
1. A. B. Mollohan (D)
2. H. O. Staggers, Jr. (D)
3. R. E. Wise, Jr. (D)
4. N. J. Rahall II (D)

Wisconsin
1. L. Aspin (D)
2. R. W. Kastenmeier (D)
3. S. C. Gunderson (R)
4. G. D. Kleczka (D)
5. J. Moody (D)
6. T. E. Petri (R)
7. D. R. Obey (D)
8. T. Roth (R)
9. F. J. Sensenbrenner, Jr. (R)

Wyoming
D. Cheney (R)

*elected in 1986
all others: re-elected in 1986

UNITED STATES SUPREME COURT

Chief Justice: William H. Rehnquist (1986)

Associate Justices:
William J. Brennan, Jr. (1956)
Byron R. White (1962)
Thurgood Marshall (1967)
Harry A. Blackmun (1970)
Lewis F. Powell, Jr. (1971)
John Paul Stevens (1975)
Sandra Day O'Connor (1981)
Antonin Scalia (1986)

UNITED STATES CABINET

Secretary of Agriculture: Richard E. Lyng
Attorney General: Edwin Meese III
Secretary of Commerce: Malcolm Baldrige
Secretary of Defense: Caspar W. Weinberger
Secretary of Education: William J. Bennett
Secretary of Energy: John S. Herrington
Secretary of Health and Human Services:
Otis R. Bowen
Secretary of Housing and Urban Development:
Samuel R. Pierce, Jr.
Secretary of the Interior: Donald P. Hodel
Secretary of Labor: William E. Brock III
Secretary of State: George P. Shultz
Secretary of Transportation: Elizabeth
Hanford Dole
Secretary of the Treasury: James A. Baker III

In 1986, Antonin Scalia became an Associate Justice of the United States Supreme Court.

STATE GOVERNORS

State	Governor	State	Governor
Alabama	Guy Hunt (R)*	**Montana**	Ted Schwinden (D)
Alaska	Steve Cowper (D)*	**Nebraska**	Kay A. Orr (R)*
Arizona	Evan Mecham (R)*	**Nevada**	Richard H. Bryan (D)**
Arkansas	Bill Clinton (D)**	**New Hampshire**	John H. Sununu (R)**
California	George Deukmejian (R)**	**New Jersey**	Thomas H. Kean (R)
Colorado	Roy Romer (D)*	**New Mexico**	Garrey E. Carruthers (R)*
Connecticut	William A. O'Neill (D)**	**New York**	Mario M. Cuomo (D)**
Delaware	Michael N. Castle (R)	**North Carolina**	James G. Martin (R)
Florida	Bob Martinez (R)*	**North Dakota**	George Sinner (D)
Georgia	Joe Frank Harris (D)**	**Ohio**	Richard F. Celeste (D)**
Hawaii	John Waihee (D)*	**Oklahoma**	Henry Bellmon (R)*
Idaho	Cecil D. Andrus (D)*	**Oregon**	Neil Goldschmidt (D)*
Illinois	James R. Thompson (R)**	**Pennsylvania**	Bob Casey (D)*
Indiana	Robert D. Orr (R)	**Rhode Island**	Edward D. DiPrete (R)**
Iowa	Terry E. Branstad (R)**	**South Carolina**	Carroll A. Campbell, Jr. (R)*
Kansas	Mike Hayden (R)*	**South Dakota**	George S. Mickelson (R)*
Kentucky	Martha Layne Collins (D)	**Tennessee**	Ned R. McWherter (D)*
Louisiana	Edwin W. Edward (D)	**Texas**	William Clements (R)*
Maine	John R. McKernan, Jr. (R)*	**Utah**	Norman Bangerter (R)
Maryland	William Donald Schaefer (D)*	**Vermont**	Madeleine Kunin (D)**
Massachusetts	Michael S. Dukakis (D)**	**Virginia**	Gerald L. Baliles (D)
Michigan	James J. Blanchard (D)**	**Washington**	Booth Gardner (D)
Minnesota	Rudy Perpich (D)**	**West Virginia**	Arch Moore (R)
Mississippi	Bill Allain (D)	**Wisconsin**	Tommy G. Thompson (R)*
Missouri	John Ashcroft (R)	**Wyoming**	Mike Sullivan (D)*

*elected in 1986
**re-elected in 1986

CANADA

Capital: Ottawa
Head of State: Queen Elizabeth II
Governor General: Jeanne Sauvé
Prime Minister: Martin Brian Mulroney (Progressive Conservative)
Leader of the Opposition: John Turner (Liberal)
Population: 25,550,000
Area: 3,851,809 sq mi (9,976,185 km²)

PROVINCES AND TERRITORIES

Alberta
Capital: Edmonton
Lieutenant Governor: Helen Hunley
Premier: Donald R. Getty (Progressive Conservative)
Leader of the Opposition: Ray Martin (New Democratic Party)
Entered Confederation: Sept. 1, 1905
Population: 2,384,200
Area: 255,285 sq mi (661,188 km²)

British Columbia
Capital: Victoria
Lieutenant Governor: Robert G. Rogers
Premier: William Vander Zalm (Social Credit)
Leader of the Opposition: Robert E. Skelly (New Democratic
   Party)
Entered Confederation: July 20, 1871
Population: 2,901,000
Area: 366,255 sq mi (948,600 km²)

Manitoba
Capital: Winnipeg
Lieutenant Governor: Pearl McGonigal
Premier: Howard Pawley (New Democratic Party)
Leader of the Opposition: Gary Filmon (Progressive
   Conservative)
Entered Confederation: July 15, 1870
Population: 1,077,200
Area: 251,000 sq mi (650,090 km²)

New Brunswick
Capital: Fredericton
Lieutenant Governor: George F. G. Stanley
Premier: Richard B. Hatfield (Progressive Conservative)
Leader of the Opposition: Frank McKenna (Liberal)
Entered Confederation: July 1, 1867
Population: 720,900
Area: 28,354 sq mi (73,436 km²)

Newfoundland
Capital: St. John's
Lieutenant Governor: W. Anthony Paddon
Premier: A. Brian Peckford (Progressive Conservative)
Leader of the Opposition: Leo Barry (Liberal)
Entered Confederation: March 31, 1949
Population: 580,000
Area: 156,185 sq mi (404,517 km²)

Nova Scotia
Capital: Halifax
Lieutenant Governor: Alan R. Abraham
Premier: John M. Buchanan (Progressive Conservative)
Leader of the Opposition: Vincent J. MacLean (Liberal)
Entered Confederation: July 1, 1867
Population: 883,100
Area: 21,425 sq mi (55,491 km²)

Ontario
Capital: Toronto
Lieutenant Governor: Lincoln Alexander
Premier: David Peterson (Liberal)
Leader of the Opposition: Larry Grossman (Progressive
   Conservative)
Entered Confederation: July 1, 1867
Population: 9,164,400
Area: 412,582 sq mi (1,068,582 km²)

Prince Edward Island
Capital: Charlottetown
Lieutenant Governor: Lloyd G.MacPhail
Premier: Joseph A. Ghiz (Liberal)
Leader of the Opposition: James M. Lee (Progressive
   Conservative)
Entered Confederation: July 1, 1873
Population: 128,000
Area: 2,184 sq mi (5,657 km²)

Quebec
Capital: Quebec City
Lieutenant Governor: Gilles Lamontagne
Premier: Robert Bourassa (Liberal)
Leader of the Opposition: Pierre-Marc Johnson (Parti Québécois)
Entered Confederation: July 1, 1867
Population: 6,618,500
Area: 594,860 sq mi (1,540,700 km²)

Saskatchewan
Capital: Regina
Lieutenant Governor: F. W. Johnson
Premier: Grant Devine (Progressive Conservative)
Leader of the Opposition: Allan E. Blakeney (New Democratic Party)
Entered Confederation: Sept. 1, 1905
Population: 1,020,200
Area: 251,700 sq mi (651,900 km²)

Northwest Territories
Capital: Yellowknife
Commissioner: John H. Parker
Leader of the Elected Executive: Nick Sibbeston
Reconstituted as a territory: September 1, 1905
Population: 51,000
Area: 1,304,896 sq mi (3,379,684 km²)

Yukon Territory
Capital: Whitehorse
Commissioner: J. Kenneth McKinnon
Government Leader: Tony Penikett (New Democratic Party)
Leader of the Opposition: Willard Phelps (Progressive Conservative)
Organized as a territory: June 13, 1898
Population: 22,800
Area: 186,299 sq mi (482,515 km²)

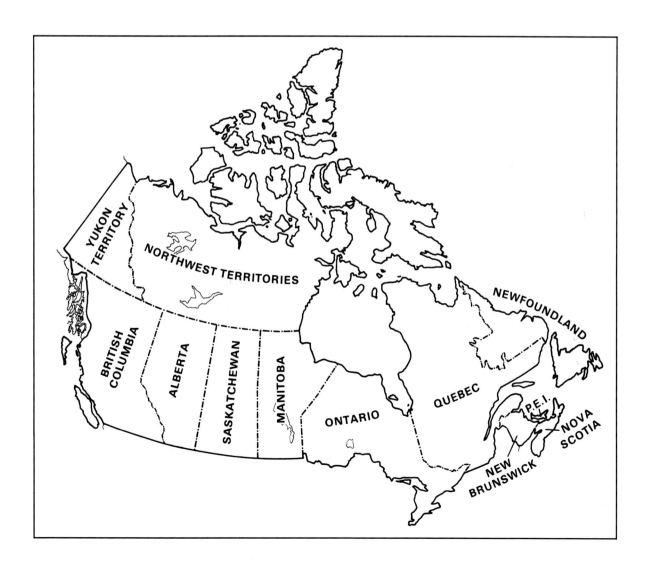

INDEX

C

D

G

H

Islam, religion
    Indian Muslim art 247, 249–51
    Iran 54
    Lebanon 51–52
    Philippines 40
Islamic Holy War, terrorist group 52
Isle of Man
    commemorative coins 153
    postage stamp, picture 142
Israel 54, 352
    Lebanon 52
    oil prices affected by Arab-Israeli conflict 62–63
    Palestinian homeland, problem of 53
    secret arms sales to Iran 39
    Shamir, Yitzhak, prime minister 35
    Shcharansky, Anatoly B., picture 66
    Syria 53
Issa, Kobayashi, Japanese poet 288–89
Istanbul, Turkey
    synagogue attack 32, 55
Italy 352
    economic summit conference, Tokyo, Japan 24
    Expo 86 pavilion 102
    family names 209
It's Mine, story by Leo Lionni, picture 278–79
Ivory-billed woodpecker, bird, picture 78
Ivory Coast 352

J

Jackal, animal 76
Jackson, Janet, American singer 254
Jacobsen, David P., American hostage in Middle East 52
Jamaica 352
    Peace Corps volunteers 201
Japan 352
    economic summit conference, Tokyo 24
    Expo 86 pavilion 102
    haiku, verse form 286–89
    neon signs, shopping district, Tokyo 245
    Philippines 40
    space exploration 96
Jarvis, Gregory B., American astronaut 17, 121
Jason Jr. (JJ), robot 113
Jazz music
    Goodman, Benny, death of 26; picture 27
Jenco, Lawrence Martin, American priest 52
Jewelry
    art deco designs 217
    art nouveau designs 213–14
    bracelet designs 151
Jewish people
    Babylonian conquest 333
    family names 209, 211
    Rome synagogue, Pope John Paul II's visit to, picture 65
    Shcharansky, Anatoly B., picture 66
    synagogue attack, Istanbul, Turkey 32, 55
Joan of Arc, French patriot
    OM competitions problem 222; picture 221

Joel, Billy, American musician 255
John Paul II, Pope
    Rome synagogue, visit to, picture 65
Johnson, Don, American actor 256
Johnson & Johnson, manufacturer of Tylenol 19
Johnston, Philip, American athlete 163
Jonathan, Leabua, prime minister of Lesotho 17
Jones, Carolyn, American playwright
    Coup d'Etat, play 224; picture 225
Jordan 352
    Palestinian homeland, problem of 53
Joyner, Jackie, American athlete 183
Jungle Books, The, stories by Rudyard Kipling
    story of Rikki-tikki-tavi 290–99

K

Kampuchea *see* Cambodia
Karlen, John, American actor 276
Kennedy, John F., American president
    Peace Corps, formation of 200
Kennedy, Joseph P., II, American senator 36
*Kennedy Center Honors, The: A Celebration of the
    Performing Arts,* television program 276
Kenya 352
    postage stamps 143
Khalifa, Omar, Sudanese athlete, picture 183
Khomeini, Ayatollah Ruhollah, religious leader of Iran
    54
Kidnappings
    Lebanon 52
Kilburn, Peter, American hostage in Middle East 52
Kipling, Rudyard, English writer
    Jungle Books, The, story from 290–99
Kirov Ballet, Soviet dance troop 103; picture 270
Kizim, Leonid D., Soviet cosmonaut 123
Knight, Ray, American athlete 161–62; picture 160
Korea, Democratic People's Republic of (North Korea)
    352
Korea, Republic of (South Korea) 352
Krugerrand, South African coin 152
Kuwait 352

L

LaBelle, Patti, American singer 254; picture 255
Labor movement
    Haymarket Affair, Chicago, Illinois, story about
        308–18
    South Africa 49
Labor Party, Israel 35, 54
Laboulaye, Édouard-René Lefebvre, French historian
    186–87

M

N

O

Presidential Medal of Freedom, U.S. award
    Horowitz, Vladimir, picture 271
Prince Edward Island, province, Canada 360
Prizes and awards
    Academy Awards 252–53
    Caldecott Medal 303
    Canada Council children's literature prize 304
    Emmy Awards 276–77
    Grammy Awards 259
    Newbery Medal 302
    Nobel prizes 35
    Presidential Medal of Freedom, picture 271
    Scholastic/Kodak Photo Awards Program winners,
        pictures 238–41
Product tampering incidents 19
Protoavis, bird 30; picture 31
Pterodactyl, extinct reptile
    mechanical replica, picture 79
P'u Hsin-yu, Chinese artist
    commemorative postage stamp 143
Pulitzer, Joseph, American newspaper publisher 188

Q

Qaddafi, Muammar el-, Libyan leader, 22, 55
Qatar 354
Quebec, province, Canada 361
    La Mauricie National Park commemorative postage
        stamp 143
    Little League baseball team, Valleyfield 163
Queen Anne's lace, flower 132
Quetzal, bird, picture 108
Quetzalcoatlus northropi, extinct reptile
    mechanical replica, picture 79
Quilting, handicraft 149–50
    heart designs 262, 265
Quincy Market, Boston, Massachusetts, picture 206

R

Raccoon, animal 72, 75, picture 76
Racial segregation, South Africa see Apartheid
Radioactivity
    Chernobyl nuclear accident, Union of Soviet Socialist
        Republics 23, 44–45
Railroads
    English Channel rail tunnels 16–17
    Roundhouse, train shed shown at world's fair 100
Rainfall 326–27
Rain forests 106–111
    ferns 124
    sloths 84–87
Ramos, Fidel, Philippine military leader 43
Ramsay, Sir William, British chemist 244
Rattlesnake, reptile 73–74
Reagan, Nancy, American first lady, picture 80

Reagan, Ronald, president of the United States, pictures
    13, 80
    economic policies 56–57
    immigration reform 36
    Iran, arms sales to 52
    Libya 16, 22
    pre-summit meeting, Reykjavik, Iceland 35, 58
    Secretary of Agriculture, nomination of 17
    South Africa 34, 50
    space exploration 121–22
    Statue of Liberty centennial 191
    Supreme Court appointments 26
    tax reform 33
    White House crisis 39
Recession, economic, a period of reduced economic
    activity
    budget deficits 56
Recipes 156–57
Reed, Frank Herbert, American hostage in Middle East 52
Rehnquist, William H., American Supreme Court Justice
    26; picture 64
Religion
    heart, symbolism of 263
    India 247
    see also specific religions and religious denominations
Remedial English, play by Evan Smith 224
Republican Party, United States 36
Resnik, Judith A., American astronaut 17, 121
Revel, Bernard, American educator
    commemorative postage stamp 140
Reykjavik, Iceland
    pre-summit meeting 35, 58; picture 12–13
Rhine River, Europe
    chemical spill, Switzerland 36
Richie, Lionel, American singer and songwriter 255;
    picture 269
Riddle, Nelson, American music arranger and conductor
    255
Rikki-tikki-tavi, character in *The Jungle Books,* stories by
    Rudyard Kipling 290–99
Riley, James Whitcome, American photography program
    winner, picture 241
Ringwald, Molly, American actress, picture 269
Robinson, A. N. R., prime minister of Trinidad and
    Tobago 39
Robinson Crusoe, novel by Daniel Defoe 320–21
Robots 113
Rock and Roll Hall of Fame, Cleveland, Ohio 259
Rohrer, Heinrich, Swiss physicist 35
Roman Catholic Church
    John Paul II, picture 65
    Philippines 43
Ronstadt, Linda, American singer 255–56
Roscoe, William, British historian and writer
    Butterfly's Ball, The, poem 307
Rose, flower 32
Rowe, Star, American friend of Katerina Lycheva,
    picture 228
Roy, Patrick, Canadian athlete 171; picture 170
Ruckus Manhattan, sculpture by Red Grooms, picture
    271
Rumania 354
Ruska, Ernst, German physicist 35
Russia see Union of Soviet Socialist Republics
Rutan, Burt, American airplane designer 112
Rutan, Richard, American airplane pilot 112
Rwanda 354

S

U

V

W

X

Y

Z

ILLUSTRATION CREDITS AND ACKNOWLEDGMENTS

The following list credits or acknowledges, by page, the source of illustrations and text excerpts used in this work. Illustration credits are listed illustration by illustration—left to right, top to bottom. When two or more illustrations appear on one page, their credits are separated by semicolons. When both the photographer or artist and an agency or other source are given for an illustration, they are usually separated by a dash. Excerpts from previously published works are listed by inclusive page numbers.

12– © John Ficara—Newsweek
13
16 © Sygma
17 Courtesy NASA
19 Artist, Michèle A. McLean
20 © Philippe Halsman
21 AP/Wide World
22 © Ray Fairall—NY Times
23 © Sygma
25 Gary Hardwood—UPI/Bettmann Newsphotos
27 Culver Pictures, Inc.
28 © Edward Klamm—Fotowest
29 © Charles Rex Arbogast
30– Courtesy National Geographic Society
31
33 Artist, Michèle A. McLean
34 © S. Bassouls—Sygma
37 Bettmann Archive
38 AP/Wide World
39 Artist, Michèle A. McLean
40– © A. Hernandez—Sygma
42
45 © Gamma/Liaison
46 © AFP
48 © Louise Gubb—JB Pictures
49 © Arthur Grace—Newsweek
51 © Roger Auque—Gamma/Liaison
53 © A. Nogues—Sygma
54 © Kazeni—JB Pictures
55 © Chris Laffaille—JB Pictures
57 Artist, Michèle A. McLean
58 AP/Wide World
59 © J. L. Atlan—Sygma
60 © Peter Main—The Christian Science Monitor
61 AP/Wide World
62 © Tom Sobolik—Black Star
64 UPI/Bettmann Newsphotos; © Gamma/Liaison
65 © Donatello Brogioni—Sygma; Jacques Langevin—Sygma
66 Reuters/Bettmann Newsphotos; © François von Sury—Sygma
67 AP/Wide World
68– © Dave Woodward
69
70 © Alex Kerstitch
71 © Chris Newbert
72 © Tom McHugh—Photo Researchers, Inc.
73 © Joseph R. Pearce—DRK Photo
74 © Jack Dermid—Bruce Coleman, Inc.; © S.J. Krasemann—DRK Photo
75 © Carol Hughes—Bruce Coleman, Inc.
76 © Wolfgang Obst
77 © Joe & Carol McDonald—Tom Stack and Associates; © Farrell Grehan—Photo Researchers, Inc.

78 © Courtesy The Walt Disney World Company; © James T. Tanner—Photo Researchers, Inc.
79 © Barry Shaver—People weekly, © 1986 Time Inc.; © Ed Kashi
80 AP/Wide World; Pete Souza—The White House
81 © Hans and Judy Beste—Animals Animals; © Ron Garrison—Zoological Society of San Diego
82 © Laurie Winfrey—Carousel
83 © Susan Copen Oken
84– © Michael Fogden
85
86 © Alex Kerstitch
87 © Michael Fogden—Animals Animals
88 © L. West—Bruce Coleman, Inc.; © Walter E. Harvey—Photo Researchers, Inc.; © Chip Isengart—Tom Stack and Associates
89 © K. G. Preston-Mafham—Animals Animals; © Peter Ward—Bruce Coleman, Inc.
90 © Walter Chandoha
91 © Jane Latta—Photo Researchers, Inc.; © Richard Hutchings—Photo Researchers, Inc.
92 © Walter Chandoha; © Dagmar—Animals Animals
93 © Reynolds Photography; © Walter Chandoha
94– © 1986 Royal Observatory Edinburgh
95
96 AP/Wide World
97 Courtesy Max Planck Institut fur Aeronomie
98 The Granger Collection
99 © Peter DeSeve
100– © Bob Clarke—The Stock Market, Inc.
101
102 © Gordon J. Fisher—The Stock Market, Inc.
103 © Image Finders
104– Artist, Michèle A. McLean
105
106 © G. I. Bernard—Oxford Scientific Films/Earth Scenes
108 © Renate Jope—Photo Researchers, Inc.; © B. G. Murray, Jr.—Earth Scenes; © Michael Fogden—Animals Animals
109 © C. W. Perkins—Earth Scenes; © Richard K. La Val—Animals Animals; © Raymond A. Mendez—Animals Animals
110 © Donald R. Perry
112 © François Duhamel—Sygma
113 © Woods Hole Oceanographic Institution; AP/Wide World
114– Artist, Michèle A. McLean
116
117 © Sabine Weiss—Photo Researchers, Inc.
118– © Larry Ulrich
119
120 © Sisson—SIPA
121 © Sygma
122 © Jet Propulsion Lab

123 © 1986 Time Inc. Adapted by permission from Time magazine
124 © Rod Planck—Tom Stack and Associates
125 © Patti Murray—Earth Scenes; © Stephen P. Parker—Photo Researchers, Inc.; © Larry West
126 © K. G. Preston-Mafham—Earth Scenes
127 © Milton Rand—Tom Stack and Associates
128– Artist, Frank Senyk
129
130– Paper dolls designed and created by Jenny Tesar
131 Tesar
133– © Paul Williams
135
136– Artist, Susan M. Waitt
137
138– Caterpillars designed and created by Michèle
139 A. McLean
144– Crafts by Jenny Tesar
145
146– Artist, Kim Kelly
147
148– Courtesy Crafts 'n Things magazine
151
152– Courtesy Krause Publications, Inc.
153
154 Hat designed and created by Jenny Tesar
155 SOLUTION: Crustaceans
156– From Many Friends Cooking: An International
157 Cookbook for Boys and Girls. Text © 1980 by Terry Touff Cooper and Marilyn Ratner. Illustrations © 1980 by Tony Chen. Used by permission of Philomel Books, a division of the Putnam Publishing Group
158– Gamma/Liaison
159
160 © Focus on Sports
161 AP/Wide World
163 Vannucci Foto Services
164 © Focus on Sports
166 © Bob Brown—Focus on Sports
167 © Focus on Sports
168 © UPI/Bettmann Newsphotos
169 © Focus on Sports; UPI/Bettmann Newsphotos
170 © Focus on Sports
172 Rick Wilking—UPI/Bettmann Newsphotos
173 © Steve Powell—All-Sport
174– © Duomo
175
176 © David Cannon—All-Sport
177 Reuters/Bettmann Newsphotos
178 © Focus on Sports
179 Reuters/Bettmann Newsphotos
180 Reuters/Bettmann Newsphotos
181 © Louis DeLuca—Dallas Times Herald; © Jerry Wachter—Focus on Sports
182 Tass from Sovfoto

Grolier Enterprises, Inc. offers a varied selection of both adult and children's
book racks. For details on ordering, please write:

Grolier Enterprises, Inc.
Sherman Turnpike
Danbury, CT 06816
Attn: Premium Department